Since Beck

Continuum Literary Studies Series

Also available in the series:
Active Reading by Ben Knights and Chris Thurgar-Dawson
Beckett's Books by Matthew Feldman
Beckett and Decay by Kathryn White
Beckett and Ethics edited by Russell Smith
Beckett and Phenomenology edited by Ulrika Maude and Matthew Feldman
Canonizing Hypertext by Astrid Ensslin
Character and Satire in Postwar Fiction by Ian Gregson
Coleridge and German Philosophy by Paul Hamilton
Contemporary Fiction and Christianity by Andrew Tate
Ecstasy and Understanding edited by Adrian Grafe
English Fiction in the 1930s by Chris Hopkins
Fictions of Globalization by James Annesley
Joyce and Company by David Pierce
London Narratives by Lawrence Phillips
Masculinity in Fiction and Film by Brian Baker
Milton, Evil and Literary History by Claire Colebrook
Modernism and the Post-colonial by Peter Childs
Novels of the Contemporary Extreme edited by Alain-Phillipe Durand and Naomi Mandel
Recalling London by Alex Murray
Romanticism, Literature and Philosophy by Simon Swift
Seeking Meaning for Goethe's Faust by J. M. van der Laan
Sexuality and the Erotic in the Fiction of Joseph Conrad by Jeremy Hawthorn
Such Deliberate Disguises: The Art of Phillip Larkin by Richard Palmer
The Palimpsest by Sarah Dillon
The Measureless Past of Joyce, Deleuze and Derrida by Ruben Borg
Women's Fiction 1945–2000 by Deborah Philips

Since Beckett
Contemporary Writing in the Wake of Modernism

Peter Boxall

continuum

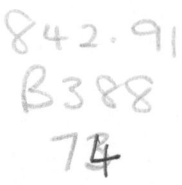

Continuum International Publishing Group
The Tower Building   80 Maiden Lane
11 York Road   Suite 704
London SE1 7NX   New York, NY 10038

www.continuumbooks.com

© Peter Boxall 2009

All rights reserved. No part of this publication may be reproduced or transmitted in any form or by any means, electronic or mechanical, including photocopying, recording, or any information storage or retrieval system, without prior permission in writing from the publishers.

Peter Boxall has asserted his right under the Copyright, Designs and Patents Act, 1988, to be identified as Author of this work.

British Library Cataloguing-in-Publication Data
A catalogue record for this book is available from the British Library.

ISBN: 978-1-4411-7813-8

Library of Congress Cataloging-in-Publication Data
Boxall, Peter.
Since Beckett : contemporary writing in the wake of modernism / Peter Boxall.
  p. cm.
ISBN: 978-1-4411-7813-8
1. Beckett, Samuel, 1906-1989–Influence. 2. Beckett, Samuel, 1906-1989–Criticism and interpretation. 3. Literature, Modern–20th century–History and criticism. 4. Modernism (Literature) 5. Influence (Literary, artistic, etc.)–History–20th century. I. Title.

PR6003.E282Z5766 2009
848'.91409–dc22
                                                         2008047951

Typeset by Newgen Imaging Systems Pvt Ltd, Chennai, India
Printed and bound in Great Britain by the MPG Books Group

For my mother

Contents

Acknowledgements — viii
List of Abbreviations — x
List of Illustrations — xii

Introduction: Since Beckett — 1

Part One: Back Roads: Beckett, Banville and Ireland
1. Edgeworth, Bowen, Beckett, Banville: A Minor Tradition — 21
2. Spectrality and Eclipse: Beckett and Banville — 38
3. Unknown Unity: Ireland and Europe in Beckett and Banville — 53

Part Two: Tune Accordingly: Beckett, Bernhard and Sebald
4. Faint Clarity: Tuning in Beckett — 69
5. All Balls: Quotation and Correction in Beckett and Bernhard — 86
6. A Quite Singular Clarity: Beckett, Bernhard, Sebald — 109

Part Three: How It Ought To Be: Beckett, Globalization and Utopia
7. From Joyce to Beckett: From National to Global — 135
8. Knowledge Within Bounds: Beckett, Globalization and the Limits of Perception — 148
9. Slow Man, Dangling Man, Falling Man: Beckett in the Ruins of the Future — 166

Notes — 200
Bibliography — 217
Index — 227

Acknowledgements

This book has had a long genesis, and has been shaped by conversations over many years. My stepfather, Andrew Neil, was the first person to introduce me to Beckett's work, and he remains obscurely associated with Beckett, for me, to this day. The late Jim Smith ran an undergraduate course on Samuel Beckett at Southampton University in 1991, and the fondness of my memories both of this course and of Jim himself make it easier for me to see the warmth in Beckett's writing. Conversations with Drew Milne over the course of my years as a student at the University of Sussex were an uninterrupted lesson on how to read Beckett, a lesson which I am still trying to learn.

I first laid out the arguments developed in this book in an essay entitled 'Since Beckett', which appeared in *Textual Practice* in 2006, and my thanks go to Pete Nicholls and to Daniel Katz for their insightful work on this essay. I have since given parts of the book as papers at conferences in Tokyo, Rome, Osnabrück, Oxford, Durham, Reading, Belfast, Birmingham, London and Brighton. My thanks go to all those who responded to these papers, and made this book a great deal better as a result. I have also published some essays in the last two years that have been related to chapters in the current volume. These include essays in Mark Nixon and Matthew Feldman's collection *Samuel Beckett: Debts and Legacies*, in Russel Smith's *Beckett and Ethics* and Sean Kennedy's *Beckett and Ireland*. My thanks go to the editors of these volumes for their comments and thoughts.

This work has also been supported by a very large number of friends, colleagues and students. These include, in particular, Steven Connor, Leslie Hill, Enoch Brater, Laura Salisbury, Jo Brooker, Simon Morgan Wortham, Shane Weller, Daniela Caselli, Paul Sheehan, Laura Marcus, Peter Brooker, John Pilling, Rick Crownshaw, Andrzej Gasiorek, Roger Luckhurst, Mary Bryden, James Knowlson, Ronan McDonald, Ulrika Maude, Sam Thomas, John Calder, Andrew Hadfield, Steve Burman, Nicholas Royle, Keston Sutherland, J. D. Rhodes, Lara Feigel, Pamela Thurschwell, Vicky Lebeau, Margarete Kohlenbach, Daniel Steuer, Sebastian Franklin, Kumiko Kiuchi, Anthony Leaker, Victoria Blunden, David Tucker and Alvin Birdi. I owe a debt of gratitude also to all my colleagues and students at the University of Sussex.

Acknowledgements

Anna Fleming and Colleen Coalter at Continuum have been supportive throughout this project, and made the final stages a pleasure. The London National Gallery kindly gave permission for me to reproduce Hieronymus Bosch's 'Christ Mocked'.

This book is at its heart about the relationship between parents and children. In writing it, I have been supported above all by my own family, by my partner Hannah and my children Ava and Laurie. The Jordans, Boxalls, Moenchs, Losassos, Chamberlains and Neils, as always, have my thanks. My parents have never been far from my mind when writing what follows, both my mother who brought me up, and my father who was not able to. This book is dedicated with love and gratitude to my mother, and to the memories I preserve of my father.

List of Abbreviations

E   John Banville, *Eclipse*
S   John Banville, *Shroud*

CDW   Samuel Beckett, *Complete Dramatic Works*
CP   Samuel Beckett, *Collected Poems 1930–1978*
CSP   Samuel Beckett, *Collected Shorter Prose*
D   Samuel Beckett, *Dream of Fair to Middling Women*
Di   Samuel Beckett, *Disjecta*
HII   Samuel Beckett, *How It Is*
Mo   Samuel Beckett, *Molloy*
MD   Samuel Beckett, *Malone Dies*
Mu   Samuel Beckett, *Murphy*
NO   Samuel Beckett, *Nohow On*
PTD   Samuel Beckett, *Proust and Three Dialogues with Georges Duthuit*
U   Samuel Beckett, *The Unnamable*
W   Samuel Beckett, *Watt*

DM   Saul Bellow, *Dangling Man*

C   Thomas Bernhard, *Correction*
Ex   Thomas Bernhard, *Extinction*
OM   Thomas Bernhard, *Old Masters*
WN   Thomas Bernhard, *Wittgenstein's Nephew*

CS   Elizabeth Bowen, *The Collected Stories of Elizabeth Bowen*

DtP   J. M. Coetzee, *Doubling the Point*
SM   J. M. Coetzee, *Slow Man*
EC   J. M. Coetzee, *Elizabeth Costello*

A   Don DeLillo, *Americana*
FM   Don DeLillo, *Falling Man*

List of Abbreviations

Mao   Don DeLillo, *Mao II*
WN   Don DeLillo, *White Noise*

CR   Maria Edgeworth, *Castle Rackrent*

Du   James Joyce, *Dubliners*
P   James Joyce, *Portrait of the Artist as a Young Man*

UdM   Heinrich von Kleist, 'Über das Marionettentheater'

A   W. G. Sebald, *Austerlitz*
Un   W. G. Sebald, *Unrecounted*

List of Illustrations

Figure 5.1 Bosch, 'The Crowning with Thorns' 100
Figure 8.1 *Ill Seen Ill Said* 158

Introduction: Since Beckett

Samuel Beckett's writing is at once a poetics of exhaustion, and a poetics of persistence. It is a writing which stages the end of an entire range of cultural and literary possibilities, but it is also a body of work which extends these possibilities, inventing new and richly productive ways to 'stir', as 'Beckett' puts it in one of his dialogues with Georges Duthuit, 'from the field of the possible' (PTD 103). The moment in his work at which these two antinomial conditions come into closest proximity, and which has become a signature moment in Beckett's writing, comes at the end of Beckett's extraordinary novel *The Unnamable*, when the narrator brings his maelstrom of words to a close with the blankly aporetic line 'I can't go on, I'll go on' (U 418).

Any attempt to understand or to inherit Samuel Beckett's legacy has to reckon, at the outset, with this contradiction between a writing which continues to go on, and a writing which is unable to go on. On the one hand, we have to ask how we can think of ourselves as living in a moment that is 'since Beckett', when one of the principle effects of his writing is to make its own ending, or ending in general, unthinkable.[1] This book sets itself, in part, the task of tracing Beckett's 'influence' on those who come after him, of identifying a Beckettian legacy that plays itself out across a range of contemporary writers, in various national and political contexts. But it is difficult to imagine how we can approach Beckett's legacies when his work itself seems reluctant to end, when those who thought to have come into his fortune find themselves still lingering by his death bed. Hamm declares at the beginning of *Endgame* that 'it's time it ended', that whatever temporal disturbance that had allowed him to live on after the destruction of his world has now to be corrected. 'It's time it ended', Hamm declares, but he admits, hesitantly, that 'I hesitate to . . . to end' (CDW 93). It is this hesitation, this stuttering tendency for time to slow down, to enter into a kind of slow, arrested duration, that characterizes the persistence of Beckett's writing, its singular capacity to live on after the conditions that allow it to come into being have passed away. But, on the other hand, if Beckett hesitates to end, it is also the case that he finds it rather difficult to start, that he struggles to be properly born as much as he finds himself unable to die ('I gave up', the narrator of 'Fizzle 4' says, 'before birth' [CSP 234]). As the narrator of Beckett's late prose work *The Lost Ones* puts it, the 'beginning' is as 'unthinkable as the end', the 'first day' as 'unthinkable' as the last (CSP 212, 213). The tendency to persist, the difficulty that Beckett's narrators and characters have in consummating their own devoutly wished for deaths, is balanced, in Beckett, against this incapacity to begin, in the same way that the unnamable narrator balances the imperative that he must 'go on' against his inability to do so.

To start to think about what it is to come after Beckett, to be 'since Beckett', it is perhaps necessary to tease out these opposing tendencies, to separate those drives in his work that are directed at diminishment and termination from those that aim towards persistence and enlargement. But it is one of the peculiarities of Beckettian temporality that these tendencies are not only opposed to one another, but they are also won from one another, and become part of the same movement. (This is one of the reasons, incidentally, that dialectical thinking is so difficult in relation to Beckett's writing. He sets dialectical oppositions in motion, but repeatedly allows such oppositions to collapse into a kind of identity, a kind of slack unity.) When the narrator of *The Unnamable* finally beaches himself on that last line, he gives concise expression to one of Beckett's fundamental contradictions, but he also suggests that these opposing forces in Beckett conspire with one another, that the very quality of passing time in Beckett's writing is determined by an uncanny collaboration between persistence and termination. The predicament that the narrator articulates at the close of the novel is not one that emerges only here, in the embers of Beckett's 'middle phase', but is rather the underlying condition of possibility and of impossibility that guides the production of narrative in Beckett's writing more generally. Throughout the novels of the trilogy, there is a persistent confusion between beginning and ending, as if this is the medium in which Beckett's writing comes into being, rather than a disabling destination that is reached by the narrator of *The Unnamable*. When Molloy attempts to describe his 'world', for example, he suggests that it is conjured in some sense from this confusion, from this intimate co-mingling of antinomial oppositions. It is a 'world', he says, that is 'at an end, in spite of appearances', a world which at once ends and continues to go on, a world, indeed, which owes its capacity to endure from its having ended. 'It's end brought it forth', Molloy writes, 'ending it began' (Mo 40). This curious interdependence between ending and going on is suggested, indeed, by the sense that the final expression of contradiction at the end of *The Unnamable* is itself an echo from earlier in Beckett's writing. The narrator of *The Calmative* ends his narrative in a manner which predicts or shadows forth the end of *The Unnamable*, as if that ending, which has come to mark a watershed not only in Beckett's writing career but in the passage of twentieth-century literature, had already been written, giving rise to Beckett's work rather than bringing it to a kind of halt. When *The Calmative* closes with the narrator's declaration that 'the memory came faint and cold of the story I might have told, a story in the likeness of my life, I mean without the courage to end or the strength to go on' (CSP 99), he stages at once a prediction and a recollection, he looks at once to the future and to the past. The ending of the earlier novella seems, to those of us who are 'since' *The Unnamable*, to be overwhelmed by the moment it appears to predict, seems to suggest that here Beckett's narrator is simply preparing the deadlock between continuing to go on and being unable to go on that closes perhaps his most important work (the 'story' that the narrator of *The Calmative* 'might have told'). But even this work of prediction comes to the narrator as a memory, as if such a deadlock is an ancient, originary condition, as if remembering and predicting are one, as if being at once able and unable to go on is what brings Beckett's work forth, giving it a kind of still birth, imparting to it a still stirring.

It is to some degree this insistently recurring confusion between beginning and ending, between persistence and termination (a confusion that is caught in that wonderful Beckettian word 'still') that makes Beckett's work difficult to place historically. Beckett published his various works, his novels, poems, essays, short stories, novellas, prose poems, stage plays, works for television, radio and film, mimes and so on, between 1929, when he published his essay 'Dante . . . Bruno. Vico . . . Joyce', and 1989, when he published *Comment dire*. For much of that time, Beckett has been regarded, in a variety of contexts, as one of the most important writers of his generation. He has been thought of as the heir of Kafka, of Joyce, of Proust, and is contemporary at once with Virginia Woolf, Elizabeth Bowen, Gertrude Stein, Iris Murdoch and Angela Carter. Given his pre-eminence, his longevity, and his contribution to a number of literary cultures over seven decades of the twentieth century, one might expect his work to influence and be influenced by the contexts that produce him, and that he has helped to produce. We might reasonably expect his work to represent some kind of bridge from modernism to postmodernism to the contemporary. We might even expect his work to help us to produce a literary historical narrative that would make sense both of his own development as a writer, and of the various historical figures with whom he came into contact. But the unfolding of the body of Beckett's reception, through its various stages, has suggested that this is not the case. Despite Beckett's prevalence, his reputation for so much of his career as one of the world's 'greatest living writers', his work has stood at a very peculiar, oblique angle to the cultures that have produced it. It is difficult, for example, to accustom oneself to the fact that Beckett's *Ghost Trio* was first televised in the year that *Star Wars* was released, that *Mal vu mal dit* was published in the same year that Salman Rushdie published *Midnight's Children*, or that *Quad* was first published in the year that Martin Amis published *Money*. It is not simply that Beckett's work responds to the world in a different way than that of Amis, or Rushdie, or George Lucas, but that it appears to inhabit a different history altogether, a history that cannot easily be slotted between 1929 and 1989. Beckett's work has seemed to belong to a world of its own, to be sealed into an historical and geographical cylinder, like that imagined in *The Lost Ones*, that has no connection with the world that produced *Dallas*, or *East Enders* or even *The Play for Today*.

Now, there are very many reasons for this peculiar relationship between Beckett and his contemporaries, some of them no doubt contradictory, but one aspect of this disconnect, I suggest, is the odd confusion that I have been tracing between beginnings and endings, and the characteristically stalled, stretched and contracted temporality that Beckett's work produces as a result. It is difficult to think of Beckett's work as part of a broader historical current, developing in response to a wider environment, when it produces such a singular form of duration, when it seems at once to persist beyond its own limits, and to evade the business of beginning altogether. The kind of time that Beckett's writing produces might best be thought of as an endless moment, an endless, dislocated now, that does not obey the laws that require time to pass, and that recreates the effects of duration only by extending a pause, by allowing a frozen moment to come unstuck, to stretch like elastic. The repetition that one finds in Beckett's work, the resurfacing of a static impasse at the end of *The Calmative* and of *The Unnamable*, is one sign of this singular duration, this becalmed wallowing within the infinitely distant horizons of a single moment. It is not simply that the repetition restates the contradiction between continuing and ending that determines, to a degree, Beckett's writing career, but also that the repetition itself suggests that Beckett's writing does not move on, or that, as in the late work *Worstward Ho*, it manages somehow to conflate forward and backward motion, to make of the continued insistence on going on a kind of going back ('back', says the narrator of *Worstward Ho*, 'back is on' [NO 121]). The work moves, endlessly, tirelessly to the place that it has always been. Time and time again in Beckett's oeuvre, such repetitions occur, as if Beckett's entire oeuvre were created at the same instant, already fashioned and complete. In Beckett's novel *Watt*, for example, written towards the beginning of Beckett's career, Watt reflects on his perception that time seems to slow down, to become endless, as he approaches the heavy gravitational field of Mr Knott's house and grounds. Recalling the incident of the 'Galls father and son', who visit Mr Knott's establishment to tune the piano, the narrator writes that the visit 'resembled all the incidents of note proposed to Watt during his stay in Mr Knott's house'. 'It resembled them', the narrator goes in, 'in the sense that it was not ended, when it was past, but continued to unfold, in Watt's head, from beginning to end, over and over again' (W 69). In many ways, Watt thinks of this extended stasis as a kind of utopia, as a haven, but he also finds it troubling, and feels the need to anchor himself in relation to a wider, shared history, to a time which passes in a more consecutive fashion. He compares the endlessly recurring visit of the Galls, for example, to an earlier incident in which he was visited, like a less grave Hamlet, by his dead father. Despite the spectrality of this paternal visitation – which itself might suggest that the time of inheritance was somehow out of joint – Watt remembers it with fondness, as an instance of an event which obeyed a kind of historical propriety. 'He could recall', the narrator writes, 'as [an] ordinary occasion, the time when his dead father appeared to him in a wood, with his trousers rolled up over his knees and his shoes and socks in his hand' (W 70). This incident, Watt thinks, unlike the difficult visit of the Galls, was one of which he was 'content to say, "That is what happened then"' (W 70). Of the incident of the Galls, however, the narrator says that 'Watt did not know what had happened':

> He did not care, to do him justice, what had happened. But he felt the need to think that such and such a thing had happened, the need to be able to say, when the scene began to unroll its sequences, Yes, I remember, that is what happened then. (W 71)

Watt's approach to Mr Knott's endless emptiness might be thought of as an increasing proximity to that still time of which Beckett's writing is made, that time compounded of persistence and exhaustion. The novel stages a gradual immersion in Beckettian time, the time that is 'not ended, when it was past', and one of the signs of this immersion in such a static temporality is the peculiar recurrence of its elements, which emerge again and again in Beckett's writing, just as the 'purely plastic' (W 69) features of the Galls' visit unfold endlessly in Watt's head. There is something deeply uncanny, for example, about the resurfacing of Watt's desire to re-enter historical time, nearly forty years later, in Beckett's novella *Company*. This late work is set, like so much of Beckett's writing, in a time that is composed at once of past, present and future, that mingles remembrance of the past with a description of the present and an evocation of the time to come. Here, towards the close of Beckett's career, it is as if we have set up camp at the heart of Mr Knott's establishment, in which things 'continue to unfold, from beginning to end, over and over again'. The 'voice' in the novella speaks to a figure who lies on his back in the dark, telling him stories about how his life was, how it is, how it will be, and at one point he imagines that the figure might finally be able to tell his own stories, to take ownership of the life that is being given to him. 'If he were able to utter after all?' the voice proposes to himself:

> What an addition to company that would be! You are on your back in the dark and one day you will utter again. One day! In the end. In the end you will utter again. Yes I remember. That was I. That was then. (NO 16–17)

For the reader of Beckett's work, this moment, this recurrence of Watt's need to be able to say 'Yes, I remember, that is what happened then', comes as a lurch, producing a kind of vertiginous déjà vu. Just as the voice in *Company* imagines that the figure might move towards an end, might eventually come to an independent existence in which he is able to remember his own life, to say that 'such and such a thing had happened', this fragment from *Watt* surfaces from the dark, returning Beckett's writing to the extraordinary temporal stasis that it has inhabited from the unthinkable beginning to the no less unthinkable end. The voice imagines the end here, imagines that the story might come to a conclusion with the figure's birth into his own life, into his own memories. But this echo from *Watt* alerts us to the underlying Beckettian predicament, in which the only way that the work can end is by continuing to go on. As the novella draws to a close, there is no re-entry into historical time, no recovery of historical sequence or historical community. Rather, the narrative ends with the voice telling the figure that 'you are as you always were. Alone' (NO 52).

It is in part this production of a kind of still time, then, that has made it difficult to place Beckett's writing within an historical trajectory. It has been hard to see how Beckett's writing emerges from or engages with its historical contexts, when the work itself is so concerned with a form of historical and geographical isolation. The solitude with which *Company* ends suggests that Beckett's writing does not belong to historical or geographical communities, but that it lives in its own endlessly recurring instant, removed from the world of sequential events that it tries and fails to remember. Seeking to understand how Beckett inherits a legacy from his predecessors – from those parental figures that haunt him as Watt is haunted by his dead father – or to understand how Beckett passes his own legacy on to those who come after him, would seem to require us to read against the grain of his writing, which so resists such forms of historical sequence. It would require us to repress or to forget Watt's insistence that questions of provenance and influence have no bearing on the quality of the empty time that he spends idling with Mr Knott. He lives at Mr Knott's, he tells us, in the space of an 'interval', an evacuated space and time has nothing to do with the 'ordaining of a being to come by a being past, or of a being past by a being to come' (even though, Watt condescends to concede, such forms of influence might be the subject of 'a fascinating study' [W 134]). Partly as a result of this difficulty, Beckett's readers and critics have tended to regard him either as a writer without precedent, occupying a time and place that does not refer to specific histories or geographies beyond itself, or they have situated him as a figure in which the historical forms with which he does have an oblique connection reach a kind of suspension. The first of these tendencies most commonly takes the form of a humanist insistence upon the 'timelessness' of Beckett's work, particularly in the earlier decades of Beckett criticism. If Beckett's work represents an extended single moment, a stretch of empty time that continues endlessly to go on, then it does so because it gives expression to the fundamental, ahistorical experience of being in time. The early work of critics and readers such as Martin Esslin and Alain Robbe-Grillet was extremely influential in providing a critical language in which to express this version of Beckettian temporality, as a time drained of history.[2] The quality of this ahistoricism has changed with the passing phases of Beckett's reception, particularly with the development from humanist to more avowedly theoretical, poststructuralist, psychoanalytical, Deleuzian and Derridean approaches,[3] but it has nevertheless

Introduction

persisted, even if it tends to be regarded as a function of the failure or the undecidability of language, rather than of the timelessness of the human condition. The second tendency has developed alongside the first, and is sometimes difficult to separate from it. Perhaps the most influential early attempt to historicize the waning of the historical in Beckett's work is Theodor Adorno's essay 'Trying to Understand *Endgame*', in which Adorno characterizes Beckett as a writer in whom the historical forces that drive earlier aesthetic forms congeal, freeze or dry up. Adorno famously wrote that 'to write poetry after Auschwitz is barbaric', because, he argues, the horror of Nazism ushered in the 'final stages' of Benjamin's 'dialectic of culture and barbarism'.[4] Auschwitz, for Adorno, marks the 'absolute reification' of the mind, the arrival of a 'total society' which has absorbed its own margins, which tends to absorb the cultural space which makes critical intelligence, which makes poetry itself possible.[5] Culture becomes the barbarism which it seeks to critique. If it is impossible to write poetry under these conditions, then it is Beckett's work, for Adorno, which best performs this impossibility. In Beckett's work, what survives of history is only the residue of historical forces, the residue that tells us history is over. *Endgame*, Adorno argues, gives a kind of static expression to this residue. In the play, Adorno writes,

> History is kept outside because it has dried up consciousness' power to conceive it, the power to remember. Drama becomes mute gesture, freezes in the middle of dialogue. The only part of history that is still apparent is its outcome – decline.[6]

If Beckett's work is historical, for Adorno, it is so only in that it gives an expression to the exhaustion of history itself. He reads Hamm's freighted and nearly unreadable comment that 'It's the end of the day like any other day' as evidence of this salvaging of a frozen continuation from the experience of termination itself, a frozen continuation that gives conjoined expression both to the horrors of the past and of the future, constituting, as W. J. McCormack has astutely remarked, both 'an echo from the fascist past [and] an image of the thermo-nuclear future'.[7] 'Like time', Adorno writes, 'the temporal has been incapacitated; even to say that it didn't exist any more would be too comforting. It is and it isn't, the way the world is for the solipsist, who doubts the world's existence but has to concede it with every sentence.'[8] Time and history continue in Beckett's writing, but they have been 'incapacitated', emptied out, and display in their continuation only the suspended effects of this incapacity. These interwoven tendencies, to think of Beckett as ahistorical, or as a figure in whom historical narratives are held in abeyance or suspense, have combined to produce a powerful impression of Beckett as in some sense the 'last writer'. The contradictory continuity between persistence and exhaustion that runs through his work has given rise to a repeated characterization of Beckett as a writer in whom the dwindling possibilities of previous writers, and of previous

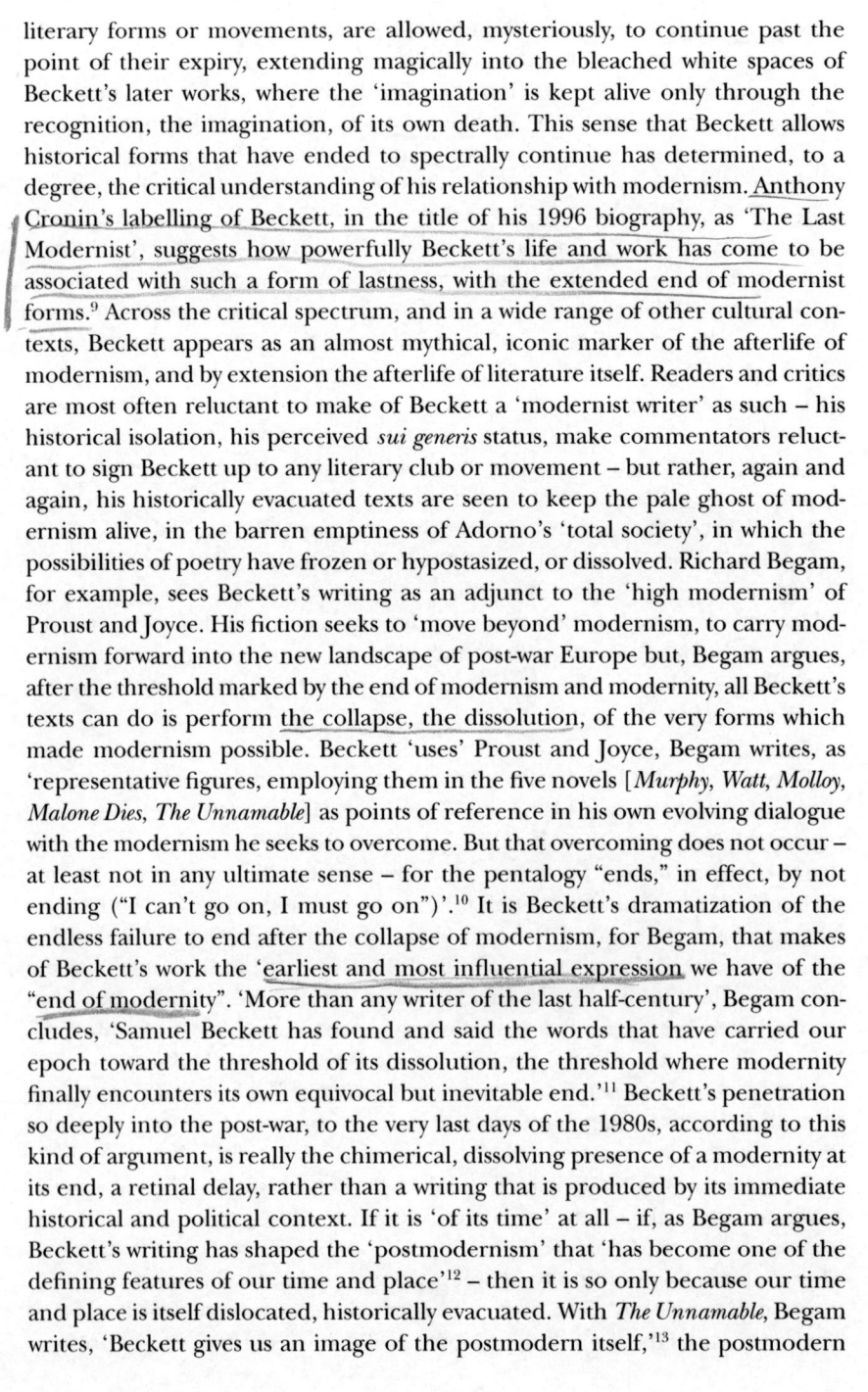

literary forms or movements, are allowed, mysteriously, to continue past the point of their expiry, extending magically into the bleached white spaces of Beckett's later works, where the 'imagination' is kept alive only through the recognition, the imagination, of its own death. This sense that Beckett allows historical forms that have ended to spectrally continue has determined, to a degree, the critical understanding of his relationship with modernism. Anthony Cronin's labelling of Beckett, in the title of his 1996 biography, as 'The Last Modernist', suggests how powerfully Beckett's life and work has come to be associated with such a form of lastness, with the extended end of modernist forms.⁹ Across the critical spectrum, and in a wide range of other cultural contexts, Beckett appears as an almost mythical, iconic marker of the afterlife of modernism, and by extension the afterlife of literature itself. Readers and critics are most often reluctant to make of Beckett a 'modernist writer' as such – his historical isolation, his perceived *sui generis* status, make commentators reluctant to sign Beckett up to any literary club or movement – but rather, again and again, his historically evacuated texts are seen to keep the pale ghost of modernism alive, in the barren emptiness of Adorno's 'total society', in which the possibilities of poetry have frozen or hypostasized, or dissolved. Richard Begam, for example, sees Beckett's writing as an adjunct to the 'high modernism' of Proust and Joyce. His fiction seeks to 'move beyond' modernism, to carry modernism forward into the new landscape of post-war Europe but, Begam argues, after the threshold marked by the end of modernism and modernity, all Beckett's texts can do is perform the collapse, the dissolution, of the very forms which made modernism possible. Beckett 'uses' Proust and Joyce, Begam writes, as 'representative figures, employing them in the five novels [*Murphy, Watt, Molloy, Malone Dies, The Unnamable*] as points of reference in his own evolving dialogue with the modernism he seeks to overcome. But that overcoming does not occur – at least not in any ultimate sense – for the pentalogy "ends," in effect, by not ending ("I can't go on, I must go on")'.¹⁰ It is Beckett's dramatization of the endless failure to end after the collapse of modernism, for Begam, that makes of Beckett's work the 'earliest and most influential expression we have of the "end of modernity". 'More than any writer of the last half-century', Begam concludes, 'Samuel Beckett has found and said the words that have carried our epoch toward the threshold of its dissolution, the threshold where modernity finally encounters its own equivocal but inevitable end.'¹¹ Beckett's penetration so deeply into the post-war, to the very last days of the 1980s, according to this kind of argument, is really the chimerical, dissolving presence of a modernity at its end, a retinal delay, rather than a writing that is produced by its immediate historical and political context. If it is 'of its time' at all – if, as Begam argues, Beckett's writing has shaped the 'postmodernism' that 'has become one of the defining features of our time and place'¹² – then it is so only because our time and place is itself dislocated, historically evacuated. With *The Unnamable*, Begam writes, 'Beckett gives us an image of the postmodern itself,'¹³ the postmodern

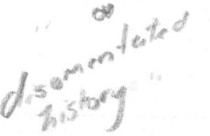

which, according to one of Frederic Jameson's 'five symptoms of postmodernity', inaugurates what he calls a 'weakening of historicity'.[14] Beckett might orient us historically, but to a disorientated history which recognizes itself only as an extended end of modernity. It is perhaps this conception of Beckett as a symptom of the end of modernity that prompts Bill Gray, the writer at the centre of Don DeLillo's 1991 novel *Mao II*, to declare that 'Beckett is the last writer to shape the way we think and see' (Mao 157). For Bill Gray, Beckett marks the end of a critical fiction, a fiction which can reimagine and reshape the world, can bring into being what Watt thinks of as 'the new day at last, the day without precedent at last' (W 63). With Beckett's death, in the gloaming of December 1989, literature itself dies, leaving the work of shaping thought and vision to terrorists, to men of violence. 'Beckett is the last writer to shape the way we think and see', Gray says. 'After him, the major work involves midair explosions and crumbled buildings' (Mao 157).

While this picture of Beckett as a writer who stages the stretched termination of modernism and modernity continues to have currency, however, the close connections between Beckett and the end, Beckett and lastness, have begun in recent years to give way to a dawning sense that Beckett is also the source of new beginnings, of new possibilities. In the conception of Beckett that I have been describing, in which he is posted as the final marker of a kaput modernism, the capacity of his writing to go on has been fused somehow to his articulation of the end, so Beckettian persistence has become a spectral after effect of literary possibility, rather than in any sense its continued embodiment. But with this shift, with this growing recognition of Beckett as origin rather than as destination, the insistence upon going on that his work produces has, as it were, found a new outlet, a form of expression that extends, in some fashion, beyond that unbearably stalled dialectic sketched by Adorno, in which history continues in Beckett only as a function of its incapacity. This shift can be detected in many different ways, and across a range of responses to Beckett's writing. It can be registered, for example, in the new phase that is opening up in the 2000s in Beckett studies, which is dedicated to tracing, more accurately than has been possible before, the ways in which Beckett belongs to literary histories, both in terms of his debts and his legacies. There are several different aspects to this new turn in Beckett criticism. It is generated in part by the growing availability of archival material, as Beckett's writing becomes increasingly mined and monumentalized, which allows for a whole range of scholarship that is able more accurately to determine what Beckett read, and how his reading and thinking helped to produce a writing which as a result becomes historically legible and engaged, rather than the detached and self-enclosed oeuvre with which we were more familiar. This kind of criticism is exemplified by work such as Matthew Feldman's *Beckett's Books: A Cultural History of Samuel Beckett's 'Interwar Notes'*, as well as by Feldman and Mark Nixon's collection, *Beckett's Literary Legacies* which demonstrates the extent to which an understanding of Beckett's literary and historical debts can help us to trace his legacies, to understand more clearly how Beckett's work influences and produces new forms.[15] Daniela Caselli's *Beckett's Dantes* is another example of a work which uses an increasing critical access to unpublished Beckett material to produce the fullest account to date of Beckett's oeuvre wide engagement with Dante, and there has been a number of recent works that have been devoted to uncovering a growing range of work that is avowedly indebted to Beckett.[16] James Knowlson's collection *Beckett Remembering / Remembering Beckett*, and the recent collection *After Beckett*, by Anthony Uhlmann Sjef Houppermans and Bruno Clément, eds, published as a special edition of *Samuel Beckett Today / Aujourd'hui'* are two examples of this recent trend.[17]

But much more striking than this critical retuning is the increasing proliferation and diversity of Beckett's legacies themselves, across a truly vast range of cultural practices and contexts. From early on in Beckett's reception, there have been a number of writers who sought affiliation with his work, and who it was possible to imagine as working under his 'influence'. It is possible to see a dramatic tradition, for example, that emerges from Beckett's writing, in the form of Harold Pinter's version of Beckettian 'absurdism', or Tom Stoppard's, and there has long been a perception that writers such as Christine Brooke-Rose, Malcolm Lowry, B. S. Johnson or Alain Robbe-Grillet are working in some kind of dialogue with Beckett.[18] One reason that this set of influences came so readily to critical expression, however, is that these writers, in various ways, are themselves often regarded as spokespersons for a late modernism, and the Beckett that readers have found in these writers is the Beckett that is historically marooned, that marks the extended termination of modernism. Beckett's presence in Pinter's earlier work, for example, can be thought of as a rather static presence, a fixed point, rather than as a source of new dramatic possibilities. But in more recent years, Beckett's influence has found a new kind of expression, and has begun to emerge in forms that seem in some ways inimical to his own artistic practice. Harold Pinter's later, more politically engaged work, for example, has suggested some of the ways that Beckett's dramatic language might extend beyond the kind of impasse marked out by Adorno, and this widening or loosening of the features of the Beckettian dramatic stamp can be seen in the new dynamism of his influence on the drama.[19] Sarah Kane, for example, has a strong affiliation with Beckett, just as it is possible to see Pinteresque shapes in her work, but both Beckett and Pinter come to a new kind of expression in Kane's work, a different kind of contemporaneity, and carry a different kind of political charge.[20] This adaptation of Beckett's stage can be seen across the world, both in terms of dramatists who adapt a Beckettian influence to new political, theatrical and formal environments, and in terms of the range of productions of Beckett's works, which demonstrate an extraordinary sensitivity to context. Vaclav Havel, for example, demonstrates how little one has to inflect Beckett's plays, or Beckett's dramatic shapes, to produce an intensely contemporary political theatre.[21] Bruce Naumann's work is extraordinarily effective in reimagining Beckett in various media,[22] and recent productions of Beckett's *Breath* by Damien Hirst, Nikos Navridis and Adriano and Fernando Guimarães demonstrate the widening purchase of Beckett's work on world theatre. In film and television, also, Beckett exerts a peculiar, almost uncannily wide and elastic influence. Strains of his comedy can be heard reverberating through a whole range of popular television shows, from the Irish sitcom *Father Ted* to the British suburban drama of meandering old age, *One Foot in the Grave*. His influence can be felt in cinema from Bergman and Godard to David Mamet and David Lynch, where Beckett's influence can be seen filtered to a degree through Kafka.[23] In contemporary poetry, Beckett's work achieves a similarly wide resonance, where he is refracted in various ways in the poetry of Derek Mahon, John Ashbery, J. H. Prynne and in the work of Susan Howe, whose own reflection on influence, *My Emily Dickinson*, suggests intriguing ways in which Beckett's influence might mingle and merge with that of Dickinson, a poet with whom Beckett has a rich but elusive affiliation.[24] It is possible to divine Beckett's presence in dance, in video art, in various forms of contemporary music, as well as across the range of contemporary fiction, in Europe, North America, South Africa and around the globe. Beckett is a striking presence, for example, in Ismail Kadare's novels, which seek to imagine the outlines of an Albania which might be part of a new, global Europe.[25] J. M. Coetzee's novels, in their attempt to invent a language for the new South Africa, in their experiments with producing a voice which can cross the divide between man and woman, between human and animal, are engaged, throughout, in an ongoing dialogue with Beckett.[26] Thomas Pynchon's novels, from *Crying of Lot 49* to *Mason and Dixon* (a kind of expanded version, seen in a certain light, of *Mercier and Camier*) stage a singular, if oblique engagement with Beckett. It is possible to see a Beckettian strain running from Thomas Bernhard to W. G. Sebald, which has the effect of recasting Beckett's persistent but unworded engagement with the Holocaust (see Part Two). One can see Beckett moving in Marguerite Duras, in Houellebecq, in James Kelman, in John Banville, in Paul Auster.[27] In a recent novel *Pattern Recognition* by William Gibson, a writer of 'cyberpunk' who seems to have nothing in common with Samuel Beckett, the plot turns around a cult who are obsessed with fragments of a film broadcast on the internet known as 'the footage', a dislocated, empty set of images whose slow dissolution is held in contrast to the speed of the global, high-tech plot. The novel concerns the protagonist Cayce Pollard's search for the auteur of this Beckettian scrap of auratic film, a search which is centrally involved with a figure who sells Curta calculators, a man who 'looks just like a scary portrait of Samuel Beckett on a book [Pollard] owned in college', as if it is some descendent of Beckett who has brought this counter-intuitive slowness, this aesthetic aura, into the heart of a globalized world, into the heart of Gibson's science fiction.[28]

Again and again, across genres, styles, media, and with a diversity and proliferation to which it is impossible to do justice in this kind of list, Beckett's work emerges in contemporary forms of expression, where it suggests not the end, not the death of the imagination, but the possibility of a new means of shaping the way that we think and see. Even in DeLillo's novel *Mao II*, where Bill Gray suggests that Beckett's power to shape has expired, one can feel this continuing influence, this burgeoning set of possibilities. DeLillo's novel is inhabited by the spirit of the countercultural writer, the spirit of a Beckettian aesthetic that continues to make its shaping presence felt, despite Gray's suggestion that a Beckettian poetics is no longer possible, and despite Gray's own failure to publish the critical fiction that he withholds in the novel, protecting it from contact with the 'culture industry' in which it cannot readily find a place. Even as Gray gets involved in that conversation in which he mourns the passing of Beckett's influence, the dialogue catches at something from Beckett, keeping Beckett's rhythms alive even in the throes of their death. Gray makes his remark about Beckett to a character named George Haddad, as the two prepare to meet a terrorist by the name of Abu Rashid, and the dialogue goes as follows:

> 'He calls himself Abu Rashid. I honestly think you'd be fascinated by the man.'
> 'Isn't it always the case?'
> 'And I'm still hopeful he'll turn up here.'
> 'But in the meantime.'
> 'We're here to talk.'
> 'To have a dialogue.'
> 'Exactly', George said. (Mao 156)

If it is possible to hear the bantering rhythms of Gogo and Didi's cross talk here, then throughout the novel there are snippets, phrases, shapes, that drift to DeLillo from Beckett. Bill Gray, heading towards his own death in the darkness of 1989, searches for a painkiller to palliate the mortal injuries from which he is suffering, but discovers that 'there was no more medication' (Mao 159) – a diagnosis of general incurability in which, as Mark Osteen has commented, one can hear Clov's assertion to Hamm that 'there's no more painkiller' (CDW 127).[29] Indeed, it is possible to think of Bill Gray as a version of Hamm, as a version of a Beckettian writer whose 'chronicle' is unable to come to an end. One can think of Gray as a figure in whom Beckett's and DeLillo's writing reaches for a kind of accommodation, as if Gray's death in the empty space between the decades marks a passing of Beckett's spirit into the body of DeLillo's writing. When Gray says of Beckett that he is the 'last writer to shape the way we think and see', he uses a phrase that has an extraordinary resonance in DeLillo's prose, that reaches back through his writing to the earliest incarnations of a DeLillian late modernism, suggesting a peculiar intermingling between the Beckettian and the DeLillian writer. Gray's phrase echoes DeLillo's first auteur, the Godardian film maker and advertising executive David Bell, protagonist of DeLillo's first published novel *Americana*. Bell thinks of himself as an inheritor of a Beckettian aesthetic, imagining himself 'sitting in my living room' with

'James Joyce and Antonioni and Samuel Beckett' (A 220), but it is advertising rather than modernism that makes this conjunction between David Bell, Bill Gray and Samuel Beckett. Speaking of his job in an advertising firm, Bell says that 'in a curious way I liked my job – in the beginning at least. It made me think and see as I never had done before' (A 36). And in *White Noise*, 13 years later, the phrase comes up again, where again DeLillo forges a connection between a persistent, late modernist avant-garde and an aesthetically bankrupt culture of consumption. Jack Gladney, who is often regarded as the figure of a retrenched modernism in the novel, meets up in the supermarket with Murray Jay Siskind (regarded equally often as the representative of a DeLillian post-modernism),[30] and Murray says to Jack that he likes the supermarket, finding its bare white interiors more conducive to critical thinking than the university library or quad. It is the supermarket, he says, that represents 'the last avant-garde' that is the custodian and progenitor of 'bold new forms' (WN 19). 'It's all much clearer here', he tells Jack, quoting David Bell and predicting Bill Gray, 'I can think and see' (WN 36). So, when Bill Gray suggests to George Haddad that Samuel Beckett is the last figure to help us to think and see, he makes a conjunction between the DeLillian and the Beckettian artist that crosses a broad divide, between Europe and the United States, between high art and consumer culture, between modernism and whatever comes in its wake. He suggests some of the ways in which Beckett's modernism lives on, adapting itself to the contours of the contemporary, giving the possibilities of contemporary literary expression a shape and a form.

In the following chapters, this book traces some of these shapes in which Beckett's writing inhabits the contemporary, while at the same time reading back through Beckett to the modernist and proto-modernist forms that Beckett himself inherits. The book consists of three large movements, each of which is broken into three chapters. The first movement reads Beckett back through an Irish tradition that includes W. B. Yeats, Elizabeth Bowen and Maria Edgeworth, before plotting a course through Beckett to John Banville, in order to determine the extent to which Beckett's blocked engagement with homeland reaches a freer expression in those Irish writers that come after him. In Banville's fiction, I argue, it is possible to see the partial emergence of a new, post-national accommodation between Ireland and Europe, an accommodation which is shadowed forth in Beckett's writing, but which remains for Beckett unnameable and almost unthinkable. This delicate conjunction between Ireland and Europe in Beckett and Banville opens onto the second of the book's three movements, in which I trace Beckett's involvement with a European rather than an Irish tradition. Here, I read Beckett not through Bowen and Edgeworth, but back through Wittgenstein to Heinrich von Kleist, before reading the ways in which Beckett and Kleist together stretch through the prose of Thomas Bernhard to that of W. G. Sebald. In reading this European, Germanic tradition, alongside the Irish Beckett plotted in the first movement, I argue that Beckett's writing helps to produce the forms in which Bernhard and Sebald stage the recovery of historical material lost in the darkness of the Holocaust. If the Holocaust marks the limits of a certain modernist form of remembrance, the modes of remembrance developed by Proust and by Joyce, then I argue it is Beckett's writing that adapts these modes, and that forges a kind of Kleistian poetic remembrance that is able to bring lost histories to the point of a mute expression. The final movement of the book circles outwards, from the Irish and European contexts of the first two chapters, to trace the development of a proto-global perspective in Beckett's writing. The first part of this last chapter reads Beckett's inheritance of Joyce's nationalism, before following the ways in which Beckett's later work performs a dissolution of the 'partitions' which mark out national boundaries, allowing for the imagining of a new, unboundaried relationship between the local and the global. The third and final part of the last chapter then reads Beckett's engagement with a range of writers, including Saul Bellow, J. M. Coetzee and Don DeLillo, who seek to imagine the form that democracy might take, under the conditions brought about by the globalization of capital and of culture. The decline of national sovereignty makes the task of imagining democratic institutions a pressing one, and, I argue, one of the perhaps surprising legacies of Beckett's writing is a means responding to this task, a means of thinking a new global democracy, a new 'way', as Beckett puts it in 'The Capital of the Ruins', of 'being we' (CSP 277).

So, this book is part of an ongoing critical attempt to free Beckett's works from the deadlock which has caused him to become hypostasized as the 'last modernist'. In it I seek to give expression to some of the ways in which Beckett's capacity to persist has allowed his work to generate new possibilities, to extend the modernism that he inherits in new and exciting ways, rather than freezing it in mid-gesture. In doing so, however, in seeking to sketch an historical narrative that might make sense of Beckett's work as a bridge from Joyce and Proust, Kleist and Edgeworth and Bowen, to Banville, DeLillo, Coetzee and Sebald, I am mindful at all times of the other half of the Beckettian equation – mindful that Beckettian persistence is only ever a function of exhaustion, that the beginnings that are occasioned by his work are won from and return to an ongoing termination. In tracing Beckett's influence and his influences, I have no intention of placing his work securely into an historical current. I do not want to claim that it is possible after all to see where Beckett begins and where he ends, or to suggest that increasing critical familiarity with Beckett's writing and the archival material that surrounds his published oeuvre have allowed us finally to understand where his work comes from, and to understand where it leads to. On the contrary, if this book traces Beckett's debts and legacies, it does so in the spirit of the temporality that is fashioned in Beckett's writing, and in the unthinkable tense that Molloy demands when he seeks, himself, to talk of his 'life' ('at the same time it is over and it goes on', he writes, 'and is there any tense for that?' [Mo 36]). It seeks to orient the contemporary in relation to Beckett's writing, but it does so in the conviction that Beckett's work is a fugitive and restless landmark, or timemark, which does not remain securely contained within the borders 1929–1989, which seems at once impossibly old and at the same time unthinkably new, almost unborn. I seek here to give critical expression to the meaning of the phrase 'since Beckett', while seeking to respond to the sense in which he is at once not over, and still to come. Indeed, it is one of the peculiarly recurring features of Beckett's legacy that he is characterized, even by those who regard him as a key influence, as in some sense still in the future, as if he is at once behind us and ahead of us. J. M. Coetzee, for example, says in an interview with David Atwell that 'Beckett has meant a great deal to me in my own writing – that must be obvious. He is a clear influence on my prose' (DtP 25). But while Coetzee implies that Beckett is in a sense where he has come from, he also suggests that Beckett is ahead of him still, in the unmade, unborn time of the future. Coetzee sees the trajectory of Beckett's work as a steady progression towards such a future, a development, he suggests, in which he himself is lagging behind. '*Molloy*', Coetzee writes,

> was still a very embodied work. Beckett's first after-death book was *The Unnamable*. But the after-death voice still has body, and in that sense was only halfway to what he must have been feeling his way toward. The late pieces speak in post-mortem voices. (DtP 23)

It is this same sense that Beckett has developed an 'after-death' voice in his later prose that is the substance of Thomas Bernhard's only known comment on Beckett's writing. When Bernhard was asked by Rita Carrio how he responded to Beckett's influence, he replied that 'as far as I'm concerned Beckett has been dead for ten years, he merely sends brief messages from the hereafter'.[31] And in W. G. Sebald and Jan Peter Tripp's collaborative work *Unrecounted*, the lithograph of Beckett's eyes gazes back at us as if from the future, suggesting that he is not an influence but a destination. The verse that accompanies Tripp's image also resonates with Coetzee's and with Bernhard's sense that Beckett is over us, above us, rather than in any sense behind us. 'He will cover / you with his / plumage', the verse reads, '& / under his wing then / you will rest' (Un 79). Time and time again, Beckett's work seems displaced in this way, removed to the time to come, suggesting that Beckett's haunting of the culture follows the spectral logic of the influence of Marx traced by Jacques Derrida in *Spectres of Marx*. The phrase 'since Marx', Derrida writes, 'names a future-to-come as much as a past'. '"Since Marx" continues to designate the place of assignation from which we are *pledged*', Derrida argues,

> [B]ut if there is pledge or assignation, injunction or promise, if there has been this appeal beginning with a word that resounds before us, the 'since' marks a place and a time that doubtless precedes us, but so as to be as much

in front of us as before us. Since the future, then, since the past as absolute future.³²

If Derrida is able, in *Spectres of Marx*, to develop a means of thinking this 'to come' of Marx, then it is partly because Beckett's writing, Beckett's poetics of persistence and exhaustion, has given him a vocabulary with which to do so, a vocabulary upon which the possibility of deconstruction itself to some extent rests.

In tracing Beckett's presence in contemporary culture through the three movements of this book, then, I aim to develop a model of influence that can account for and arises from the peculiar temporal effects produced by his writing, a model that departs from the historical sequentiality, the struggle to overcome the past, that is the burden of Harold Bloom's enormously influential and elegant model of literary influence *The Anxiety of Influence*. In Bloom's account, the passage of literary history is a violent struggle between 'strong poets', in which each generation of writers seeks to master those that have come before them, aiming for what Bloom calls the 'absolute absorption of the precursor'.³³ Bloom reads influence as a 'Battle between strong equals, father and son as mighty opposites, Laius and Oedipus at the crossroads'.³⁴ But one of the most significant of Beckett's legacies, I would argue, is a conception of legacy itself, a conception of influence, which does not depend upon such opposition between past and future generations, between father and son, between parent and child. In Beckett's writing, the father is as likely to belong to the future as he is to the past, just as those who register Beckett's influence tend to think of him not as parent to be slain, but as a possibility to be glimpsed, the spectral boy in the wasteland outside the refuge rather than the progenitors in the trashcans. The task of this book is to give a critical expression to the ways in which Beckett brings the past into contact with the future, us into contact with them, here into contact with there, in ignorance of the kinds of struggle for supremacy, for supersession, that is the burden of Bloom's account of the passing generations. Beckett does not obey the historical logic of Bloom's model of influence, I argue here, but if his work undermines or troubles such forms of historical sequentiality, this is not because we have entered a post-phase, not because Beckett's writing marks the transition from modernism to postmodernism that is suggested by Begam, and others who regard Beckett as an architect of the postmodern.³⁵ Rather than presiding over the end of history, the postmodern weakening of historicity, I argue that his work keeps histories alive, bringing the modernist forms he has inherited from Joyce and Proust into a peculiar contact with the contemporary. Beckett's writing, I argue, invents bleakly utopian forms which bring almost unthinkable continuities and unities to the verge, to the threshold of expression. If what Begam thinks of as the 'end of modernity' ushers in an historical phase that seems to many to be the end of history, and if the second half of the twentieth century appears to stage the decline of sovereignty,

Introduction

the end of the nation state as the prime administrator of political power and identity, then it is easy to see why Beckett has been read as the expression of such an end. His historical and geographical dislocation and disengagement seem clearly symptomatic of such forms of termination. But in the chapters that follow I suggest that Beckett's writing is one which not only stages these modes of political exhaustion, but also invents delicate forms in which we might extend ourselves into a new future, and give expression to new forms of political and poetic identity; forms which are still, since Beckett, coming to the point of perceptibility.

Part One

Back Roads: Beckett, Banville and Ireland

Chapter 1

Edgeworth, Bowen, Beckett, Banville: A Minor Tradition

To think about Beckett and Ireland is to think about the back. His relationship with an Irish tradition, and his bequest of singular form of engagement with Ireland, is conducted through a poetics of the back, in all its various and delicately shaded connotations.

This connection in Beckett between Irishness and what David Wills has called 'dorsality' has, I suggest, deep roots in the Irish literary tradition.[1] Maria Edgeworth's novel *Castle Rackrent*, for example, is one which is centrally concerned with formulations of the back. At one point in Edgeworth's novel the hopelessly spendthrift landlord Condy Rackrent gallantly returns to his Irish ancestral home with a new bride, whose possession of fine jewellery and a large personal fortune, he fondly hopes, will save him from impending bankruptcy. On arrival at the house, the bride and groom find that, through neglect and consequent dilapidation, the front entrance is impassable. As a result, the servants gather to greet their new mistress not in the arcaded front hall, but jostling at the 'back gate'. The disappointed bride Miss Isabella asks her husband 'am I to walk through all this crowd of people, my dearest love?', and he replies 'My dear, there is nothing for it but to walk, or to let me carry you as far as the house, for you see that back road is too narrow for a carriage, and the great piers have tumbled down across the front approach; so there's no driving the right way, by reason of the ruins' (CR 46–7). As Miss Isabella makes her way into the house through the cramped back kitchen, the narrator Thady Quirke recounts, with his customarily oblique glee, that the 'feathers on the top of her hat were broke going in at the low back door' (CR 47).

This moment in the novel makes a conjunction between thresholds, thoroughfares and minority that finds echoes across the following centuries of Irish writing. The back road, the back gate and the back door are signs, in this novel, of the failure of an Anglo-Irish tradition, signs that the major lines of communication, the forms of congress and community that have made the Anglo-Irish ascendancy possible, are now impassable. The back door through which the bewildered Miss Isabella is forced to pass cannot accommodate her feathered grandeur, a grandeur which is in any case starting to look a little fragile, a little ridiculous. It is Thady Quirke, and more importantly Thady's calculating son Jason, who are better accustomed than their masters to the back passage ways, and more adroit in the navigating of minor routes. Jason Quirke's capacity to slip in by the back door, to enter the house as servant and leave it as master, is the central focus of Edgeworth's narrative. Jason's incremental and somehow inevitable prising of the house and of the land away from the exhausted grasp of his Protestant masters suggests that capital will pass, from now on, through the back doors, that the front entrances and driveways that the absentee landlords had allowed to fall into disrepair would never again be the main channels of commerce and power.

As Edgeworth writes the novel, in the months before the 1800 Act of Union, she suggests that this migration from front to back, from dominant to emergent, should be seen in the context of a larger shift in the balance of power. The homely tale of Thady's dogged devotion to his slovenly masters, and of Jason's canny betrayal of them, is a mildly cautionary one, but it is nevertheless possible to laugh at it because, Edgeworth insists, 1800 will inaugurate a new age in which the Quirkes and the Rackrents will speak to each other in an entirely new language. 'There is a time', Edgeworth writes in the preface to the novel,

> when individuals can bear to be rallied for their past follies and absurdities, after they have acquired new habits and a new consciousness. Nations as well as individuals gradually lose attachment to their identity, and the present generation is amused rather than offended by the ridicule that is thrown upon their ancestors. (CR 5)

The new consciousness that Edgeworth invokes here, perhaps anticipating the 'uncreated conscience' that Joyce's Dedalus ascribes to his 'race' in *Portrait* over a century later,[2] will give rise to a new cosmopolitanism, in which the local struggle between dominant and emergent cultures in Ireland will become a charming irrelevance. 'When Ireland loses her identity by an union with Great Britain', Edgeworth goes on, 'she will look back with a smile of good humoured complacency on the Sir Kits and Sir Condys of her former existence' (CR 5). This assured confidence that the Union will effect a transformative cultural renaissance, however, is always somewhat strained in Edgeworth's account. In her preface there is a curious temporal slippage – it is the 'present generation' who thinks with a new consciousness, and yet the Union is still in the future, and evoked in the future tense – which echoes or anticipates the temporal confusion of the novel itself. Thady's narrative begins on '*Monday Morning*' (CR 7), and Edgeworth explains in her glossary that this Monday marks a stalled time that is a feature of provincial Irish culture. Thady 'begins his Memoirs of the Rackrent family by dating *Monday Morning*' Edgeworth explains in the glossary to the novel,

> because no great undertaking can be auspiciously commenced in Ireland on any morning but *Monday morning.* – 'Oh please God we live till Monday

morning, we'll set the slater to mend the roof of the house – On Monday morning we'll fall to and cut the turf – On Monday morning we'll see and begin mowing – On Monday morning, please your honour, we'll begin and dig the potatoes,' &c.

All the intermediate days between the making of such speeches and the ensuing Monday are wasted, and when Monday morning comes it is ten to one that the business is deferred to *the next* Monday morning. (CR 99)

In a sense, the novel sets out to remedy this collapse of linear time into a single, eternal Monday. The narrative is peppered with footnotes in which the editor of Thady's narrative insists that the Monday in which Thady is marooned has well and truly passed away. Thady says, for example, that 'Sir Murtagh had no childer', and the editor politely points out at the foot of the page that 'this is the manner in which many of Thady's rank, and others in Ireland, *formerly* pronounced the word *Children*' (CR 18). This word 'formerly', meaning before the Act of Union, comes up time and again in the narrative, where it marks a gap between Thady's blindly static narrative and the editorial apparatus of glossary, preface and footnotes that reflects upon it, and that belongs to a post-Union culture that has re-entered historical time.[3] But in the preface, already, it is possible to detect this same stalling, this same confusion between past and future, between next Monday and last. The union which will build a new, broad road across the Irish channel, allowing the comically circuitous back roads of Thady's narrative to pass into obscurity, has both already occurred in the preface, and is still to come, suggesting that the confident separation between the future and the past upon which the novel is predicated is in fact far from clear. The scholarly voice of the preface and the notes is infected, as a result of this temporal confusion, by the idiomatic provincial voice in which the narrative is told. The former should belong to a utopian period after the Union, the latter should fall away into the pre-Union gloom. But the possibility of a unified cosmopolitan perspective which would allow Ireland to join with Britain – to enter into modernity – seems always just beyond the novel's grasp. Edgeworth conceives of the Union not only as a political act, but also as a sundering of the imagination from the coils, the back roads of a pre-modern Irish identity. This imaginary sundering, though, belongs to a future which cannot quite arrive – which even the 1800 act of Union cannot deliver – while the editorial voice of *Castle Rackrent* is returned to a troubling complicity with the 'former' Irish culture which it tries to mock.

One sign of this failure in Edgeworth to detach the cosmopolitan from the provincial might be the continuing resonance in Irish writing of the back – the back door, the back room, the back road. It is possible to draw a line from Edgeworth through Elizabeth Bowen to Samuel Beckett and to John Banville – to map a kind of back road – which suggests that there is something like a tradition to be found here, a tradition of the back, or of the minor; a shadow of the Anglo-Irish tradition plotted by W. J. McCormack in *From Burke to Beckett*.[4]

To take some examples more or less at random, we might trace a line from Edgeworth's back road, to Bowen's extraordinary ghost story 'The Back Drawing Room', to Beckett's late, nostalgic evocation of the 'dear old back roads' in *Company* (NO 18), *Stirrings Still* (CSP 260) and . . . *but the clouds* . . . (CDW 422), to the 'dappled back roads' in Banville's *Body of Evidence* (BE 102), and the 'back roads' that were prowled in his youth by Alexander Cleave in Banville's *Eclipse* (E 33). In each of these instances, it might be argued, the back road or the back room is asked to carry the burden of an Irishness that has not yet been accommodated within the unified cosmopolitanism that Edgeworth was reaching for in 1800, but that is also unable to find a major language in which to articulate itself, or to put itself into the foreground. In all of these writers, the failure of the kind of reconciliation that Edgeworth imagines in her preface to *Castle Rackrent* has produced a curious shroudedness in reference to Ireland, a kind of occlusion, as if Ireland can no longer be looked at other than squintwise, as if it can be named only through the suspension of the name. Where Edgeworth imagines that the back roads of Thady's narrative will fall into a kind of disuse as Ireland is refashioned and renamed through its union with Britain, these writers suggest instead that Ireland's difficult relationship with modernity and with Europe has led to a kind of failure of reference, a failure that is already anticipated in the curious contradictions exhibited by Edgeworth's narrative. The Ireland imagined in Thady's story cannot be translated into the language of European modernity, as Brian Friel's play *Translations* attests, but neither is there a language available in which to preserve the rural culture to which Thady belongs. Rather, the naming of and reference to Ireland in these writers takes place in a kind of hidden back room, stowed somewhere beneath a surface which tends towards placelessness and geographical anonymity.

This connection between Ireland and the minor, or the back, tends, in Elizabeth Bowen, to produce a certain spectrality. The spectral can be felt in many of her novels – in works such as *The Last September* and *To the North* – but it is in her short stories that she explores this relation between Ireland and the ghostly most effectively, and particularly in her story 'The Back Drawing Room' – a story explicitly about the ghostliness of the back. This story, despite the article in the title, is in fact a tale of two back drawing rooms. The first of these, in which the story opens, is the scene of an intimate gathering of cosmopolitan intellectuals, a salon of some kind, in a place which remains unnamed and unspecified, but which we are led to assume is in England, possibly London. The conversation is lofty, self-conscious and pompous, and turns around the possibility of the survival of the soul after death. The question that the company are addressing as the story begins is whether it is fitness or tenacity that guarantees the survival of the soul; is it a Darwinian principle, or something more mysterious – some blind, willed tenacity – that allows a trace of life to linger on after the conditions of its possibility has lapsed. Into this company blunders an unnamed stranger – 'Somebody who came in late had brought him, with an apology' (CS 200). The stranger, who has none of the sophistication of the salonnière and her guests, misreads the tone of the conversation, and sees the discussion of the post-mortem soul as a cue for a ghost story; 'Hell', says one of the guests, 'bring in the Yule log, this is a Dickens Christmas' (CS 203). It is the ghost story that the stranger tells, against the mocking protests of the other guests in the salon, that takes us to the story's second back drawing room; the back drawing room of an Irish big house that has been burnt down by republicans during the troubles, but that has somehow lingered on, somehow survived the passing of its age through a blindly willed tenacity, rather than through any Darwinian fitness. Everything in the story hinges round the seam that the stranger opens here between the two rooms, a conjunction that produces a number of contradictory effects. Bowen's story tells of the movement from the first room to the second, but it quickly becomes apparent that the journey from first to second, from front story to back story, is haunted, from the beginning, by a simultaneous movement in the opposite direction. As the mocking guests who repeatedly interrupt the stranger's story are quick to point out, this is a clichéd tale of a journey towards a haunted house, a journey from the real and the quotidian towards the spectral, the absent, the strange. 'What was the house like' one of the guests interjects: 'Was it very obviously haunted? *Weren't* there any dark windows' (CS 206). But while the journey is, in one sense, from the real to the spectral, in another sense the story moves in the opposite direction, from the vague to the defined. While the first back drawing room remains unlocated, adrift, the second room is located, from the beginning, in Ireland. The movement towards the centre of the stranger's story is one that takes us from placelessness to place. With the stranger's journey, the anonymity of the story's setting is gradually broken, as the narrative takes us from a generalized cosmopolitan locale, across the Irish channel towards a realized space that becomes increasingly concrete, until the stranger himself is riding bumpily along on a bicycle on a country road that is given more substantiality, more descriptive colour, than anything that belongs to the shadowy environs of the first back drawing room. Indeed, the salonnière herself, Mrs Henneker, registers this sense that the stranger's story is taking us across a threshold from vagueness to the vividness of a specific place, but even as she does so she registers also the opposite direction in which the stranger's story moves. The stranger begins his story by saying that last year he 'went over to Ireland', and Mrs Henneker interrupts him:

> 'Ireland', said Mrs Henneker, 'unforgettably and almost terribly afflicted me. The contact was so intimate as to be almost intolerable. Those gulls about the piers of Kingstown, crying, crying: they are an overture to Ireland. One lives in a dream there, a dream oppressed and shifting, such as one dreams in a house with trees about it on a sultry night.' (CS 203)

The stranger's fictional journeying towards the second back drawing room takes him over the threshold marked by Kingstown, a name which might be thought of, itself, as a royal English mask for the Irish Dun Loaghaire. For Mrs Henneker, this journey towards the heart of Ireland is a journey towards an intimacy, towards a kind of *contact* that is unbearable in its overwhelming presence. But at the same time, it is a journey towards a dream, a journey away from the real. As the story continues, this confusion between the dreamlike and the concrete becomes increasingly marked, until we arrive at the heart of the story, a dead centre composed at once of the real and the spectral, the clichéd and the original, the present and the absent.

As we enter this dead centre – the heart of the back – the word back starts to repeat itself uncontrollably, as if the word is part of the haunting, one of the revenants in the stranger's story. The stranger, out for the day on a bike ride in the Irish countryside, arrives at the ghostly big house, where he lets himself timidly into the hall (his bicycle has had a puncture, and he is looking to the house, as per the generic convention, for help and shelter from the rain). The house seems deserted, until 'a door at the back of the hall opened' (CS 207), and the figure of a woman appears. Losing his sense of propriety, as if hypnotized or possessed, the stranger follows the woman into 'a drawing room, a back drawing room' (CS 207). ('Here was I', the stranger says, reliving his bafflement with a quiet, ironic reference to his uninvited presence as narrator in the first back drawing room, 'Here was I, unintroduced, in a back drawing room, really quite an intimate room, where I believe only favoured visitors are usually admitted' [CS 208]). As the stranger enters this intimate back room, there is an immediate sense that both he and his narrative are becoming somehow submerged, immersed in the backness of this place that seems lost to time and to history. With his entry into this ghostly dimension, the voices belonging to the first back drawing room that have been haranguing him and holding him back fall away, and a new voice starts to speak, from the back, as it were. Adding to the overwhelming sense of immersion, the unnamed voice suggests that the woman, who is now sobbing silently before the stranger on the couch, is 'drowning'. When the drowning woman looks up at the stranger, he says, he is startled, and the unnamed voice interrupts again, 'as if you had not known she had a face' (CS 208). This encounter between the stranger and the drowning woman, mediated by an unanchored voice coming from the back heart of the narrative (a voice belonging at once to the drowning woman and to salonnière Mrs Henneker, but also to neither), is one in which the back shows its face, in which we discover that the back does indeed have a face, if not one which is describable or thinkable or knowable. The sight of this face, the stranger says, 'made me feel the end of the world was coming':

'I couldn't speak to her again; she – she . . .'
  'Beat it back'.
  'Beat it back'. (CS 208–9)

With this repetition of 'beat it back' – a repetition in which the voice of the stranger merges hypnotically with the unnamed, dislocated voice – the story is over. The woman 'put down her face again', and the stranger 'went back into the hall', and out of the house, back along the country road to the cosmopolitan present, and to the first back drawing room in which he tells his tale (CS 209).

The convention of the ghost story within the story dictates that the return of the teller to the scene of telling effects a closure, in which the spectral or the monstrous that is encountered at the story's heart is somehow neutralized. The return to the normative setting with which we began allows us to put things back together, as if waking from a dream, having exorcized our fear of the other which the story has both banished and assimilated. But in Bowen's story, the encounter with the back does not allow for such a return. The directional and spatial effects that are produced around the word back mean that return itself, coming back, becomes entangled with its opposite. The back becomes the face, returning becomes a form of going on, producing what, in *To the North* Bowen calls a 'shadowy continuity' between opposing states.[5] The drowning woman, the stranger and the unnamed voice all join in the hypnotic and uncanny mantra 'beat it back', and there is a suggestion that the spectral woman is somehow containing her grief, pushing it back beneath the surface of the story, to release the stranger back to the first back drawing room. But back has mingled with the front in this story, as the strangers back drawing room has taken the place of Mrs Henneker's; the back has been grafted on to the face, and to be beaten back is not only to be suppressed or enshrouded, but also to be revealed, to be brought out of hiding. As the story ends, there is no simple return to solidity of the first room from the slippy spectrality of the first. Rather, the boundary between front and back has been disturbed, disabling any interpretive attempt to distinguish the one from the other. The background has become part of the foreground, the minor has been spliced into the major, in such a way that both rooms become unplaceable, suspended in relation to one another. The frame narrative does not enclose the stranger's story, but rather the two narratives, and the two rooms, lie adjacent to one another, in an unmappable and unframable side by side, connected and separated by that back door through which the stranger first glimpsed his drowning ghost.

Bowen herself offers what might be thought of as a diagnosis of this condition, this appearance on the face of the back. In her series of essays 'Pictures and Conversations', she emphasizes her own commitment to place in her writing, asking rhetorically 'Am I not manifestly a writer for whom places loom large?'.[6] But for Bowen this importance of place does not mean that her writing is placed, or placable; place remains somehow located in the back, even as it looms large. While she is centrally interested in the regional, specific locations of her writing, she also insists that 'the Bowen terrain cannot be demarcated on any existing map'.[7] Her commitment to place sits alongside a curious failure of place, as, she says, 'I have thriven on the changes and chances, the dislocations and the contrasts which have made up so much of my life.'⁸ These contrasts, these dislocations, are to some degree a symptom, she says, of the Anglo-Irish condition. She suggests that, 'possibly, it was England that made me a novelist', speculating that this might be so because it is her arrival in England as an Anglo-Irish immigrant that introduced her to the dislocations that motivate her writing. She says, of the moment of her arrival in England, that

> from now on there was to be (as for any immigrant) a cleft between my heredity and my environment – the former remaining, in my case, the more powerful. Submerged, the mythology of this 'other' land could be felt at work in the ways, manners and views of its people, round me.⁹

This evocation of a submerged land hidden beneath the surface of another suggests a rich resonance between this moment in Bowen's autobiographical sketch, and her earlier story. The drowning woman in 'The Back Drawing Room', herself a figure cloven, in mysterious ways, to the cosmopolitan figure of Mrs Henneker, becomes, through reference to Bowen's later essay, emblematic of a wider cultural condition. It is the fate both of the drowning woman and of the displaced Anglo-Irish to feel suspended, cleft between these two spaces that work such a strange influence upon one another. Maria Edgeworth's dream of union has become, in Bowen's rendering, a much more partial and uncanny cleaving. England and Ireland cleave together and asunder, their separation and their connection effected by the work of the back.

Indeed, Bowen herself suggests that this condition might be thought of as producing a tradition of Irish writing, a tradition born out of a certain deterritorialization. 'To most of the rest of the world' she writes in *Pictures and Conversations*,

> we [Anglo-Irish] are semi-strangers, for whom existence has something of the trance-like quality of a spectacle. As beings, we are at once brilliant and limited; our unbeatables, up to now, accordingly, have been those who best profited by that: Goldsmith, Sheridan, Wilde, Shaw, Beckett. Art is inseparable from artifice: of that, the theatre is the home.¹⁰

Condemned to be 'semi-strangers' everywhere, this line of Irish playwrights have conjured a dramatic art from the necessity for artifice that such strangeness produces. The brilliance that Bowen finds in these writers is intimately related, for her, to their limits: it is the disabling, damaging effects of homelessness that produce a paradoxical, trance-like comfort with the uncomfortable, with the unaccommodating. Declan Kiberd, among others, has pursued this possibility in relation to Samuel Beckett, the last figure on Bowen's list. For Kiberd, Bowen's 'ladies and gentleman' betray a perhaps surprising resemblance to 'Beckett's clowns', in that, despite the disparity in means, both are dispossessed, both are products of what he calls 'empty, contextless space'.[11] Reading directly from Beckett's Anglo-Irish context to the placelessness of much of his writing, Kiberd suggests that Beckett 'set up shop in the void' in response to the unrootedness of the Anglo-Irish predicament.[12] The estrangement suffered by the middle-class Protestant culture to which Beckett belonged is mirrored in the dislocation of Beckett's dramatic and fictional landscapes. Considering that Beckett belongs to a generation of Anglo-Irish who 'feel like strangers in their own country',[13] it is 'small wonder that the protagonist of his early stories comes to conclude that his true home is "Nowhere as far as I can see"'.[14] This nowhere is given a particularly emphatic form of expression in Beckett's stage spaces, Kiberd suggests. Plays such as *Waiting for Godot*, he goes on, enact 'the amnesia which afflicts an uprooted people'.[15] Beckett's empty stage is representative of a landscape which, shorn of any historical identity which might place it or colour it, has become blank and unreadable. Didi and Gogo are 'presented as characters without much history', who find themselves adrift in a world which 'has no overall structure, no formal narrative'.[16]

Like Elizabeth Bowen, Kiberd seeks to read this alienation from a national consciousness as forming part of a national tradition. The 'nowhere' in which the Anglo-Irish find themselves living, and which for Kiberd is the location of Beckett's writing, is revealed to be not only a limit or a privation, but also an 'artistic blessing', since it 'would make of Beckett the first truly Irish playwright, because the first utterly free of factitious elements of Irishness'.[17] The removal of 'elements of Irishness', according to this argument, allows Beckett to become 'truly Irish'. An Irish tradition here is founded upon the disappearance of Ireland, because it is only through such disappearance, such failure of reference, that the experience of living in cultural suspension can be accurately or authentically evoked. Kiberd's neat folding of absence into presence here, his transformation of a lack into a surfeit, is familiar from a long tradition of Beckett criticism which has discovered value and meaning in Beckett's dramatic articulation of valuelessness and meaninglessness. But there is an important difference between Kiberd's sketch of a negative Irish tradition, and that briefly glimpsed by Bowen in *Pictures and Conversations*. Where Kiberd describes the Anglo-Irish as 'strangers', Bowen calls them 'semi-strangers'. In Bowen's writing, as well as in her criticism, the Anglo-Irish condition is not determined by a lack of reference, by what Kiberd calls 'empty contextless space', but by a troubling tension between location and dislocation, the strange and the familiar, belonging and alienation. She writes that the 'Bowen terrain' cannot be mapped, going on to describe it as 'unspecific'.[18] But despite this lack of specificity, she insists, there is something 'under the surface' that locates her writing, a network of references that holds her stories together.[19] Indeed, she is evidently frustrated that 'few people questioning me about my novels, or my short stories, show curiosity as to the places in them. Thesis-writers, interviewers or individuals I encounter at parties all, but all, stick to the same track, which by-passes locality.'[20] Such an assumption that locality doesn't matter offends Bowen's sense that place 'looms large' in her work, and misses the point that, for her, understanding the geographical imperative that drives her writing would provide something like a key to reading it. 'Since I started writing', she claims, 'I have been welding together an inner landscape, assembled anything but at random.'[21] It is the mysterious forces that dictate this unrandom assemblage, this mosaic drawn, she says, from references to Irish and English places, that 'predetermines the work', to a greater extent, even, 'than I may have know at the time'.[22] If Bowen's writing might be thought of as part of a tradition that finds a national consciousness in the experience of dispossession, then such a tradition has to accommodate at once her lack of geographical specificity, and her attachment to place, an attachment which expresses itself in submerged connections, in rooms and spaces secreted in the back. And to position Beckett within this tradition similarly requires us to respond to the semi-strange in his work, rather than simply the strange. To read Beckett's 'nowhere' as an Ireland for the dispossessed, an Ireland free of Irish elements, is to make light of a struggle between reference and failure of reference – a struggle that produces what W. J. McCormack, after Adorno, calls a 'vestigial referentiality'[23] – that runs throughout his oeuvre. It is to assume that Beckett speaks of Ireland by freeing himself from it – in Kiberd's terms freeing himself from it 'utterly' – when I would suggest that Beckett's relationship with Ireland is best imagined in terms of cleavage rather than separation or union. To place Beckett within a minor tradition, to understand how a back road might run from Edgeworth to Bowen to Beckett to Banville, it is necessary to respond to the double implications of this cleavage, this joining and severing of the face to and from the back.

This task has become more pressing in recent years, partly because the critical orthodoxy that has insisted on Beckett's placelessness has started to give way to a sense that his work, like Bowen's, is more engaged with a specific geography than the colourless placelessness of his 'surfaces' might suggest. A number of recent critics have begun to argue, for a range of different critical and ideological reasons, that his work is in fact bound up with place, that it stages a confrontation between a universal, placeless surface – a blank face – and a submerged connection to place, to homeland.[24] Throughout his oeuvre, an autobiographical Irish landscape can be felt moving beneath the surface of an internationalized, sometimes European, sometimes nonspecific space. Just as, in Bowen's story, an Irish space is hidden in the back, beneath a space which is at once unnamed and European, so in Beckett there is a constant movement between a submerged Irish location, and exile in a place that is both European and displaced. In the very earliest prose, this struggle is more or less explicit. In Beckett's first novel *Dream of Fair to Middling Women*, the protagonist Belacqua describes himself as undergoing a three-way struggle between Europe, Ireland and an Edgeworthian dream of 'emancipation, in a slough of indifference and negligence and disinterest, from identity' (D 121). 'At his simplest', the narrator says, Belacqua was 'trine':

> Centripetal, centrifugal and . . . not. Phoebus chasing Daphne, Narcissus flying from Echo and . . . neither [. . . .] The chase to Vienna, the flight to Paris, the slouch to Fulda, the relapse into Dublin and . . . immunity like hell from journeys and cities. (D 120)

As Beckett's work continues, this three-way struggle becomes less overt. Throughout the *Four Novellas* and the three novels of his first Trilogy, the secreting of an Irish space beneath a universalized European surface becomes more canny, as Beckett's experiments with the threshold between the revealed and the hidden, between the face and the back, become more subtle and innovative. It is partly the growing complexity of Beckett's dramatization of the relationship between the local and the universal, the located and the adrift, that leads to the perception that his work is empty of geographical content – the perception, lamented by Bowen in her own critical reception, that the local doesn't matter. The connection with place in Beckett becomes so obscured as to be barely perceptible; the very possibility of home, as in Beckett's late piece 'Neither', becomes 'unspeakable' (CSP 258). As Beckett enters into his most austere phase, from the sixties onwards, it is easy to imagine that there has been a final purging of all detail, of all local colour. There is not much scenery in the late stories, such as *Imagination Dead Imagine*, or in the late dramatic works. But I would argue that it is in his concentrated, short late works that the threefold negotiation between Ireland, Europe and nowhere, first staked out by Beckett's footsore Belacqua, reaches its most concise expression. It is in the sparse plays for television *Ghost Trio* and . . . *but the clouds* . . ., and in the somewhat gentler late novella *Company*, that Beckett's poetics of the back, in relation to a submerged, unspeakable homeland, reaches its most intense form.

Company is a work that is concerned in equal measure with the back and with the face.[25] The story tells of a figure lying on his back in the dark, listening to a voice which speaks to him, from somewhere above his 'upturned face' (C 12), telling him stories about his life. These stories, unusually for a late Beckett work, are rich in geographical detail. The autobiographical content of the stories, their nostalgic evocation of Beckett's Irish childhood, is well documented.[26] For this reason, it might appear that in this work Beckett relents from the cruel austerity of his other late works, revealing the nostalgic attachment to place that has been there all along, but that he has been at great pains to disguise. It is easy to imagine that this story, written originally in English unlike the majority of Beckett's later prose, sees a returning home to those Irish spaces that have lain hidden beneath the sparse, dislocated French language texts such as *Ping* and *The Lost Ones*. It is tempting to think that here we find that we are finally walking again along the 'Ballyogan Road', that 'dear old back road'. Where Beckett's and Belacqua's European wanderings have left him stranded 'nowhere in particular on the way from A to Z', the sudden remembrance that the voice grants the hearer, at this late stage in life and career, allows him to 'say for verisimilitude the Ballyogan road', to find himself walking 'the Ballyogan Road in lieu of nowhere in particular' (NO 18). We are no longer in the bleached out desert space of *Imagination Dead Imagine*, but walking again hand in hand with the mother and the father, towards Croker's Acres, or home from Connolly's Stores. But to read this story as allowing for such access to the back roads of Beckett's memory, those rural lanes whose passing is mourned in Beckett's radio play *The Old Tune*, would be to overlook the singular way in which the back that is so longed for here is placed in relation to the face. This story might be an exception to other late works, in that it speaks so clearly of a remembered Irish landscape, but I would argue that this is not a sudden return to the back, but the playing out of a relation between the blank face and an inaccessible but nevertheless haunting back space that has run throughout the sixties and the seventies, and that can be seen clearly in the less obviously located plays *Ghost Trio* and . . . *but the clouds*. . . .

One impediment to reading *Company* as a nostalgic return, as a going back to the back roads, is the troublingly multiple and layered referents in the novella of the word back. The back, in *Company*, signals a return home to a remembered childhood, as it suggests the pre-modern rural seclusion of the back road, the minor route, but it also names the bodily back upon which the hearer lies, as the voice recounts those memories that he so longs and so refuses to accept are his. This cleavage in the use of the word back complicates any attempt to locate the back, to place it or to assimilate it into the story's spatial economy. Much of the energy of the work is dedicated to finding a way of allowing the hearer to own these memories, to take them into his body, to make the voice itself *his* voice, carried on *his* breath. As *How It Is* is narrated by a 'voice once without qua qua on all sides then in me', an 'ancient voice in me not mine' (HII 7), so the voice of *Company* tries to make a home for itself inside the body of the hearer. For this story to signal a return home, the body must become a cage for these memories, these 'past moments old dreams back again' (HII 7). The back and the face must form two sides of a closed unit – a 'sealed jar', in Molloy's terms (Mo 49) – that can house the voice. But the dynamics of the story do not allow for this bodily arrangement of back and face. As I have already suggested above (p. 5), the desire for the hearer to be ale to say 'Yes I remember. That was I. That was then' (NO 16–17) is consistently thwarted in the novella. Rather, the back is continually becoming the face, just as back and face become uncannily merged in Bowen's ghost story. Rather than forming a three-dimensional storage unit in which the voice might rest or dwell, back and face continually merge, or lie side by side in a peculiar, flat adjacency. As in Bowen's story, the back has a face here, and the face lies flatly on the back, or alongside the back. Any coming together, any melding of voice, body and memory into a single, self-identical subject, is stymied by the insistent collapse of back into face, of face into back. The fantasy of a return home, of a reclaiming of place and of self, gives way to a scenario in which zones lie side by side, seeking but unable to find a means of becoming a whole. The unnamed, dislocated space in which the hearer lies is brought into contact with the richly evocative Irish space he 'remembers', as the voice is brought into contact with the hearer, flirting continually with the prospect of *becoming* the hearer, of revealing its identity with the body that lies on its back in the dark. But as much as the story yearns for a means of putting these zones together, of finding a voice, emanating from within the face, that can say 'yes I remember', there is no means of producing such a union. The zones cleave to one another, but cannot join, leaving the voice to float outside of the face which remains uncannily coterminous with the back.

It is in the paired television plays . . . *but the clouds* . . . and *Ghost Trio*, first broadcast in 1977, that this cloven relation between back and face is given its clearest visual manifestation.[27] Both these plays turn around the relationship between the bowed back and the revealed, uplifted face, and both try and fail to find a form in which to join face and back in a single body. *Ghost Trio* depicts a closed grey room – the 'familiar chamber' – in which a seated figure is bowed over a cassette recorder which apparently plays Beethoven's Fifth Piano Trio (known as *The Ghost*). The face of the figure can barely be seen, as it is covered by his matted hair; the faint light that falls upon him lies along the ridge of his bowed back. This closed figure is held in a tense relation to the three moments in the play when a face is suddenly, magically revealed – the face of a boy who comes to visit the figure in his room, and the face of the figure himself seen once reflected in a mirror that is hanging on the wall, and once at the end of the play, as he raises his head to face the camera in the closing moments. . . . *but the clouds* . . . is set not in an enclosed space, but in three different locales. The first is the place from which the narrator (M) apparently speaks, and consists of a near shot of a seated figure, in which it is only possible to make out his clasped hands. The second is a kind of vestibule in which M appears as character – M1. In this interstitial space, a circle of light surrounded by thick shadow, M1 acts out the movements described by M, as he moves between the 'roads' upon which he tramps by day which are located to the west, a closet in which he changes from tramping gear to robe and skullcap which is located to the east, and a 'sanctum' which is located in the North. As M1 walks in his circle of light between roads, closet and sanctum, he adopts the bowed posture that he shares with the figure in *Ghost Trio*, the light again catching the curve of his bowed back. The third space is an entirely spectral dimension, and consists of a painfully tight close up of a woman's face, drowning in white light, her wide eyes, brimming with unshed tears, averted from the viewer's gaze.

This relationship between face and back is determined by the struggle, in both plays, to find a connection between the former and the latter. As in *Company*, and in Bowen's 'The Back Drawing Room', both of these plays depict a scenario in which the voice has become disconnected from the body, has been expelled from the scene of its own bodily production. The movements from back to face, controlled in both cases by a voice which is located outside of the dramatic space, are symptomatic of this expulsion. In both cases, also, this movement is orchestrated by the haunting presence of a remembered place, and a remembered time, the absence or unavailability of which is partly what has led to this curious dislocation of face from back, of voice from body. Both plays are about broken channels of communication, which have condemned the figures on set to become isolated from a loved one and a loved time, and to be broken from themselves, to be cleft in two. In *Ghost Trio*, this broken communication is evoked most immediately by the grey room in which the seated figure is enclosed. The box of faint light, commanded into being, as in *Company*, by the faint voice which describes it, is a televisual representation of those late prose spaces in which Beckett's bodies lie immured, in stories such as *Ping* and *Imagination Dead Imagine*. There is a powerful sense here of incarceration, of the figure's absolute enclosure within his box, as the 'skull' of the figure in 'Fizzle 8' is 'alone in the dark the void no neck no face just the box last place of all' (CSP 243). The stage space itself suggests a profound separation of the figure from the voice which animates him, and from the boy who comes to visit him. But despite this suggestion that the box is sealed, a central focus of the play is of course the door – the 'indispensable door' (CDW 408) – and the 'opaque' window (CDW 408), which offer a compromised access to the outside, from which the boy visits and from which the voice speaks. Throughout the performance, the stage directions tell us, both door and window are 'imperceptibly ajar' (CDW 408), suggesting that at all times there is some possibility of communication between inside and outside. Indeed, it is the exploration of this possible communication that is the main action of the play, as the figure moves around the room, opening door and window, peering into the shadowed space that surrounds him, gazing through these semi-opaque thresholds towards the places from which he has been cut adrift. This lost place and time is summoned most evocatively by the Beethoven Trio, which comes only partly from the cassette recorder locked within the room, but also from those remembered places that lie beyond the window and the door. If there is an imperceptible connection between inside and outside in the play, the music, belonging to both frames at once, marks this connection out, suggesting both the availability of the past that the music summons, and its spectrality, its imperceptibility. The music suggests the partiality of the threshold, its function both as a closed and as an open boundary, and it is this uncertainty at the boundary, this undecidability, that gives the play such a strange, mysterious power. There is an extraordinary affect produced by the view that we are granted through the window to the darkness scored with rain, and through the door to the corridor, in which the boy appears, dressed in glistening oilskins. These views across the threshold, this near contact with an outside, suggest an epiphanal, Proustian encounter with lost time. The rain – always evocative, however obliquely, of an Irish landscape in Beckett's writing – seems to belong to the lost past itself, as Beethoven's music is located, still, in the remembered past, even as it is reproduced on that tinny cassette recorder. The boy, drenched in remembered rain, seems to have travelled through time itself to deliver his enigmatic negative; it is of course a spectre of himself that both boy and man encounter across this simultaneously open and closed threshold. But while these moments in the play at which door and window are opened might suggest epiphanal, Proustian communication, they are also moments at which the incommensurability between past and present, between the inside and the outside, is at its most emphatic. The play depicts a situation in which the possibility of a channel between the expelled and his homeland, the possibility of a back road that might take this stranded figure home, back to himself as child, is recognized only as a condition of its impossibility. The door that is imagined here is one that makes spaces which are radically divorced from one another – which belong in different dimensions in time and in space – magically adjacent. As in Deleuze and Guattari's reading of Kafka, in which 'two blocks on a continuous and unlimited line, with their doors far from each other, are revealed to have contiguous back doors that make the blocks themselves contiguous',[28] Beckett's door is a back door that summons adjacency, contiguity, from radical separation. But the price of such adjacency is that the back road itself is impassable, or passable only imperceptibly, as ghost or spirit.

In . . . *but the clouds* . . . the oblique reference to an Irish landscape suggested by the teeming rain in *Ghost Trio* becomes a much stronger nostalgia for homeland. The play, of course, is possessed by the spirit of Yeats' poem 'The Tower',[29] and seeks, like the poem, to

> send imagination forth
> Under the day's declining beam, and call
> Images and memories
> From ruin.[30]

The figure in Beckett's play, like the stranger in Bowen's story, calls images from ruin, in particular the image of the woman's face, as he vanishes in his little sanctum through the night. And he too sends his imagination forth, when the time comes,

> with break of day, to issue forth again, void my little sanctum, shed robe and skull, resume my hat and greatcoat, and issue forth again, to walk the roads. [*Pause.*] The back roads. (CDW 421–2)

The back roads here become both the locus of a remembered Irish landscape – the 'dear old back roads' of *Company* and of *Stirrings Still* – and the route towards the recovery of such a landscape, the back road along which the imagination might return to its lost home. But this play, like *Ghost Trio*, is a play about broken channels of communication; the back road here offers only a partial access to rural Ireland, or to the woman's face that so magically appears in the deepening shade of the inner sanctum. One of the ways in which this broken communication expresses itself in the play is in the failed relationship between back, face and voice – the bowed back of the male figure, the revealed face of the spectral woman, and the disembodied voice that directs the action. The play, like most of Beckett's work for television, experiments with the effect on the dramatic space of the failure of suture.[31] The work of suturing in television and film is to fuse a flat succession of adjacent images – the face and the back, for example – into an embodied, three-dimensional world. It is to stitch together a coherent life world out of a montage of discrete, unconnected images. But Beckett's film and television work pushes in the opposite direction, so that voice, music, body and space do not cohere into a recognizable unit but rather lie alongside each other in a manner that defies the perception of an integrated whole. In . . . *but the clouds* . . ., this refusal of suture expresses itself most powerfully in the broken relationship between face and back. The extraordinarily disorientating editing together of the woman's silently mouthing face with the pacing, bowed figure of the man and with the extra-diegetic narrative voice prompts us to make of these elements a whole, prompts us to find a bodily harmony between face, back and voice. And indeed, the sense of contiguity that is produced by the play does suggest a certain coming together here, a coming together that Richard Bruce Kirkley describes as a 'fleeting moment of unified consciousness'.[32] The appearance of the woman's face, mouthing a Yeatsian effort to recollect, does suggest a kind of presence, a kind of bodily relationality between the man and the woman, as if the play is inventing a new body in which man, woman and memory might become united. But at the same time, this is an unthinkable body, conceived from a deeply uncanny form of suturing which performs discontinuity and separation as much as union and possession. The central moment of the play – the moment at which this cleft relation between man and woman expresses itself most forcefully – comes as the voice quotes the close of Yeats' poem – 'but the clouds of the sky . . . when the horizon fades . . . or a bird's sleepy cry . . . among the deepening shades . . .' (CDW 422)[33] – in time with the woman's inaudible speech. This moment suggests an extraordinary coming together of woman, man, voice and memory, a coming together that has an uncanny resonance with the moment in Bowen's story at which man and woman speak together, in their hypnotic injunction to 'beat it back'. The man's voice itself shapes to come from within the woman's lips, to emerge on her breath from some internal body space in which profoundly separate entities have become merged. This moment is one in which face and back, man and woman, Beckett and Yeats, bodily and spectral, Ireland and nowhere, reach for a kind of accommodation, a kind of union more complete, and more transformative of the very conception of identity, than any imagined by Edgeworth. But this accommodation, this new bodily relation, is deeply unsettling, disturbing the very boundaries of the thinkable, or of the perceptible. The body that is suggested here is not only one that holds together, but one that breaks apart, as the indispensable door in *Ghost Trio* marks the separation between adjacent spaces as well as their impossible contiguity. The body made of face and back in *. . . but the clouds . . .* is one that suggests a different kind of thinking about the possibility of communication and community. It suggests an almost perceptible form in which separate entities, which remain profoundly alienated from one another, might share presence. But in suggesting this form, the play produces a collapse of the possibility of form itself. The placing of the Yeatsian voice within and outside the woman's spectral face makes tremble the boundaries and the thresholds which have allowed for the placing of a body within a place.

It is this simultaneous incorporation and rejection of a remembered voice and a remembered landscape that characterizes Beckett's belonging to a minor Irish tradition. In ventriloquizing Yeats' voice, Beckett keeps this tradition alive, through a kind of unDarwinian tenacity that allows it to continue even after its enabling conditions have passed away, even in its deterritorialized, dispossessed state. But the formal means by which Beckett inherits this tradition are also those that undermine the very possibility of inheritance. In allowing his ghosts to speak, Beckett disrupts the spatial and temporal boundaries which allow us to position ourselves in space and time, suggesting a new accommodation between present and past, between body, voice and memory, for which there is not yet a major language. Anna McMullen suggests in a recent essay that 'placing Beckett's oeuvre within the frames of Irish and postcolonial studies troubles their boundaries', because 'Beckett's work performs a dislocation of the frames of nation, identity, or theory'.[34] It is this dislocation of the frame, this troubling of the mechanisms of spatial and temporal orientation, that marks Beckett's inheritance of a minor tradition. For those who come after Beckett, it is necessary to find a way of belonging to this broken, dislocated tradition, to find a way of speaking with a voice that comes at once from within and outside the face.

Chapter 2

Spectrality and Eclipse: Beckett and Banville

In John Banville's 1989 novel, *The Body of Evidence*, the narrator and character Freddie Montgomery dwells for a paragraph or two on the death of his father – the paternal death that he describes in another novel, and with a clear Beckettian echo, as a 'slow dissolution'.[1] Freddie's father died by increments, he says, and took, in his last days, to spending much time in a gloomy cellar, away from the sun of late summer. 'Light was not his medium any more', Freddie recalls, 'he preferred it down here, in the mossy half-dark, among the deepening shades' (BE 48).

This moment in the novel is a freighted one, combining as it does a guarded nostalgia for the dying father with an appeal both to Yeats and to Beckett. The deepening shade of the Montgomery cellar is at once the Celtic twilight of forgetting in Yeats' poem 'The Tower', and the same Yeatsian twilight as summoned by Beckett in . . . *but the clouds* . . . . It calls forth at the same time Yeats' gently resigned ode to the inevitable death of the imagination, and Beckett's resistance to such inevitability – his struggle to continue to imagine even when the imagination is dead. Among the deepening shades in which the father dies in Banville it is possible to make out the dark shapes both of Yeats and of Beckett.

This fleeting coming together of Beckett and Yeats in Banville's paternal remembrance might suggest that Banville seeks a means of accommodating both Yeats and Beckett in his fiction, a means of extending and producing an Irish tradition in which both Beckett and Yeats might be at home. If Beckett's attempt, in . . . *but the clouds* . . ., to make a sounding board for Yeats' dying voice produces a kind of estrangement, a form of dislocation and disjuncture, then perhaps Banville's prose is the place where a rapprochement between Beckett and Yeats might be managed more seamlessly. Indeed, it might be argued that Banville's reception not only of Yeats and Beckett, but also of Bowen and Edgeworth, gives a new voice to an Irish literary tradition. If there is a back road that stretches from Banville back through Beckett, Bowen and Yeats to Edgeworth, a connective thread that allows us to organize these writers into a minor tradition, then maybe it is in Banville's polyphonic, haunted and many-voiced writing that this path might be divined. Banville himself has famously proclaimed that 'I've never felt myself part of any movement or tradition', declaring that the culture to which he belongs is one that he has 'manufactured'.[2] But if Banville feels unable to belong to any existing tradition, he is nevertheless prepared to give us orienting marks that help us to imagine a kind of tradition to which his work might belong, even if one invented, manufactured by his own writing. In another well-known interview, Banville gives a fairly heavy hint to help us work out what this tradition might look like. He comments, in his 1996 interview with Hedwig Schall, that 'every writer has to choose between a Joycean or Beckettian tradition', insisting that 'I go in a Beckettian direction',[3] a direction that might take us along the back road that I plotted above, and which passes from Beckett through Yeats and Bowen to Edgeworth.

It is perhaps in Banville's 2000 novel *Eclipse* that the Beckettian direction that he invokes in 1996 opens up most clearly. This is a novel, in fact, about taking directions, about plotting a course back home, to the house of the narrator's childhood – and in particular to the mother's bedroom – and in following this route the novel evokes an extraordinarily rich sense of Beckett's landscapes, as if the narrator is not only returning to a Banvilleian home but also to a Beckettian one, as if the landscape across which he travels home reaches for a unity with that fetishized, partly autobiographical Irish landscape that shifts under the nameless surface of Beckett's writing.[4] (This sense of a shared Banville-Beckett landscape, indeed, comes into the open after a fashion in Banville's later novel *The Sea*, in which the narrator calls the town and village in the novel is played out 'Ballymore' and 'Ballyless', after the Bally, Ballyba and Ballybaba of *Molloy* [Mo 134].)[5] The opening of *Eclipse*, indeed, evokes Beckett's novel *Molloy* with a peculiar intensity, merging Banville's ambivalent struggle to return to the mother's house with Beckett's. Molloy's narrative is driven by his inarticulate urge to see his mother, and his attempt to make his way to her bedside by finding the 'right road', the 'one that led to her' (Mo 31). Banville's *Eclipse* is propelled, similarly, by a son's baffled need to return to his mother's house. The novel begins with the narrator, Alexander Cleave, finding himself lost on a country road in the winter twilight:

> For miles I had been travelling in a kind of sleep and now I thought I was lost. I wanted to turn the car around and drive back the way I had come, but something would not let me go. (E 5)

This something that holds Cleave captive is obscure to him, until he realizes that his lostness is in fact a kind of finding, that he has driven himself unknowingly home:

> I walked forward to the brow of the hill and saw the town then, its few glimmering lights, and, beyond, the fainter glimmer of the sea, and I knew where unknowingly I had come to. I went back and got behind the wheel again and

drove to the top of the hill and there I switched off the engine and the lights and let the car roll down the long incline in bumping silence, dreamily, and stopped in the square, before the house standing in its darkness, deserted, its windows all unlit. (E 5)

The town that Cleave glimpses from the hill, here, calls to the town that Molloy sees 'faintly outlined against the horizon' at the close of his narrative (Mo 90), suggesting again that there is a kind of double vision in Banville's novel, that the town of Cleave's youth and the town which Molloy has 'never left' are in some fashion the same.

As *Eclipse* continues, this mingling of a Banville-Beckett landscape, haunted by an eroticized mother and a spectrally absent father, unnamed but also Irish, becomes ever more marked. Cleave's town, with its 'few glimmering lights, and, beyond, the fainter glimmer of the sea' evokes not just the landscape of *Molloy*, but that over-determined, partly autobiographical landscape that emerges across the range of Beckett's writing. The view of the town in *Eclipse* that draws the most echoes from Beckett is that which Cleave has from his mother's bedroom window, the parental bedroom that is the origin and destination of *Molloy*, and that acts as a kind of primal scene throughout Beckett's oedipally charged writing. Cleave, like Molloy, comes to occupy his mother's bedroom on his return to his childhood home ('I am in my mother's room', Molloy writes, 'It's I who live there now' [Mo 7]), and the memories of his mother that come to him when he is there, as well as the landscape that he can see through the windows, are immersed in a Beckettian medium, refracted through Beckett's parental remembrance. Cleave remembers, as he sets up camp in his mother's room, how he would visit her in the days of her dying, her slow dissolution. 'I would sit down beside her on one haunch on the side of the bed', he remembers,

> the bed in which I had been born – had been got, too, most likely – and put an arm around her shoulders and draw her forward and look on as she drank, her puckered, whiskery lips mumbling the rim of the cup, and feel the water going down in hiccupy swallows. (E 61)

If this scene calls irresistibly to those scenes in *Molloy* in which Molloy visits his mother's bedside, reproducing that strange mixture of violence, tenderness and repressed desire that characterize encounters with the mother in Beckett, then this scene also evokes Beckett's *Company*. Banville's novel summons a moment from Beckett's novella, in which the narrator's memories of his parents' nuptial bed are mixed with his view from the window, a view on to that charged Beckettian landscape that is so evocative of home:

> You first saw the light in the room you most likely were conceived in. The big bow window looked west to the mountains. Mainly west. For being bowed it

looked also a little south and a little north. Necessarily. A little south to more mountain and a little north to foothill and plain. (NO 9–10)

It is this view that comes back in *Eclipse* again and again, seen at once through the windows of Cleave's mother's house, and of the Beckettian parental window. On his first return to the house, Cleave describes his fearful approach to his mother's room, 'the big back bedroom' (E 18), focusing the oedipal energy of the encounter on the view through the window (which mixes Beckett here with something from Poussin):

> It was light still. I stood at the tall window [and looked out at] the garden straggling off into nondescript fields, then a huddle of trees, and beyond that, where the world tilted, an upland meadow with motionless miniature cattle, and in the furthest distance a fringe of mountains, matt blue and faint against the sky where the sun was causing a livid commotion behind a heaping of clouds. (E 18)

When Cleave enters the room again much later in the novel, this counterpointing of the remembered landscape against a maternal sexuality is complicated further, given an even more illicit sexual charge, by the mingling of the erotic presence of his mother with that of his daughter. He walks into his mother's room to find Lily Quirke, who is both a surrogate for his missing daughter and an illicit sex object, splayed girlishly and pornographically on the bed, a figure who now recalls Lolita, rather than Jocasta. As Cleave regards her, through several interlocking frames of reference, her figure is framed against that parental bedroom window, causing a deeply unsettling confusion of sexual drives with a nostalgic longing for home:

> She was in her room – I think of it as hers now, no longer my mother's [. . .] – lying on her belly on the bed with her legs up and ankles crossed, reading an inevitable magazine. She was in a sulk and would not look at me, hesitant in the doorway. Her bare feet were filthy, as usual; I wonder if the child ever bathes. She swayed her legs lightly from side to side in time to some dreamy rhythm in her head. The window was a big gold box of light; the far hills shimmered, dream blue. (E 172)

This moment is also inhabited by another Beckettian scene, in which a strikingly similar set of tensions are set up between conflicting erotic drives and the view from a parental window, recalling as it does the landscape that the narrator of *First Love* sees from his lover's bedroom. Beckett's narrator recounts the episode in which Anna/Lulu informs him that she is pregnant with his child, a moment at which a loved landscape is refracted through a lens coloured at once by love for the father, a horrified and reluctant desire for a lover who is also a mother, and by the becoming father of the son. Anna/Lulu, the narrator writes, 'had drawn back the curtain for a clear view of all her rotundities', but the narrative eye is drawn, past the pregnant curves of Anna's body, to the rotundities of the landscape revealed by the open curtains:

> I saw the mountain, impossible, cavernous, secret, where from morning to night I'd hear nothing but the wind, the curlews, the clink like distant silver of the stone-cutter's hammers. I'd come out in the daytime to the heather and gorse, all warmth and scent, and watch at night the distant city lights, if I chose, and the other lights, the lighthouses and lightships my father had named for me, when I was small, and whose names I could find again in my memory, if I chose. (CSP 44)

So, the landscape of Banville's novel *Eclipse* is occupied, haunted by Beckett's 'unspeakable home' (CSP 258), a landscape shaped by the body of the mother and bearing the names given to it by the dead father, even if those names are put under erasure. But while Banville's novel is so deeply engaged in a difficult relationship with Beckett, this occupation is never complete, because, as is so often the case in Banville's writing, the novel is haunted also by a host of other Irish dead. The fleeting coming together of Beckett and Yeats in Banville's quotation from 'The Tower' and . . . *but the clouds* . . . is part of a richly associative pattern of reference, in which Beckett's work harmonizes with a chorus of Irish voices. The suspended, unnamed Beckett-Banville landscape, it might be argued, is given a richer Irish quality by virtue of this association, as if Banville is retuning Beckett to a degree, bringing his repressed Irishness to the light. Take, for example, the opening of *Eclipse*, in which Cleave describes his view of his mother's house from the garden:

> I turned and looked back at the house and saw what I took to be my wife standing at the window of what was once my mother's room. The figure was motionless, gazing steadily in my direction but not directly at me. [. . .] Day reflecting on the glass made the image in the window shimmer and slip; was it she or just a shadow, woman-shaped? (E 3)

This scene comes through the parent's window from the other side, as it were, and merges the Beckettian window with a number of other spectral presences. The scenario in which the son gazes up at the mother's window might faintly capture something from Beckett, particularly from the scene in *Krapp's Last Tape* in which the son watches the window of his dying mother's sick-room from the street. And the troubling mingling of the images of wife and mother might again recall moments in Beckett's prose, such as Molloy's confession that 'my mother's image sometimes mingles' with those of his various lovers, 'which is literally unendurable', he says, 'like being crucified' (Mo 59). But the appearance of Cleave's almost-wife at the high window has a number of other associations that interfere with the Beckettian image, making it 'shimmer and slip'. When Cleave first enters his mother's room, to encounter the view of the Beckettian landscape from the window, these associations interfere again with the view:

> I turned and went down a flight, to the first floor, and entered the big back bedroom there. It was light still. I stood at the tall window, where that other day I had seen my not-wife not-standing, and looked out at what she had not-seen. (E 18)

At this moment, as the narrator looks from his mother's window onto what Eion O'Brien has called 'the Beckett country', it is not only Beckett that is evoked, but also a rather different tradition. There is a fascination here, which recurs in Banville, with the window, and the window frame, as a threshold that can be looked through from either side. The effect of this passage derives from its resonance with the earlier passage, quoted above, in which Cleave gazes up at the same window from the outside. In moving from outside to inside here, Cleave occupies the space of that spectral presence – his 'not-wife' – that he glimpsed in the earlier passage, while at the same time looking down on himself looking up, from her spectral vantage point. The movement from outside to inside, it is suggested, is a movement from one dimension to another, a crossing of some threshold which separates the real from the ghostly. In crossing this Rubicon, it is further suggested, Cleave leaves something of his fleshy self standing at gaze in the garden – he sees what she had not-seen, which, among other things, is a version of himself – and enters into the shimmering, slippy dimension occupied by the shadow, woman shaped, that he glimpses through the mother's window. It is this interest in the window frame as threshold – its capacity to divide the onlooker from him or herself – that lies at the heart of Banville's earlier trilogy of novels, *The Body of Evidence*, *Ghosts* and *Athena*, and that runs throughout his oeuvre, manifesting itself in a near obsession with the space of the threshold, with the hesitation in the doorway.[6] While Banville derives some of this fascination from Beckett's experiments with the threshold, he also draws here on the ghost stories of Henry James and of Elizabeth Bowen. James' novella *The Turn of the Screw*, for example, turns around the threshold marked by the window pane. As Cleave sees his ghosts from both within and outside the window, so James' novella is organized around an exquisitely turned series of encounters through the window. The haunting begins in James' story when the governess Mrs Grose sees the ghostly Quint twice: first from the garden, as he is framed in a high window, and second from within the house, when Quint appears outside the dining room window, 'his face [. . .] close to the glass'.[7] Everything that happens subsequently in the story is positioned by this double encounter across a transparent boundary – a boundary that separates house from garden, inside from outside, and the living from the dead. It is difficult not to read the window in *Eclipse* as a somewhat oblique reference to the window as organizing principle in James. But if the ghost story as developed by James has an influence on Banvillean spectrality, then it is also the case that Bowen's short stories, themselves markedly influenced by James, are a somewhat more visible presence in *Eclipse*.[8] The appearance of a ghostly woman in a back bedroom, shimmering on the threshold of presence and of visibility, recalls not only Bowen's story, 'The Back Drawing Room', but also a wider tradition of Big House writing, of which Bowen's work is to some degree a part. As Cleave stands outside and within his family home, feeling himself haunted and occupied by an unnamed history that cannot quite make itself present, perhaps the most nearly palpable ghost is the big house tradition itself, and the tenacious spectre of the demesne as imagined by Edgeworth, Bowen and Somerville and Ross.[9] Cleave's stay in his mother's house is peopled by ghosts that are drawn from this tradition, by spectres that crowd the peripheral vision but that cannot withstand the level gaze. Cleave refers at one point to the family of ghosts that occupy the house – a woman, a child and a spectral version of himself – as a 'ghost trio' (E 55), as if to bring this peculiar blend of Beckett and Bowen almost to the surface of the prose. As Cleave's haunting brings Beckett and the big house tradition into a kind of shared presence, it offers to place Beckett's television play *Ghost Trio* more firmly within the Irish tradition that whispers at its edges. In Banville's reimagining of Beckett and Bowen, the rain that scores the darkness in Beckett's play takes on a more distinctly Irish quality, and the box in which F is trapped, dislodged from space and time, becomes imaginable, fleetingly, as a big house.

While Bowen's presence in *Eclipse* remains peripheral, however, something of a pale haunting, perhaps the most vividly realized presence is that of Maria Edgeworth, a figure who has exerted a major influence on Banville's writing. The becalmed time in which Edgeworth's *Castle Rackrent* is set – the eternal 'Monday Morning' that characterizes life in rural Ireland, and that Edgeworth imagines will finally come to an end with the inauguration of the Union – is the stalled, empty time in which Banville's fictions take place. The narrator of *The Body of Evidence* returns, at the close of his narrative, to his Nabokovian prison cell in which he writes his confession, on just such an Edgeworthian Monday morning. 'Monday morning', he writes, 'Ah, Monday morning. The ashen light, the noise, the sense of pointless but compulsory haste. I think it will be Monday morning when I am received in Hell' (BE 205). The purgatorial nature of this Monday, the sense that imprisoned time does not progress but rather remains static, unnarratable and unplacable in an historical trajectory, infects Banville's writing throughout. In *Eclipse*, this idling time is also the time of an out-of-time mourning – a belated mourning for Cleave's parents, and an anticipatory mourning for his daughter, in the lee of whose distant death the narrative wallows, unable properly to progress or to recede. The quality of this mourning also derives, like the nature of its temporality, to a considerable extent from Edgeworth. The moving account of the narrator's incapacity to respond to a call either from his parents or from his daughter – the poignancy both of his love for these missing people and of his inability to articulate or somehow realize such love – is laced with something from Edgeworth, and contains something of her capacity to depict a nation and a class in the arrested swoon of a kind of static decay.

Indeed, *Eclipse* can be read as a loose retelling of *Castle Rackrent*. The story of an absentee landlord's return to his family pile, which has been languishing under the so-called care of a retainer named Quirke, is so closely modelled on Edgeworth's tale as sometimes to blend with it uncannily, as if in a kind of *déjà vu*. Throughout *Eclipse*, *Castle Rackrent* can be felt as an understory, a background which supports and underlies Banville's novel, and which sometimes rises up to occupy it completely. The initial encounter, for example, between Cleave and Quirke, in which the pair drink into the night in Cleave's mother's house, is inhabited by the spirit of Edgeworth's novel, to the point of losing its own identity, its own location in fictional time and space. In Banville's telling of the scene, Cleave and Quirke

> sat at the oilcloth covered table in the kitchen and drank while the day died. Quirke was not to be got rid of. He squirmed his big backside down on a kitchen chair and lit up a cigarette and planted his elbows on the table, regarding me the while with an air of high expectancy. [. . .] He told of the history of the house before my family's time – he had gone into it, he said, it was a hobby of his, he had the documents, the searches and affidavits and deeds, all done out in sepia copperplate, beribboned, stamped, impressed with seals. (E 22)

As Cleave and Quike face each other across the kitchen table getting drunker with the dying of the light, it is impossible not to feel the same scene in Edgeworth's narrative, between Sir Condy of Castle Rackrent and the Quirkes (both father and son) rising up beneath the surface, threatening to usurp Banville's story. In Edgeworth's narrative, it is Jason Quirke who sits with the landlord Sir Condy, plying him with whiskey, while setting before him on the table the deeds to Castle Rackrent:

> 'Here's the punch! (says Jason, for the door opened) – here's the punch!' – Hearing that, my master stirs up in his chair and recollects himself, and Jason uncorks the whiskey – 'Set down the jug here', says he, making room for it beside the papers opposite to Sir Condy, but still not stirring the deed that was to make over all. (CR 77)

Such moments in Banville's novel have the character of a possession. It is of course the case that this scene, shared between *Eclipse* and *Castle Rackrent*, is a scene of *dis*possession. Banville's Quirke is a kind of hybrid of Edgeworth's Thady and Jason Quirke – he is at once the loyal old retainer and the pushy young entrepreneur, plotting to take the house off the master's hands – and this moment in both novels is one at which ownership of the house begins to change hands. As Castle Rackrent ends up in Jason Quirke's possession in Edgeworth's novel, Cleave gives his big house to Lily Quirke at the close of *Eclipse*. But while Cleave's dispossession starts here, with Quirke's wolfish hoarding of the deeds to the house, the effect during this scene in Banville's novel is one of an uncanny and profound inhabitation. Edgeworth, always lying somewhere beneath the surface of the novel, rises here into a near perfect alignment with Banville. Cleave's mother's house and Castle Rackrent become one, and the gulf between Edgeworth and Banville closes up, again after the fashion of a *déjà vu*. This coming together, this possession by Edgeworth of Banville, itself crosses over with the experience of possession and haunting that characterizes Cleave's stay in his mother's house. The ghosts that haunt Cleave, compounded of his parents and his daughter, of Beckett, Bowen and Edgeworth, lie under the surface of the here and now, just as Castle Rackrent inhabits the fibres of Cleave's house. 'There is something in them', Cleave writes, 'of those ancestral resemblances that will spring unnervingly up at one from the cradle or the death bed'. The ghosts

> lend to this or that piece of the humble appurtenances of my new life a passing, spectral significance. When I speak of them being at the table, or the range, or standing on the stairs, it is not the actual stairs or range or table that I mean. They have their own furniture, in their own world. It looks like the solid stuff among which I move, but it is not the same, or it is the same at another stage of existence. Both sets of things, the phantom and the real, strike up a resonance together, a chiming. If the ghostly scene has a chair in it, say, that the woman is sitting on, and that occupies the same space as a real chair in the real kitchen, and is superimposed on it, however ill the fit, the result will be that when the scene vanishes, the real chair will retain a sort of aura, will blush, almost, in the surprise of being singled out and fixed upon, in this fashion. (E 48)

It is this blush rising to the skin of the novel, this coming to the surface of spectral presences, that characterizes the living of the dead in *Eclipse*, and in Banville more generally. In giving a kind of auratic animation at once to Beckett, and to Bowen, and to Edgeworth, in finding a way to make these Irish voices 'chime' and 'resonate', Banville's prose offers itself as a house in which an Irish tradition might find itself at home, might find itself possessed of itself, even if this possession is only won through an acceptance of a history of dispossession.

Spectrality in Banville's fiction, then, might offer a means of conjuring the tradition that he himself is reluctant to belong to in the flesh. It is in the deepening shade of Banville's haunted, whispering novels that we glimpse a kind of harmony. To brush up against Bowen's story once again, it is in Banville's ghosts that we might find a fitness, a fit between present and past, however ill, a kind of union. In Banville's writing a certain 'sameness' can be divined, a sameness crossing through other 'stages of existence', joining these writers, bringing them into a shared presence, retuning each into an uncanny harmony with the others. But I would suggest that to discover such fitness in spectrality, such sameness, is to attend only to one half of another kind of pairing in Banville, another kind of union. Spectrality, in Banville, is only thinkable through its difficult conjunction with eclipse, with occlusion, with the figure of the shroud. A fusion between the return of the dead and the phenomenon of the eclipse is already made, in fact, by Yeats, in his poem 'The Tower'. In this poem, the power of memory and of the imagination to bring the past into the present, to 'call / Images and memories / From ruin',[10] to bring back from the dead an 'ancient bankrupt master of his house',[11] is intimately, fundamentally linked to blindness, to darkness, to an occlusion of the sun. 'If memory recur', the poet says, 'the sun's / Under eclipse and the day blotted out'.[12] Memory in Yeats is not only snuffed out by the deepening of the shade, it is also composed of it; memory causes and is summoned from the darkness of eclipse. The remembering poet demands that 'the moon and sunlight seem / One inextricable beam';[13] a beam that issues from eclipse – from the merging of sun and moon – and that shines a darkness on the land, a darkness in which loss becomes somehow fused with remembrance. But while Yeats makes a kind of unity out of memory and eclipse, forging from such unity an 'inextricable beam', in Banville, as in Beckett, the two remain in a somewhat more dialectical tension. Where Yeats finds unity, Banville finds cleavage. Spectrality and eclipse are cloven together and apart, just as the moment of eclipse itself marks a kind of cleavage between memory and forgetting. The occlusion of the sun brings separate states together, producing a strange, delirious continuity between light and darkness, between night and day; but at the same time it separates such states, thrusts them apart, blocks the lines of contiguity and continuity that it seems at the same time to open. To eclipse, to occlude, is both to cloak and to reveal. Banvilleian spectrality is won through the revealing power of the eclipse, its capacity to find a dark unity between opposing states. But at the same time, to eclipse is to place an impassable boundary between the spectral and the real, the living and the dead, to cover the face of the dead with a shroud.

Early in the novel, the narrator arrives at an image which is suggestive of this cloven relation between separate states, and which builds on the cleavage that echoes, of course, in Cleave's very name. One of the factors which drew Cleave back to his childhood home, he explains to his wife, was a dream, in which it was Easter at his parent's house, and he had been given a plastic chicken, which laid plastic eggs:

> The egg was made of two hollow halves glued together slightly out of true, I could feel with my dreaming fingertips the twin sharp ridges at either side.
> (E 6)

The egg, symbol of smooth, perfect unity, the singularity of an enclosed, sealed life, becomes, in this dream image, alarmingly seamed. Rather than comprising a single life, the dream egg is the composite of two halves imperfectly sutured together, as the two 'zones' of Beckett's *Ill Seen Ill Said* are joined 'to form a roughly circular whole. As though outlined by a trembling hand' (NO 59). That the oneness of the egg should yield, in this way, to an out-of-true pairing, that it should produce that disturbing, sharp ridge that separates self from skewed self, is in keeping with the novel's fascination with the imperfect join, with the cleavage that lies at the heart of the self-same. Indeed, this dream-egg becomes curiously central to the novel, and returns rather insistently in various ways. When the narrator describes his first haunting, in which he encounters his dead father in the attic, he remembers that, for a while after seeing the apparition, 'everything was bathed in a faint glow of strangeness, an unearthly radiance.' The effect of the haunting, he goes on, was that the 'world seemed tilted slightly out of true' (E 45). As the egg was glued out of true, to reveal a hidden faultline running through Cleave's dream, a suggestion of difference from self, so this same out-of-trueness lying at the heart of things is revealed to Cleave through the presence of his father's ghost. And the resonance between these two moments, between egg and apparition, is deepened further later in the novel, when Cleave reflects upon his frustrated longing for a true union with himself, the union that is envisaged, in different ways, both by Edgeworth and by Yeats:

> For is this not what I am after, the pure conjunction, the union of self with sundered self? I am weary of division, of being always torn. I shut my eyes and in a sort of rapture see myself stepping backward slowly into the cloven shell, and the two halves of it, still moist with glair, closing around me. (E 70)

This fantasy of pure conjunction, of perfect union, returns Cleave to the dream egg that opens the novel. He imagines here that he might encounter himself not as an other, but through some mode of knowing that does not require reflection, or division. The return to the egg, like the return to the mother's womb, is a fantasy of retreat into a pre-symbolic unity, in which one knows of no distinction between oneself and the world. But the egg into which Cleave retreats is already cloven, already broken into hollow halves, which reveal the out of true that inhabits the very possibility of seeing and knowing. Pure conjunction is not possible, for Banville; all forms of joining involve, instead, a disjunction. To join, here, is to cleave.

The role of the eclipse in administering this cleavage, in marking the boundary that divides the novel from itself, the spectral from the real, the object from its reflection, is revealed most clearly in the imperceptibly open passage that is crafted in the narrative between Cleave and his daughter, Cass. Cass' death takes place off stage, in Italy. Her life and death in the Mediterranean remain beyond the far horizon of the novel, and only reach into Cleave's seclusion by way of poor telephone lines, and various kinds of miscommunication. Cass is hidden, throughout the novel, behind a shroud; she can only be glimpsed through a gauzy curtain that separates her from her father. But while Cass fails to appear (the etymological root of 'eclipse', incidentally, is from the Greek to 'fail to appear'), the novel is entirely animated by her presence, by a spectral version of her that crosses this boundary, to inhabit her father's house as surely as he himself, and the other surrogates with which he is surrounded, his ghostly family and the fleshy Quirkes. The mechanism that effects this simultaneous absence and presence in the novel is the eclipse. The eclipse both brings Cass to her father – more completely, it is suggested, than through any bodily visitation – and separates her from him, removing her to a realm entirely beyond the reach of his imagination. The novel is balanced around the event of this solar eclipse, that hangs over the novel's late summer. Everything about the pacing and the dramatic structure of the narrative is determined by this astronomical event, but the eclipse itself does not take place with any certainty. Rather, it manifests itself in a series of phantom occlusions that surround the novel's climax, which falls during a circus performance in the square outside Cleave's mother's house. As Cleave waits outside the circus with Lily Quirke, a surrogate for Cass, the eclipse can be felt gathering under the novel's skin. Cleave remarks the 'steadily darkening air', 'the peculiar light insipid and shrouded, like the light in a dream' (E 179), and in this gathering dreamlight the novel starts to register a peculiar loss of orientation, as if the midday night that is preparing to dawn is releasing the bonds that hold Cleave in time and place, in the unnamed Beckettian town of his Irish childhood. As Lily and Cleave wait, in the darkening noon light, in the lee of a vast celestial event, Cleave's Irish town begins to lose its definition, just as the image of his not-wife at the opening of the novel shimmered and slipped through the flawed window pane of his mother's bedroom. The Northern European locale stars to merge with a Mediterranean space, the space in which, it is suggested, Cleave's daughter is at that moment preparing to die. 'It must have been this deserted atmosphere', Cleave says,

> the noon-tide stillness, and the tree, and the glare of the whitewashed lavatory wall beside us and the faint understink of drains, that made it seem that we were in the far south, somewhere hot and dry, on some harsh coast, with peeling plane trees and cicadas chirring under a merciless sky. *What seas what shores what granite islands* . . . (E 174)

This blending of northern and southern Europe suggests the spectral power of the eclipse, its capacity to bring discrete things into shared presence. Under its shrouded light, Cleave's town becomes possessed, revealing some underlying sameness that it shares with the 'far south'. The snatch of Eliot's poem 'Marina' that drifts in here ('What seas what shores what granite islands towards my timbers / And woodthrush calling through the fog / My daughter'[14]) builds upon this sense that the eclipse is eroding the barrier between north and south, between here and there, between absence and presence. Eliot's extraordinary poem is a reflection on the leaving and the return of 'my daughter', in which loss becomes compounded with rediscovery, and impossible distance becomes an equally impossible proximity; in which, the poet says, 'I have forgotten / And remember'. The focus in Eliot's poem is on the image of the daughter's face as a surface upon which the contradiction between the immeasurably close and the immeasurably far away is written. 'What is this face', the poet asks,

> less clear and clearer
> The pulse in the arm, less strong and stronger –
> Given or lent? more distant than the stars and nearer than the eye.

The daughter's face, at once clear and obscure, is both a part of the poet – made by and of him – and utterly lost to him, living beyond his reach on the other side of a far boundary. 'This form, this face, this life', he says,

> Living to live in a world of time beyond me; let me
> Resign my life for this life, my speech for that unspoken.

In Banville's novel, as the eclipse works its alchemy, this plea that the daughter's face might be brought to presence, brought closer than the eye itself that beholds, is in some sense answered. It is during the novel's climax in the circus tent that the eclipse finally falls, unbeholden, and Cass materializes, after a fashion, transported from 'a world of time beyond me' to her father's presence, at the occluded moment of her death. Lily is coaxed into the ring, where she is hypnotized by an abusive and sinister circus performer, and Cleave finds himself walking on to the stage, to rescue Lily from her hypnotic trance, and claim her for his daughter:

> 'My name is Alexander Cleave', I said, in a loud, firm voice, 'and this is my daughter.'
> Before I rose I had not known what I would do or say, and indeed, I still do not rightly know what I was saying, what doing, but at the touch of Lily's chill, soft, damp hand on mine I experienced a moment of inexplicable and ecstatic sorrow such that I faltered and almost fell out of my standing; it was as if a drop of the most refined, the purest acid had been let fall into an open chamber of my heart. (E 187)

This is the unrevealed moment of eclipse in the novel. It is at this moment that Cass is brought into an extraordinarily intimate proximity, brought closer indeed than the eye. The eclipse has produced a merging here of the absent and the present daughter – the surrogate, flesh bound Lily and the absent, ethereal Cass – joining them in its inextricable beam. The 'touch of Lily's chill, soft, damp hand' speaks of a spectral possession that is the climax of all the hauntings in the novel, all of the possessions. But at the same time, the eclipse marks a profound and absolute severance, in which the daughter becomes 'more distant than the stars'. Cleave's words, 'this is my daughter', perhaps work the kind of resignation that Eliot imagines in 'Marina'.[15] Cleave seeks here to 'resign my life for this life, my speech for that unspoken'. He becomes the father of Lily, becomes himself a Quirke, in order that he might speak his other daughter's unspoken name, might remain, unspeaking, her father. But this attempt to speak the spectral merging produced by eclipse condemns Cleave to an ecstatic difference from self, returns him to the cloven condition that he has suffered from the outset. It is an 'ecstatic sorrow' that he experiences at this moment of spectrality and eclipse; a sorrow which knows at once the ecstasy of possession, of consubstantiality with the spirit of the other, and the ecstasy of loss, in which one is beside oneself; divided, torn, cloven.

It is this contradiction at the heart of the Banvilleian eclipse, I would suggest, that determines his engagement with literary tradition, and that leads him in a 'Beckettian direction'. While the spectral presences of Beckett, Bowen, Yeats and Edgeworth might suggest that Banville's fiction manufactures a new kind of accommodation, producing an Irish tradition in which all of these spirits might find themselves at home, such a spectral gathering should be seen through the cracked frame of the eclipse, and in its dark light. If Yeats seeks to discover a unity in eclipse, an erasure of difference that has its origin, to some extent, in the fantasy of a fully realized Anglo-Irish union, then the eclipse as imagined by Banville is one that produces only an imperfect unity, one forged from difference and disjunction; one that is closer in spirit to Beckett than to Yeats. When Cleave claims Lily as his daughter, when he tries to speak at once as Cleave and Quirke, asking the phrase 'my daughter' to refer in the same breath to Lily and to Cass, he does not achieve a Yeatsian inextricability, or an Edgeworthian Union. There is no shudder in the loins that can engender, here, the broken wall, or conjure poetic unity from separation.[16] If Yeats' voice does speak in Banville, it does not articulate a spectral unity that might be found among the deepening shades. Rather, his voice is heard as it is refracted through the silently mouthing face in Beckett's . . . *but the clouds* . . ., different from itself even as it reaches for self-identity and perfect remembrance. Distance and proximity, the living and the dead, cannot be resolved into a unity, but remain at odds with one another, out of true, as the Dickinsonian contradictions in Eliot's poem remain the more insistently unresolved the more tightly the poet knots them together. To go in a Beckettian direction, in Banville's fiction, is to travel in the knowledge and in the spirit of this separation, this cleavage at the heart of the self same. It is not to travel towards a space that might be recognizably Beckettian, an unnamed Irish space that Beckett and Banville share, and which can almost reveal its hidden identity; it is not to find oneself rehoused, like Molloy and Cleave, in the familiarity of the mother's bedroom, and the mother tongue. It is not to find oneself at home in a tradition, or a nation or a language. Rather, it is to travel along a road that remains a back road, towards a place that, even in its homeliness, retains an unhomeliness secreted in the back. It is this place that is Beckett's legacy to Banville; a place which is at once Ireland and not, at once home and exile, a place 'complete with missing parts' (PTD 101).

Chapter 3

Unknown Unity: Ireland and Europe in Beckett and Banville

In Banville's fiction, the tension between home and exile that is one of his most striking inheritances from Beckett manifests itself also in a difficult relationship between Ireland and Europe, and between Irish and European traditions.[1] I argued in the last chapter that Banville's is a haunted writing, that it gives voice to a spectral Irish tradition of which Beckett might form a part, however partially. But, throughout Banville's oeuvre, this Irish lineage blends with his evocation of a European tradition. In *The Untouchable*, for example, a biographical portrait of Louis MacNeice is merged with a portrait of Anthony Blunt, producing a new European and Soviet context for MacNeice's thirties Ireland. And in Banville's paired novel's *Eclipse* and *Shroud*, Cleave's return to his unnamed Irish home in *Eclipse* is placed side by side with the Europe of *Shroud*, and with a return to the shadows of the Holocaust. While *Eclipse* tells the story of Cleave's mourning for his daughter – a story in which the daughter fails to appear – *Shroud* is a kind of parallel text, which tells the daughter's story, and in which Cleave is a haunting absence. Where Edgeworth's *Castle Rackrent* is a guiding text in *Eclipse*, modelling Cleave's house on an Anglo-Irish architecture, Paul de Man is the figure upon whom *Shroud* is hung. The central character of *Shroud*, Axel Vander – an academic whom Cass Cleave sets out to expose as the anti-Semitic author of pro-Nazi articles written during the Second World War – is loosely based on de Man, and positions Banville's novel in a European philosophical and theoretical tradition that goes back through de Man to Heidegger and Nietzsche. The investigation of spectral and uncertain identities, that is fed through the history of Anglo-Irish dispossession in *Eclipse*, is read back, in *Shroud*, to intellectual traditions that gave rise to and emerge from the Holocaust. Vander's anguished failure to find a means of articulating a stable identity is spliced into a reflection on the difficulty of producing an historical account of the Holocaust, when that event is so destructive of the very forces which produce historical narrative.

In placing these two traditions side by side, Banville's novels suggest a kind of hybrid tradition, a peculiar conjunction of the Irish and the European, in which Beckett functions as a knot, or a bridge, belonging to both traditions at once.

As I have argued, Beckett's voice is allowed to resonate with a chorus of Irish voices in Banville's prose, but he is equally immersed in the European traditions upon which Banville draws. One of the major intertexts for *Eclipse*, for example, is Kleist's *Amphitryon*, which Banville loosely adapts to an Irish locale in his play *God's Gift*, published in the same year as *Eclipse*.[2] It is while performing as Amphitryon in Kleist's play, and as he prepares to deliver the clinching line 'Who if not I, then, is Amphitryon' (E 89),[3] that Cleave experiences the crisis that leads him to abandon the stage, and sends him on his journey back to his mother's house. The moment of self-abandonment in Kleist – at which Amphitryon realizes that his identity has been usurped by a stranger – is the occasion for Cleave's evacuation of his life-long role as actor. It is partly this central interest, in Kleist's play, in the possession of the self by others – Amphitryon's identity is stolen by Jupiter in order that the latter might seduce Amphitryon's wife – that makes it such a resonant intertext for Banville. Like *Eclipse*, it focuses on inhabitation and possession and, like *Eclipse*, the play is itself inhabited by other versions of itself: Kleist's play is a retelling, a usurpation, both of Molière's *Amphitryon*, and of the Greek myth upon which Molière, Kleist and Banville base their adaptations. This fascination with multiple identities makes Kleist a central figure not only in *Eclipse*, but also in *Shroud*: Cass Cleave, for example, is at work on a project which involves cataloguing the last moments of Kleist's life, and Axel Vander recalls attending a conference 'on Molière, Kleist and *Amphitryon*' (S 163). This Kleistian vein running through the two novels produces a European, Germanic flavour to the texts, which sits alongside the Edgeworthian cast of *Eclipse*. But while Kleist remains at odds with Edgeworth, exerting a kind of parallel influence, the Kleistian legacy is fed through and merges with the Beckettian legacy in Banville. If Kleist is a structuring presence in Banville, then it is also the case that he exerts a shaping influence in Beckett's work. Beckett's play *Ghost Trio*, for example, is inhabited by the spirit of Kleist. The figure stranded in his rectangular box in Beckett's play, straining to reach across its porous borders towards the spirits that might animate him – the spirit both of himself and of his loved ones – lives through a predicament investigated by Kleist not only in his plays, but also in his essays. Indeed, Beckett famously suggested to the director of the BBC version of *Ghost Trio*, Ronald Pickup, that it was to Kleist's essay 'Über das Marionettentheater' that he should refer, in order to visualize the figure's movements as he paces around his room.[4] Kleist's essay on the marionette theatre – which incidentally is one of the texts that Cleave schools himself to read, in *Eclipse*, as part of his training to become an actor (E 37) – turns around his perception that the puppet moves with a kind of grace, balance and harmony which eludes the human dancer or actor, because the puppet can move without the constrictions and flaws that are imposed on the body by consciousness of self. The body of the puppet, empty of the distorting presence of consciousness, achieves a 'more natural arrangement of the centres of gravity' than is possible for a living actor

(UdM 15). Kleist suggests that the natural movement of puppets allows us to see, by contrast, how unbalanced our own movements are, how imperfectly the soul is housed within the human body. It is this contrast between the flowing, graceful movements of the unconscious actor, and the awkward, unbalanced movements of the conscious actor, that Beckett asked Pickup to articulate in *Ghost Trio*. The figure in Beckett's play, as James Knowlson suggests, is 'poised midway between two worlds',[5] the human world and the inanimate world, separated by the imperceptibly open boundary marked by window and door. His movements as he attempts to negotiate between them, between remembering and forgetting, between clinging to and abandonment of self, are inhabited by Kleist, just as Amphitryon is inhabited by Jupiter. It is this close occupation of Beckett by Kleist that Banville inherits in *Eclipse*. The Kleistian frame that holds the novel in place, that animates Cleave's movements both as Amphitryon and as himself, is inhabited also by Beckett, as if Beckett, Kleist and Banville are coming together here, merging into a single, overpopulated body. The extent of this co-habitation is suggested, in fact, at a moment in *Eclipse* that I have already quoted above, in which Cleave reflects on his own possession by spectres. Puzzling over the meaning of his haunting at his mother's house, he asks

> what am I to make of this little ghost trio to whose mundane doings I am the puzzled and less than willing witness?
> Trio? Why do I say trio. There is only the woman and the even more indistinct child – who is the third? Who, if not I? (E 55)

This is a multiply haunted moment in *Eclipse*. Beckett is present here, both in the title of his television play *Ghost Trio*, and in the title of his play *Not I*, which was broadcast alongside *Ghost Trio* as part of the *Shades* trilogy on BBC 2 on 17 April 1977. But even as *Ghost Trio* and *Not I* come together here, producing a spectral Beckettian undertone to Cleave's hauntings, Kleist can be felt under the surface also, joining with Beckett, and recalling the moment of Cleave's collapse on stage, the moment at which he became too conscious of himself to act. 'Who, if not I', calls not only to the denial of self-identity in Beckett's play, but to that moment in Kleist and in Molière at which Amphitryon demands 'who if not I, then, is Amphitryon'.

Beckett, then, inhabits both the European and the Irish cultures that Banville draws on in his 'manufacturing' of his own tradition. In Beckett's oeuvre, Banville finds a means of bringing Edgeworth and Kleist, a Germanic and an Irish tradition, into a cloven unity. In Beckett, these traditions offer themselves up to a kind of merging, even while they remain distinct from one another. His work, written both in French and in English, harbours the possibility of a unity between Ireland and continental Europe, a new kind of transcultural accommodation that would see beyond the national politics that have separated them; but at the same time, it performs the impossibility of finding such a unity, as

Irish and European strands in his writing assert their opposition to each other, their historical, cultural and political specificity, even at the moment of their fusion. Banville's inheritance of Beckett's legacy builds on this simultaneous merging and separation of the Irish and the European, this search for an underlying unity that cannot quite come to the surface. Banville's poetics of eclipse, in which discrete things betray a hidden sameness, emerges partly from this legacy. If the ecliptical mechanics that I have described above turn around the relationship between Cleave and his daughter, then it is also the case that the same mechanics, the same difficult combination between proximity and distance, determines the relationship in Banville between Ireland and Europe. As I have argued, Banville's paired novels *Eclipse* and *Shroud* lie beside each other, occurring in a peculiarly simultaneous manner. The two novels belong to different landscapes and different traditions, but while they occupy such discrete national, political, cultural and philosophical arenas, they are written in such a way that it is possible, at all times, to read across from one to the other, to glimpse the shadows of one novel moving behind the thin partition that separates it from the other. The telepathic relationship between Cleave and his daughter, in which the distance that separates them is continually threatened with sudden extinction, opens a kind of back passage between *Shroud* and *Eclipse*, between Ireland and Europe, like that imperceptible passage between home and exile that is opened up in *Ghost Trio*. Just as the square in Cleave's Irish town reveals its capacity, at the moment of eclipse, to become a Mediterranean piazza, so, throughout both novels, there is an insistent interference across the boundary, an insistent possibility that the Irish might at any moment merge with the European, and vice versa.

The eclipse, in fact, that occurs and fails to occur in *Eclipse*, is one of the mechanisms by which this interference is effected. The title of the later novel first appears, in a kind of premonitory fashion, as the eclipse gathers in *Eclipse* – 'I remarked the peculiar light', Cleave says, 'insipid and shrouded' (E 179) – and the moment of eclipse that is somehow deferred in *Eclipse* is registered in *Shroud*, as if the occluded light of one novel shines through a thin curtain to illuminate the other. As the eclipse is struggling to take place in Ireland, a Turin square across which Axel Vander is wandering will start to darken, the 'sun being stealthily swallowed by a fat, barely moving cloud' (S 50). And later in the novel, Axel remembers the moment in his cloven, de Manian past, at which he stole his namesake's identity, and the eclipse emerges again, an 'enormous, grape blue cloud nudg[ing] its way up out of the low west, like a slow, sullen thickening of nameless possibilities' (S 227). Throughout both of these novels, the eclipse produces these 'nameless possibilities', in which an unnamable, hybrid space promises to emerge from the interstices. Vander, like Cleave, only partly occupies his space, finding part of himself always located elsewhere, on the other side of the boundary that separates the two novels, and that separates Ireland from Italy. Echoing Cleave's name, as if Cleave is an Irish alter ego to this European intellectual, he suggests that he 'is cloven in two' (S 13), that his 'true source and destination are always elsewhere' (S 69). In a near quotation from Beckett's play *All That Fall*, where the 'dark Miss Fitt' comments ruefully that 'the truth is that I am not there, Mrs Rooney, just not really there at all' (CDW 182–3), Vander says that 'the fact is, I was never there, not really' (S 90). Even in his youth, when like Cleave he would 'prowl the back roads' (E 33), when he would 'walk in the narrow secret streets' of the 'city where I was born' (S 90), Vander felt himself occupied by this other spectral presence, felt himself somehow displaced from himself, absent from the scene of his own becoming. Throughout both novels Axel and Alex – cloven, axial anagrams of each other – communicate in this way, finding their true source and destination, their Kleistian centre of gravity, thrown across the threshold that is produced and erased by the eclipse. And the figure that intervenes between them, that is closest to the imperceptible boundary marked by the eclipse, is Cass. Cass, in her empathic hyper-sensitivity, offers a kind of window or door through which Axel and Alex, Ireland and Europe, might flow into each other. On the first, disturbing occasion that Cass and Axel have sex, this sense of a nameless possibility, of some kind of imperceptible, unnamable communication, starts to assert itself. The 'first time', Cass recalls in the third person, 'when he had come out of the bathroom at last and heaved himself on top of her, she had thought of one of those huge statues of dictators that were being pulled down all over Eastern Europe. Crash' (S 118). This is a peculiarly freighted moment, combining as it does a sense of the new Europe that is in the process of becoming, with the possibility of a merging between *Eclipse* and *Shroud*, a kind of nameless communication between them. There is an insistent preoccupation, in *Shroud*, with the shifting of the boundaries that divide nation states and direct the flow of capital in late twentieth-century Europe – with the fate of those 'statelets wedged like boulders of basalt, though beginning rapidly to crumble now, between the straining continental plates of East and West' (S 43) – and the crashing down of European dictators at this moment in the novel resonates with this concern. It is as if the molestation of a young girl by an aged European intellectual, in a skewed version of Yeats' 'Leda and the Swan', is inaugurating here a new European regime, a new distribution of knowledge and power. But this moment also calls, if faintly, to *Eclipse*, and to Cass' father. The straining continental plates of East and West double, here, as a tectonic conjunction between *Eclipse* and *Shroud*. Cass' comparison of the rampant Vander with a falling statue blends uncannily with the same comparison attributed to Cleave in *Eclipse*. A newspaper covering the incident at which Cleave corpses during his performance in *Amphitryon* reports that watching Cleave dry on stage 'had been like witnessing a giant statue toppling off its pedestal and smashing into rubble on the stage' (E 88). While this appearance of the father's shadow in the daughter's boudoir remains a fleeting visitation, however, on the second occasion that Vander and Cass have sex the paternal presence is much ruder. If the first sexual encounter was rather abrupt, the 'second time', Cass remembers, 'was different': 'he was all chest and churning elbows and quaking thighs, straining and heaving, until she thought she might split in two down the middle' (S 119). The repellent violence of Vander's assault opens a divide in Cass, through which the father might enter less obliquely. 'While Vander was busy goughing and grunting at her that second time', the narrative goes on,

> Daddy had opened the door of the room and walked in, speaking. He was barefoot, and was wearing an old pair of faded blue baggy trousers of the kind that he always wore when he was on holiday. (S 129)

The door that separates *Shroud* from *Eclipse*, that remains imperceptibly ajar throughout, yawns wide here, as Cass suffers beneath Vander's foul onslaught. Where Cleave glimpses something of his home through the parent's window, past the erotically draped figure of Lily his surrogate daughter, Cass sees here across a spectral threshold to a home that lies somewhere in the impossible interstices of the novel, in which she is once again in the comfort of the father's shade.

It is this 'unspeakable home', lying as a dormant possibility in the fold between Ireland and Europe, that is Beckett's final legacy to Banville. To travel in a Beckettian direction is to orient oneself to the unspoken possibility that this space harbours, a space which remains hidden in the back, which cannot show its face, but which nevertheless comes to a form of expression. Cleave himself thinks of this nameless possibility growing beneath the surface of the text, pushing up to occupy the furniture of both novels, as an 'unknown unity', a form of utopian possibility that Banville inherits from Beckett and that shimmers just beyond the borders of perception. Seeking yet again to understand the meaning of his haunting at his mother's house, Cleave reflects that

> [S]ome intricate system, elaborate yet mundane, an *unknown unity*, some little lost and desolated order, is trying to put itself into place here, to assemble itself within the ill-fitting frame of the house and its contents. (E 47. My emphasis)

In Banville's out of true novels, Beckett's legacy is a kind of unity between opposing states that cannot be accommodated within the 'ill fitting frame' that Banville makes for it, but that nevertheless lies in wait under the surface of the novels, and in the impossible space between them. In Beckett's writing, as I have argued above, this possibility is fashioned from an impossible coming together of face and back. Beckett's late works both perform the failure to stitch face and back into a proper unity, to make them fit, and suggest a new kind of accommodation between them, a newly sutured body which might experience a negatively utopian unity, but which, in Ernst Bloch's terminology, cannot yet come to consciousness.[6] In Banville's writing, Beckett's remade but as yet unthinkable body reaches for a new kind of articulation. Some of the cultural pressures that exert themselves upon Beckett, that defer the utopian possibilities that his writing produces, have passed away at the beginning of the third millennium, or reshaped themselves. The straining between continental plates that doubles, disturbingly, as the bodily struggle between Vander and Cass in *Shroud*, has freed some pressures while producing others. The struggle to reimagine and rename Ireland that is one of the defining exertions in Beckett's writing has eased somewhat as Beckett is reimagined by Banville. The repositioning of nation states in relation to a newly federalized Europe, and in the context of globalized capital, has lifted some weight from the relation between Ireland and Europe that is so blocked in Beckett but that reaches for a greater fluency in Banville. But while Banville's inheritance of Beckett registers this easier exchange between Ireland and Europe, what this inheritance illuminates most starkly are the barriers that remain, the obstacles that stand in the way of thinking the forms of utopian unity and community that struggle for expression in Beckett. If Banville gives expression to an Irish Beckett placed in the context of globalized capital, then he reveals not only the possibility of a reconciliation with the difficulties of national belonging, but also the development of a new set of cultural forces which stand in the way of the 'unknown unity' that Banville inherits from Beckett.

In Banville, as in Beckett, one of the ways in which this continuing failure of the utopian imagination expresses itself is in the broken relation between the face and the back. Both *Eclipse* and *Shroud* are novels that are centrally preoccupied with faciality. The forms of communication and miscommunication that occur between Cass and his father, across the boundary between Ireland and Europe, are shaped by the image of Cass' face. It is the case, as I have said, that Cass fails to appear in *Eclipse*, remaining hidden behind the partition that separates Ireland from Italy, and *Eclipse* from *Shroud*. But her body does eventually make it across this boundary, at the close of the novel, returning from Turin to Cleave's unnamed Ireland in the cargo hold of an Aeroplane. The cost of this transgression of the boundary, however, is not only Cass' life, but also her face. On the only occasion in the novel that Cleave is in the physical presence of his daughter, when he identifies her body in an Italian morgue, this defacement is poignantly revealed:

> The sheet was drawn back. *Stella Maris*. Her face was not there, the rocks and the sea had taken it. We identified her by a ring, and a little scar on her left ankle that Lydia remembered. But I would have know her, my Marina, even if all that was left of her was the bare, wave-washed bones. (E 204)

Eliot's poem 'Marina', his keening evocation of the daughter's face, at once immeasurably close and more distant than the stars, is a powerful presence at this moment in the novel. Taking possession of his daughter's body, here, does not bring Cleave any closer to her face, but rather reasserts its distance. To bring her home is to peel the back from the face, to bring to light that unthinkable plane that lies behind the face, featureless, unmade and uncanny. To bring her body home is to effect some kind of separation between face and back, and to recognize that they can only be rejoined, can only achieve their unknown unity, elsewhere, in an as yet unnameable, unspeakable place where the body that strives for expression in *Shroud* and *Eclipse* can find itself fully formed; where, as in Eliot, 'this form, this face, this life' is able to 'live in a world of time beyond me'. It is as if *Shroud* and *Eclipse* are separated by a partition which acts like a shroud, which speaks of a persistent presence only by separating face from body. In his essay 'The Exhausted', Gilles Deleuze notes Beckett's recurrent interest in faciality, and in the figure of the shroud. 'In . . . *but the clouds* . . .', Deleuze writes,

> the female face has 'almost no head, a face without head suspended in the void'; and in *Nacht und Träume*, the dreamed face seems as if it were wrested from the cloth which mops away its sweat, like a face of Christ, and is floating in space.[7]

Deleuze is no doubt thinking here of the well-known anecdote in which Beckett suggested to his cameraman Jim Lewis that the cloth which wipes the dreamt face in *Nacht und Träume* 'alluded to the veil that Veronica used to wipe the brow of Jesus on the Way of the Cross. The imprint of Christ's face remains on the cloth'.[8] In *Nacht und Träume*, Deleuze is suggesting, the handkerchief which wipes the dreamt face brings Beckett's figure into a kind of paradoxical contact with the face of Christ. In 'wresting' the face from the shroud, from the veil, an act of defacement becomes also a moment of communication. A young Beckett, frustrated at the limits of language in expressing the inexpressible, thinks of his language as a 'veil that must be torn apart in order to get at the things (or the nothingness) behind it' (Di 171). By the time that Beckett writes *Nacht und Träume*, this violent attitude to the veil has to an extent passed away. For this later Beckett, the veil which hides, which occludes, is also the surface which offers a fleeting contact between things and nothingness, between presence and absence. The veil both defaces, and bears an inscription of what the director in Beckett's *Catastrophe* thinks of as a 'trace of face' (CDW 459). The face of Christ, the face of the mother in *Company*, which, like the face of the daughter in Eliot's poem seems at once more and less distant 'than in reality it is' (NO 8), is brought to the point of a wordless communicability by the very shroud which covers it; the 'billowing shroud' (CDW 394) that separates the voices in Beckett's play *That Time* while also offering the possibility of some fleeting union. In Banville's paired novels, the shroud works, similarly, as a simultaneously separating and connecting fabric. The unknown unity that lies under the surface both in Beckett and in Banville, that would allow a measure of peace to the seeker weary of 'wandering to find home' (Mu 6), cannot yet express itself in the work of either writer, cannot show itself plain. Rather, the surface of the page, like the fabric of the shroud, or the 'little fabric' of which the whiteness is made in *Imagination Dead Imagine* (CSP 182), can only image forth the possibility of unity from its performance of disunity, its separating of face from back, of figure from ground. The narrator of *The Unnamable* gives perhaps the most painful articulation of this aporia, in which connection can only be established through disjunction, and in which the expression of unity is a condition of its inexpressibility. The narrator thinks of himself, at one point in the novel, as a thin sheet which intervenes between separate states. 'Perhaps that's what I feel', he writes,

> an outside and an inside and me in the middle, perhaps that's what I am, the thing that divides the world in two, on the one side the outside, on the other the inside, that can be as thin as foil, I'm neither one side nor the other, I'm in the middle, I'm the partition, I've two surfaces and no thickness, perhaps that's what I feel, myself vibrating, I'm the tympanum, on the one hand the mind, on the other the world, I don't belong to either. (U 386)

In imagining himself as a partition here, the narrator casts himself as a page, or as a shroud, a marked surface which brings opposed states together, but only at the cost of a terrible dismemberment. In order to imagine the world whole, it is necessary to cleave the world in two. To bring inside and outside together, to conjoin face with back, mind with world, is to find oneself ejected from the world, to find oneself composed of a surface with no thickness. This is the predicament that so tortures the narrator of *The Unnamable*, as it determines the expressive possibilities of Banville's fiction. *Eclipse* and *Shroud* are joined by a shroud, by a vibrating partition which brings Europe and Ireland together, which brings a daughter to her father, which sutures the face to the back. But for Banville, still, to summon this unity, to imagine this conjunction, is to find oneself divided, from others and from oneself. As Axel Vander has it in one of his de Manian essays – an essay that Kristina Kovacs suggests might have been written about the shroud of Turin – 'Real Presence' is a function of 'effacement' (S 156).[9]

If there is continuity between Beckett and Banville here, however, there is also difference. The forces which govern the speakability of unity between Ireland and Europe are different for Banville than they are for Beckett. Beckett's writing belongs partially and tangentially to a tradition of Irish writing, stretching from Edgeworth to Bowen and Yeats, that seeks to imagine a union between Ireland and Europe, that strives for a poetic reconciliation between spaces which remain materially irreconcilable. In engaging with this tradition, Beckett transforms the terms in which such unity might be imagined. His work suggests a new way of envisaging a cloven unity between Ireland and Europe, between face and back, which is won through and seamed with an expression of disunity. The utopian possibilities in Beckett's writing, the images of peace and unity which are threaded through his oeuvre, are more intimately related to disunity, to the dystopian failure of an expressive or political project, than in any preceding writer. The complete body, the body at home in its world that comes excruciatingly close to expression in Beckett's writing, is fashioned from torture, from dismemberment, from unhomeliness. This homeliness and this unhomeliness is Beckett's double-faced gift to those of us who come after him. But Banville's receipt of such a gift occurs at a time when the relation between Ireland and Europe is itself being reimagined and rewritten. Where Beckett's engagement with Ireland was with a post-war nation state engaged in a difficult, pseudo-colonial relationship with Britain, Banville's Ireland is a state in the process of incorporation into a new, arguably post-nationalist Europe. The lines of blocked communication between Ireland, England and continental Europe that run through Beckett's writing, and determine to an extent both its failures and its capacity to 'fail better' (NO 101), have as a result been redrawn. When Banville imagines a continuity between Ireland and Southern Europe, he is no longer imagining against the geopolitical grain, in quite the same way that Beckett does, as Ireland has reached a political accommodation with Europe that has allowed it, in a limited and difficult fashion, to reconceive its difficult relationship with the United Kingdom.

This sense of a new facility in the communication between Ireland and Europe expresses itself, in Banville's fiction, in terms of roads. As Alexander Cleave makes his way back to his childhood home, at the opening of *Eclipse*, he journeys not only backwards into the past, but also along a newly built road, a road which is part of Ireland's newly upgraded infrastructure, built on European and US inward investment.[10] As Cleave travels with his wife, 'bowling along through the country-side's slovenly and uncaring loveliness', the effect of this new infrastructure on the accessibility of the past becomes a direct focus. On the road the Cleaves overtake a circus – the circus in which Cleave will be re- and dis-united with his daughter, the circus in which he will experience and fail to experience the eclipse – and the caravanserai speaks of an obsolete form of travel, a form of travel that the Cleaves leave behind as they smoothly glide by. 'We passed by a circus', Cleave writes, 'going in our direction, one of the old-fashioned kind, rarely to be seen any more, with garishly painted horse-drawn caravans, driven by gipsy types with neckerchiefs and earrings' (E 14). The sight of this antiquated equipage leads Cleave to a brooding reflection, to a nostalgia which becomes closely intermingled with the condition of his own journeying:

> I brooded on words. Sentimentality: unearned emotion. Nostalgia: longing for what never was. I remarked aloud the smoothness of the road. 'When I was young this journey took three hours, nearly.' Lydia threw up her eyes and sighed. Yes, the past again. (E 14–15)

The smooth, newly surfaced road, here, offers easy access to the past while also threatening the past with erasure. The horse-drawn circus paraphernalia seems to belong to a past 'that never was', a past whose spectral persistence is reliant on the circuitousness of the back road. The Ireland to which Cleave belongs is one that is entering into a new relationship with modernity, one which is yielding up the secrets that have been hidden in the folds of the poorly maintained back roads. But at every stage of the novel there is a sense that the very structures, political as well as infrastructural, that allow for a new access to Ireland's past also work to delete it, as if national memory relies for its preservation on the uneven surface, on the roughness and obscurity of the way. As Michael Cronin has argued, in his Virilian analysis of the new speed of culture in 'Irish late modernity', 'the faster you go, the quicker you forget'.[11] This fascination with the route back to the past is balanced in the novel against an equal interest in the way forward, the path towards Ireland's European future. While Cleave travels at the beginning of the novel towards the past along a newly built road, he travels at the novel's close by aeroplane towards the Italian village in which his daughter dies. And, again, the focus of the narrative is on the tension between ancient and modern forms of travel:

> On the endless journey out – in real time it took only from early morning until the middle of the afternoon – woe sat like lumpy satchels on our backs, weighing us down. I thought of a pair of mendicant pilgrims out of a Bible scene, bent under our burdens, making our toilsome way along a hot and dusty road leading off into an infinite perspective [. . .] I sat slumped in the narrow aeroplane seat, numb of mind and heart, stewing in my crumpled clothes, my bilious frog's stare fixed on the stylised patchwork world passing slowly far below us. (E 202)

This final journey is one that takes place in two time frames at once. The journey is both endless and brief; it is both an impossibly slow tramp along an infinitely long, dusty road, and a peculiarly weightless annihilation of distance. The long road that takes Cleave back to his daughter, that takes him back to his home, becomes a kind of fantasy here, as the temporality of air travel – called here 'real time', for all its counter-intuitive unreality – produces a new proximity, a kind of simultaneity, between Ireland and Europe. The 'passing of the stylized patchwork world' beneath the slowly speeding aeroplane suggests that the future does not belong to roads, that the globalization of capital has led to a reorganization of space in which different places become strangely contiguous, of a piece. The 'defaced daughter' (E 209), hidden in the cargo hold of the aeroplane, brings the back back home, but *Eclipse* and *Shroud* suggest that there is now a new relation between back and face, that the back is no longer to be preserved in the twists and turns of a premodern rurality. If the back exists at all, if it is possible to preserve and maintain a contact with that part of oneself that is secreted in the back rooms in Edgeworth, in Bowen, in Beckett, then it has become necessary to look for it elsewhere. Back and face come together, in Banville and in Beckett, in that imperceptible space that Beckett imagines in his short piece 'Neither' – a space 'between two lit refuges whose doors once neared gently close, / once turned away from gently part again' (CSP 258), the space of the interval, in which a utopian unity waits to come to consciousness. As global capital produces a global communicability, the back does not and cannot hide away in those places that modernity has not yet reached. The globalization of capital has meant that the back has become part of the face. The struggle to remain faithful to the local as opposed to the general, to distinguish between the provincial and the cosmopolitan, between home and exile, is no longer oriented by the relation between town and country, between the back road and the major thoroughfare, between the modern and the antiquated, or at least not to the same extent. Globalization tends towards a situation in which all is at once brand new and already obsolete. As a UK advertising campaign for the global bank HSBC has it – in its slogan 'the world's local bank' – globalization shapes to make the local universal.

So Banville's figuring of the relationship between Europe and Ireland takes place in a global context that was not fully available to Beckett. But if Banville is responding to the possibility of a post-nationalist Ireland in his fiction, a possibility that has come into a newly sharp focus since Beckett, it is nevertheless the case that Beckett's writing, in its blocked, agonized depiction of an unknown unity between Ireland and Europe, imagines the shape which a European Ireland might take, *avant la lettre*. If Beckett's work bears the stamp of a failed relationship between Ireland, Britain and continental Europe, if his poetics of failure and exile are determined, to a degree, by the impossibility of resolving the political contradictions of post-war Europe, then it is also the case that his writing gives a pale, utopian expression to a post-nationalist consciousness, however uncreate (a utopian globalization that I will examine in more detail later in this book [see pp. 133–199]). And it is this unspoken possibility that characterizes Beckett's presence in Banville. This is not to say that the increasingly rapid globalization of culture since 1989 has allowed Banville to articulate a utopia that remains latent and unimaginable in Beckett; I would argue, on the contrary, that the Banville's fiction is alive to the politically regressive consequences of globalization, just as it registers the inchoate possibilities of new communities that it harbours. But it is to suggest that Beckett's writing, as it is reflected in Banville, suggests a mode of post-national consciousness that is coming to the point of a new expression, as the boundaries that divided Europe in the immediate post-war begin to give way to new configurations. Terry Eagleton has warned against the easy assumption that European integration might resolve some of the more intractable problems of Irish nationalism. It is tempting, Eagleton suggests, 'to leap suitably streamlined and amnesiac into Europe',[12] to find in a federal, corporate European culture a solution to the contradiction between Ireland's history and its relationship with modernity. But such a solution, he argues, involves not only a cultural amnesia, a loss of commitment to one's 'unspeakable home'; it involves also the replacement of subservience to a national colonial power with subsumption into a new, global empire, that empire which has been theorized more recently by Hardt and Negri.[13] Banville's imagining of the relationship between Ireland and the new Europe responds to this difficulty. The challenge presented by globalization is to respond imaginatively to the possibilities for new communities and new political configurations that it creates, as Hardt and Negri have argued, while resisting the drive towards cultural uniformity and homogeneity that is the condition and the result of the globalization of capital.[14] Banville's later fiction might be thought of partly as a response to this challenge. *Shroud* and *Eclipse*, in their peculiar relationship to one another, seek to articulate a new accommodation between Ireland and Europe, while also preserving the discrete cultural histories, both Irish and European, that are threatened with deletion by the process of post-national integration. The body that is reached for in Banville, the new relation between face and back suggested by the poetic, telepathic communication between *Eclipse* and *Shroud*, seeks to embody this possibility; it is a fragile body that emerges intact but protoplasmic from the collapsing boundaries of the new Europe. This body may still not yet be thinkable; it might still reside in the Blochian dimension of the not yet conscious. But it is this attempt to articulate a still unknowable unity emerging from the tectonic shifts in the global geopolitical landscape that is Banville's ethical and political response to the dangers and the possibilities of globalization. And it is in Beckett's writing, in Beckett's barely readable, barely thinkable articulation of an uncreated relation between face and back, that Banville sees the first stirrings of this new body, at home in the world.

Part Two

Tune Accordingly: Beckett, Bernhard and Sebald

Chapter 4

Faint Clarity: Tuning in Beckett

I argued in the final chapter of the last section that Beckett's work might be thought of as forming a bridge or a knot between Irish and European traditions. In the deepening shades of Banville's fiction, I suggested, we might see back, through a multiply haunted Beckett, both to an Irish and a European past, both to Edgeworth and to Kleist.

In part two of this book, I want to follow some of the lines of European descent that run through and beyond Beckett's writing, and that form a parallel to the minor Irish tradition that I proposed in the first. If one holds Beckett's writing against the light at a certain angle, or a certain slant, it is possible to see the shades of Joyce, Yeats, Bowen, Edgeworth, Swift, a sort of Irish host that gathers around Beckett's curiously conflicted nostalgia for homeland; if one turns it slightly, one can catch other shapes, other spiralling routes back through European literary traditions that effect a kind of shift in the Beckettian landscape, a remaking and making strange of the Beckett country analogous to the change that comes over Arsene and his surroundings when he experiences what he thinks of, in *Watt*, as his 'little slip'. As Alexander Cleave, in Banville's *Eclipse*, experiences a certain Europeanization of his Irish home at the moment of eclipse, and at the eclipsed moment of his daughter's death (see p. 56), so, in *Watt*, Arsene suffers a becoming other of Mr Knott's house and grounds, as a result of his 'little slip of one or two lines maybe' (W 41), the mystical little slip in which 'millions of things mov[e] all together out of their old place, into a new one nearby' (W 41). 'The sun on the wall', Arsene remembers in his speech to Watt on his arrival at Mr Knott's house,

> underwent an instantaneous and I venture to say radical change of appearance. It was the same sun and the same wall, or so little older that the difference may safely be disregarded, but so changed that I felt I had been transported, without my having remarked it, to some quite different yard, and to some quite different season, in an unfamiliar country. (W42)

It is by virtue of some such 'little slip', some such reordering of the particles of which Beckett's writing is made, that the Irish terrain that I have mapped so far gives way soundlessly to other traditions, revealing other exiles, other 'countries' of reference that lie within it. Beckett's affiliation with Joyce, for example, runs alongside a conflicted kinship with Kafka (a kinship suggested not least in the ways in which Beckett's and Kafka's influences tend to mingle in writers that follow them, such as Coetzee and Auster),[1] which might suggest a middle European, Germanic dimension to Beckett's writing, which reaches back through Wittgenstein and Thomas Mann to Kleist.[2] Or turn the work another way, and Beckett's writing opens itself to a French speaking tradition that includes Proust, Sartre and Robbe-Grillet and Camus and that reaches back to Molière and forwards to Robert Pinget, Marguerite Duras, Jean-Philippe Toussaint, Marie Redonnet and Michel Houellebecq;[3] or Beckett becomes part of the wider European absurdist tradition, mapped so influentially by Martin Esslin, that includes Eugene Ionesco and Arthur Adamov, Harold Pinter and Vaclav Havel.[4]

So, reading the different traditions that go to the making of Beckett's writing, and reading such traditions as they are transformed by Beckett as he passes them on to the writers that come after him, might be thought of as a kind of tuning. We can tune Beckett, as it were, to an Irish frequency, and find a narrative of sorts that works back from Banville to Edgeworth and beyond; a turn of the dial, and we can hear a French Beckett, a Beckett indeed composed in French, who belongs to a French tradition that transforms his writing, as Arsene is transformed, while leaving it somehow the same. Or we can tune ourselves to a line – the line that I am going to pursue here – that runs back from W. G. Sebald to Thomas Bernhard through Beckett and Kafka and Wittgenstein to Kleist.[5] My title – Tune Accordingly – suggests precisely such a tuning process, suggests that we can tune Beckett according to a Germanic tradition which takes us from the Kleist that Beckett himself thinks of as an animating spirit to what might be thought of as the Austrian late modernism of Bernhard and Sebald.

To make use of such a concept, to think of Beckett as a kind of radio through whom various voices pass at various wavelengths, however, requires us to attend, in the first instance, to a peculiarity of tuning in Beckett, a peculiarity which will be central to the forms of historical transmission that I will be developing throughout the chapters of this section (indeed, it may be possible to detect in what follows a certain tension between *tuning* and *developing*, between the radiophonic and the photographic, between the aural and the visual). The phrase 'tune accordingly' comes, of course, from Beckett, and from Beckett's television play *Ghost Trio*, where some of the difficulties and the possibilities of Beckett's poetics of tuning come into a certain focus (*focussing* is another term that will enter into a tension here with *developing* and *tuning*). The play which, as I have argued above, is concerned with opening up channels through which one might 'tune in' to the past, begins with a directive that we should undertake such a tuning ourselves. In line with the now outmoded convention by which television presenters instruct us not to 'adjust our sets' when there is a fault in transmission, the voice in Beckett's play opens as follows:

> Good evening. Mine is a faint voice. Kindly tune accordingly. [*Pause.*] Good evening. Mine is a faint voice. Kindly tune accordingly. [*Pause.*] It will not be raised or lowered, whatever happens. (CDW 408)

The demand that we tune to this faint voice is a difficult one to respond to, however. The suggestion is that there is a frequency to which we should tune our listening apparatus that would allow us to hear this voice clearly, but of course we have no mechanism with which to effect such a tuning. The most perfectly tuned receiver on which we might watch this play, or with which we might read it, will not render this voice any less faint, because the faintness is attributed to the voice by the voice itself. The faintness of this voice is not an imperfection that we can correct by 'adjusting our sets', but rather a condition that the voice is ascribing to itself, is insisting upon in fact with the utmost clarity. The untroubled repetition of that first line, the insistence that the voice will 'not be raised or lowered, whatever happens', suggests the unswerving clarity of this faint voice. The more clearly we hear the voice, the more perfectly we tune ourselves to its frequency, the more clearly we hear its level insistence on its own faintness. As the play goes on, this faintness multiplies, becoming an emphatic, underscored presence, infecting both the visual and the aural dimensions of the play with its avowed indistinctness. The woman describes not only her voice as faint, but also the grey light in which the set is bathed. 'The light', the voice intones at the opening of the play: 'faint, omnipresent. No visible source. As if all luminous. Faintly luminous' (CDW 408). The faintness of voice and light then reaches out across the play, to encompass the music in which the male figures memories are to some degree embalmed ('faint music audible for first time at A' [CDW 411]), the rain which is to some degree a sign of homeland ('faint sound of rain' [CDW 413]), the footsteps which presage to some degree the arrival of the figure's own boyhood across the threshold that separates present from past ('faint sound of steps approaching' [CDW 413]), and the knocking with which, to some degree, he announces his arrival ('faint sound of knock on door' [CDW 413]). Faintness repeats itself, here, again and again, until faintness itself becomes the medium in which this play takes place, but a faintness which is made into a clarity, made visible and audible by the clear-faint voice, to whose clair-obscurity we are asked to tune.

Such a conception of tuning might seem to render tuning itself redundant, negating the sense that tuning requires or allows the tuner to see into the dark, to find a wavelength which rescues a particular voice, a particular channel, from the static, the white noise. The tuning that the voice asks of us at the beginning of *Ghost Trio* is one that requires us to take no action, to make no adjustment to our 'sets'. It requires us to tune ourselves only to what is already apparent, to listen and search only for that which we have already heard and seen. 'Look', the voice says:

> The familiar chamber. [*Pause.*] At the far end a window. [*Pause.*] On the right the indispensable door. [*Pause.*] On the left against the wall, some kind of pallet. [*Pause.*] The light: faint, omnipresent. No visible source. As if all luminous. Faintly luminous. (CDW 408)

Just as we can hear the voice with which the woman speaks – decide for ourselves whether it is faint or not – so we can see the light in which the room is bathed, can see the window, the door, the pallet. The voice does not bring anything to this scene, does not reveal anything that we cannot hear or see, so to tune to her voice is only to tune to what is already on the surface. The monologue intoned by the voice indeed resembles nothing more than the stage directions that produce it, in which the voice reveals here only the codes that have brought the scenario, including the faint voice itself, into being. But even as the clear-faint voice of *Ghost Trio* suggests such a flat, monophonic surface – suggesting with the later Wittgenstein that everything is 'laid open to view', that 'nothing is concealed'[6]– it continues to whisper, to speak under its breath, to harbour the depths that it denies, as if there is a faintness here that refuses the interpellating power of the voice, that remains indistinct, partially hidden. The faint voice in *Ghost Trio* does not remain identified with the scene which it so closely describes but rather reaches out, beyond the walls of the room and of the play, calling to other faint voices in Beckett's oeuvre, and producing a kind of layered, double-voiced harmonics that is at odds with its own monotone, its refusal to be raised or lowered. The faint voice of *Ghost Trio*, for example, has a twin in the voice – 'a faint voice at its loudest' (NO 13) – that speaks in a different medium to one on his back in the dark in Beckett's novella *Company*, and that 'sheds', itself, a 'faint light' over the space in which the figure is immured (NO 15). And these twin voices reach back right across the decades of Beckett's writing, from the 1980s to the 1930s, becoming entangled with a very much older voice, a voice which reaches back, through Dante, to Virgil. The faint voice in *Company* and *Ghost Trio* carries an echo, however faint, of the weak voice with which Pim whispers to his tormentor in *How It Is*, 'that voice ruined from long silence' (HII 100) of which the narrator, like Sam in *Watt*, can hear only 'a third', or 'two fifths' (HII 100).[7] This ruined voice, in turn, calls to an earlier voice, that of the narrator/character in Beckett's novella *The Calmative*, who struggles to make himself understood because of the weakness of his voice, a weakness that he thinks of as a 'speechlessness due to long silence, as in the wood that darkens the mouth of hell' (CSP 66). In both of these earlier instances, the faintness of the voice is implied – the faintness that rises to the surface in *Company* and *Ghost Trio* – but also withheld, in that the adjective 'faint' is not used. It is only through the reference to Dante's *Comedy* that runs through this complex of associations that it is possible to tune in to the undertow of faintness in these scattered moments of vocal weakness. From *Company* and *Ghost Trio* back through *How It Is* to *The Calmative*, the weak, ruined voice of Beckett's narrators calls to the shaded voice of Virgil, who first whispers to Dante as the latter finds himself stranded in the 'wood that darkens the mouth of hell' at the opening of *Inferno*, having 'lost', as Dante puts it, the 'straight way' ('la diritta via').[8] The Dantean source that runs through these faint communications is found, as Daniela Caselli has pointed out, still earlier in Beckett's writing, in the 'Whoroscope notebook', in which Beckett jots down the line from Dante 'hoarse from long silence: Virgil to Dante (chi per lungo silenzio parea fioco: inf. I)'.[9] Even here, the faintness is still withheld, Beckett translating *fioco* as 'hoarse'. But as Caselli observes, in the 'critical tradition of the *Comedy*, "che per lungo silenzio parea fioco" is usually interpreted as an "acoustic metaphor," as a translation of a "phonic emotion into a visual one" to indicate a blurred image, surfacing from the surrounding darkness as if from a long absence'.[10] Some English translations, Caselli informs us, 'render 'fioco' by 'hoarse", as Beckett does in his notebook. However, she goes on, 'this is not the case with Cary's translation, owned by Beckett, which reads: "I fell, my ken discern'd the form of one / Whose voice seem'd faint through long disuse of speech"'.[11]

So, the faintness which seeks to reveal itself in *Ghost Trio*, which shapes to become a clarity, holds within itself also a kind of obscurity, a kind of darkness in which Virgil's voice can just be divined, speaking without speech, trembling on the very brink of imperceptibility. To tune according to this faint voice requires us to develop a mode of reading that can attend at once to the clarity of this voice, and to its faintness, to respond to the peculiarly paradoxical sense that Virgil's voice is preserved, and made audible to us, only through a denial of the depths from which he speaks. It is to tune at once to what lies revealed on the surface of the text and the screen, and to what is hidden beneath a veil, buried in darkness and absence. To tune in this way requires us to hear Virgil's voice as an undertone to the woman's voice in *Ghost Trio*, while hearing at the same time that there is one voice speaking here, not two. It is to hear sameness and difference at once, as in Beckett's poem 'they come', in which 'each' is 'different and the same' (CP 41). In the terms that I developed in the last chapter, the faint voice that opens *Ghost Trio* summons an undervoice, a kind of back road from Beckett to Virgil that branches off from what Dante calls, at the opening of Inferno, the 'straight way'; but it does this through a denial of the back, through a splicing of the back onto the face, a fusing of the underneath with the surface, as the lineaments of Arsene's 'unfamiliar country' are written on the very face of the familiar, the homely.

It is this cleaving of the double with the singular, of sameness with difference, of the faint with the clear, of the back with the face, that characterizes Beckett's engagement with the Germanic tradition that I will be tracing here, and that determines to a degree the ways in which Beckett's legacy is passed on to those who extend the Germanic line, those writers such as Bernhard and Sebald who engage with an Austrian-, Swiss-, Czech-Germanic writing that includes Kafka and Kleist, and that is blended with, cloven to, something that they take from Beckett. Indeed, as I have argued above (pp. 54–55), Beckett's reception of Kleist might be thought of as a kind of cleaving or fusing, in which the figures in Kleist's essay 'Über Das Marionettentheater' become one, after the logic of *Amphitryon*, with the figure who paces on stage in *Ghost Trio*. As has been noted above, and by John Pilling and James Knowlson in their work on Beckett and Kleist, Beckett's directions were that the puppets in Kleist's essay should inhabit the body of the male figure, directing his 'sustained economical and flowing movement' within his chamber, just as Kleist's artificial figures themselves are occupied by their 'centres of gravity'.[12] In Kleist's essay, it is the perfect alignment between a body and its centre of gravity that allows for aesthetic and ethical 'grace', and that points towards the unity of being that is sacrificed by humanity at the moment of the fall – a unity of being enjoyed, in a postlapsarian state, only by Gods and inanimate objects. If Kleist's essay might be thought of as 'influencing' Beckett's play, then, this influence is expressed as possession or inhabitation, as Edgeworth's figures inhabit the spooked houses of Banville's fiction.

But if it is possible to see Kleist moving in this way in the play – if Beckett's dramatic work as a whole, as Pilling and Knowlson argue, 'finds an unusually faithful echo in Kleist's remarkable essay'[13] – it is also the case that his presence in Beckett's work remains affiliated with the back, the underneath. As the narrator's voice carries and undervoice, a faintness that refuses the play's assertion of clarity, monophony and unity of being, so Kleist's presence in Beckett's play brings with it an underside, a sort of back space that cannot rise to the surface, and that inhabits Beckett's figures only as an absence, or an unnamability. Indeed, this back space, this absence seamed into presence, can be found at the heart of Kleist's essay. The argument that Kleist makes in 'Über Das Marionettentheater' is that it is only through this back space or back road – what the speaker in the essay calls an 'opening at the back' (UdM 15) – that a fallen humankind can reach redemption, can find a way of returning to Paradise, to self-presence and unity of being. The essay is composed of three discrete narratives – two told to the first person narrator (hereafter called K) by his old friend Herr C, which sandwich a central narrative told by K to Herr C – and all three narratives turn to some degree around the possibility of discovering this back route, this back passage to the Paradise that we have lost. All three stories concern C's (and to some extent K's) perception that grace relies on unselfconsciousness. The first is C's story of the dancing puppets (and incidentally of a human who dances gracefully with a wooden prosthetic limb), and suggests that marionettes move more gracefully than humans because their movements are determined by a 'more natural arrangement of the centres of gravity' (UdM 15). The second story, told by K to Herr C, concerns a beautiful, graceful young man, whose elegance is suddenly and permanently ruined when he glimpses an image of himself in a mirror. The mirror image, which reveals to the boy his statuesque beauty, also makes him self-conscious, and that consciousness destroys his freedom and naturalness at the very moment that it makes it visible to him. From the moment that the boy saw himself in the mirror, K tells C,

> an extraordinary change came over him. He began to spend whole days before the mirror. His attractions slipped away from him, one after the other. An invisible and incomprehensible power seemed to settle like a steel net over the free play of his gestures. (UdM 17)

In the third story C tells K of a fencing bear, whose occupation of his body is so natural, so unreflective, that he has an uncanny ability to recognize the difference between false and natural movement. C takes the bear on in a fencing match, and finds that the bear 'not only parried my thrusts like the finest fencer in all the world; when I feinted to deceive him he made no move at all' (UdM 18).

All three stories, then, suggest that consciousness of bodily existence is the enemy of grace. The more dimly the light of consciousness burns within a body, the more that body is able to achieve beauty and economy of movement. From this perception of an inverse proportion between grace and self-awareness, C develops his argument about the possibility of human redemption after the fall. We became self-conscious the moment Eve ate of the tree of knowledge, C argues. The history of fallen humanity is the history of the awkwardness that comes in the wake of that ruinous moment. While animals and plants and things are spared this excruciating consciousness of an ill fit between spirit and body, it is the human lot to live in its shadow. In seeking to correct this awkwardness, to recover an equilibrium, C argues, we cannot swim against the historical current that runs from Genesis to Revelations. We cannot return to the easy grace, the unity of body and spirit, that our first parents enjoyed in the Garden of Eden, any more than we can transform ourselves into Gods. Gracelessness, C tells K, 'is unavoidable now that we've eaten of the tree of knowledge'. Paradise, he goes on, 'is locked and bolted, the cherubim stands behind [hinter] us'. But if there is no way *back* to a paradise which lies behind us, C nevertheless suggests there is a circuitous way to restore humanity to grace, to allow us in Milton's words to 'regain the blissful seat'.[14] 'The cherubim stands behind us', C argues, so 'we have to go on and make the journey round the world to see if it is perhaps open somewhere at the back [hinten]' (UdM 15).[15] To return to bliss is not to attempt to swim upstream, against the historical current and against the hierarchy that places Gods above men, and men above things. Rather, as in Beckett's late novella *Worstward Ho*, the only way back is to continue onwards. We should not look backwards to Paradise and God, but forward to destruction and death, because it is there, at the end of the world, when the pilot light of spirit has finally burnt out, and we have returned to the dead ashes of which we were made, that we find a back way to grace, that we find that Paradise is 'open somewhere at the back'. We should continue our 'journey around the world' because, as the circularity of this metaphor suggests, the further we travel, the further away from God we get, the closer we come to a reunion with him. It is this sense that distance from God is also proximity, that going on is also going back, that allows us to see the grace of God in inanimate things. 'Where grace is concerned', C says to K, 'it is impossible for man to come anywhere near a puppet. Only a God can equal inanimate matter in this respect' (UdM 15). While humans are still close enough to God to be aware of the great gulf between his knowledge and ours, the puppet has travelled so far away from God that such disequilibrium no longer makes itself felt, no longer unbalances and perverts. So, for this reason, the puppet starts to resemble God, and to perform a circular return to grace. 'This', C says to K, this peculiar unity of absolute contraries, is 'where the two ends of the circular world meet' (UdM 16). As we travel from God to human to puppet, puppet and God discover a near identity, an identity which suggests the Viconian circularity and infinite reproducibility of history that Beckett dwells on in his early essay on *Finnegans Wake*.[16] But this is a *near* identity; God and puppet are nearly the same but not quite. Their sameness and difference here is expressed as the meeting of the impossible 'ends' of a circle, a meeting which makes of the circle something imperfect, something penetrable (as, for the narrator of *The Unnamable*, 'Eden' is penetrable: 'Quick, a place', the narrator writes, 'With no way in, no way out, a safe place. Not like Eden' [U 351]). While Paradise might be 'locked and bolted', hermetically sealed and impervious to our attempts to re-enter it, this meeting between puppet and God in a near identity forms a breach in the 'circular world', a kind of hole at the bottom through which we might smuggle ourselves back to Paradise. As the sealed box of *Ghost Trio* is imperceptibly open – as the smooth unbroken surface is broken and not broken by the windows and doors which are 'imperceptibly ajar' – so in Kleist's essay it is the near sameness between God and puppet that leads to a certain disjuncture, which forces a breach or opening that, like the 'trapdoor' and 'secret passage' in *The Lost Ones*, offers a way back to Paradise (CSP 206).

This broken meeting between God and puppet in Kleist's essay finds its most productive and suggestive expression in a series of mirror metaphors that run throughout 'Über Das Marionettentheater', and that help to develop an understanding of the question of 'tuning' both in *Ghost Trio*, and across Beckett's oeuvre. Kleist's essay is centrally concerned with mirroring. The puppet mirrors to some degree both the human and the God, the fencing bear offers a kind of reflection of C that passes across the species barrier, and the relationship between K and C itself is presented as a mirrored relationship, a reflective dialogue which recalls the similarly mirrored relationship between More and Raphael Hythloday in Thomas More's *Utopia*.[17] This larger interest in mirroring turns around two moments in Kleist's essay where a mirror image is explicitly evoked. The mirror image that I shall look at first here is the one that comes last, and that closes the essay. C brings the lesson that he gives to K to a close with a complex double analogy that is drawn from mathematics and from optics. 'We see that in the organic world', C says,

> as thought grows dimmer and weaker, grace emerges more brilliantly and decisively. But just as a section drawn through two lines suddenly reappears on the other side after passing through infinity, or as the image in a concave mirror turns up again right in front of us after dwindling into the distance, so grace itself returns when knowledge has as it were gone through an infinity. Grace appears most purely in that human form which either has no consciousness or an infinite consciousness. That is, in the puppet or the God. (UdM 18)

In this final evocation of a mirror image, C suggests that the concave mirror might present a surface upon which puppet and God can be brought together or reunited, and as a result might be a means of capturing infinity, rendering us whole again, restored from the dismembering effects of being in time. Rather than 'making the journey around the world' towards that hind point at which puppet and God discover a broken unity, this call to the vertiginous effects of looking into a concave mirror suggests that we might see through the world, through history itself, bringing God and thing, absolute knowledge and absolute absence of knowledge, into a peculiarly intense proximity and simultaneity, a proximity to recall Eliot that is 'more distant than the stars and nearer than the eye' (see pp. 49–51). As the image suddenly reappears, as it is brought from the deepest of depths to the surface 'right in front of us', the suggestion is that the bottomless pool that separates the beginning of time from the end, the origin from the goal, is suddenly eliminated. The concave mirror allows us to tune to the other side of infinity, to prematurely evoke that cancelling of oppositions that Christian teleology has scheduled, as C puts it, 'for the final chapter in the history of the world' (UdM 18), fusing together the 'two ends of the circular world'. The opening to Paradise that lies 'somewhere at the back' is brought, through the magic of that optical spiral through infinity, to the very surface of the mirror, and of the page. As in that haunting line from Eliot, distance is preserved at this moment, but also cancelled, as the mirror records both a 'dwindling into distance' and a recovery from distance, both a doubling and a unity of being.

The other moment at which a mirror image is evoked in the essay, however, produces a rather different effect. This moment comes, of course, in the middle story of the three narratives that make up the essay, as the beautiful young man catches sight of himself so disastrously in the mirror. 'It happened', K tells C, that he and the boy

> had recently seen in Paris the figure of the boy pulling a thorn out of his foot. The cast of the statue is well known; you see it in most German collections. My friend looked into a tall mirror just as he was lifting his foot to a stool to dry it, and he was reminded of the statue. (UdM 16)

There is a complicated set of mirror images at play at this point in the essay, that is organized around that glimpse that the boy catches of himself in the 'tall mirror'. The boy finds his gesture reflected not only in the mirror, but also in the statue of the boy removing the thorn from his foot, the Spinario that he and K had recently seen in Paris. This play of different forms of reflection is further complicated by its relationship with the essay's mirrored narrative structure. This point in the essay is the moment at which K tells his story to C, thus inverting the dominant relation in the essay between first person narrator and his interlocutor or educator. The essay sets up a scenario in which K looks to C for guidance and knowledge, just as More looks to Raphael for an explanation of the perfection of Utopia. C is a mirror in which K (and by extension the reader) might find himself transfigured, as More finds himself transfigured and perfected in the mirror image he finds in Raphael. But here, at this moment, K is offering a mirror to C, offering to C a reflection of his own stories about grace and self-consciousness. When the boy catches sight of himself in the mirror, then, the essay offers the fleeting possibility of a convergence of the factors of which the essay is made. The boy sees himself as a statue, sees himself as an inanimate, unconscious object, frozen in an attitude of permanent grace available only to puppets and other lifeless things, and he does so at a moment in the narrative at which C finds his stories reflected in K's mirrored response. The mirror offers the possibility of a coming together in which the stasis of the statue becomes one with the supple motion of the young man, in which the animate finds itself sharing a form with the inanimate, and in which the student and reader becomes one with educator and author. But, of course, here, at the centre of the essay, the possibility of unity and redemption offered by this glimpse in the mirror quickly gives way to its opposite, to disunity and a kind of eternal damnation. When the boy saw himself so reflected, K tells C,

> He smiled and told me of his discovery. As a matter of fact, I'd noticed it too, at the same moment, but . . . I don't know if it was to test the quality of his apparent grace or to provide a salutary counter to his vanity . . . I laughed and said he must be imagining things. He blushed. He lifted his foot a second time, to show me, but the effort was a failure, as anybody could have foreseen. He tried it again a third time, a fourth time, he must have lifted his foot ten times, but it was in vain. He was quite unable to reproduce the same movement.

It is from this moment that the boy develops an obsession with mirror images, and falls prey to the paralysing self-consciousness that 'settles over him' like a 'steel net' – a precursor perhaps to the net in which Lucky imagines himself entangled in *Waiting for Godot* (CDW 39). The mirror image here does not provoke the promised coming together of movement and stasis, of educator and educated, or of animate and inanimate, but rather provides the form in which these things are cast in a kind of unending disequilibrium. Both the peculiarly violent dishonesty with which K denies the apparent continuity between boy and statue, and the comic pathos of the boy's vain attempts to catch again at the paradoxically statuesque movement of which the mirror had given him a glimpse, speak of this disequilibrium, this disarticulation. The mirror, in this tale of the vain young man, provides a surface in which the oppositions of which the essay is made – that between soul and body, the front and the back, animation and stasis, knowledge and ignorance – are held fast in an unbalanced, disarticulated suspense. Rather than summoning that 'opening at the back' to a premature unity with the surface, it condemns the back to a permanent dislocation from the face, leaving the body of the erstwhile graceful young man permanently unbalanced, and disfigured.

So, the two mirror images in Kleist's essay offer strikingly different ways of responding to the relationship between grace, self-consciousness and the possibility of redemption. The mirror image with which the essay closes suggests that the reflective surface – the reflective plane both of the critical essay and of the work of art – allows for a recovery of lost time, a recovery which manages to rescue a graceful unity of being from the alienating effects of being in historical time after the Fall. In bringing the face of God and puppet into a kind of intimate contact, the mirror provides a bounded form in which the infinite is brought into the simultaneity of presence and absolute knowledge. But the mirror image in the heart of the essay has an opposite effect, and speaks instead of the failure of the representative surface to capture or to master time. Here, the mirror becomes a brittle glass, a static plane which can only represent the failure of the art surface to make of the self a graceful whole, and which rather than freeing the young man from time and self-consciousness condemns him, in Paul de Man's resonant phrase, to 'remain frozen in deadly self-alienation'.[18] It is this doubleness – this performance at once of the capacity and the failure of art and criticism to recover a unity of being from what an avowedly Proustian Beckett calls 'that double-headed monster of damnation and salvation – Time' (PTD 11) – that determines the presence of Kleist in Beckett, both in *Ghost Trio*, and across Beckett's writing. The voice that opens *Ghost Trio*, that instructs us to adapt our listening and seeing apparatuses to the audiovisual faintness that is seamed through light and sound in this play, is tuned to this Kleistian doubleness. To tune according to the faint voice of *Ghost Trio* is to see through the plane of the television screen, as C sees through the concave mirror; it is to find the faint speech that whispers from Virgil through Dante to Beckett preserved and recovered in its depths. But it is also to find in the flat grey surface of the screen the kind of disarticulated stasis which freezes Kleist's young man in de Man's 'deadly self-alienation', which performs a radical disarticulation between front and back, surface and depth, and which delivers both Kleist's young man and Beckett's male figure to a stalled, alienated temporality.

The way in which this double Kleistian inheritance expresses itself in Beckett's play is related, as in Kleist's essay, to the mirror image. If the movements of Beckett's figure are choreographed to some degree by Kleist's puppets – if the figure is animated by a Kleistian centre of gravity – then the grace of this occupation, the balance between body and centre of gravity, is modulated and determined by the various mirror images in which the figure finds himself reflected. As I have argued above, the figure's enclosure in his box performs a separation between his bowed form and the remembered presences that press on him from the outside, and from the past. The smooth, unbroken dramatic surface that is narrated by the voice, in which faintness itself is rendered clear, is troubled by the pressure of this ghostly outside (a remnant perhaps of Murphy's 'big world'), which threatens at any moment to penetrate the sealed inside in which the figure is both exiled and asylumed, in which he is cut adrift, like the Krapp of *Krapp's Last Tape*, both from his loved one and from past versions of himself. The voice bids us 'look' at the 'smooth grey' material of which this enclosure is made, to 'look closer' at the 'floor' and the 'wall' (CDW 408), as if demonstrating the hermeticism of the dramatic surface. But while the floor and the wall offer, in close up, identical 'smooth grey rectangles' of '0.70 m × 1.50 m' (CDW 408), the door and window, of course, delicately refuse the kind of smoothness that is demanded by the voice. While they present the same smooth grey surface to the camera, and to our gaze, the stage directions (importantly *not* the voice) tell us that door and window are 'imperceptibly ajar' (CDW 408), breaking both the bond between narrator and narrated and the sealed boundary between inside and outside, bringing the male figure into an imperceptible contact with the past time which presses against door and window, and which it exceeds the capacity of the voice to bring to clear expression. Where the voice seems, at the opening of the play, to be at one with the stage directions, to merge with them, even to the extent of indicating its own faintness, here the voice and the stage directions diverge, breaking the faint-clear surface summoned by the voice and marking a faultline in the screen, even if imperceptibly, a faultline which is perceived only at the level of the printed text, and even then only as an invisibility. As broadcast voice and printed stage directions part company here, an imperceptible gap is opened 'somewhere at the back' between the faint and the clear, a gap that it is the work of the play to explore, to test. The Kleistian movements of the figure in his room are organized around his attempt to discover the penetrability of the borders that contain him, and the extent to which there is a gap that escapes the narrating power of the voice, a rift in the sealed container in which he dwells, a rift that opens at the point where the 'ends of the circular world meet', and that recalls the breach in the structure of the cylinder in

The Lost Ones which, for 'amateurs of myth' (CSP 207), offers a way back to 'nature's sanctuaries' (CSP 206). If the doors and windows offer one means by which this gap might be opened, however – one chink in the smooth surface summoned by the faint voice – the other weakness in the dramatic surface is marked by the mirror that hangs on the wall (the wall stage right that is not broken by the door [stage left] or by the window [upstage]). In the voice's confident description of the scene in the first act of the play, she itemizes all of the elements of which the set is comprised, following the list given in the stage directions at the opening of the play, offering us close ups of the floor, the wall, the door, the window, the pallet and finally introducing us to the male figure. But what is striking about this tour of the scenery is that it misses out the mirror altogether, as if the voice senses that the mirror represents a kind of threat to her capacity to narrate the scene. The mirror does not make an appearance in the play until half way through the second act when, remarkably, the figure himself appears to disobey the narrative voice that is animating him. Direction 21 in Act 2 declares that 'F turns to wall at head of pallet, goes to wall, looks at his face in the mirror hanging on the wall', and in doing so he draws from the voice a 'surprised' 'Ah' (CDW 411), as if he has broken free from his deviser, like a puppet that has come to life. At this point in the play, we do not see into the mirror itself; it simply marks the moment at which the figure exceeds the control of the voice. But in the final act, as the voice falls silent, relinquishing in some wise her hold on the scene that she narrates, the mirror becomes a central presence in the room. The camera in Act 3 repeats the movements around the room previously directed by the voice, but now the smooth sealed surface presented by the voice is broken by a lingering view into the mirror of which the voice could not bring herself to speak. First, the camera offers us a 'close up of mirror reflecting nothing' (CDW 413), a mirror that is presented, like door and wall, as a 'grey rectangle' (CDW 413), before the camera returns to the mirror, when it shockingly offers us a close up of F's reflected face (CDW 413). This face is then mirrored again in the raised face of the boy who comes to F along the corridor that leads from the door – to some degree F's own boyhood face (CDW 413–4) – before the play closes with F raising his own head, presenting us for the first and only time with an unreflected view of his open face (CDW 414).

The mirror in *Ghost Trio*, then, works like the door and the window to break the sealed surface presented by the voice. When we are presented with the first close up of the empty mirror in Act 3, it offers only a grey view of the room (with our own viewpoint and viewing apparatus troublingly absent). The mirror's grey rectangle is nearly identical to the close ups of the door and floor, and it is specified in the stage directions that it should have identical dimensions to the close up of the grey rectangular cassette recorder that F holds in his lap, and which plays the Beethoven trio which gives the play its name (CDW 413, direction 24). But if this structural identity should emphasize the fact that the mirror simply gives us a view of what we have already seen, it is nevertheless the case that the mirror works less as a reflective surface than a kind of opaque portal to another dimension, a Carrollian, spiralling hole that takes us beyond the closed horizons of the room, rather than reflecting back from them. As the rectangular cassette recorder offers a contact with the past, with remembered music as well as the music tinnily reproduced from within the room, the mirror too opens a pathway to lost time. This effect is strikingly amplified when we see the first close up of F's face in the mirror. It is only at this moment in the play – and across the peculiarly open and closed threshold provided by the mirror – that the male figure reaches for a completion, or a unity of being. Until this stage, we have only been given a view of the figure's bent back as he hunches over his cassette recorder, but here, as we see his lifted face gazing out of the mirror, we are able for the first time to suture face to back, to imagine the figure as a whole, to imagine a fit between his body and his centre of gravity. As, in Kleist's essay, C's closing mirror image allows us to see through the dismembering effects of being in time, to imagine a coming together between God and puppet that will anticipate aesthetic and ethical unity at the close of history, so here Beckett's mirror image offers the fleeting possibility of unity between inside and outside, between face and back. The image of the figure's face that we are given at this point does not seem to come from within the sealed grey room, but rather seems to bring the figure's face back to him from an exorbitant, absolute outside, an outside to which the face has been banished (like Banville's and Eliot's faces) and to which the mirror grants us a magical access. The figure's face seems to regard us not from a reflective surface but through an imperceptibly open window here, as the frightful face of Quint regards us through a window separating death from life in James' story *The Turn of the Screw* (see p. 43). As, in Kleist's essay, the concave mirror brings together beings that are absolutely different from each other, somehow crossing the infinite reaches of space and time that separate them, so here the mirror offers to cancel the utter difference from self that is the condition of being in time, as Krapp seeks to cancel his difference from himself through the recuperative power of the cassette recorder. The boy who comes to the figure along that dark corridor towards the end of the play is another version of this mirror image, as if the mirror has the power to summon not only one's face as it is now, but to bring to you the face that you have always had, and will always have; as if the mirror, as in Kleist's essay, can salvage an image of the raised face, one's true, eternal face, from the work of time itself.

But if C's closing mirror image can be seen reflected in Beckett's play, then so, too, can the mirror image at the heart of K's story, the mirror image which freezes the beautiful young man in deadly self-alienation. The mirror offers a coming together of the figure in the room with the versions of himself that are banished to the outside; but this is a unity that is won only at the cost of disunity, a regaining of time that is also a delivery to a stalled temporality, in which the figure is frozen in a permanent alienation, in disarticulated disequilibrium, like Clov in his strange freeze frame at the end of *Endgame* (CDW 132–4). As the spell of the mirror in Kleist's essay condemns the beautiful young man to neurotic repetitive gestures in which he seeks to catch at the graceful unity of being of which the mirror has robbed him, so Beckett's figure's jerkily mechanical, repetitive movements speak of the failure to meet his mirror image with any grace, or to experience the unconscious unity that the mirror seems so tantalizingly to offer both to Beckett and to Kleist. The boy's enigmatic refusal at the close of the play might in part be a recognition of this failure, a recognition that boy and man, origin and goal, cannot fuse after all in the space of the mirror, but are rather held in this stalled, repetitive disequilibrium. In a peculiar echo of the faint voice which opens the play, and of the faintness that the voice attributes to light and sound throughout, the stage directions state that, with 'white face raised to invisible f', the 'boy shakes head faintly' (CDW 413). The mirror in Beckett's play might bring outside and inside, adult and child, face and back, into a kind of uncannily close proximity, as the mirror at the heart of Kleist's essay fleetingly conjoins the supple young man with the statue, the educator with the student, K with C. But the boy's faint shake of the head suggests that this proximity, this side by side, does not lead to a unity but rather to a stasis, in which the oppositions that are brought into close contact remain balanced against each other, reaching for but never achieving the kind of reconciliation that C glimpses in his image of the concave mirror at the close of Kleist's essay. Here, as the boy offers this faint gesture of refusal to the male figure, the deep recuperative power that the mirror seems to offer – the sense that it opens a gap in the dramatic surface through which past might merge with present, outside with inside – gives way to a mere reflection of what is already here. The boy 'turns and goes', the camera following his 'slow recession till he vanishes in the dark at the end of the corridor' (CDW 414), leaving us with the final image of the figure's raised face, identical to the image that we saw earlier in the mirror, as if now, at the end of the play, the mirror no longer functions as a breach to the outside, but only as a reflection of the room, whose boundaries are synonymous, as in *The Lost Ones* and *Endgame*, with the knowable. The boy's faint shake of his head suggests here that faintness cannot after all be contained within clarity, cannot make itself felt as distance and difference preserved within the self-same, the simultaneous, the present. The possibility that the play might give expression to the faint, to the imperceptible, might open a gap between narrator and narrated that will allow for that recuperation of the other, of past time, of difference and distance; this possibility fails as the play closes, giving way to the thin tautology with which the voice opens the play, in which faintness is rendered as clarity, rather than preserved as faintness, in which faintness and clarity merge in the smooth grey dramatic surface, not as a result of the vast historical reconciliation with which C closes Kleist's essay, but as a symptom of the historical stasis which is the burden of the story that K tells to C, and in which mirrored oppositions are frozen in an undialectical identity which is also an antinomy.

So, Kleist's presence in Beckett, in *Ghost Trio* and throughout his writing, marks and is marked by both a failure of historical transmission, and a kind of historical possession, a collapse of the historical and geographical borders that separate Beckett from Kleist. To tune to this Germanic presence in Beckett's writing is to develop a mode of reading that can respond at once to this failure and to this possession, to develop a way of thinking and seeing that can find in its mirrored plane both a recovered historical depth, and a frozen, alienated surface. It is to look at Beckett's work rather as Watt looks at Erskine's painting in *Watt*. This painting might be thought of as a representation of Kleist's essay, a pictogram of the broken circle that takes us around to the world to the opening 'at the back'. The painting depicts 'a circle, obviously described by a compass, and broken at its lowest point' with, in its 'eastern background', a 'point or dot' (W 126). To look at this painting, for Watt, is to seek a relation between the broken circle and its centre of gravity, to understand the spatial and temporal forces that place the centre within the circle, that make of the circle and its centre a balanced, Kleistian unity. The painting moves Watt, perhaps because it suggests to him that back route to paradise that C finds in the broken unity of God and puppet. In studying the painting, Watt experiments with its orientation, 'holding it upside down, on its right side, and on its left side', but, the narrator says,

> in these positions the picture pleased Watt less than it had when on the wall. And the reason for that was perhaps this, that the breach ceased to be below. And the thought of the point slipping in from below at last, when it came home at last, or to its new home, and the thought of the breach open below perhaps for ever in vain, these thoughts, to please Watt as they did, required the breach to be below, and nowhere else. (W 128)

The painting 'pleases' Watt here, suggesting as it does that moment when the centre of gravity returns to its true home through this hind breach. Even the thought of the 'patient breach for ever below' (W 128), waiting for ever in vain, maintains the possibility of this back opening to paradise, which predicts the 'way out' celebrated by the searchers of *The Lost Ones*. But if the painting is pleasing because it evokes such spatial and temporal harmony, what elicits the most striking reaction in Watt is not harmony, but rather a kind of frozen, disarticulated disharmony. Watt considers, in his neurotic way, the range of different possible relations in the painting between the circle and its centre, before settling on a reading of the painting that seemed to him, if not the most correct, then at least the most moving. The last relation Watt suggests is that the painting represents 'a circle and a centre not its centre in search of a centre and its circle respectively, in boundless space, in endless time', and, we are told, at the thought that it was perhaps this, a circle and a centre not its centre in search of a centre and its circle respectively, in boundless space, in empty time, then Watt's eyes filled with tears that he could not stem, and they flowed down his fluted cheeks unchecked, in a steady flow, refreshing him greatly. (W 127)

If circle and centre move towards equilibrium, if they find a kind of coming together in the plane of the painting, then they also perform the kind of disequilibrium that freezes Kleist's beautiful young man in endless alienation, a disequilibrium in which the circle and centre do not even belong to each other, but remain forever 'in search' of a spatial and gravitational unity that is forever denied them. The painting sustains the 'illusion of movement in space, and it almost seemed in time', and this movement works on the one hand as a movement towards Kleist's union of God and puppet. Watt wonders as he looks at the circle and centre 'sailing steadfast in the white skies with its patient breach forever below' how 'long it would be before point and circle entered together on the same plane', or whether, indeed, 'they had not done so already'. But he speculates also that they might remain unconnected and indifferent to one another, exerting upon one another no shaping force. 'He wondered', we are told, 'if they would eventually pause and converse, and perhaps even mingle, or keep steadfast on their ways, like ships in the might, prior to the invention of wireless telegraphy' (W 127).

To read the presence of Kleist in Beckett, to tune to a Kleistian wavelength, requires us to read with both of these possibilities in mind. It is to read at once for the union of centre and circle – to find in Beckett's writing a mingling of Beckett and Kleist – and to read for this frozen disequilibrium, this uncoupling of elements that endlessly fail to cohere.

Chapter 5

All Balls: Quotation and Correction in Beckett and Bernhard

The question of Beckett's inheritance of a Germanic tradition, discussed in the previous chapter, takes on a particular significance when one considers Beckett's influence on those German language writers, such as Thomas Bernhard and W. G. Sebald, who come after him. For these writers, the concept of tuning to a wavelength which will bring us into contact with the past, the possibility of recovering voices from silence and darkness, becomes one of the primary aesthetic and political motivations of their work. Bernhard and Sebald, in different ways, are engaged with the attempt to bring the absent, obliterated past – the histories that are lost in the shadows of World War II, and in the dark, unspeakable atrocities of the Holocaust – into a kind of intimate contact with the present. In reading the presence of Beckett in Bernhard and Sebald, I will argue, it is possible to trace the development of a specific mode of historical transmission and recovery, a poetic articulation of the relation between past, present and future that is shared by Beckett, Bernhard and Sebald, notwithstanding their manifold differences. It becomes possible to identify a Beckettian mode of remembrance, of witnessing, that allows for a new understanding of the difficult relation between Beckett and the Holocaust, a relation that has long been recognized by Beckett's readers, but which has proven troublingly resistant to critical articulation.[1]

In an essay on the current historiographical understanding of the accessibility of the past (after Hayden White), Eelco Runia suggests that the past 'as presence' is at once 'dramatically present', and 'radically absent'. 'It is as presence', he argues,

> that the past is more dramatically present than naïve historical realists assume. And it is as presence, too, that the past is more radically absent than historical constructionists claim. For, as presence, the past is terribly close, though it can never be reached. As presence, the past is the exact opposite of what historians think it is. Historians – especially representationalist historians – assume that the past is 'lost', that it is gone forever, but that it can be 'represented' in 'representations' that can be taken along in the hand luggage with

which we traverse time. As presence, however, the past is the exact opposite, the cruel Proustian irony: indestructible, uncannily close, and – despite its closeness and its durability – utterly impossible to conserve in 'representations'.[2]

It is this uncanny proximity of the past, combined with its radical, 'unrecountable' absence, that determines the texture of temporality in Beckett, Bernhard and Sebald. In another essay on the 'presence of the past', indeed, Runia cites Sebald's work as an example of a form of representation which gives expression to the closeness of the past, claiming that the photographs and illustrations that are included in Sebald's novels 'function as fistulae or holes through which the past discharges into the present', and that 'Sebald's illustrations are a kind of "leak" in time through which "presence" wells up from the past into the present'.[3] The concept of tuning that I develop here suggests that Beckett's work produces a form which gives expression to a kind of temporal and spatial continuum, that brings Kleist, Bernhard and Sebald into the same plane, that bears witness to Zuckerman's insistence, at the close of his Holocaust memoir, that 'the past lives in the present and in the future'.[4] But, as Beckett performs at once the completion of historical time envisaged in Kleist's essay, and the collapse of time into a single, endlessly repeated moment suffered by Kleist's vain and beautiful young man, so his recovery of the past is won at the cost of a kind of temporal stalling or freezing, in which we are dismembered by time, rather than delivered from it. It is this difficult relation to the past that Beckett bequeaths to Bernhard and Sebald, and that determines what Runia thinks of as the 'welling up' of the past into the present in Sebald's work. I will argue in what follows that Beckett's work produces a new form with which to express Zuckerman's persistence of the past in the present and the future, a new way to represent, in Runia's terminology, the unrepresentable and uncanny presence of the past – a form which has a shaping influence on the German language writers that come after Beckett. But this continuity, this persistence, can only be expressed, in Beckett as in Bernhard and Sebald, as a radical form of discontinuity, the temporal discontinuity that is given perhaps its clearest physical expression in Beckett's work in the spooled, boxed cassettes of *Krapp's Last Tape*.

In the work of Thomas Bernhard – and particularly in his prose, which I will concentrate on here – this simultaneous continuity and discontinuity is expressed in terms of what he most commonly calls 'correction', in terms of the tendency towards editing and literary destruction that is perhaps Bernhard's dominant concern. Bernhard's major work, *Correction* (*Korrektur*), takes the process of correction as its main focus, the process whereby the novel's narrator 'sifts and sorts' the literary papers of his friend Roithamer, which Roithamer bequeaths to the narrator on his suicide (a gesture which Paul Auster reprises in his Bernhardian, Beckettian novel *The Locked Room*, and which recalls Kafka's bequest of his literary estate to the destructive care of Max Brod).[5] *Correction* offers itself as an account of the narrator's 'plan of working on Roithamer's papers' during his stay in their mutual friend Hoeller's garret in the Aurach gorge, his plan of 'sifting and sorting Roithamer's papers and even, as I suddenly decided, simultaneously writing my own account of my work on these papers, as I have here begun to do' (C 1). The narrator sets out, he tells us at the beginning of the novel, to remake Roithamer's work, to 'reconstitute its original coherence as envisioned by Roithamer' (C 7). But the 'correction' of the title refers not only to the narrator's ordering and reconstruction of Roithamer's papers, but also to the literary method developed by Roithamer himself, a method which generates 'authentic' manuscript not from a process of creation and construction, but from one of 'elimination' and gradual paring down. Roithamer's 'major work' entitled 'About Altensam and Everything Connected with Altensam, with Special Attention to the Cone' (C 118, 243) – an account of his building of a conical construction for his sister that is also a broad attack on the provincialism of family home in Austria – is a manuscript that he has steadily corrected and reduced, from an 'eight-hundred-page draft', to a 'second three-hundred-page revision of this first draft', to a 'third version, boiled down to only eighty pages, of the second version' (C 118). This gradual reduction of the manuscript, the narrator says, is part of what he calls a 'monstrous process of total correction' (C 56), a process of correction that produces a 'complete' work only through the unwriting, the negation of that which has already been written. For Roithamer, editing a manuscript means 'correcting it out of existence' (C 55), so that he makes a work only through the erasure of the work, by reducing it to nothing, or by transforming it into a completely different work, by 'correcting it into the exact opposite of what he had started out to say' (C 55). 'It was precisely through this process', the narrator writes, 'of always overturning every earlier conclusion throughout the whole work and correcting it and ultimately, as he believed, totally destroying it', that Roithamer arrives at a finished work:

> it was nevertheless by this process of boiling down a work of over eight hundred pages to one of only four hundred pages and then a mere one hundred fifty pages and then no more than eighty pages and then finally one of not even twenty pages and in fact, ultimately leaving absolutely nothing of the entire work behind, that all of it together *came into being, all this taken together is the complete work.* (C 119)

As the novel progresses, from the first part entitled 'Hoeller's Garret' to the second and final part entitled 'Sifting and Sorting', the focus shifts from the narrator's method of correction to Roithamer's, from the narrator's ambivalent desire to make a coherent whole out of Roithamer's legacy to Roithamer's own desire to correct himself out of existence (his suicide itself being described as the 'ultimate correction' [C 223], the ultimate editing). As the novel draws to a close, the narrator's voice steadily dwindles, leaving us increasingly to the ravening, self-correcting voice of Roithamer himself, the voice which makes itself heard only through a murderous, suicidal negation of itself. 'I'd seen at once', Roithamer says in the final pages of the novel, 'that everything in my manuscript was all wrong, that I'd not only described some things badly, but that I'd described everything all wrong'. 'When I make corrections', he goes on, 'I destroy, when I destroy I annihilate [. . .] . What I used to consider an improvement, formerly, is after all nothing but deterioration, destruction, annihilation. Every correction is destruction, annihilation [. . .] This manuscript too is nothing but a mad aberration' (C 244). As Beckett's novel *Molloy* famously closes with the blank and total negation of the manuscript that had gone before it (Mo 176), as Malone's notes in *Malone Dies* have a 'curious tendency to annihilate all they purport to record' (MD 261), as the Unnamable narrator sets out to 'proceed' by 'affirmations and negations invalidated as uttered' (U 293), so, in *Correction*, the process of writing becomes bound up with, indistinguishable from, the process of erasure, and of negation.

The extent to which this process might be thought of as producing a kind of discontinuous historical continuity, or as offering a form of access to an occluded past, however, is suggested more clearly, and more directly, in Bernhard's late work *Extinction* (*Auslöschung*), than in his earlier *Correction*. In this later work, the relation between literary destruction and the preservation of a threatened history becomes overt, rather than implicit. The narrator of this novel, Franz-Josef Murau, is a writer, like Roithamer, whose literary method consists of a process of reduction, and annihilation. The novel takes the form of a monologue, partly addressed by the narrator to his student Gambetti, which details the narrator's discovery of the death of his parents and brother in a car crash, and his subsequent journey to his family estate, Wolfsegg, to attend the funeral. In the midst of this richly comic diatribe, Murau outlines his plan to write a novel called *Extinction*, an autobiographical novel which, 'if I ever manage to get it down on paper' (Ex 236), will provide a 'valid account' of the narrator's life in his despised family home (an estate which bears a similarity to the 'Altensam' which is the object of Roithamer's diatribe in 'About Altensam and Everything Connected with Altensam, with Special Attention to the Cone'). The novel ends, rather in opposition to the end of *Molloy* and of *Correction*, with Murau declaring that his plan to write *Extinction* has been realized, that the account of Wolfsegg that he has given in the novel's previous 651 pages (in the original German) in fact constitutes the novel that he tells Gambetti earlier in the narrative that he is planning to write. 'From Rome, where I now live', the novel ends, 'I have written the work entitled *Extinction*' (Ex 335). But if the novel closes by making such a claim, by suggesting that *Extinction* is writeable and publishable and that Murau's *Extinction* and Bernhard's *Extinction* are one and the same, all the way through the narrative Murau's novel takes on a more spectral form, where it appears to be not only unwritten, but unwriteable. 'The only thing I have fixed in my head', Murau tells Gambetti about a third of the way through the narrative,

> is the title, *Extinction*, for the sole purpose of my account will be to extinguish what it describes, to extinguish everything that Wolfsegg means to me, everything that Wolfsegg is, everything, you understand, Gambetti, really and truly everything. When this account is written, everything that Wolfsegg now is must be extinguished. My work will be nothing other than an act of extinction, I told Gambetti. It will extinguish Wolfsegg utterly. (Ex 102)

This act of destruction, it is clear, annihilates not only that which it describes, but the description, the record itself. 'We may recoil' from this act of writing, Murau says, 'we may shrink from such an almost superhuman enterprise', because it involves us in an act of self-annihilation, in which we ourselves are erased as part of our act of erasure. 'I'll call my account *Extinction*', Murau tells Gambetti, 'because in it I intend to extinguish everything: everything I record will be extinguished' (Ex 103). As Roithamer recognizes that correction is indistinguishable from suicide, so Murau recognizes that his planned extinction requires a kind of self-destruction. 'When I take Wolfsegg and my family apart', he says,

> when I dissect, annihilate and extinguish them, I am actually taking myself apart, dissecting, annihilating and extinguishing myself. I have to admit that this idea of self-dissection and self-extinction appeals to me, I told Gambetti. I'll spend my life dissecting and extinguishing myself, Gambetti, and if I'm not mistaken I'll succeed in this self-dissection and self-extinction. (E 150)

The 'success' that Murau envisages here, like the successful completion of his novel that he declares at the close of the narrative, is a success won from failure, a version, as Jean-Michel Rabaté and Catharina Wulf have commented, of Beckett's determination to 'fail better' (NO 101).[6] The completion of this manuscript, which looks so difficult and unlikely as the narrator's monologue is in process ('we think we can embark on such an undertaking', Murau says to Gambetti, 'yet we can't. Everything's always against us, against such an undertaking, so we put it off and never get around to it. In this way many of the works of the mind that ought to be written never see the light of day, but remain just so many drafts that we constantly carry around in our heads for years, for decades – in our heads' [Ex 102]) marks at once the becoming of the novel *Extinction* and its destruction, the completion of Murau's account of himself and his family and its annihilation.

It is this success won from failure, this becoming won from '*auslöschung*', that opens on to Murau's and Bernhard's bid to recover and preserve histories that are threatened with erasure. The failure of 'the Austrians' to adequately address or remember their traumatic and violent recent past is one of Bernhard's most recurrent and vitriolic complaints. The character Reger, in his novel *Old Masters*, declares that there 'is no political atrocity, no matter how great, that is not forgotten after a week, no crime, no matter how great' (OM 117), and Paul Wittgenstein, in Bernhard's *Wittgenstein's Nephew*, deplores the 'society of today, which resolutely denies its own history and which consequently, as he once put it, has *neither a past nor a future*' (WN 99). In *Extinction*, the narrator declares that his method of *auslöschung* can be employed to correct this forgetfulness, to bring the crimes that were committed 'during the Nazi period' out of historical hiding, and to express a new, continuous relation between past, present and future. Murau dwells for a period on his friend Schermaier upon whom, he says, the 'full horror of National Socialism had been visited' (Ex 237). 'I remembered', Murau says,

> how Schermaier had never spoken about the time he spent in the prisons, the penitentiaries and the concentration camp in Holland, and decided that if he did not speak about it I would one day write about it. In *Extinction*, the book I'm planning, I'll write about Schermaier, about the injustice he suffered and the crimes committed against him, I thought. His wife still wept when forced to think of those bitter years that had brought them both such unhappiness, but she too never said why she wept. It's my duty, I thought, to write about them in my *Extinction*, to cite them as representatives of so many others who never speak about what they suffered during the Nazi period [. . .] . I promised myself that in my *Extinction* I would find a way of drawing attention to him, even if I could not restore to him the rights of which the Nazis had deprived him. My *Extinction* will provide the best opportunity to do this, I thought, if I ever manage to get it down on paper. (Ex 236)

Murau declares here that his *Extinction* will give a voice to the silent suffering not only of Schermaier but of the 'so many other' victims of Nazism, but this claim to speak for Schermaier at this moment in the novel, to recover his history from erasure, is itself held in a peculiar suspense. Schermaier is named here, his story briefly told, but only because Murau's *Extinction* is to some degree not yet written, is in some sense still a 'work of the mind' that has yet to be 'put down on paper'. If *Extinction* provides the 'best opportunity' to 'draw attention' to Schermaier, then it does not do it here, in this draft form, but only as *Extinction*'s work of extinction reaches its completion, only as the account of Schermaier that is envisaged here is annihilated, extinguished, destroyed. To successfully recover Schermaier from silence it is necessary to return him to it, as recuperation of the past and its loss become, for Bernhard, part of the same process. Murau is emphatic that the past is susceptible of recovery, that it presses, as Runia would have it, 'uncannily close'. He insists that 'we do not have the slightest difficulty' in calling the past to mind, 'in reliving it, as it were'. 'The same is true', he goes on, 'of the motions of a face we once saw years ago [. . .]. What we witnessed years ago can still be seen and heard precisely, if we can master the mechanism that makes this possible' (Ex 319). The past is still alive, still with us, but we need a 'mechanism' with which to retrieve it, to tune into it, and, Murau says, 'I believe I have developed this natural mechanism into an art, which I practise every day and intend to perfect' (Ex 319) – the art that has produced Murau's *Extinction*, and that seeks to recall, to preserve, to relive the past, through an act of aesthetic destruction. Murau insists that this art can be brought to bear on his own childhood, that his childhood is present to him still, as the narrator of *Old Masters* can summon his past into presence, can 'gaze into his childhood', can 'surrender totally' to his 'long-past' (OM 21). But the process of bringing this present history to expression is not only to restore it, as Murau plans to 'restore' Schermaier's suffering if not his rights, but also to destroy it, to restore it by destroying it. Murau had planned, he says, to restore a part of the estate at Wolfsegg known as the 'Children's villa', because he had believed it was in the children's villa that his childhood was to be found. 'I had believed', he says, 'that if I had the Children's villa thoroughly restored – or renovated as my sisters would say – I would be restoring or renovating my childhood'. But he now realizes, he says, that 'it would be senseless to restore the Children's villa', that his childhood is not to be preserved through such acts of renovation. If there is a 'mechanism' for the retrieval of his childhood, it derives not only from Runia's dramatic presence of the past, but also its radical absence. When we go to 'a house where as children we spent such happy hours', Murau says, 'we believe we're revisiting our childhood, but all we find is a *gaping void*. Entering the Children's Villa means nothing more than entering this notorious *gaping void*' (Ex 309–10). It is this condition that Murau's *Extinction* seeks to recreate, in which the past is preserved as absence, as negation. If 'revisiting our childhood meant staring into this uniquely sickening void', if 'all you see when you look back is a *gaping void*', if 'not only your childhood, but the whole of your past, is a *gaping void*' (Ex 310), then the mechanism that gives the surest expression to this past is one that that depicts it in its absence, in its void annihilation, what Reger, in *Old Masters*, calls a 'mechanism of dissection and disintegration' (OM 113). To restore Schermaier's history is not to renovate him, as Murau's sisters think of renovating the Children's villa, but to find a mechanism for the dramatic expression of his extinction, to express his unspeakable history, as Wittgenstein puts it at the end of the *Tractatus*, by passing over it in silence.[7]

So, both Beckett and Bernhard develop a form with which to express the uncanny presence of the past, but for both writers this presence, this continuity between present and past is achieved only through a kind of radical discontinuity, through the erection of a boundary between present and past, between the inside and the outside of the room in which the male figure is enclosed in *Ghost Trio*. For both writers the work of tuning into the past, or revealing its dramatic presence, is thus bound up with, and indistinguishable from, a destruction of the past, an annihilation or 'correction' of the very history that is brought to the point of presence. Many of the several commentators who have reflected on the close relations between Bernhard's and Beckett's work have focused on this structural feature as one of the key points of comparison. Michael Jopling, for example, in his 1997 essay 'Bernhard as Company for Beckett', argues that both writers' 'pessimism is reflected in the thematics of failure and despair, which dominate their writing. This "sense of failure" is a central component of their attitude towards language'.[8] As Beckett produces a 'literature of the unword', and as Bernhard develops his 'method' of *auslöschung*, so both Beckett and Bernhard make failure articulable through a kind of reductive aesthetic practice, which, Jopling argues, 'create[s] narrative paradoxically out of its apparent impossibility, out of the seemingly endless stories of figures and writers who are unable to write'.[9] It is the argument, similarly, of Catharina Wulf's book on Beckett and Bernhard that the work of both writers is driven by an imperative to narrate that is also and at once a 'commitment to failure'.[10] While Beckett's narrator in *Worstward Ho* seeks to 'Fail again. Fail Better', Wulf points out, Bernhard has written of his own artistic practice that 'to me, the risk of failure seems to be an essential stimulation'.[11] While Beckett writes that 'language is most efficiently used when it is most efficiently misused' (Di 171–2) and Molloy declares that 'you would do better, at least no worse, to obliterate texts than to blacken margins' (Mo 13), Bernhard's narrator in *Der Italianer* insists that,

> I am a destroyer of stories, I am a typical destroyer of stories. If there is a hint of a story anywhere in my work, or if I see somewhere in the distance behind a hill of prose a first symptom of a story, I would shoot on sight. It is the same with sentences, I would almost like to eliminate in advance the least complete sentence that might take shape.[12]

This comparison leads Wulf to the conclusion that

> Beckett's and Bernhard's writing is then characterized by a constant process of self-examination and the precarious borderline between the continuation to write and the wish to reach silence. The writing draws its energy and determination from this conflict.[13]

But if the shared procedure of drawing the possibility of narration from the failure of narration is where the writers seem to be most similar, it is also in the attitude to failure, to exhaustion and silence, that the two have been seen to differ. Wulf argues, for example, that 'it has become apparent that Beckett's and Bernhard's literary works move in opposite directions', declaring that 'whereas Beckett's late prose becomes evermore elliptical and condensed, Bernhard never ceases to present us with a habitual and uninterrupted maelstrom of words'.[14]

Jopling similarly sees a direct opposition between a Beckett who tends towards silence and a Bernhard who grows increasingly prolific and verbose, arguing that this difference makes any comparison between the two writers 'superficial', 'by no means as significant as may appear at first sight'.[15] He writes that 'it is precisely in their responses to the negativity which pervades their writing that Beckett and Bernhard differ most fundamentally'. Molloy might share with the Bernhard narrator the desire to 'eliminate', to 'obliterate' text, the desire, as he puts it, to 'fill in the holes of words till all is blank and flat', but this shared desire belies a profound difference; 'Where Beckett reduces words to holes', Jopling writes, 'Bernhard fills holes with words'. Bernhard has commented that he seeks to 'fill the 'void' with 'sentences', and it is this need to combat lessness with verbal proliferation, Jopling argues, that distinguishes Beckett's pale, exhausted prose from Bernhard's rambunctious, vitriolic work. Jopling argues that 'the reconstructive element of Bernhard's conception of "Auslöschung" is very different from Malone's notes' "curious tendency, as I realize at last, to annihilate all that they purport to record"', because, as he puts it, 'the concentration on self-realization in Bernhard's autobiographical texts overcomes the extreme pessimism of his early fiction, at least in part'.[16] Where Bernhard's conception of self-correction, as I have already argued, is driven by a determination to preserve a self and a history from the 'void', Jopling argues that in Beckett this determination is lacking, that Beckett performs the dwindling of the urge, the imperative to express, 'aspiring', as Jopling puts it, 'to write the very end'.[17] Accordingly, while Bernhard's prose remains bound up with the need to recover, to 'reconstruct' an Austrian past, Beckett's writing, Jopling argues, loses its attachment to a specific geography, to a specific history. 'The almost mythological presence of Austria in [Bernhard's] work', Jopling argues, 'is only paralleled in Beckett by the Irish setting of his early prose, after which his writing becomes increasingly abstract'.[18]

So, for Jopling, while Beckett and Bernhard both draw the continuing possibility of narrative from the failure of narration, they do so for opposite reasons, or in different spirits. Beckett's is a writing of gradual lessening, which writes itself out of history and geography towards a final absence, whereas Bernhard uses his encounter with failure as a kind of assault on the reader and on the culture, which far from winding down becomes ever more violent and comically abrasive. 'If Beckett moves towards breath's end, "the right to silence"', Jopling writes, 'Bernhard uses language as a kind of weapon: relentless repetition and spiralling sentence structures beat their subject into submission'.[19] Now, while this difference is borne out to some degree by the trajectory of each writer's oeuvre, I would argue that the distinction that is made here between a Beckettian reduction and a Bernhardian proliferation risks overlooking the extent to which, for both writers, correction and negation remain bound up with the task of recuperation, of 'tuning in' to the past. When Jopling suggests that, after his richly coloured and located early prose such as *Dream* and *Murphy*,

Beckett's works become more abstract, more effectively cancelling themselves through the process of negation, he is taking a well-established position on Beckett's oeuvre. It is a (now loosening) orthodoxy of Beckett studies that, after *Watt*, and with Beckett's adoption of the French tongue, Beckett's work empties itself of reference, as though, in Ludovic Janvier's arresting analogy, 'an anchor were raised, permitting the work to set out slowly toward its own myth'.[20] As the narrator of *The Calmative* puts it in the early stages of Beckett's use of French as a language of composition, 'All I say cancels out, I'll have said nothing' (CSP 62). For Jopling, this cancellation, in Janvier's terms this 'dissolution of reality', amounts to an abandonment on Beckett's part, an abandonment to which Bernhard never succumbs. Beckett, Jopling argues, 'felt compelled to give up the easy facility of his English for French', whereas Bernhard 'chose to "unword" his language from within, stretching it, torturing it, rather than abandoning it'.[21] But, as several critics have begun to suggest, and as I argue in various ways throughout this book, it may be the case that Beckett's writing does not abandon its historical and geographical referents in quite the way that Jopling and many others suggest. Rather than moving steadily towards an increasingly empty abstraction, I have argued that Beckett's writing develops an increasingly subtle form in which to express a continuing engagement with a set of historical and geographical referents that place it and shape it, an engagement which is also a refusal, an engagement which emerges indeed from such refusal. It is this formal innovation that Beckett bequeaths to Bernhard, and that helps Bernhard to develop his characteristically destructive relationship with a history that he preserves through aesthetic 'extinction'. So, far from the two writers moving in opposite directions, I would argue that it is Beckett's discovery of a peculiar continuity between reduction and proliferation, between extinction and restoration, between an abandonment and a preservation of the past, that germinates in Bernhard's writing, and that gives rise to what Wulf calls his 'maelstrom of words'.

This continuity between Beckett and Bernhard, this shared tendency to summon persistence from termination, to produce, in Moran's words, an 'atmosphere' of 'finality without end' (Mo 112), can be most clearly seen, I would suggest, in the relation that the two writers forge between *correction* and *quotation*. For both writers, the process of correction, the process of editing towards inexistence, is intimately bound up with a poetics of quotation, in which a narrator opens a space in which another voice is allowed to speak from elsewhere – as More gives a voice to Raphael in *Utopia*, as K gives a voice to C in Kleist's 'Über das Marionettentheater'. The process by which both writers draw narrative possibility from correction, from the destruction and extinction of narrative apparatus, opens onto and determines the process by which Beckett's and Bernhard's narrators open fields of quotation, allowing quoted voices to come to a kind of existence which survives or persists beyond the collapse of the machinery of narration that is brought about by the narrators' 'correction towards inexistence'.

The narrative of Beckett's *How It Is*, for example, is drawn, in some way, from that voice that remains beyond the horizons of the work, that voice that speaks from an unimaginable geography 'beyond part three', that it is the work of the narrative to 'quote', but which the narrative fails, endlessly, to capture in ink, or in breath. 'How it was', the narrative opens, '*I quote* before Pim with Pim after Pim how it is three parts I say it as I hear it' (HII 7, my emphasis). Throughout the work, the quoting voice acts in this way as a conduit through which this other voice is channelled, the voice that speaks from beyond part three and that the narrator repeats (he tells us) verbatim, quoting the voice as he hears it to the mud. It is from this voice, the narrator says, this voice that was 'once without', 'on all sides', and 'then in me', that the narrator learns about himself, about Pim, about his long struggle through the mud. 'From it', the narrator says, 'from it everything I know how it was before Pim before that again with Pim after Pim how it is' (HII 139). Just as the narrator in Beckett's *Watt* insists repeatedly that 'all I know on the subject of Mr Knott, and of all that touched Mr Knott, and on the subject of Watt, and of all that touched Watt, came from Watt and from Watt alone' (W 123); and just as the narrator of Bernhard's *Correction* finds that he 'thinks Roithamer's thoughts' (C 22), that everything that he thinks and writes 'came from Roithamer' (C 13); so, in *How It Is*, the narrator denies his own agency in the narration, passing the responsibility for the words of the text onto another, absent agent. The entire movement of the narrative is aimed at catching up with this spirit that animates it, crawling relentlessly towards that unworded moment beyond part three when the voice will speak for itself, when quotation will give way to direct speech, when double-voicing will give way to the revelation of a unified voice, speaking at last in its own language, and its own 'land' (in a 'language', as the voice would have it, 'meet for me', 'meet for here' [HII 19]). But of course, as the narrator reaches the far threshold of the narrative, the end of part three at which he is due to meet with the voice that he quotes, to find himself at home at last in his own body, he carries out that most dramatic, most suicidal of corrections, admitting at the climax that in fact there is no animating voice, that 'this business of voices' is 'all balls', that there is 'only one voice here yes mine', that there is 'only me yes alone with my voice', and that the whole tale of Pim and his crawl through the mud, of 'sacks deposited yes at the end of a cord no doubt yes of an ear listening to me yes', all of the details of this little narration, are 'all balls' (HII 158–9). In *How It Is* quotation conspires in this way with correction to allow a voice to speak while freeing the voice from the collapsing, disintegrating mechanism of narration, just as Bernhard's Murau simultaneously preserves and extinguishes Schermaier's account of his suffering at the hands of the Nazis. The narrative of *How It Is* is shaped by, emerges from the quoted voice as the narrative of *Correction* emerges from the inside of the absent Roithamer's head; but in both texts, as we arrive at the critical moment, as the narrative builds a bridge from its own material, written condition to that spirit which it seeks to recover or restore, the voice abruptly denies its own validity, consigning itself, like Beckett's Malone, to nonexistence – to what Malone calls 'the blessedness of absence' (MD 223) – bringing the textual edifice that has given it birth around its own ears, committing a kind of perfect suicide which eradicates not only the future, but also the present and the past, an act of 'self-correction' (C 222) in which the suicide vanishes knowing nothing of his own act of destruction, in which the suicide remains utterly free in an empty space beyond part three, beyond the far horizons of the collapsing, extinguished work.

At one point in Bernhard's novel *Wittgenstein's Nephew* (*Wittgensteins Neffe*), this conjunction between quotation and correction, and between Beckett and Bernhard, comes to the point of a rich expression. Partly, this conjunction is expressed at this moment in terms of influence, in terms of Bernhard's near quotation of Beckett, and particularly of Beckett's novel *Watt*. In Bernhard's novel, the narrator, 'Thomas Bernhard', relates his conversations with Paul Wittgenstein, who, at the opening of the novel, is an inmate of a mental institution which borders the hospital in which Bernhard himself is a patient. While Bernhard, a lung patient, is housed in what he calls the 'Hermann Pavilion' ('dem Pavillon Hermann'), Wittgenstein, we are told, is laid up 'some two hundred yards away in the Ludwig pavilion' ('dem Pavillon Ludwig'[22]) (WN 4). Part of the drama of the novel is the struggle that the narrator undertakes to cross from his pavilion to that of his friend, in order to stage the dialogue between narrator and quoted speaker that is the substance of *Wittgenstein's Nephew*, as it is of so many of Bernhard's other novels.[23] The narrator comments that it is 'strictly forbidden for the chest patients to leave their compound and visit that of the mental patients'. 'It is true', he goes on,

> that there were high fences separating the two areas, but these were in places so rusty as to be no longer secure; there were big gaps everywhere, through which it was possible *at least to crawl* from one area to the other. (WN 10)

It is perhaps this porosity of the boundary between the two pavilions that allows – on an occasion that 'had the most shattering effect' on the narrator and that marks a clearing in the novel, a suspended centre of gravity – for the narrator and Wittgenstein finally to meet, in the space between the two pavilions. 'We met', the narrator recorded, 'halfway between the Hermann Pavilion and the Ludwig Pavilion and sat on a bench just inside the chest patient's territory. *Grotesque, grotesque!* he said and began to weep uncontrollably' (WN 45). Now, this meeting between Bernhard and Wittgenstein draws multiple echoes from Beckett's writing – from the peculiar relation between Murphy and Endon in *Murphy* (Mu 134–40), as well as from the deranged scenes in the gardens of 'House of Saint John of God' asylum in *Malone Dies* (MD 276–81), but the echo that is strongest and clearest here is from *Watt*. As Marjorie Perloff has commented:

Two friends or acquaintances who meet in the 'garden' between their respective 'Pavilions' in what seems to be a mental hospital: it is the setting [. . .] for the strange encounter of Sam and the protagonist in Chapter III of Beckett's *Watt*. In a novel (or is it an autobiographical memoir?) written some forty years later by the Austrian writer Thomas Bernhard, this paradigm recurs.[24]

The meeting that Bernhard and Wittgenstein conspire to accomplish in *Wittgenstein's Nephew* is inhabited, to a degree, by that earlier meeting between the pavilions in which Watt and Sam are incarcerated. As in Bernhard's institution, Beckett's pavilions are separated by fences, by a 'high barbed wire fence, greatly in need of repair, of new wire, of fresh barbs' (W 154), and like Bernhard, Sam feels a desperate urge to cross this boundary, to cross from his own pavilion to join Watt in his. Seeing Watt pressed against his side of the fence, Sam says, 'I believe, that in my anxiety to come at Watt then, I would have launched myself against the barrier, bodily, if necessary' (W 157–8). But just as he is preparing to force himself through the fence, he realizes that his enclosure, like Bernhard's, is imperfectly sealed, that there is a 'hole, in the fence, a large irregular hole', through which, like Bernhard, it is possible for him to 'pass, without hurt or damage to my pretty uniform' (W 158).

When Bernhard and Wittgenstein meet in *Wittgenstein's Nephew*, then, they are staging, at the same time, a kind of meeting between Bernhard and Beckett, as if Bernhard and Beckett are regarding each other, here, through a flimsy fence that separates Ireland from Europe, the 1940s from the 1980s. But if this moment suggests such a conjunction, such an act of quotation or homage, it is also a moment, in the work of both writers, at which the mutually shaping relation between quotation and correction is held in a particularly delicate and suggestive balance. As Sam looks at Watt through the broken boundary between their respective pavilions, as he looks forward unbeknownst to the Bernhardian scene still hidden in the future, he says that he feels as if he is looking into a mirror, a mirror that might recall the reflective surfaces that appear in Kleist's 'Über das Marionettentheater', and that reappear in Kleistian vein in Beckett's *Film*, and in *Ghost Trio*. Sam describes how Watt approaches him until he 'lay against the fence',

> and I saw his face, and the rest of his front. His face was bloody, his hand also, and thorns were in his scalp. (His resemblance, at that moment, to the Christ believed by Bosch, then hanging in Trafalgar square, was so striking, that I remarked it.) And at the same instant suddenly I felt as though I were standing before a great mirror, in which my garden was reflected, and my fence, and I, and the very birds tossing in the wind, so that I looked at my hands, and felt my face, and glossy skull, with an anxiety as real as unfounded. (W 157)

At this moment, as Sam gazes into Watt's bloody face, the quotational structure of the novel is given a kind of manifest form. The narrative comprises Sam's 'sifted and sorted' version of Watt's garbled story of his journey to the house of Mr Knott. This journey, told to Sam by Watt in elaborate forms of mirrored, inverted language, takes Watt across a kind of Carrollian threshold, through the Kleistian mirror and into that empty space represented by Mr Knott. As Sam regards Watt here, as in a mirror, it is as if he can see through the looking glass, can see through the mirror to the other side, as C sees through the concave mirror at the end of 'Über das Marionettentheater', and as the male figure in *Ghost Trio* sees through the mirror to the ghostly face that occupies an exorbitant outside, that occupies a space on the other side of that play's imperceptibly open boundary. It is as if, here, the narrator of *How It Is* had been brought face to face with that 'not one of us' (HII 150) that speaks from beyond part three, or as if the narrator of *Correction* had been brought face to face with Roithamer. In giving a form to the quotational structure of the novel, this *vis a vis* marks a threshold between here and there, between life and death, between the present moment and the occluded time (be it past or future) from which the disembodied voices of Beckett's and Bernhard's fictions emanate. Watt's resemblance to the Christ depicted in Bosch's painting 'The Crowning with Thorns' adds to this sense that Watt is coming to us from elsewhere, from an other space and time with which the plane of the page, the surface of the canvas, gives us a kind of magical contact (as for Deleuze the 'cloth' makes such contact fleetingly imaginable in Beckett's play *Nacht und Träume* [CDW 465–6; see p. 60]). In Bosch's painting, the face of Christ forms a quiet, still centre of gravity, around which the crazed, violent elements of the painting circle, as if around a vortex. A pale Christ is surrounded by four lurid tormentors who encircle him, two kneeling in front of him in the foreground, two looming over him from behind. The tormentor who holds him from behind, whose mouth is inclined towards his left ear, and whose hand is on his right shoulder, suggests in fact another Beckettian narrative structure, assuming precisely the posture that the narrator adopts in relation to Pim in part two of *How It Is* ('in the dark the mud my head against his my side glued to his my right arm around his shoulders' [HII 60]). But if the tormentors adopt a violent attitude towards Christ, inflicting a pain upon him for which his calm gaze, seeking our own, seems to ask forgiveness, the peculiar ambiguity of this painting stems from the sense that his tormentors are also beseeching him – as the narrator of *How It Is* violently beseeches Pim – that their violence is also a form of worship. The tormentor who clasps Christ from behind, who I suggest might be thought of as a model for the narrator of *How It Is*, has an expression on his face that is suspended, wonderfully, between a violent hatred and a compassionate pleading. It is as if the tormentors are not only setting out to mock and finally to exterminate Christ, but also beseeching him to come to existence, to come to the canvas from whatever unimaginable space and time he originates, and towards which he is bound.

FIGURE 5.1 Bosch, 'The Crowning with Thorns'

So, when Sam looks at Watt, seeing in him a version of Bosch's Christ, he looks across the threshold that is marked in the novel between the knowable and the unknowable, between material presence and spiritual absence. But while this moment suggests the power of Beckettian quotation to summon this other into existence, to call to a Christ-like Watt who lives on the other side of a far horizon, it does so only in relation to the violent, annihilating power of correction. As Bosch's painting seems both to summon and to eradicate Christ, to stage a peculiar and delicate push and pull, so Sam both brings Watt uncannily close here, and forces him out of the plane of the picture, banishing him to an outside, to Runia's 'radical absence'. While in one sense the mirror offers access to the empty space from which Mr Knott and Bosch's Christ regard us, in another sense the same mirror image of course refuses such access, reflecting back from the horizon rather than offering any route through it or across it. As Sam gazes at Watt, he both tunes through to the other side of the text – using Watt's backwards language as a kind of bridge or Wittgensteinian ladder that takes him towards Mr Knott's calm emptiness – and finds himself gazing only at himself, as the narrator of *How It Is* discovers at the end of his narrative that there is 'only one voice here yes mine' (HII 158), as the narrator of *Company* finds at the end of his narrative that 'you are as you always were. Alone' (NO 52).

The surface that Watt's face offers to the observer here, at once transparent and opaque, at once mirror and window, returns again and again in Beckett's writing, and strikingly in *How It Is*, where the narrator adopts that pose from Bosch's painting, and where the flesh of Pim's back presents a similarly open and closed threshold. As the narrator crawls towards Pim through the mud of part two, as he reaches him and lies over him, adopting the posture of Christ's tormentor in 'The Crowning with Thorns', he uses the exposed skin of Pim's back as a kind of parchment, as a written surface upon which he imagines that the crawl through the mud might be recorded, or witnessed. Making of Pim's back a kind of Freudian 'Mystic Writing Pad', the narrator records how 'with the nail then of the right index',

> I carve and when it breaks or falls until it grows again with another on Pim's back intact at the outset from left to right and top to bottom as in our civilisation I carve my Roman capitals. (HII 77)

As the narrator continues to write upon Pim's back, with a violence that recalls the scourging of Christ as well as the punishment meted out to the prisoner in Kafka's 'In the Penal Settlement',[25] it becomes clear that the back here is becoming a version of the page that we are reading, that the page and the back are becoming one. The story that the narrator writes on Pim's back contains, like the narrative of *How It Is* itself, 'no paragraphs', 'no commas', 'not a second for reflection', and the contents of this breathless script mirror also Beckett's narrative, telling as they do of

> that childhood said to have been mine the difficulty of believing in it the feeling rather of having been born octogenarian at the age when one dies in the dark the mud upwards born upwards floating up like the drowned and tattle tattle four full backs of close characters the childhood the belief the blue the miracles all lost never was. (HII 78)

In becoming one with the narrative in which it is contained, as Murau's *Extinction* becomes one with Bernhard's *Extinction*, this back/page offers an extraordinary bridge that connects the above with the below, that connects the face and the back, that brings the back and the front of the mirror into a kind of unity, as Freud's 'Mystic Pad' brings the conscious into contact with the unconscious.[26] The narrator writes the stories of his childhood 'above in the light' on Pim's back, so that Pim will give these stories a voice, will mutter them in turn into the waiting ear of the narrator. The narrator crawls towards Pim, travelling from west to east, from above to below, so as he reaches Pim and inscribes his stories upon his back, he connects the above to the below, west to east, preserving and recording in bloody text that childhood above in the light in which he finds it so difficult to believe. The words of the text become a fleshy connection between above and below, between here and there. The narrator comments, recalling again the posture adopted by Christ and his tormentors in Bosch's 'Crowning with Thorns', that 'the coming into contact of mouth and ear leads to a slight overlapping of flesh in the region of the shoulders', and concludes that this bodily contact, expressed in the form of words inscribed on the back/page, produces an 'imbrication of flesh without breach or fissure', a flesh–word bridge that joins the front and the back, the above and the below, that 'glues together' the 'unthinkable first' and the 'no less unthinkable last' (HII 153). But while the narrator crawls towards Pim from above, while he tells stories of his (and Pim's) childhood to Pim, the story that he is telling is, of course, already a quotation. The story that he writes on Pim's back is not only a story of the childhood that he tries to remember, those brief images that he sees of his life above in the light when a curtain parts and a light goes on; it is also the story that is being told to him by that voice that was 'once without on all sides and then in me', the voice that speaks not from the above but from the below, from that empty space beyond part three towards which the narrator relentlessly crawls. Rather than burrowing down from above, the voice comes from beneath, as Kafka's story 'The Burrow' comes not from the above but from the below.[27] As the story written on Pim's back suggests, the direction of transmission is not (only) down from the above, from the 'unthinkable first', but is rather (also) a 'floating upwards' from beneath, from the 'no less unthinkable last', coming up to us from a dark future rather than from a fleetingly light past. Not only is the figment of a life up above in the light a story that is told to Pim by the voice, a story that comes from the future rather than the past, but Pim himself, and the story of the crawl through the mud, the story of the writing in blood on Pim's back – all are elements of a story told to us by that unimaginable voice, living beyond the reach of flesh or of page. In rendering that absent voice in fleshy words, in imagining the page as the surface of Pim's back, the narrative offers here a fleeting and remarkable coming together of the spectral voice that speaks from beyond part three with the (literally) embodied voice of the narrator's childhood, the voice that speaks with the language, like Moran at the close of *Molloy*, that he 'had been taught when he was little' (Mo 176). The plane of the back / page here, like that window-mirror that brings Sam together with a Christ-like Watt, is a double surface which offers to join the above with the below, a written plane which allows us, like the narrative of *How It Is* itself, to hear at once the voice that speaks from beyond part three, and the voice that recalls a life above in the light.

How It Is is written, I would argue, to produce that moment of utopian double voicing, to allow the page to bring future into contact with the past, to bring the above into contact with the below. But if the script gouged so painfully into Pim's flesh offers such contact, it does so only by virtue of its denial of this contact, as the capacity to speak with two voices is won from the imperative that there is 'only one voice here' (HII 158). The page might work as a kind of Riemann surface bringing narrator and quoted voice into intimate unity, finding a form in which More and Raphael, Kleist's K and C, might speak together, in the same breath. But this is only made possible by that revelation of monovocalism which ends *How It Is*, as it ends *Company* and *Correction* – the revelation of monovocalism which at once enables double voicing and eliminates the grounds of its possibility. As the narrator crawls over Pim's prone form, as he presses his ear against his mouth like Christ's tormentor, he hears a voice coming to him from elsewhere, receiving that voice like a radio tuned into tomorrow, or into yesterday. But at the same time, the voice that he hears gives him back only the words that he himself has sent out, as the words that he quotes emanating from beyond the far horizon of the work are only his words bouncing back to him. The words that come from part three belong, we are told, to an 'intelligence', 'not one of us', a loving agent who is responsible for the 'justice' and 'harmony' of the little people who crawl through the mud (HII 150). It is the miracle of *How It is* that we are able to hear this wordless voice speak. But, as that drastic moment of self-correction at the close of the narrative makes abundantly clear, the voice speaks only in the words that we have given it. That living, divine agent, that 'not one of us' towards whom we crawl and from whom we have come, towards whom we direct our prayers and our curses, 'listens', when we call to it, 'only to himself'; 'when he lends his ear to our murmur does no more than lend it to a story of his own devising' (HII 151). His words do not lead from here to there, do not pass as in prayer across the threshold that divides life and death, before and after, but rather they come only from us to us. As the narrator of *The Unnamable* rather wittily puts it, 'what doesn't come to me from me has come to the wrong address' (U 353). We see in these words not an entry to another world, to the distant past or to the distant future, but only a mirror in which we see ourselves alone, as, at the end of *Ghost Trio*, the mirror shifts from an imperceptibly open portal to the outside, to a reflection of that unbroken grey room in which the male figure is enclosed. As, in Kleist's essay, the mirror works both as a lens that focuses the other side of infinity, and as a steel net which holds us imprisoned in a stalled time that refuses to pass, so, in *How It Is* and in *Watt*, the possibility of an open channel between here and there, between past and future, between man and God, is only wrested from the blank, pitiless refusal of such communication. When Sam looks across the threshold towards a Wattish Christ, when he 'tunes according' to the faint voice that he hears drifting across the Stygian gulf that separates them, he sees Watt's face only to the extent that he sees his own. Quotation is made possible only through an act of correction.

So, when Bernhard and Beckett regard each other across the flimsy boundary that separates their respective pavilions, they achieve a kind of communication, a kind of conjunction, that is won from separation, from correction. Bernhard reaches back to Beckett, quoting him, animating him, just as Beckett reaches forward to the future, to this scene in Bernhard that lies beyond part three. But as Bernhard reaches back, this intimate contact with a voice from the past obeys the Bernhardian logic of *auslöschung*, in which the past, the voice of the other, is preserved only by virtue of extinction. Beckett is brought to presence in *Wittgenstein's Nephew*, in the same contradictory way that Paul Wittgenstein himself is recovered in the novel by 'Thomas Bernhard'. Bernhard's novel reaches at once towards Beckett and towards Wittgenstein, towards a Wittgensteinian Beckett and a Beckettian Wittgenstein, but it allows both Beckett and Paul Wittgenstein to speak only to the extent that *How It Is* gives breath and colour and muddy ink to that voice that speaks from beyond part three. Ludwig Wittgenstein famously remarked of his *Tractatus Logico-Philosophicus*, in a letter to his friend von Ficker, that 'my work consists of two parts: of the one which is here, and of everything which I have *not* written. And precisely this second part is the important one'.[28] In *Wittgenstein's Nephew*, and in the figure of Paul Wittgenstein, Bernhard gives a kind of mute articulation to that unwritten half of Wittgenstein's philosophy. The novel passes over the published body of the *Tractatus* in silence – 'we never once talked about the *Tractatus*' (WN 63), Bernhard observes – reaching instead for contact with Paul Wittgenstein's elusive genius, a kind of mad, deathly genius which remains unpublished, in Murau's terms not yet 'put down on paper'. Paul is a 'great, original, revolutionary thinker', like his uncle, but the philosophy that he produces, the philosophy that it is the aim of *Wittgenstein's Nephew* to approach, is one that remains, like the 'more important' half of Ludwig's work, unwritten and unpublished. Roithamer asserts in *Correction* that 'what we publish is destroyed in the instant of publication' (C 236), and Bernhard insists, in *Wittgenstein's Nephew* that Paul Wittgenstein managed to preserve himself from such destruction by not publishing in the first place. 'Ludwig published his philosophy', Bernhard says, 'Paul did not: Ludwig was the born publisher (of his philosophy), Paul the born nonpublisher of his philosophy' (WN 63). But in order to achieve some kind of access to this unpublished genius, the novel has to cross the threshold that separates the written from the unwritten, the Hermann Pavilion from the Ludwig Pavilion, that separates Sam from Watt, presence from absence. In order to reach Paul, Bernhard realizes, he has to reach across the boundary that separates life from death, he has to stage what he calls a '*direct* confrontation with death' (WN 99). The novel that he has written, Bernhard realizes towards the end of the narrative, comprises simply of this Malonian confrontation with death, this attempt to give death a voice. 'I now realise', he writes, 'that these notes [. . .] were the record of a man dying', that they '*traced* [*verfolgt*[29]] his dying over a period of more than twelve years' (WN 99), that in the dialogue that he stages in the novel between himself and Paul, he was 'basically nothing but the twelve year witness of his dying' (WN 99). In the only known direct reference that Bernhard made to Beckett, in an interview in 1982, it is possible to hear a resonance between this 12 years' record of Wittgenstein's death, and the persistent presence of Beckett's work in his own. 'As far as I'm concerned', Bernhard said, 'Beckett has been dead for ten years, he merely sends brief messages from the hereafter' (see p. 15). Both Beckett and Wittgenstein speak in Bernhard's work from the 'hereafter', from 'beyond the grave', as, in *Old Masters*, Reger speaks as a 'dead man, as a 'dead man who has to go on living' (OM 126). Bernhard's fiction brings these dead voices to the point of speech, he fashions a language which can allow these voices to leave a trace, but he only does so by allowing his work itself to die, to enter with Beckett, Wittgenstein, Schermaier and Reger, into the realm of death. His prose brings these voices to life, to print, only at the moment of their destruction.

It is in *Correction* that Bernhard finds the most flexible form with which to perform this Beckettian relation between quotation and correction. In this novel the page, as in the excruciating dynamics of *How It Is*, acts as a plane that connects the dead and the living, the past and the future, here and there. The Bernhard page might be thought of not only as the page made from the skin of Pim's back, but also as the 'little fabric' (CSP 182) from which Beckett fashions his barely perceptible inhabitations in his late short prose, those messages that Bernhard says Beckett sends us from the hereafter. The rotundas of Beckett's most transparent works are made from this little fabric, that can only trace (verfolgen) a white mark in the whiteness, and it is this fabric also that Bernhard and Roithamer use to build their cone in the centre of the Kobernausser forest, to which they send Roithamer's (Wittgenstein's) sister to die, the cone which is organized too around a central 'rotunda' (C 149). The cone, like the narrative of *Correction* itself, is a construction that comes into being in the impossible clearing between life and death, between the written and the unwritten. It is a fabric, a material, that marks the meeting point between the seen and the unseen, between Roithamer's 'impossible thinking' and the narrator's 'notes' which seek to capture such thinking, to sift it and sort it; but it only marks this meeting, this clearing, by dissolving, because the price and prerequisite of witnessing such a meeting is dissolution. The clearing in the Kobernausser forest made and marked by the cone doubles, in *Correction*, with another clearing, the clearing between Stocket (home of the narrator) and Altensam (home of Roithamer), in which the two meet, as Sam and Watt, Bernhard and Wittgenstein, meet between the fences of their pavilions. These clearings, between Stocket and Altensam and in the heart of the Kobernausser forest, constitute the grounds for, the very possibility of, the artwork. Roithamer, indeed, had written an early work (now lost), the narrator tells us, entitled *The Clearing*, about their meetings in this clearing between their respective homes, and which predicted, or became, Roithamer's death by hanging, which took place in the same clearing (C 53–4). This lost work, the cone, the narrative itself, all are conjured from an exchange between the impossible and the possible, the written and the unwritten, an exchange which weaves a collapsing form out of an encounter with formlessness. When the narrator recalls, recounting his meetings with Roithamer, that 'it often happened that our paths crossed, his downward path toward Stocket, my upward path toward Altensam, crossing at the same midpoint, the clearing in the forest', he is giving a kind of physical form to the narrative structure of the novel, as that meeting between the fences makes narrative structure manifest in *Wittgenstein's Nephew*. The written page of *Correction* is made from the crossing of these two paths, and seeks to present a surface upon which each path can leave a trace. Like Roithamer's lost early work, which offered a 'description of the road from Altensam to us in Stocket and a description of the road from Stocket to Altensam, naturally two entirely different descriptions' (C 54), *Correction* offers a single form in which these two paths can come together, a work in which these two 'entirely different descriptions' find a unified expression. The first half of *Correction* might be thought of as leading from Stocket to Altensam, from the narrator to Roithamer, while the second might be thought of coming to us from Altensam to Stocket, from beyond the far horizon marked by Roithamer's death, his self-correction. But the 'little fabric' of which this novel is made is a peculiarly double-sided one that allows and requires both voices to speak at once. The voice of the narrator is occupied, throughout, by the voice, by the thought of the absent Roithamer, to the extent that the narrator himself seems at times to disappear, or as he puts it to be 'extinguished by Roithamer's thinking' (C 22). For long swirling swathes of the novel, Roithamer takes over the narrative completely, pushing aside the agent that quotes him. But equally, and conversely, Roithamer is only present to the extent that he is animated by the narrator, to the extent that he allows himself to be thought by him. Roithamer might occupy the far side of the text, might live in absence in the empty space beyond part three; but in meeting with the narrator that quotes him, in coming to that clearing between Altensam and Stocket, he has in a sense to forfeit or to defer that freedom that he has won through suicide. 'One day', Roithamer says, towards the close of the novel, 'one day, in a single instant, we'll break through the final barrier, but the moment hasn't come yet' (C 248). As that moment in which the voice will reach the quiet peace beyond part 3 is continually deferred in *How It is*, so Roithamer, in meeting with the narrator, in clothing himself in his speech, has repeatedly to defer his death, to put off the death that he has already died. Just as Bernhard's narrator, in reaching for Roithamer, enters the unwritten, unpublished space of impossible, deathly thinking, so Roithamer, in reaching for the narrator, has to undie the death that allowed him to stir, in Beckett's words, from the field of the possible.

It is the figure of correction, inherited from Beckett and from Wittgenstein, that allows Bernhard to keep these two competing voices housed in a single textual clearing. The draft of the novel, like the crawl through the inky mud of *How It Is*, is cast as a kind of process, a kind of editing that is still taking place. 'Actually', Roithamer says at one point, in the draft of his work on the cone that is being quoted, sifted and sorted by the narrator:

> Actually I'm shocked by everything I have just written, what if it was all quite different, I wonder, but I will not correct *now* what I've written, I'll correct it all when the time for such correction has come and then I'll correct the corrections and correct again the resulting corrections andsoforth, so Roithamer. (C 222)

It is the deferral, in this way, of the final correction, of the final draft, that allows Roithamer to share space with the narrator, to allow them, between themselves, to weave that little fabric of which the cone, and of which *Correction* is made. It is its peculiar, delicate unfinishedness that allows the work to make a bridge between the narrator and Roithamer, between before and after, between life and death. But if the text allows these voices to come together, it does so only, finally, to free them from one another, or as Beckett's narrator says of the voice that he is quoting in *How It Is*, to

> eliminate him completely and so admit him to that peace at last while rendering me in the same breath sole responsible for this unqualified murmur of which consequently here the last scraps at last very last (HII 157).

The final correction is deferred just long enough for that absent voice from part three, for Roithamer's death-shaded voice, to declare that the text that gave them a voice is 'all balls'. The delicate textual clearing that these fictions open up, that gives the narrator of *Correction* his last, double-voiced word ('The end is no process', the novel ends, 'Clearing.' [C 249]), survives on the impossible, out of joint temporality that also dismembers and disintegrates it. At the close of the *Tractatus*, that published work that Bernhard and Paul Wittgenstein refuse to discuss, Wittgenstein suggests that his work, too, is really only a deferred correction. 'My propositions', he says,

> serve as elucidations in the following way: anyone who understands me eventually recognizes them as nonsensical, when he has used them – as steps – to climb up beyond them. (He must, so to speak, throw away the ladder after he has climbed up it.)

The Tractatus serves, Wittgenstein suggests, only as a ladder to get beyond the far horizon, to reach that space beyond part three in which the narrator of *How It is* 'has his life'. Like the narrative of *How It Is* and of *Correction*, the *Tractatus* lives in word and sound and print just long enough to bring student in contact with teacher, to bring the beginning into contact with the end. After that, it returns to silence.

Chapter 6

A Quite Singular Clarity: Beckett, Bernhard, Sebald

I argued in the last chapter that Beckett and Bernhard summon a certain contact with the past, a certain recovery of lost time, from the experience of a particular dismemberment by time, a dismemberment which finds expression in the experience of literary correction and disintegration; and I argued that, in finding this continuity between Beckett and Bernhard, it is possible to place Beckett within a tradition that passes from Kleist to Wittgenstein and Kafka to Bernhard. It is possible not only to tune Beckett to this Germanic frequency, but also to find in Beckett's work the crafting of an innovative tuning mechanism for the recovery of lost histories, a mechanism which adapts a Kleistian inheritance, and which Bernhard in turn adapts to his own aesthetic and political ends.

The line that I have been tracing here, that one can see disappearing into the recovered depths of a Kleistian mirror, reaches an end point, of sorts, with W. G. Sebald, a writer in whose work it is possible to see the shared presences of Bernhard and Beckett, Wittgenstein and Kleist. While Bernhard has been famously described as an 'Alpen-Beckett', W. J. McCormack has described Sebald as an 'Anglo-German Beckett without the humour'.[1] And if Sebald, like Bernhard, can seem inhabited in some way by Beckett, then he has also been frequently allied with Bernhard, the primacy of whose influence Sebald dwelt on rather eloquently in a radio interview shortly before his death.[2] Indeed, Amir Eshel has commented on the presence of Bernhard in Sebald's work, and has suggested that Bernhard's influence can be felt primarily in the ways in which Sebald 'faces' the dead, in which he seeks to bring the dead and the past to a kind of suspended presence in the literary work. Eshel writes in his essay 'Against the Power of Time: the Poetics of Suspension in W. G. Sebald's *Austerlitz*', that

> Like authors such as Ingeborg Bachmann, Thomas Bernhard, and Alexander Kluge, but also like Claud Simone, if one were to expand the view into the perspective of contemporary European literature, Sebald's significance lies precisely in the manner in which his work continually faces the dead through

an opening up of the literary as a space of reflecting the present, as a space for reflection.[3]

As Kleist deploys the image of a convex mirror as a reflective plane in which one might see through to the other end of time, in which one might make the broken ends of the circular world meet, so for Eshel, Sebald's work presents a (Bernhardian) reflective surface in which the faces of the dead might be recovered, 'suspended', as Eshel puts it, recalling the well-known essay on Kleist by William Ray, 'in the mirror'.[4]

This recovery of the dead in Sebald's work is staged most often, as it is in Beckett and in Bernhard, in terms of a meeting between narrator and character, across the kind of threshold marked out by the gap between Beckett's and Bernhard's 'pavilions', or by what Sebald's Austerlitz thinks of as an 'invisible barrier' (A 56). As Kleist's K looks across such a gulf towards C, as Sam looks towards Watt, as the narrator of *How It Is* crawls towards Pim, as the narrator of *Correction* reaches towards Roithamer, as Bernhard reaches towards Wittgenstein, as Atzbacher, in Bernhard's *Old Masters*, faces Reger, so Sebald's fiction consists, in *Austerlitz*, in *Vertigo*, in *The Emigrants*, of a narrator who works towards his interlocutor or character, who seeks to tunnel into a space 'somewhere behind his eyes' (A 197). In *Austerlitz*, indeed, this reaching towards the space of the other is cast to a degree in terms of the relationship between Thomas More and Raphael Hythloday that More forges in *Utopia*, a relationship that I have suggested can be felt beneath the surface of the dialogues staged in Kleist, in Beckett and in Bernhard. The narrator of *Austerlitz* opens his narrative by describing the European journeys that he took 'in the second half of the 1960s' when, he writes,

> I travelled repeatedly from England to Belgium, partly for study purposes, partly for other reasons which were never entirely clear to me, staying sometimes just one or two days, sometimes for several weeks. On one of those Belgian excursions which, as it seemed to me, always took me further and further abroad, I came on a glorious early summer's day to the city of Antwerp, known to me previously only by name. (A 1)

It is here, in Antwerp, that the narrator meets Austerlitz, just as it is in Antwerp in 1516 that Thomas More meets Raphael Hythloday, himself a character who, like Austerlitz, is returning to the world from his time spent in absence, in Hythloday's utopian 'no-place'. It is one of the many jokes woven into More's narrative that Hythloday is recognizable by his characteristic habit of standing 'with a cloak slung carelessly over one shoulder', a characteristic that, according to Roger Ascham, Hythloday shares with More,[5] thus slyly invoking the mirror structure that runs throughout *Utopia*, suggesting that Hythloday is only ever a perfected mirror image of More himself. When Sebald's narrator first meets Austerlitz in Antwerp, he recognizes in him a similar characteristic gesture, that recurs every subsequent time that he runs into Austerlitz, and that suggests not only a comparison with More's Raphael, but also with Wittgenstein. On the first occasion that Austerlitz and the narrator meet, Austerlitz has not his jacket but his 'rucksack' 'slung over his shoulder' (A 23). And when they meet again, 20 years later, the narrator recognizes this gesture again in Austerlitz, remarking that 'he had not changed at all either in his carriage or clothing and even had the rucksack still slung over his shoulder' (A 54). It is this rucksack, the narrator says, that not only came to represent Austerlitz for him, but also to mark the similarity that the narrator divines between Austerlitz and Wittgenstein. 'I believe it was mainly the rucksack', the narrator says, 'which put into my mind what on the surface was the rather outlandish idea of a certain physical likeness between [Austerlitz] and the philosopher who died of the disease of cancer in Cambridge in 1951' (A 55), a resemblance that, while outlandish, brings the narrator eventually to remark that

> whenever I see a photograph of Wittgenstein somewhere or other, I feel more and more as if Austerlitz were gazing at me out of it, and when I look at Austerlitz it is as if I see in him the disconsolate philosopher, a man locked into the glaring clarity of his logical thinking as inextricably as into his confused emotions, so striking is the likeness between the two of them. (A 56)

So, when Sebald's narrators set out to meet those characters that people his fictions, such as Jacques Austerlitz, Paul Bereyter or Ambros Adelwarth, they restage that coming together of More and Hythloday imagined by Thomas More in *Utopia*, that coming together of Bernhard and Wittgenstein imagined by Thomas Bernhard in *Wittgensteins Neffe*. And, as in More, Beckett and Bernhard, these meetings are cast both as a physical journey – crawling through the mud towards Pim or sailing across the channel towards Antwerp – and as a word journey, in which the narrator builds word bridges that take him across that 'invisible barrier' that separates here from there, us from them, and that allow him to enter that most intimate space 'behind the eyes' of the other, behind those eyes that gaze at us so compellingly from the pages of Sebald's and Jan Peter Tripp's collaborative work *Unrecounted*. One of the most striking formal characteristics shared by Bernhard and Sebald, and derived to an extent from Beckett, is this tendency to open long lines of quotation, in which a narrator builds his way into the wordspace, into the very pronoun, of the character whose voice he quotes. In this, again, all three writers catch at something that comes to them from More. It is the task of More's *Utopia* to craft a double-sided form in which Raphael and More share a single voice, in which Raphael can give expression to a utopian perfection that remains beyond the scope of More's political pragmatism while nevertheless clothing that unspeakable perfection in More's lucid political discourse. If Raphael can be thought of as a mirror image of More, an image of More freed from the compromises of court politics, and if Utopia itself can be thought of as a negative version of England – the unmapped, uncharted England of the future, that has not yet come to consciousness or to possibility – then the quotational structure of the work is crafted to allow More's narrative to contain the echoes of Raphael's voice, speaking from somewhere on the other side of the mirror, or from a space in a utopian future, beyond part three. In Sebald's writing, this working towards the space of the other is cast more often as a journey into the past than into the future. In *Austerlitz*, for example, the process by which Austerlitz recovers his memory – the process by which he 'restores' and 'renovates' his boyhood in Prague, resurrecting in the process his mother, his father and a host of Jewish dead – is indistinguishable from the way in which the narrator quotes Austerlitz who quotes in turn those from whom he pieces together his story. If the recovery of memory in *Austerlitz*, as in *How It Is*, is figured as a parting of the curtain or a veil that separates the present from the past, then these strings of quotation are the bridges or the lines of flight that grant the narrator and the reader passage from one zone to the other. As the narrative approaches the scenes in Nazi-occupied Prague during the period when Jews were forced to flee their homes, for example, the thread that takes us from the narrator to the scene he is recovering, becomes extremely stretched. Austerlitz's mother Agáta, we learn, did not want to leave Prague without her husband Maximilian, Austerlitz's father, and this reluctance, this adhesion to Prague and to her family, comes to us through this long series of quoted agents. 'For her part', the narrative reads,

> Agáta was not prepared to go to France ahead of Maximilian, although he had repeatedly advised her to leave, and so it was that your father, Vera told me, said Austerlitz, then in the utmost danger, did not leave until it was almost too late, on the afternoon of the 14th of March, by plane from Ruzyně to Paris. I still remember, said Vera, that when he said goodbye he was wearing a wonderful plum-coloured double-breasted suit, and a black felt hat with a green band and a broad brim. (A 242)

At this moment, as the narrative stretches back to the darkness of 1940s Prague, giving us this strange glimpse of the father waving goodbye in a plum-coloured suit, the novel connects five distinct narrative personae – the narrator, Austerlitz, Vera (the Austerlitz family's housekeeper), and finally the father and the mother, in the very act of disappearing. These delicate chains are of course everywhere in the novel, and continue to stretch as the novel goes on, into the heart of the Theresienstadt where the narrator finally recovers an image his mother's face, and then, at the close of the novel, towards the still unrecovered father.

In reaching in this way towards the darkness, *Austerlitz* uses the 'mechanism' that he inherits, in part, from Bernhard and from Beckett before him, to retrieve from the historical vacuum of the World War II the voices and faces of Austerlitz's parentage, a sort of utopianism in reverse that produces a negative image of the ungraven possibilities of the past, rather than those of the future. Throughout his fiction, Bernhard too employs those chains of quotation that proliferate in Sebald to make curious and delicate transitions from one narrative perspective, one temporal and spatial field, to another. In *Correction*, for example, the narrative moves restlessly from the perspective of the narrator, sitting in Hoeller's garret, to that of Hoeller, and most insistently to the very inside of Roithamer's 'impossible thinking', and the particular structure of the Bernhard sentence allows this restlessness to unsettle and loosen the bonds that hold narrative in place and in time. The deliciously deranged scene towards the close of the novel's first half, for example, in which the narrator looks down from his garret to Hoeller's workshop where Hoeller is stuffing a 'huge black bird', effects a peculiar to and fro between garret and workshop, between narrator and Hoeller. Hoeller is working in the dark in his workshop, while the narrator stands at the lit window of the garret, and the narrator becomes obsessed by the idea that Hoeller has turned out his workshop light so that he can see the narrator, without being seen himself. The narrator decides, in a kind of paranoid panic, that he should 'step back' from his lit window, 'step back so far that Hoeller can no longer see me', and thinks to himself that

> now that I've stepped back Hoeller might turn the light on again in his workshop, because he'll assume that I'm no longer interested in him now that I've stepped back from the window, he can feel free to turn on the light, as I'm no longer looking down there, I thought, he may well think, now I can turn the light on again here in the workshop, because he (me) is no longer looking down. (C 123)

This is a peculiar moment in the novel that predicts the near collapse of the boundary between the narrator and Roithamer that occurs in the novel's second half. The narrator's decision to 'step back' from the window in order to maintain his bird's eye view of Hoeller while defending himself from Hoeller's reciprocal upward gaze leads, peculiarly, to this alarming shift in perspective, in which we suddenly find ourselves in Hoeller's head looking through Hoeller's eyes, in which Hoeller suddenly occupies the novel's 'I', and in which the narrator equally suddenly becomes 'he'. This usurpation of the narrative I builds throughout the second half of the novel, as the narrative gives itself in the first person to Roithamer's impossible thinking. As Roithamer reaches endlessly towards the suicidal emptiness of the cone and of the clearing, his death-bound thinking is separated from the narrator's increasingly fragile outpost in the garret only by the repeated phrase 'so Roithamer', which functions, like 'said Austerlitz' in *Austerlitz*, to mark the shift in quotation fields from the narrator to Roithamer, to allow for this passing further and further from the given place of narration to the depths of Roithamer's Wittgensteinian genius. Or, to give another example, at one moment in Bernhard's novel *Old Masters*, Bernhard uses the frame of a painting, of Tintoretto's 'White Bearded Man' hanging in the Kunsthistorisches Museum in Vienna, to open up a narrative window that transports us from one viewpoint to another, one place and time to another. The Tintoretto painting, which functions as a kind of anchor for the novel throughout, takes on this peculiar transparency during the richly comic story, told by Reger to Atzbacher (the narrator), of the 'Englishman from Wales'. This Englishman from Wales, Reger tells Atzbacher, one day sat next to Reger on the Bordone settee in front of the 'White Bearded Man' in the Kunsthistorisches Museum, where Reger had sat to look at the Tintoretto every morning for the last 36 years. The Englishman comes to look at the painting because, he explains to Reger, he had been told by his nephew that the 'White Bearded Man' hanging in Vienna was identical to the 'White Bearded Man' that the Englishman himself owns. He had 'come to the Vienna Kunsthistorisches Museum to study the *White-Bearded Man*', he tells Reger,

> because *back home he had just such a White-Bearded Man* hanging over his bed in his bedroom in Wales, *in actual fact the same White-Bearded Man*, the Englishman said, Reger said. (OM 74)

As this story unfolds, and as the chain of narration reaching from Atzbacher to Reger to the Englishman from Wales gets stretched further and further, the Tintoretto hanging in the Kunsthistorisches Museum, standing in the midst of its Benjaminian aura, becomes an opening, a portal of sorts that leads from Vienna to the Englishman's bedroom in Wales. The Englishman walks up to the painting to inspect it closely, to check that it is indeed 'not merely the same but absolutely identical' (OM 77) to his own Tintoretto hanging at home, and Reger tells Atzbacher that 'I watched the Englishman stepping up quite close to the *White-Bearded Man* and staring at him'. 'Naturally', he goes on,

> As I was watching him from behind, I could not see his face, Reger said to me, but I knew of course, even though I was watching him from behind, that he was staring at the *White-Bearded Man*, now more or less disconcerted. (OM 77–8)

As the tormentors crowd behind Christ's back in Bosch's 'Crowning with Thorns', approaching the plane of the painting as if it were a contested boundary between here and there, between material presence and spiritual absence, (see pp. 98–101) so the Englishman's approach to the painting here offers to take him out of the Museum, away from the space narrated by Atzbacher, and through Tintoretto's canvas back to his bedroom in Wales. Reger's positioning at the Englishman's back, with Atzbacher in turn behind him, suggests that the Beckettian chain of quotation which takes us from Atzbacher to Reger to the

Englishman from Wales will take us, eventually, beyond the horizon of the novel altogether, as the chain of quotation, the 'imbrication of flesh without breach or fissure', leads, in *How It Is*, beyond the mud of the text to the quiet space beyond part three. Reflecting on how it could be that the two identical paintings could hang at once in Wales and in Vienna, the Englishman decides that one or other must be a fake. 'It is perfectly obvious', Reger says to Atzbacher

> that one of these Tintoretto paintings is a forgery, the Englishman then said, Reger said, either this one here at the Kunsthistorisches Museum, or mine, which hangs over my bed in my bedroom in Wales. (OM 78)

The riddle of the two identical Tintorettos is never solved – the Englishman from Wales exits the narrative at this point never to return – but it nevertheless serves to make of the painting this peculiar, uncertain boundary through which the narrative moves beyond itself, remaking Reger as an Englishman from Wales, delivering him to 'my bed in my bedroom in Wales'.

So, when Sebald builds those chains of quotations that run through his work, using that characteristic 'said Agáta, Vera told me, said Austerlitz' to recover times and spaces that have been repressed or forcefully extinguished, he is quoting also a stylistic characteristic of Bernhard's, which itself has echoes of Beckett's quotational patterns. And, as Bernhard uses Tintoretto's 'White Bearded Man' as a means of folding together discrete times and spaces, so Sebald's word bridges are organized around recovered images, those images that Runia suggests function as 'holes through which the past discharges into the present'.

Two such images, which suggest the capacity of photography to effect this folding together of discrete entities, are the photographs of Wittgenstein's eyes (A 3), and of a family of deer, who regard us from the other side of what Marie, a character in the novel, thinks of as a 'breach of incomprehension' (A 369). The narrator includes a picture of Wittgenstein's (and by extension Austerlitz's) eyes at the opening of his narrative, when he describes his visit to a nocturama in which he was entranced by the wide eyes of owls, and other nocturnal creatures. 'All I remember of the denizens of the Nocturama', the narrator writes,

> is that several of them had strikingly large eyes, and the fixed, inquiring gaze found in certain painters and philosophers who seek to penetrate the darkness which surrounds us purely by means of looking and thinking. (A 3)

This observation is illustrated by photographs of pairs of eyes, those of the animals of the Nocturama, as well as of Wittgenstein himself who gazes at us directly from the page. Now, to some degree these photographs have the effect of distancing us from their object, rather than opening Runia's 'holes' which allow 'here' to 'discharge' into 'there', 'now' to flow into 'then'. The close ups, as in the collection of images and poetry in Sebald's and Tripp's *Unrecounted*, are contained in small, cropped rectangles, which give the impression that we are looking at them through a letterbox, that they are contained somewhere on the other side of a wall, or on the other side of the page. But if the page seems, in one sense, to act as a barrier between us and them, to recreate the sense that Wittgenstein is 'locked into the glaring clarity of his logical thinking' (A 56), in another sense the image punctures the page, allowing for a new and intense form of exchange between us and them, allowing whatever is on the other side of the page to 'leak' across that 'invisible barrier', that 'breach of incomprehension'. The power of Wittgenstein's gaze to 'penetrate the darkness' is harboured here also to erode that barrier, to burn a hole in the page that separates us from him. This double function of the image, both to separate us from they eyes that gaze at us, and to give us a more direct access to them, conspires with the work of quotation to build from here to there, from us to them, to find a passage into that space 'behind the eyes' of the other. The chains of quotation fashioned by the prose allow the voice of the narrator to become occupied by that of Austerlitz, who himself channels the voices of his father and his mother. The experience of reading the novel is to find oneself repeatedly resituated on the other side of the fence, or the 'breach', that separates narrator from character, here from there, as the voices that the narrator quotes appear to usurp the first person, to wrest control of the narrative away from him. So when one looks through the plane of the printed page into the eyes of Wittgenstein/Austerlitz, as one looks through the back/page of *How It Is* towards that space beyond part three where the narrator 'has [his] life', one does not simply look *into* those eyes but also to some degree *with* them, as the coordinates that orientate you on one side of the page or the other become confused, or recalibrated.

One of the moments in the novel when this specular effect is most pronounced comes mid way through the narrative, as Austerlitz wanders in the uncannily deserted town of Terezín. It is here, as Austerlitz returns to the scene of his mother's detention in the ghetto at Theresienstadt, that the novel reaches deeply into the shrouded past it seeks to recover, coming close to 'penetrating the darkness' in which the history of Austerlitz's lost family is hidden. Austerlitz's journey to Terezín (present day Theresienstadt), is prompted to a degree by his discovery of a picture of himself as a 5 year old dressed as a page boy, a photograph that produces in him that strange confusion, that strange disorientation that is suggested by the image of Wittgenstein's eyes at the opening of the novel. The sight of the picture leads Austerlitz to reflect that we do not 'understand the laws governing the return of the past'. 'I feel more and more', he goes on,

> as if time did not exist at all, only various spaces interlocking according to rules of a higher form of stereometry, between which the living and the dead can move back and forth as they like, and the longer I think about it the more it seems to me that we who are still alive are unreal in the eyes of the dead,

that only occasionally, in certain lights and atmospheric conditions, do we appear in their field of vision. (A 261)

This obliquely Joycean perception that it is the dead who are the more permanent inhabitants of the world than those of us who as 'still alive', comes forcefully to him as he looks at that picture of himself regarding him (and us) from the photograph (a photograph that is reproduced in the novel itself [A 258]). 'As far back as I can remember', he says,

> I have always felt as if I had no place in reality, as if I were not there at all, and I never had this impression more strongly than on that evening in the Šporkova when the eyes of the Rose Queen's page looked through me. (A 261)

At this point, as the photographed eyes of the young Austerlitz 'look through' the older Austerlitz, the narrative performs one of those peculiar reversals that occur repeatedly throughout, in which the gaze appears to change direction, to flip over. The Austerlitz who tells his story to the narrator – the middle aged Austerlitz who is preparing to travel to the Theresienstadt ghetto – no longer looks at this photograph, but becomes, himself, a speck in his earlier incarnation's 'field of vision', the field of vision produced by the eyes that gaze out of the photograph. He feels (echoing both 'the dark Miss Fitt' and Banville's Axel Vander [see p. 57]) as if he is 'not there at all', as agency, presence, 'reality' itself, is transferred from his speaking to his photographed self, from the living to the Barthesian dead, and as the eyes in the photograph shift from the objects upon which we gaze, to the organs with which we ourselves look.

This sense of 'crossing over', of passing through the plane of the page, and across the barrier of the eyeball itself, is the prelude to Austerlitz's arrival in the empty town of Terezín, a town which, like the similarly deserted town in Beckett's novella *The Calmative*, as well as the village of Llanwddyn that lies beneath the waters of the Vyrnwy dam in *Austerlitz*, feels as if it is 'under water' (CSP 54, A 71–2), as if it belongs to a different, deathly medium. As the journey to Terezín takes Austerlitz 'further and further back in time' (A 262–3), so it seems to take him across the boundary between life and death, across the boundary marked by the page of the novel itself, from which the eyes of his younger self, and the eyes of a Wittgenstein locked in the glaring clarity of his thought, gaze out at us. In the liquidy silence of the nearly deserted town, where the few inhabitants that Austerlitz sees appear bent under the weight of accumulated time, the focus of his gaze and of his camera is on doors and on widows, as if even here, in the very heartland of absence and of death, there is still a further threshold to be crossed, still more of the void to be revealed. 'What I found most uncanny of all', he says, 'were the gates and doorways of Terezín, all of them, as I thought I sensed, obstructing access to a darkness never yet penetrated' (A 267–8). As if to offer some proof of the impenetrability of the doors that face Austerlitz, the narrative includes a number of photographic close ups of shut and bolted doors, doors that offer a contrast to the partly open boundary marked by the eyes of Wittgenstein and of Austerlitz, and that recall those photographic close ups of the smooth grey doors that mark the boundary of the apparently sealed room in Beckett's play *Ghost Trio* (A 268–71). But as the doors of Beckett's play are 'imperceptibly ajar', as they offer a kind of compromised access to the other side, so Austerlitz says that he found himself, in the midst of a dislocated out-of-time dream and in a peculiarly 'half-conscious state', crossing the final boundary marked by those shut doors, 'looking into the interior of one of those Terezín barracks' (A 272), the interior in which the unspeakable itself is at home. The narrative cannot follow Austerlitz into this interior; it tries to 'hold fast' to the 'powdery grey dream image' in which it takes a brief, half conscious form, struggling to 'discover what it concealed', but the image dissolves, and is overlaid by the 'memory, surfacing in my mind at the same time' of a window, of 'the shining glass in the display windows of the ANTIKOS BAZAR on the west side of the town square' (A 273). It is through this window, through this more transparent surface, that Austerlitz sees as far into the interior of Theresienstadt as it is possible to penetrate, and it is this window also that provides the novel with two of its most penetrating photographic images. The window offers Austerlitz a view of a number of random objects, pieces of bric-a-brac that seem to him to have developed an immunity to time – 'objects that for reasons one could never know had outlived their former owners and survived the process of destruction' (A 277), as Adorno suggests that the occupants of the bunker in *Endgame* have 'survived the destruction of their world'.[6] The objects that Austerlitz gazes at have a peculiarly arrested, suspended quality redolent of Keats' figures wrought into the Grecian Urn (that 'foster-child of silence and slow time'),[7] depicting scenes that are 'perpetuated but for ever just occurring' (A 275). He dwells on a 'squirrel forever perched in the same position', and an 'ivory coloured porcelain group of a hero on horseback' – objects that are reproduced in photographs interspersed into the text. The photographs work with the text to produce a deeply uncanny sense of penetration, a sense that the page itself is giving way to the scenes which it contains and which the prose has summoned into a kind of immediate presence, producing in the viewer a sense of vertigo, a perception that the flimsy boundary that Austerlitz says separates the living from the dead has given way. But if the photographs produce this experience of free fall, this sense of falling into the suspended time of the interior of Theresienstadt, they also look two ways, as the photographed eyes of Wittgenstein and of Austerlitz look two ways. The shining glass through which we see those pieces of bric-a-brac is not only a window but also an imperfect mirror, so we see not only through it into the hidden depths, but also glimpse, caught in the glass of that 'invisible barrier' between here and there, between life and death, the ghostly image of our own viewpoint, of our own disappearing apparatus of vision. The first image, a picture of 'four still lives obviously composed entirely at random', contains a shadowy image of the town of Terezín in which 'Austerlitz' (Sebald?) is standing, so that the objects inside the shop 'appeared to have grown quite naturally into the black branches of the lime trees standing around the square and reflected in the glass of the windows' (A 274). The second image, of the porcelain horse and rider, holds within it also a shadowy image of the town, as well as the faded image of the photographer, so, Austerlitz says, 'I could now see', entwined with the objects photographed, 'my own faint shadow image barely perceptible among them' (A 277).

With this peculiar spectralization of our own view point, the sense of 'crossing over' – the feeling that the novel produces of a change of narrative direction – is given a visual form. As the Englishman from Wales, in Bernhard's novel, approaches the Tintoretto, with Reger standing behind him, with Atzbacher standing behind him, and with the reader, in turn standing behind Atzbacher and looking through his eyes, so here we approach the window of the ANTIKOS BAZAR by looking though the eyes of the narrator, who looks through the eyes of Austerlitz, at the objects that have been strangely preserved from time. The novel builds towards these objects, towards that moment in Terezín, by creating long chains of quotation which take us by degrees towards the heart of European darkness. But here, as the photograph offers us a window into that very interior, we see that chain of quotation as if from the other side, leading from Austerlitz, to the narrator, to Sebald, to us, reaching not from us towards the lost history of the Holocaust, but from the heart of that lostness outwards, towards those shadowy onlookers who become spectral, insubstantial, fleeting ephemera in 'the field of vision' that opens from the inside of the ANITKOS BAZAR. The page acts, here, as a double-sided plane, that sutures the dead and the living together, that forges a form in which we – the living – have 'grown naturally', like the lime trees in the square in Terezín, into the liquid medium of the dead, in which the fleeting present becomes a thin, insubstantial skein running through and interwoven with the dense material of the past. We do not simply look into the past here, as we do not look just into the eyes of Wittgenstein earlier in the novel; rather we are returned to an astonishing intimacy with the past, we become a part of that lost world, from which we can glimpse a barely perceptible, spectral version of ourselves, looking in from the glassy future.

It is this capacity for the page to act as a transparent surface which brings together the elements that it separates that characterizes the poetics of *developing*, of *focusing* and of *tuning* in Sebald's prose. As the window of the Antikos Bazar offers an invisible membrane through which the present passes osmotically into the past, so Sebald's writing more generally can be thought of as a kind of dissolving fabric through which darkness enters into a peculiar unity with light. It can be thought of at once visually and aurally, at once as a light sensitive plate through which images from the past pass into the present, and as a radio receiver which tunes itself to a frequency at which the voices of the dead merge and mingle with the voices of the living. Austerlitz, like Paul Rayment in J. M. Coetzee's novel *Slow Man*, is fascinated by the process of photographic developing, the process by which images rise to the surface of the photographic paper, partly because it catches at the poetics of the novel itself, the poetics of recovery of time that is so central to Sebald's work. Cotezee's Rayment describes a kind of ecstasy that accompanies the developing of the image. 'His greatest pleasure', he says,

> was always in darkroom work. As the ghostly image emerged beneath the surface of the liquid, as the veins of darkness on the paper began to knit together and grow visible, he would sometimes experience a little shiver of ecstasy, as though he were present at the day of creation. (SM 65)

In this passage, as the photographic paper parts to reveal an image that rises from underneath the liquid, that brings the darkness towards visibility, Coetzee's prose also catches at voices that carry from the past, tuning in to a chain of quotation that runs from Beckett to Emily Dickinson to John Milton. The veins of darkness which 'grow naturally' in the liquid medium towards visibility summon at once Milton's hell, in which the infernal flames give out 'no light, but rather darkness visible',[8] the peculiarly illuminated darkness of Dickinson's poetry in which 'Twas lighter – to be Blind',[9] and Beckett's *Company*, in which the faint voice 'lightens the dark', making 'darkness visible' (NO 15). It is this same sense of developing as a spectral, specular recovery or creation of the past – the making visible of the dark – that so entrances Austerlitz. 'In my photographic work', he says,

> I was always especially entranced [. . .] by the moment when the shadows of reality, so to speak, emerge out of nothing on the exposed paper, as memories do in the middle of the night, darkening again if you try to cling to them, just like a photographic print left in the developing bath too long. (A 109)

The process by which the developing image 'emerges out of nothing' mirrors that by which the novel itself allows the past to come into contact with the present, to come to presence on the surface of the page. 'Time', Austerlitz insists in an early conversation with the narrator, 'has not passed away'. 'I can turn back', he says,

> and go behind it, and there I shall find everything as it once was, or more precisely I shall find that all moments of time have co-existed simultaneously, in which case none of what history tells us would be true, past events have not yet occurred but are waiting to do so at the moment we think of them. (A 144)

The novel sets out to perform this 'turning back', this 'going behind', but it does so not by setting itself against the flow of time, but by allowing the past, as Runia says, to 'well up' from underneath. Just as Kleist's C seeks to recover the past not by climbing back against the current and the gradient to the Paradise that we have lost, but by looking in his concave mirror through time itself to that place where Paradise is 'open somewhere at the back', so developing in Sebald makes of the page itself a glass through which we can see into the past. And if the metaphor of photographic *developing* gives expression to Sebald's use of images to recover lost time, he uses the figure of *tuning* to conceptualize his recovery of lost voices, of those voices from the past that Coetzee conjures out of his visible darkness. At key moments throughout *Austerlitz*, for example, the radio offers the narrator a means of reaching those voices that the chains of the quotation build towards by other means. At one central moment in the novel, as the narrator prepares to sleep in a strangely empty room in the equally empty house owned by Austerlitz in Alderney Street, the radio offers a 'mysterious' means of channelling voices that come from somewhere outside the smooth grey walls. The 'matt grey' room in which the narrator finds himself enclosed, after Austerlitz has left him 'having latched the door carefully behind him' (A 232), is peculiarly tightly sealed, recalling the grey room in which the male figure is enclosed in Beckett's play *Ghost Trio*. Like Beckett's room, Austerlitz's room 'was quite unfurnished except for a kind of camp bed standing unfolded against one wall', a version perhaps of Beckett's 'pallet'. But if both rooms are sealed in this grey way from the outside, both rooms also contain audio equipment that serves to break the seal that separates inside from outside. The cassette recorder in Beckett's play, that reproduces the Beethoven Trio that also comes from outside, from the landscape of the male figure's memory, becomes, in *Austerlitz*, a 'bakelite radio' that tunes in to the faint voices that murmur in Beckett's play on the verge of perceptibility, that stir within the shallow depths of female narrator's faint-clear voice. The bakelite radio is twinned, in Sebald's novel, with the bakelite jars containing dead moths that are almost the only other objects contained in the room. These moths (that recall the glimpse into the 'mysterious world of moths . . . usually hidden from our sight' granted to the narrator by 'Great Uncle Alphonso' earlier in the novel [A 127–34]) are themselves receivers of a sort, tuned into the imperceptible. Their antennae, the narrator remarks, 'trembled on the edge of invisibility' (A 233), picking up frequencies beyond the normal range, frequencies that are also registered by the bakelite radio which the narrator listens to as he lies down to sleep on the pallet in Austerlitz's room. 'I turned the volume down very low', the narrator says, 'and listened to a language I did not understand drifting in the air from a great distance, a female voice which was sometimes lost in the ether, but then emerged again' (A 234). This voice drifts throughout the night into that grey room from somewhere beyond the limits of the visible and the audible, until the break of day, when 'only a faint crackle and hiss was coming from the narrow mesh over the loudspeaker', leading the narrator and Austerlitz to speculate that these faint voices, like the moths captured in uncle Alphonso's light during Austerlitz's childhood, 'shun the light of day', and 'move through the air only after the onset of darkness' (A 234).

It is this sense that the Sebaldian radio is able to pick up faint voices that travel across the border between the present and the past, between the living and the dead, that allows for the initial penetration of Austerlitz's lost past into the sealed grey room of his amnesiac present. It is when Austerlitz, while browsing in an antiquarian bookshop, overhears a radio broadcast in which two women discuss their journey to England on a special transport in 1939, that he receives the first distinct message from his shrouded past. 'It was quiet in the shop', he recalls,

> except for the soft voices coming from the little radio which stood beside [the shopkeeper], and these voices, which at first I could not make out but which soon became almost too distinct, cast such a spell over me that I entirely forgot the engravings lying before me, and stood there as if on no account must I let a single syllable emerging from the rather scratchy radio set escape me'. (A 199–200)

The radio, at this point in the narrative, effects a kind of retuning, in which Austerlitz passes from his unanchored present to the recovered past. As the voices on the scratchy radio swell from the faint to the 'almost too distinct', Austerlitz finds the world around him remade, finds that he is no longer in a bookshop in London, but standing on a quay in 1939, waiting to board a ferry called the *Prague*, to be transported from Czechoslovakia to England. 'I saw the great slabs of paving at my feet', he says, 'the grey-brown water in the harbour basin, the ropes and the anchor chains slanting upwards' (A 200), as if tuning here becomes a kind of developing, as if the becoming distinct of those voices from 1939 allows 'the shadows of reality' to 'emerge out of nothing' onto Sebald's photographic page. It is when Austerlitz, prompted by this message from the past, arrives in his old family home and meets Vera, his main interlocutor and conduit, that this emergence of a clear voice on a peculiarly poetic frequency reaches its most intense pitch. On their first meeting, which breaks the seal between present and past, Austerlitz says that Vera spoke to him 'very quietly but with what to me was a quite singular clarity' (A 216), a singular clarity which carries not only across an ocean of empty time, but also across languages and nations, from Czech to French to German. Vera speaks at first in French ('*Jacquot*, she said, *dis, est-ce que c'est vraiment toi?*' [A 216]), before passing noiselessly into a Czech which Austerlitz, miraculously, understands with utter distinctness, making him feel, he says, 'like a deaf man whose hearing has been restored' (A 219). As the voice on the radio in Austerlitz's house in Alderney street comes to the narrator faintly, in a 'language I did not understand', so this voice comes to Austerlitz in a foreign language, but a foreign language that is also a first language, and that allows him to retune, to refocus, to develop a whole set of foreign/native images that had been lost in the darkness. Carried on the current of Vera's singularly clear voice, Austerlitz says, these images of his past 'ranged themselves side by side, so that deeply buried and locked away within me as they had been, they now came luminously back to my mind' (A 221).

So, the model of tuning that Sebald develops in his writing works to create this sundering, this collapse of the present into the space of the recovered past. Rather than looking backwards, or from here to there, or from self to other, Sebald's gaze is one in which the membrane itself dissolves that separates the eye from the world. Vera remarks to Austerlitz, during one of their intense periods of recollection, that 'if I close my eyes I see the two of us as it were disembodied, or, more precisely, reduced to the unnaturally enlarged pupils of our eyes' (A 224), as if the meeting of Austerlitz and Vera takes place in the black hole of the eyeball itself, as if tuning and focusing in Sebald produces such an intimate contact between observer and observed that there is no longer any separation (see p. 163). As Vera's and Austerlitz's perspectives mingle here, it is as if that invisible barrier that separates us from Wittgenstein's penetrating gaze at the opening of the novel has melted away, causing the liquid of Wittgenstein's and of Austerlitz's vision to flood out over our own, leading to what Thomas Wirtz has called 'total reconstruction'. Now, I have been arguing so far in this chapter that the narrative mechanism by which Sebald tunes in to the past, by which he effects Wirtz's 'total reconstruction', can be read as an extension of that model of quotation that I have traced as it passes from Beckett to Bernhard. The meetings that Sebald stages between the narrator and Austerlitz, between Austerlitz and Vera, I have suggested, can be seen as owing something to those meetings in Bernhard between Atzbacher and Reger, between the narrator and Roithamer, which in turn are inhabited to some degree by the meeting between Sam and Watt, between Pim and the narrator of *How It Is* (and which themselves catch differently inflected echoes from Kleist and from More). But if this lineage might be discernible in Sebald's writing, it might be argued that there is something quite different about Sebald's reconstruction of lost time to Bernhard's or Beckett's, and this difference might be thought of partly in terms of the relationship in the three writers between *quotation* and *correction*, just as it might be formulated in terms of *tuning*. If there is something shared in Sebald's and Bernhard's method of reconstruction, if Sebald's recovery of the past resonates with Murau's attempt, in *Extinction*, to 'renovate' or 'restore' his childhood, then it might be suggested that where Sebald differs from Bernhard, and from Beckett, is in Beckett's and Bernhard's insistence upon the failure of such restoration – in their shared dedication to failure, and in their related insistence upon correction and deletion. Sebald reprises those meetings between narrator and character that run through Beckett and Bernhard, but misses out some of the comic violence of such encounters, replacing that acerbic quality shared by Beckett and Bernhard with a melancholy keening, producing what the German novelist George Klein has called a 'masochistic' 'intimacy with the dead'.[10] The meeting between Austerlitz and Vera in *Austerlitz*, for example, produces a frictionless intimacy that lacks something of the ravening Bernhard spirit, that runs against the epigrammatic and deliciously self-defeating declaration in *Correction* that 'a man approaches another only to destroy him, so Roithamer' (C 246). If in Beckett and in Bernhard, restoration is a function of destruction, of endless correction ('Correction of the correction of the correction of the correction, so Roithamer' [C 248]), in Sebald the sundering of the boundary between present and the past seems altogether less ruinous. Similarly, the model of tuning developed by Sebald arguably misses something of the difficulty, of the impossibility of tuning in Beckett. When the female narrator of *Ghost Trio* asks us to 'tune according' to her faint voice, she is asking us to hear the Dantean faintness that carries in her voice only by mishearing her, by forcibly reading against the clarity of her enunciation. To tune into the faintness in her voice is to counteract her clarity, to correct her, to destroy her. The voice carries something in its banished undertones from the outside of that sealed grey room, but one has to silence the narrator in order to hear it. In Sebald, however, the voice that speaks with such a singular clarity is forged not from destruction, but from the discovery of a kind of poetic harmonics which allows two voices to speak as one without need of such disjunction, which allows the inside and the outside, past and future, clear and faint, to 'grow naturally' into each other, as the black branches of the lime trees in Terezín grow naturally into the recovered scenes from the darkness of Theresienstadt. The voices of the past that carry by radio into Austerlitz's room in Alderney street – into Sebald's version of Beckett's sealed, grey room – seem possessed of a clarity, of a presence, that forever eludes those 'dead voices' in Beckett that rustle like leaves, like sand, like wings (CDW 57).

It is perhaps this distinction between Sebald's frictionless recovery of lost time, and the apparently more conflicted relation to the past distilled in Beckett's and Bernhard's work, that has led some critics to associate Sebald's writing more closely with Proust than with Beckett. Runia's description of Sebald's work as a place where the past 'wells up' into presence, for example, leads him to equate Sebald's model of remembrance with Proust's. Runia dwells on the key moment in the Liverpool Street station waiting room, in which Austerlitz suddenly remembers his first meeting with his adopted Welsh family. 'I felt', Austerlitz says,

> that the waiting-room where I stood as if dazzled contained all the hours of my past life, all the suppressed and extinguished fears and wishes I had ever entertained, as if the black and white diamond pattern of the stone slabs beneath my feet were the board on which the end-game would be played, and it covered the entire plane of time. (A 193)

This moment, at which the past suddenly overwhelms the present, appears to Runia to be a 'Proustian sensation of "presence"' a moment of complete recovery of lost time.[11] Now, while this quality of total remembrance in Sebald's work is indeed striking, and while there is something more effortless about the experience of retuning in Sebald than in Beckett or in Bernhard, I would argue that there is nevertheless a conflicted, disjunctive element to Sebaldian remembrance that Runia's metaphor of 'welling up', and his identification of a Sebaldian–Proustian involuntary memory, tend to overlook. Russell Kilbourn, in his essay on Architecture and Cinema in Sebald's work, shares Runia's sense that there is something Proustian about that moment in the waiting room. 'It is tempting', he agrees, 'to describe the scene in the waiting room as Austerlitz's Proustian moment, where his 'involuntary memory' is engaged through a series of serendipitous events'.[12] But Kilbourn insists that one should resist such temptation, arguing that 'the differences are telling', and that Sebald's recovery of memory is refracted through the alienating and 'mendacious' apparatus of the cinematic image. As several of Sebald's readers have argued, the mechanics with which Sebald produces Wirtz's 'total reconstruction', the photographic, cinematic devices that he employs to reach back into the past, might produce that sense of effortless retuning, that sense of a Proustian, involuntary welling up of the past, but they are themselves bound up with the failure of representation, reproducing the forms of absence and of alienation that they seek in part to counteract. Caroline Duttlinger, for example, has argued that *Austerlitz* 'illustrates the privileged but precarious role of the technical media in the representation of the Holocaust and in the process of memory more generally'. 'Photography in general' she goes on, 'plays a central role in its capacity as both a theoretical model and a mode of visual testimony that accompanies the protagonist's quest for his repressed past'. But for Duttlinger it is crucial to recognize that the recuperative power of photography is intimately related to a kind of forgetting. Both as a theoretical model and as a 'mode of visual testimony', she writes, Sebaldian photography 'is inextricably linked to the failings of memory, to the latency of remembrance and the notions of forgetting and trauma, which repeatedly disrupt and undermine the process of recollection'.[13] Sebald's singular remembrance of the Holocaust, I would argue, the model of testimony that he develops in order to respond to the demand that we give some kind of expression to that unspeakable event, is intimately and profoundly bound up with such failures, such forms of forgetting. Sebald himself has argued that writing about the Holocaust requires one not to 'focus on the horror',[14] to produce a mode of expression that both writes and does not write the event, producing what Richard Eder has called a 'Holocaust in absence'.[15] It is in part this attempt to recover and at once to annihilate the past that makes Runia's Proustian Sebald seem somewhat out of focus. However overwhelming the recovery of the past is in Sebald, however completely he dissolves that fabric that separates present from past, there is always a form of disjunction between here and there, between past and present, that brings Sebald much closer to that mode of remembrance crafted by Beckett and then by Bernhard, than that imagined by Proust. The kinds of unity that Sebald discovers in his prose, I would suggest, are much closer to the unknown, cloven unities that Banville inherits from Beckett, than the 'transparent unity' that Kristeva finds in Proust, in which discrete things are 'converted into one and the same substance'.[16] It is as if the modernist forms of recovery, the Proustian Madeleine, the Joycean epiphany, are not adequate to the kinds of witnessing that are demanded by the Holocaust. It is in Beckett's writing, in Beckett's adaptation of the modernist forms that he inherited from Joyce and from Proust as well as from (a protomodernist) Kleist, that he develops a form that can simultaneously remember and forget, that can at once preserve and annihilate. It is this restoration by destruction that Bernhard develops in his singular form of poetic historiography, and that Sebald inherits, I would argue, from Beckett and Bernhard, notwithstanding the differences in tone that obtain between them.

That key scene in the waiting room, indeed, carries a number of Beckettian shapes within its collapsing forms, suggesting a kind of fusion between Beckettian and Sebaldian remembrance, between Beckett's model of tuning and Sebald's. The part of the scene quoted by Runia, of course, in which Austerlitz imagines that the 'black and white diamond pattern of the stone slabs beneath my feet were the board on which the end-game would be played', already calls more insistently to Beckett than it does to Proust. Beckett's play *Endgame* is above all a play about the simultaneous arrest and recovery of time. The play starts with a strangely stalled chronology, in which everything is already 'finished' (CDW 93), and conjures a peculiar, extended duration from this congealing of time, precisely the kind of arrested duration that is the temporal medium of Sebald's writing. But if this relation between Beckettian and Sebaldian temporality is somewhat glancing here, as the scene in the Liverpool Street waiting room continues Beckett becomes an increasingly insistent presence, a presence which modulates the ongoing tension in Sebald between total recovery and persistent disjunction. Austerlitz's comparison of the waiting room floor to a chess board which covers the 'entire plane of time', leads him to imagine that he can see through time itself, allowing him to witness again his first encounter with his adopted parents on his arrival in the United Kingdom. 'In the gloomy light of the waiting room' he says,

> I also saw two middle-aged people dressed in the style of the thirties, a woman in a light gabardine coat with a hat at an angle on her head, and a thin man beside her wearing a dark suit and a dog-collar. And I not only saw the minister and his wife, said Austerlitz, I also saw the boy they had come to meet. He was sitting by himself on a bench over to one side. His legs, in white knee-length socks, did not reach the floor, and but for the small rucksack he was

holding on his lap I don't think I would have known him, said Austerlitz. As it was, I recognized him by that rucksack of his, and for the first time in as far back as I can remember I recollected myself as a small child, at that moment when I realized that it must have been to this same waiting room I had come on my arrival in England over half a century ago. (A 193)

This is an extraordinarily rich passage, which blends recognition and recollection with disjunction and loss so finely that they become almost indistinguishable from one another. The rucksack, that sign by which the narrator recognizes Austerlitz, and the mark of Austerlitz's peculiar unity with Wittgenstein, as well as More's peculiar mirrored unity with Raphael, becomes here a switch which both reproduces Austerlitz's unity with himself as a child, and disavows it. His approach to himself as a child, his faltering attempt to see the scene again through his own childish eyes, is subject to exactly the same reversals as those experienced by the narrator, when he attempts to see through Austerlitz's eyes, when he attempts to enter that space behind Wittgenstein's cold, clear gaze. There is a sundering, in which Austerlitz is once more his childish self, just as the Sebaldian page sunders to allow the narrator to merge with the scenes that he narrates; but this sundering reproduces a distance and a difference from self, even as it annihilates such distance, such difference. It produces that sameness and difference from self that emerges again and again throughout Beckett's writing, that becomes, in a sense, a kind of broken Beckettian signature. This is the peculiar sameness and difference that is performed when younger and older Krapp speak simultaneously through the recuperative and disjunctive magic of the tape recorder. It is, hauntingly and uncannily, the difference and sameness from self that is produced at the end of *Ghost Trio*, as boy and the man look at each other across the imperceptibly open threshold between present and past at the end of the play. And perhaps most strikingly it is the sameness and difference from self that emerges again and again throughout *How It Is*, as the narrator crawls both towards and away from himself through the inky mud, clutching the sack that is, like Austerlitz's rucksack, a faulty guarantee of self-identity. Repeatedly in *How It Is*, a 'veil' or 'curtain' parts, opening onto a scene 'above in the light', bringing the narrator face to face with his youthful self. He sees himself as a young boy sitting on his mother's knee, adopting the posture of a well-known photograph of Beckett himself sitting with his mother ('it's me', he says, 'all of me and my mother's face I see it from below' [HII 16]);[17] he sees himself as a teenager ('I see me I look to be about sixteen' [HII 31]); and he sees himself as character lying in the mud ('I see me asleep on my side or on my face [. . .] the sack under my head or clasped to my belly' [HII 26]). In each of these instances when the narrator is brought up against versions of himself, the narrative performs at once a kind of rolling together, in which the voice from beyond part three merges with the figure crawling through the mud and with the boy up above in the light, and an anguished falling apart, a kind of dismemberment in which these various versions of narrative identity fail to cohere. The narrator says that these visions, these images of himself above in the light, concern the 'question of my memory obviously', but he suggests that he has not been 'given' a memory that can fully unite these different versions of self, that can say, with Watt and the figure in *Company*, 'yes I remember. That was I. That was I then' (NO 17, W 74). 'We're talking of my memory', the narrator says, 'that it's getting better that it's getting worse that things are coming back to me nothing is coming back to me' (HII 16). In both *How It Is* and *Austerlitz*, this moment when different versions of self are brought into such proximity reveals at once the magical capacity of narrative to retune – to recover that 'yesterday' which, Beckett writes, 'is irremediably part of us, within us, heavy and dangerous' (PTD 13) – and its persistent failure to make of discrete moments, places and subjectivities a 'permanent reality'. ('The poisonous ingenuity of Time', Beckett writes in relation to Proust, but more tellingly in relation to himself, 'acts on the subject', 'resulting in an unceasing modification of his personality, whose permanent reality, if any, can only be apprehended as a retrospective hypothesis [PTD 15]).

It is as Austerlitz's narration of the scene in the waiting room draws to a close that this resonance between Beckett and Sebald comes to a climax. Austerlitz tells the narrator that he 'cannot give any precise description of the state of mind' that his recognition of himself as a child induced. But, he goes on,

> All I do know is that when I saw the boy sitting on the bench I became aware, through my dull bemusement, of the destructive effect on me of my desolation through all these past years, and a terrible weariness overcame me at the idea that I had never really been alive, or was only now being born, almost on the eve of my death. (A 193–4)

This moment produces, again, that 'crossing over' that I have been tracing in Sebald's work. As Austerlitz gazes at his youthful self, he registers first the loss of his own youth (I had never really been alive), before imagining that he is coming to life through the becoming of his own childish other, that he is being born, on the eve of his death, as the little boy that is so strange and familiar to him. To find himself born as this youth is to recast that scene in the waiting room as fresh experience rather than damaged, imperfect memory, to cast it as one of those 'past events' that 'have not yet occurred but are waiting to do so at the moment when we think of them' (A 144). But this total access to the past is bent out of shape by the echo that we hear from Beckett here, as if we are looking back partly with those Beckettian eyes that gaze past us, like Wittgenstein's in *Austerlitz*, from Sebald's and Tripp's collaborative *Unrecounted* (Un 79). This moment in *Austerlitz* summons a host of Beckettian spectres, spectres which have their origin in a lecture given by Carl Jung, in which Jung discusses the case of a child who, like Austerlitz, had never really been alive. Jung's discussion of this child turns, in fact, around a peculiar confusion between forgetting and remembering. Jung argues that in early childhood, when 'consciousness begins to dawn', the child still has memories of a collective, mythological consciousness, and is 'haunted by a constant yearning to remain with or return to the original vision'. 'Usually', Jung explains, 'at the age of four to six the veil of forgetfulness is drawn upon these experiences'.[18] But in the case of the little girl under discussion, the case that comes in turn to haunt Beckett with a yearning to return to an original vision, this forgetting does not take place, causing the girl to remain somehow indistinct, preventing her from forming her own sense of self, her own memories. 'Recently', Jung says,

> I saw a case of a little girl of ten who had some most amazing mythological dreams. Her father consulted me about these dreams. I could not tell him what I thought because they contained an uncanny prognosis. The little girl died a year later of an infectious disease. She had never been born entirely.[19]

This moment in Jung comes back in Beckett's writing time and time again. It emerges in the phrase 'never been properly born' that is adrift in the addenda to *Watt* (W 248), and it emerges in Beckett's radio play *All That Fall*, where Maddy Rooney describes how she herself has been 'haunted' by the 'mind doctor' who said in a lecture that the 'only thing wrong' with one of his patients was that 'she was dying', that 'she had never really been born!' (CDW 196). But it is perhaps in *How It is*, in a passage that I have already quoted, that this failed birth in Beckett meets most strikingly with Austerlitz's sense that he 'had never really been alive', that his birth was deferred until that moment in the waiting room in Liverpool Street station when he encounters his younger self on the 'eve' of his death. As Beckett's narrator scrawls on Pim's back, as he looks through the back/page towards that horizon beyond part three, he writes of a meeting with self that strikes an uncanny resonance with Austerlitz's experience in the waiting room. He writes in blood on Pim's back, he says, of

> that childhood said to have been mine the difficulty of believing in it the feeling rather of having been born octogenarian at the age one dies in the dark the mud upwards born upwards floating up like the drowned (HII 78)

At this stage in *How It Is* there is an extraordinary bi-directionality that predicts the bidirectionality, the crossing over, performed by Sebald. The narrator looks through Pim's back towards the voice that he is quoting, towards that space beyond part three where he 'has his life', where he can become himself, or meet with that 'permanent reality' that a young Beckett suggests can 'only be apprehended as a retrospective hypothesis'. But while we look from the above to the below, from left to right, the narrative also pulls in the opposite direction, taking the narrator, as in *Austerlitz*, back to that childhood in which he struggles so hard to believe, refashioning himself as that Beckettian child sitting on his mother's knee, resurrecting those that have been drowned, as Sebald resurrects the drowned from the underwater town of Vyrnwy, as Primo Levi seeks to resurrect the drowned of Auschwitz.[20] It is here, both in *How It is* and in *Austerlitz*, that the birth that was denied to Jung's patient is in some peculiar way endowed; but it is a birth not into presence, but into the peculiar conjunction of presence and absence that is the condition of being in time for both Sebald and Beckett. The resurrection of the drowned into birth in *How It Is* is occupied always, and at every point, by that downward pressure, by that movement towards the voice speaking from beyond part three, the voice which cannot be housed in a body, which cannot be 'entirely' born, even on the eve of death. Shane Weller has written of Beckett's obsession with Jung's lecture that it is so recurrent in his writing because it depicts so closely his own conception of *dasein* – that the girl in Jung's story resonates because for Beckett 'birth initiates something other – something less – than "life," something less than "existence"; something less, in short, than "presence."'[21] As the floor of the waiting room in *Austerlitz* gives way, it does not open onto a Proustian recovery of lost time, but rather on to this 'something less than presence', staging a return to the past that is almost soundless, in which the barrier between present and past becomes 'invisible', 'imperceptible', but which nevertheless effects a devastating removal from self and from presence, a removal as total as it is almost totally overcome.

So, in Beckett's inheritance of Kleist, in his adaptation of Kleist's simultaneous mastery of and dismemberment by time, it is possible to see a model for Sebald's recovery of lost time, a model which is adapted and passed on by Bernhard. John Banville, in a review of *Austerlitz* published in 2001, writes that 'seeking influences is particularly fruitless in the case of Sebald, for he is unique'. 'It has been apparent', he goes on, 'since literary modernism guttered out in the *noveau roman* that fiction would have to find new forms if it was to survive'. Sebald's work, for Banville, is an example of such a new form, and 'has all the marks of a new beginning'.[22] Now, while I would agree that Sebald's work appears in a sense to be *sui generis*, and while Sebald, along with other contemporary writers such as Banville himself, is clearly engaged in the invention of a new kind of novel, I would argue that it is also the case that Sebald's work extends and derives from that literary modernism that Banville sees guttering out somewhere mid century, rather than simply abandoning it. It is in Sebald's 'new beginning' that it is possible to see the coming to new expression of a mode of remembrance, a mode of witnessing, that Beckett has forged from the joint influences of Kleist, of Proust, of Joyce and of Kafka – a mode of remembrance that Banville himself adapts in different ways in his forgetful remembering of Ireland. Thomas Trezise, in his well-known essay on Holocaust remembrance entitled 'Unspeakable', suggests that Beckett's work, along with that of Celan, might be thought of as the mode of art that comes closest to witnessing the horrors of the Holocaust.[23] Beckett's commitment to failure, his willingness to 'fail as no other dare fail', is what allows him to respond to the impossible double imperative of the Holocaust – that one witness it, and that one does not seek to represent it. Beckett's art, for Adorno and for Trezise, is one that gives a negative expression to the unspeakable history of the twentieth-century Europe. In Sebald's writing, as in Bernhard's, however, it is possible to see a new kind of expression, a new kind of witnessing, emerging from those modernist forms that find an arrested duration in Beckett's work. If, in Sebald's work, the speakable and the unspeakable enter into a new kind of intimacy, it is partly because Beckett has bequeathed to him a form which summons continuity from finality, which summons remembrance from amnesia, a historical form which survives, which is born from, the death of history. If Sebald's writing marks a 'new beginning', it does so partly because Beckett's work crafts a means of going on, a means of continuing to live and to invent, after the possibility of living and of inventing has lapsed.

Part Three

How It Ought To Be: Beckett, Globalization and Utopia

Chapter 7

From Joyce to Beckett: From National to Global

If the first part of this book reads Beckett's work against an Irish context, and the second tunes Beckett to a European, Germanic tradition, then this third and final part traces the growth of a global perspective in Beckett's writing.

In thinking about Beckett's relation to globalization though, I want to start here by looking not forwards but backwards, looking not at the ways in which Beckett's writing predicts or helps us to understand the forms in which we might perceive the global, but at the ways in which the difficult relationship between modernism and nationalism, and in particular Joyce's modernism and his ambivalent nationalism, feeds into and shapes the ways in which Beckett reaches towards the possibility of a global vision. In a recent essay on Beckett and what he calls 'globalism', Steven Connor suggests that both national and global frames of reference involve a distortion of Joyce and Beckett's 'cosmopolitan modernism', and what is more that both of these organizing categories tend to conspire with one another in their distortion, to become part of the same misconception of the relationship between writing and political forms of identity and affiliation. Connor writes that it would be 'foolish' to 'search for the particular forms of universality that might account for the increasing reach of [Beckett's] work' – to find a critical expression of a 'global Beckett', or a 'world Beckett'. But neither, he says,

> do I seek to encourage the work of enforced repatriation that is being undertaken by those who seek to assert the essential regionality of Beckett's work – its 'Irishness', its 'Protestantism', and so on. I think that, following the critical work being undertaken on the work of Joyce, by writers such as Emer Nolan and Andrew Gibson (however different they may be in their approaches), which seeks to weaken the consensus about Joyce's cosmopolitan modernism made by writers such as Ellmann and Kenner and bring Joyce back home, we will see similar efforts to distort Beckett back into ethnic intelligibility.[1]

Such attempts to fit writers who offer fierce opposition to the limits of parochial nationalism into national 'intelligibility', however, are ironically perfectly in accord, for Connor, with the attempt to imagine a 'world Beckett', as the tendency towards global thinking is bound up with and reproduces the local in all its narrowness. 'Globalism', he writes, 'means many things – among them the imposition on more and more of the world of risibly particularized and parochial notions of what the world should be'.[2] It is for this reason, Connor argues, that a global Beckett and a national Beckett offer each other such little resistance. 'The global and the local', he writes, 'the historical and the atavistic, act in perfect consort here. Both Joyce and Beckett have become the PR darlings of the Celtic Tiger, with its assertions of European Ireland, cosmopolitan Ireland – "World Ireland"'.[3]

In what follows, and in seeking to understand the difficult pressures on and in Beckett's writing exerted by both the national and the cosmopolitan, the sovereign and the global, I will seek to avoid the kinds of distortion that Connor warns against here. I want neither to force Beckett's writing into 'ethnic intelligibility' by retuning it as a writing of nation, nor to suggest that Beckett's writing produces a form which might make the global intelligible. But if Beckett's work resists both national and global frames of reference, it is nevertheless the case that his work, and his reception of Joyce, is shaped to a degree by the postwar decline of national sovereignty. Joyce's articulation both of nationalism and of cosmopolitanism reaches deeply into Beckett's writing, where it exerts more of an influence on Beckett's geographical and political imagination than has been commonly recognized. But Beckett's writing also gives an oblique expression to the dissolution of some of the sovereign political institutions that exert such a shaping force in Joyce, producing bleakly utopian forms in which a limitless world – a borderless world, to recall the title of a recent 'international' Beckett conference in Tokyo[1] – might be glimpsed, if not thought. In reading the passage from the national to the global here as it is mirrored in the passage from Joyce to Beckett, I will aim to resist that easy accommodation between local and global that Connor regards as a key feature of global culture; I will argue, instead, that Beckett's writing can be seen, in a certain light, as an attempt to imagine a new and barely articulable kind of ethical relationship between the global and the local, after the waning of the sovereign nation state, a relationship which does not fit within any of the existing political, nationalist or postnationalist paradigms.

Joyce's story 'The Dead' has become an important work in Joyce criticism, partly because it seems to offer itself as an early key to this movement between the national and the international, or global, in Joyce's oeuvre. The story closes, famously, with an epiphany, in which the protagonist, Gabriel Conroy, sees anew his relationship with Ireland, and with an Irish community. Preparing to join his sleeping wife in bed, after his traumatic realization that she has an intensely lived past of which he had no conception, Gabriel gazes out of his hotel room window at the snow falling outside:

> He watched sleepily the flakes, silver and dark, falling obliquely against the lamplight. The time had come for him to set out on his journey westward.

> Yes, the newspapers were right: snow was general all over Ireland. It was falling on every part of the dark central plain, on the treeless hills, falling softly upon the bog of Allen and, farther westward, softly falling into the dark mutinous Shannon waves. It was falling, too, upon every part of the lonely churchyard on the hill where Michael Furey lay buried. It lay thickly drifted on the crooked crosses and headstones, on the spears of the little gate, on the barren thorns. His soul swooned slowly as he heard the snow falling faintly through the universe and faintly falling, like the descent of their last end, upon all the living and the dead. (Du 176)

This is an extraordinarily rich moment in Joyce's writing, which arguably frames his entire oeuvre. The passage has proved stubbornly difficult to understand, partly because it seems to set contradictory drives in motion, staging the difficult relationship between cosmopolitanism and local nationalism that Connor suggests is now in the process of being revised by Gibson and Nolan. Richard Ellmann has influentially read the end of the story as Joyce's 'first song of exile', seeing this moment as a 'linchpin' in Joyce's writing career, or what Emer Nolan describes as a '"hinge" between an early and mature Joyce'.[5] It is this elegiac close to the story, in which Ireland is buried under a blanket of white snow, that is Joyce's farewell to the parochialism of the *Dubliners*, and that marks his entry into the wider reaches of European modernism. But to read this passage as taking Joyce eastwards across the Irish Sea to continental Europe is of course to read against the westerly direction in which Gabriel decides to travel, as his soul swoons under the spell of his wife's secret love for Michael Furey. If Joyce is signalling a farewell to Ireland here, then it is also a return, prefiguring the cyclical structures of *Ulysses* and *Finnegans Wake*. The snow which falls at the close of the story bears out this doubleness. The 'newspapers were right', the passage reads, 'snow was general all over Ireland', and the suggestion is that the snow, like the binding properties of newspapers described by Benedict Anderson, is forging a nation, a community that huddles together in the festive collective isolation that colours 'The Dead' as a whole, and that makes of the paralysing closeness of *Dubliners* something briefly magical.[6] But while the snow offers this sense of belonging, this sharing of intimate space, it also of course suggests the opposite, a cold, detached blankness and loss of differentiation. As Gabriel's physical and spiritual intimacy with his wife is at once produced and annulled by his distance from her, so the snow conjures a sense of national identity from its erasure of identity. The snow falls over Ireland, but it also falls through the 'universe', summoning both the living and the dead into a post-apocalyptic shared presence that is also an annihilation. Gabriel's awakening here, his coming to a consciousness of an Irish heritage of which he has been unaware, or which he has repressed, is also a swooning, a loss of consciousness, a form of death. This passage is at once an epiphanal alertness and a kind of stupefaction, at once a remembering and a forgetting, a leavetaking and a return, a warm embrace and a cold shoulder.

It is for this reason that the passage offers itself so insistently as a key to Joyce's work, albeit one which opens his work in a number of different and contradictory ways (an 'obscure' rather than a 'simple' key, in Watt's terms [W 122]). At this critical moment in the trajectory of his career, Joyce articulates a struggle between the national, the international and the universal that shapes the rest of his writing. Despite the orthodoxy that places Joyce in opposition to Yeats, reading the latter as a cultural nationalist and the former as a modernist who rejects Ireland as the 'sow that eats her farrow' (P 220), several critics have argued, with Gibson and Nolan, that Joyce's development of an internationalist, cosmopolitan aesthetic is bound up with, haunted perhaps, by the nationalism that it seeks to overcome.[7] The curious reassertion of a national consciousnesses at the very moment that Joyce, in Ellmann's reading, reconciles himself to exile, is thus emblematic of a persistence of the nation as an organizing category in Joyce's internationalism. And if 'The Dead' can be read as a story which plays out an antagonism between Gabriel's infatuation with cosmopolitan Europe and his tenacious psychical investment in the Irish nation – an antagonism which, as we have seen, gives way to a curious kind of complicity – then this struggle between the national and the international is modulated by a third term. In 'The Dead', the contradiction between Ireland and Europe is organized around the possibility of the universal – the proto-global, perhaps – a category which transcends the national and the international, and which reaches for an absolutely inclusive expression of identity which is also a loss of identity, a simultaneous fullness and emptiness registered by the warming, obliterating snow, and by Gabriel's overwhelmed swoon. This three-way relationship between the national, the international and the universal asserts itself time and again as an organizing structure, throughout *Ulysses* and *Finnegans Wake*. Joyce, it is argued, attempts to write a world language in the *Wake*, to produce an amalgam of languages and national traditions that is universally readable, but also, by virtue of its inclusiveness, universally unreadable. But such a collective language is marked at every moment, for Joyce, by the national cultures that it tries to overcome, just as it is shaped by the struggle between Ireland and Europe, home and exile, that Gabriel lives out in 'The Dead'. It is as if, in 1939, Joyce is reaching towards a global vision, struggling, in his notoriously 'ambivalent' fashion, to divest himself of the suits and trappings of nation; but the signifying power and the political limitations of the nation state, in what we might think of as the gloaming of European modernity, are too powerful, too deeply etched into the fabric of the culture and the psyche, to allow him to conceive of a global condition that is not born out of, and always returning to, the nation state. Nationalism is written into the genetic material of Joyce's global imagination.

If Samuel Beckett might be thought of as a writer who more successfully disentangles himself from Joyce's famous 'nets' of language, nationality and religion, it is nevertheless the case that Beckett inherits some of that genetic material. It is possible to find running through Beckett's writing what the narrator of *Ill Seen Ill Said* might call the 'tenacious trace' of nation (NO 96); the same triangulation that shapes Joyce's writing, I would argue, provides a barely perceptible frame for Beckett's work. The close of 'The Dead', in fact, reappears in Beckett's first novel *Dream of Fair to Middling Women*, as the narrative draws to a close. Belacqua finds himself ejected, in the closing paragraphs, onto a Dublin street on which the 'rain fell in a uniform untroubled manner':

> It fell upon the bay, the champaign-land and the mountains, and notably upon the central bog it fell with a rather desolate uniformity. (D 239)

Joyce's elegiac passage, as it reappears in early Beckett, is stripped of much of its nostalgia for nation, and of the echoes of romantic cultural nationalism that can be heard in the former. Rain offers nothing like the simultaneous warmth and cold that Joyce discovers in snow. In Beckett's rendering, the rain produces only a damp and desolate uniformity that encompasses Dublin and the 'central bog', and that carries none of the epiphanal sense of a shared community that uniformity offers to Gabriel. But the close of *Dream* can convincingly be read, in sympathy with the climax of 'The Dead', as Beckett's 'first song of exile', and in bidding farewell to Ireland here Beckett exhibits some of the same equivocations as Joyce. Even the thin, miserable uniformity of the endless rain does pre-empt a kind of home-sickness in Beckett's exile in waiting. The rain, Belacqua reflects at the end of *Dream*, is part of Ireland's 'charm', creating the 'impression one enjoys before landscape in Ireland, even on the clearest of days, of seeing it through a veil of tears' (D 240). The rain that falls throughout Beckett's writing is an obliterating force, summoning the grey undifferentiation of what Deleuze calls an 'any-space-whatever'.[8] But, just as Joyce's snow simultaneously obliterates and preserves, so here rain becomes a less romantic, comically bathetic medium through which the landscape can nevertheless still be viewed, and in which something of its specific 'charm' is preserved. The rain here forms a 'veil' which hides the landscape from view, and which, Belacqua thinks, is responsible for the 'mitigation of contour' that he finds in the 'compresses of our national visibility' (D 240). This gauzy veil might call to mind the thick light in which Kaspar David Freidrich's landscapes are obscured (an occluding light in which much of Beckett's earlier work is bathed), as it might suggest the 'veil' of the English language that Beckett, four years later, wants to 'tear apart' in order to 'get at the things (or the Nothingness) behind it' (Di 171). Either way, rain here serves a double purpose, at once drowning out contour and relief, and serving as a kind of optic through which the homeland might be viewed, that same landscape of memory which takes fleeting shape in the rain seen falling through the imperceptibly open window of Beckett's television play *Ghost Trio* (CDW 412).

Belacqua's wanderings around Europe throughout *Dream* can be read through this simultaneously transparent and opaque medium. Thinking of his exhausting journeying across Europe, and pondering on why he goes to such trouble to travel the continent – why he persists in putting his 'trust in changes of scenery' (D 177) – Belacqua suggests a triangular model to account for his wanderlust, at a moment in *Dream* that I have quoted above in relation to Beckett's belonging to a minor Irish tradition (see pp. 30–31). 'At his simplest', he thinks, 'he was trine':

> Centripetal, centrifugal and . . . not. Phoebus chasing Daphne, Narcissus flying from Echo and . . . neither. Is that neat or is it not? The chase to Vienna, the flight to Paris, the slouch to Fulda, the relapse into Dublin and . . . immunity like hell from journeys and cities. (D 120)

Like Joyce, Beckett here choreographs the movements of his protagonist in terms of three geographical categories – European exile, Irish home and then a third category which is conceived here as a negative version of Joyce's universalism. The centripetal and centrifugal paroxysms of the novel, its systole and diastole, are orchestrated around the 'neither', the 'not', the 'immunity like hell from journeys and cities' – that 'neither' which reappears towards the end of Beckett's career in his brief piece 'Neither' (and which emerges as that 'interval' in *Watt* between a 'being past' and a 'being to come' [see W 134]). In *Dream*, as in 'Neither', the movement between home and away, the restless pacing 'to and fro as between two lit refuges', has as its fulcrum 'that unheeded neither', that 'unspeakable home' (CSP 258). And, for Beckett as for Joyce, this third term, this swooning immunity from distinction, at once structures those oppositions between to and fro, between home and exile, and serves to annul them. Both for Joyce and for Beckett, the universal, conceived either as the absolutely empty or as the absolutely full, negotiates between the competing desires for exile and for homeland. But for both the third term – that 'unspeakable home' of 'neither', that unspeakable Esperanto of *Finnegans Wake* – cannot free itself from the terms that it transcends, cannot discover 'immunity', cannot remain at rest, in the words of 'neither', 'absent for good from self and other' (CSP 258). Rather, the dead opacity it reaches for, the annulment of movement and of longing, of to and of fro, is conjured only from a certain restless transparency, as Beckett's rain both shields the Irish landscape and makes it visible, as Joyce's snow both buries Ireland and brings it into being.

To a larger degree than is often acknowledged, then, I would argue that tensions between the national and the international are grained through Beckett's indifference to place, that the fabric of Beckett's 'nowhere in particular'[9] is woven from the to and fro between the national and the international. But, as I have already suggested, it is nevertheless the case that the limitations that operate upon Joyce's leap towards a global, post-national vision, are different, historically and materially, than those that constrain Beckett's imagination. In 1939, Joyce's reaching for a global language could only be a demonstration of the organizing power of national boundaries – the very possibility of thinking or speaking globally was one, for Joyce, that was produced and constrained by the nation. But the passage of Beckett's writing career, from the triangular exploits of Belacqua in *Dream* to the restless movements of 'Neither', *Stirrings Still* and 'What is the Word', runs hand in hand with the gradual waning of the post-war nation state as the prime administrative unit in world affairs. It is the strengthening of the US and the USSR in the aftermath of World War II that marks the final demise of the European colonial powers, and that prepares the ground for the development of global markets, and a global culture.[10] With this weakening of the nation state, from 1945 to Beckett's last work written in 1989, there is a significant shift in the balance of power between the national, the international and the global, or universal – that three-way contest that dominates Joyce's writing, and that structures *Dream of Fair to Middling Women*. In the passage from 1939 to 1989, the possibility of a global community, and of a global language – that possibility which is shadowed forth but still unrealizable for Joyce – becomes not only imaginable, but the basis upon which the legitimacy of national sovereignty rests, if one which is stripped of much of the utopian energy of Wakean Esperanto. As the first major conflicts of the twenty first century have amply demonstrated, sovereignty is no longer the vehicle of power, but a privilege granted to nation states by the arbiters of international 'law' as a reward for good behaviour. For the 'rogue state' to be occupied by an international force requires no 'state of exception' and no exceptional suspension of the inviolability of national boundaries (and, as we have seen, no resolution passed by the United Nations, a body whose ineffectiveness is arguably due to its embeddedness in the anachronisms of sovereignty). Rather, national boundaries are always porous, and a given nation can only appear sovereign when such sovereignty does not come into conflict with the economic and political forces that drive global relations. National sovereignty is now, arguably, a residual political form, that is on the point of giving way to an emergent global power that is not affiliated to or legitimized by any of the democratic processes that are still conducted at the level of the state, and in the name of the sovereignty that has already passed away. One of the ironies of the war in Iraq (20 March 2003) is that, while it is prosecuted partly in the name of democracy – with the stated aim of exporting western style democracy to the Middle East – the conflict is to some degree a result of the movement from national democracy to a new form of global political power that is fundamentally undemocratic.[11]

This gradual shift from the national to the global in the exercise of state power, I suggest, finds a kind of reflection in Beckett's writing, however oblique. The national 'conscience' that is forged in the smithy of Dedalus' soul is reshaped in Beckett's writing, partly because the nation exerts pressure in a different way in the post-war. For Belacqua in *Dream*, the friction between national, international and global still produces heat. Belacqua imagines a perspective that would not be coloured by nation, that would not be refracted through that veil of Irish tears. He imagines at one point in the narrative, as he moves between Ireland and continental Europe, that he is hemmed in by the sky, as by a 'taut skin'. 'The night sky was stretched like a skin', he reflects, 'He would scale the inner wall, his head would tear a great rip in the taut sky, he would climb out above the deluge, into a quiet zone above the nightmare' (D 27). This is a fantasy of escape from the national borders that Belacqua negotiates throughout the novel, of escape from that nightmarish national history from which Dedalus sought to awake, but this early in Beckett's career, and this early in the 1930s, such a fantasy is still shaped by the geopolitics of European nationalism. Belacqua here imagines himself tearing through the fabric of the nation state, again calling to mind that tearing movement that Beckett evokes in the German letter of 1937. In *Murphy*, similarly, the movement to and fro between home and exile is conceived in terms of nation, and in terms of a struggle between London and Dublin. Here also, Murphy's movements are hemmed in by the 'soft sunless' sky, which is all that Celia 'remembered of Ireland' (Mu 27), and which, in a reprise of Belacqua's fantasy, Mr Kelly seeks to puncture with his kite ('Now', thinks Mr Kelly, as he flies his kite out of sight, through the veil of the soft, sunless, Friedrich sky, 'Now he could measure the distance from the unseen to the seen, now he was in a position to determine the point at which seen and unseen met' [Mu 157]).

As Beckett's career progresses, however, the antagonism between the national and universal or global starts to give way, to produce less friction, as if it becomes increasingly easy to force one's way through the skin of the nation, or as if national boundaries yield increasingly easily to the global forces which penetrate them, and which erode them. The narrator of *The Unnamable*, for example, masquerading as his various characters, wanders, like Belacqua and like Murphy, from place to place, and like these earlier 'vice-existers', his wanderings are determined, constrained to some degree, by the narrator's difficult, 'ambivalent' relation to nation. The narrator writes that 'Bally' is the place where the 'inestimable gift of life had been rammed down my gullet' (U 300), and this suggestion that the narrator is attached, via his 'mannikins' (U 308), to an Irish home, to the Ballys that run through Beckett's prose, resonates with other places in the novel where a remembered, Beckett/Irish landscape seems to pull at the narrator, unsettling his rejection of place. Towards the close of the novel, the narrator yearns for such placedness, pleading that 'if only I could feel a place for me', a place with the

> sea under the window, higher than the window, and the rowboat, do you remember, and the river, and the bay, I knew I had memories, pity they are not of me, and the stars, and the beacons, and the lights of the buoys, and the mountain burning. (U 403)

This characteristically self-cancelling nostalgia, this hollowed out longing for the remembered homeland that extends through Beckett's writing, and is reflected in John Banville's nameless Irish homeland, is held against an internationalist rejection of home, which again follows the pattern of *Dream*, and of *Murphy*, and which might be thought of as a version of Gabriel Conroy's and Stephen Dedalus' simultaneous rejection of and return to a homeland. But in *The Unnamable*, the movement from home to exile both involves a much wider sweep, taking the wandering narrator much further from home than the Germany, Austria and France of *Dream*, and also tends to blur the boundary between home and away, between the national and the global. The narrator, for example, devotes several pages to a description of the circuitous travels he undertakes as Mahood when, presumably as a result of having only one leg ('they whip off a leg and yip off I go again, like a young one, scouring the earth for a hole to hide in' [U 317]), he travels the globe in ever widening spirals. The narrator frets that such spirals might 'unfold ad infinitum', taking him further away from his home, where his 'dear absent ones are awaiting [his] return' in their 'small rotunda' (U 320) (this is surely a quiet parody of Donne's 'Valediction Forbidding Mourning', a work in which another wanderer traverses the earth in circles on one 'foot'). But the narrator corrects himself, realizing that the circularity of the globe means that his spiralling movement will not unfold forever, but will eventually require him, like Donne's lover, to 'end where I begun'.[12] 'It seems to me', he reasons, 'that once beyond the equator you would start turning inwards out of sheer necessity', and that, after taking him to a point at the other end of the world, his spirals would eventually find him 'returning to the fold' where 'I could be restored to my wife and parents, you know, my loved ones, and clasp in my arms, both of which I had succeeded in preserving, my little ones born in my absence' (U 320).

This kind of wanderlust, however much it might owe to the travels of Murphy and Belacqua, rests on a significantly altered conception of the relationship between the national and the global. The narrator here finds that his 'island home' is not held in Belacqua's 'trine' relationship with other European nations and capitals; this is not a grounded struggle between nationalism and cosmopolitanism, between Dublin and London, or Ireland and continental Europe. Rather, the narrator imagines himself sweeping across the globe, conducting a 'world tour'. Perhaps, he thinks,

> I left my leg behind in the Pacific, yes, no perhaps about it, I had, somewhere off the coast of Java and its jungles red with rafflesia stinking of carrion, no that's the Indian Ocean, what a gazetteer I am. (U 319)

With this enlargement of the narrator's global imaginative sweep, the nation itself loses some of its organizing power. Finding himself unconvinced by his own story of his faithful return to his family home, the narrator decides that his spiralling to a fixed point on the surface of the earth in fact owes nothing to such fidelity, but is dictated simply by the shape of the planet. Attachment to his family, he insists, 'had no part or share in what I was doing. Having set forth from that place, it was only natural that I should return to it, given the accuracy of my navigation' (U 324). The global, here, has replaced the national as a means of orientating and positioning narrative perspective. But with this reorientation, with the incursion of the global into the national, the national itself becomes to a degree global. Pages later, the narrator abruptly changes his mind about his travels as Mahood, insisting that, in fact, he has never left his 'island home', that

> I'm on the island, I've never left the island, God help me. I was under the impression I spent my life in spirals round the earth. Wrong, it's on the island I wind my endless ways. The island, that's all the earth I know. (U 329)

The sweeping global spirals, taking in Pacific and Indian Oceans, are compacted, here, into a sightseeing tour of the homeland that 'embraces entire boglands' (U 329), becoming a version of that visit to 'your own land' that the fervent Miss Ivor's recommends to a reluctant Gabriel in 'The Dead' (Du 149). 'When I come to the coast', the narrator says with a slightly embarrassed bathos, 'I turn back inland' (U 329). But what is most striking about this alternation between the global and the national as the boundaries of the narrative helix is how little these two organizing categories seem to be in conflict, how easy it is for the narrator at once to 'set out on his journey westward', and to disavow the call of nation. What Beckett discovers or registers in *The Unnamable* is a certain weakening of the boundary between nation states, as if the global and the national have come to inhabit each other. Where Belacqua tears at the skin of the nation with a certain anguish, the narrator of *The Unnamable* finds that the boundaries that position him tend to give way, to dissolve soundlessly before the eye of the imagination.

It is in Beckett's later works, in *The Lost Ones*, in *Ill Seen Ill Said*, in *Imagination Dead Imagine*, that this collapsing distinction between the global and the national plays itself out most fully. Indeed, the enigmatic novella *Ill Seen Ill Said* turns around the dissolving and reforming of a skin, of a boundary, or of what the narrator refers to in one resonant moment as a 'partition' (NO 92). The story consists of a narrator 'seeing' and 'saying' the scene before him, the scene of a spectral woman living alone in a shed in the middle of a desert. As the narrator hesitantly draws the scene, he dwells for a paragraph on the possibility that the woman's habitation might be divided by an 'inner wall':

> Next to emerge from the shadows an inner wall. Only slowly to dissolve in favour of a single space. East the bed. West the chair. A place divided by her use of it alone. How more desirable in every way an interior of a piece.

The eye breathes again. But not for long. For slowly it emerges again. Rises from the floor and slowly up to lose itself in the gloom. (NO 68)

This boundary that asserts itself only to crumble, that divides the narrative space only to return it to a unity, has a rich resonance in Beckett's work. It might recall the wall that divides and fails to divide Victor Krap's bedsit from the bourgeois sitting room of the Krap family in Beckett's first full-length play *Eleutheria*, as it might suggest the partitions, veils and skins that have fitfully divided the fictional space of Beckett's prose since *Dream of Fair to Middling Women*. From Belacqua and Murphy onwards, Beckett's narrators/characters have pressed against such boundaries, seeking to penetrate the skin that divides mind from world, language from nothingness, nation from nation, reaching for what Belacqua thinks of, in *Dream*, as an 'insistent, invisible rat fidgeting behind the astral incoherence of the art surface' (D 17), (a metaphorical echo of the rats that disturb Belacqua's sleep, scratching against the partition that divides his cramped attic room in Germany). But here, in *Ill Seen Ill Said*, the barriers that divide are always on the point of giving way, rising like an inverted stage curtain only to dissolve, as if political and aesthetic boundaries have weakened in the passage from the 1930s to the 1980s. Beckett's use of the word 'partition' to describe this dissolving boundary lends a political hue to the 'inner wall', calling to mind the partition of Ireland into North and South in 1921, as well as the countless other acts of partition that have marked the withdrawal or attenuation of colonial power in the second half of the twentieth century. And in imagining the crumbling of a wall that divides east from west, the story suggests the reunification of Germany, the fall of the Berlin wall that lay a decade in the future when *Ill Seen Ill Said* was written (the dismantlement of a last obstacle to the flow of capital in Europe that contributes to the easier availability of global paradigms that I have traced in Banville's fiction [see Part One]). The global political and economic forces that have worked to weaken the boundaries between nation states are registered in Beckett's later prose as an increasing failure to maintain the distinction between the local and the global. In these later works, the very capacity to think of the local, to imagine a place that is distinct from any other place, is threatened by the encroachment into the particular of the general, the incursion into the national of the global that Connor sees as one of the effects of 'globalism'. The 'partition', the narrator of *Ill Seen Ill Said* tells us, is 'of all the properties doubtless the least obdurate'. 'See the instant', the narrator writes as if to prove this claim, 'see it again when unaided it dissolved. So to say of itself. With no help from the eye' (NO 92). One has only to imagine a place, in these late works, for one to find oneself imagining the world, as distinctions sunder before us, releasing us into what the woman in *Ill Seen Ill Said* thinks of as an unboundaried profusion. The rotunda that lies at the heart of the unnamable narrator's spiral travels re-emerges in these late works, but now almost entirely stripped of the vacillations that are still played out, in *The Unnamable*, between the national and the global. At the opening of *Imagination Dead Imagine*, for example, the Irish view from the window in *Malone Dies* and *The Unnamable* – the sea, the bay, the beacons, the lights burning in the mountains – is resurrected in the briefest of fashions, only to be brutally dismissed, as the rotunda, erstwhile home of the unnamable narrator's loving family, is lost in the undifferentiation of Beckett's global imagination. The story opens with a command, a kind of stage direction: 'Islands, waters, azure, verdure, one glimpse and vanished, endlessly, omit' (CSP 182). As Malone puts it, with a bravado that belies his incapacity to forget the contours of homeland, 'to hell with all this fucking scenery' (MD 279). At the very opening of this agonizing slip of prose, the narrative stages the final collapse of the mechanisms that allow for the distinction between one place and another. The snow that was 'general all over Ireland' in Joyce's story returns at this moment, but only as an obliterating force, as the rotunda is conjured, magically but fatally impossibly from the endless emptiness that surrounds it, and that swallows it up. The rotunda is lost in its surroundings, 'all white in the whiteness', as the statue of O'Connell is erased by the snow in 'The Dead' (Du 194). This is figure, as Murphy might have put it, returning to ground. As, in *Ill Seen Ill Said*, the partition emerges only to dissolve, so here the material of which the rotunda is made is only imaginable at the moment of its dissolution, as if the occupation of place can only be conjured momentarily from the dissipation of place into the profuse, global emptiness. The rotunda is constructed, we are told, of a 'little fabric', a fabric which, like the spectral partition in *Ill Seen Ill Said*, vibrates on the very boundary between the seen and the unseen, that boundary that once seemed more susceptible of measurement, that was marked, in the 1930s, by the jubilant Mr Kelly's kite.

Throughout Beckett's late prose, from *How It Is* to *Stirrings Still*, this weakening of the partitions that allow for narrative placement – that allow us, as the narrator of *Worstward Ho* has it, to put a 'body' in a 'place' (NO 101) – leads the narrators towards a global vision. Beckett's late narrators, like the imaginary observer of the cylinder in *The Lost Ones*, are required to divine 'a perfect mental image of the entire system' (CSP 204), as the local divisions between one place and the next continually give way. The fragility of the partition that divides the narrative space of *Ill Seen Ill Said*, the delicacy of the vibrating fabric in *Imagination Dead Imagine*, mean that the attempt to put a discrete body in a discrete place repeatedly fails, and the limits of the fictional space unravel, unfold towards the global. The closed cylinder of *The Lost Ones*, with its 'imaginary line running midway between floor and ceiling' (CSP 203) like a kind of equator, is presented as a globe, as a complete world, a self-perpetuating machine or system which we can only see as a whole. The geography of *Ill Seen Ill Said*, in which 'The two zones form a roughly circular whole. As though outlined by a trembling hand' (NO 59); the geography of *How It Is*, in which legions of crawlers travel from west to east in an 'immense circuit' which straddles the globe (HII 131) (in the opposite to that direction taken by Gabriel at the close of 'The Dead');

the empty, unboundaried expanses of *Imagination Dead Imagine* and *Ping*; The space of *Quad*, described by Deleuze as 'a closed, globally defined, any-space-whatever';[13] all of these fictional geographies figure as worlds which one can only grasp by seeing complete, by attaining 'a perfect mental image of the entire system'. Where Joyce, in 'The Dead', in *Ulysses*, in *Finnegans Wake*, finds that the leap towards a global vision is blocked by the persistence of national categories in his creative imagination, for Beckett's later narrators, the opposite is the case. In these later works, it becomes difficult not for the narrator to think globally, but rather for the narrator to resist the global. The ambivalent need at once to speak of one's home and to leave it persists in Beckett's work, even into these whitely empty late prose pieces, which retain a certain nostalgia for nation. Even in that excruciating opening of *Imagination Dead Imagine*, one can read the trace of a struggle between persistent local reference, and the obliteration of the local. But here, in later Beckett, the possibility of thinking nationally, of placing oneself locally, is threatened by the development of a global perspective which was not available to Joyce, and which attenuates the very mechanics by which a national consciousness might recognize itself. The struggle to find an 'island home' continues in Beckett; the 'true home' of *How It Is* (HII 111), the 'unspeakable home' of 'Neither', remain entangled with the persistent need to give a voice to a remembered, semi-autobiographical, Irish landscape. But in the passage from the 1930s to the 1980s, as political and economic power migrates from colonial Europe to global America, the national comes to the point of unravelling, of giving way to the global. As Beckett's writing extends into the post-war, the struggle to speak of one's homeland, to find a form in which to give some kind of expression to one's 'unspeakable home', is balanced against this encroachment of a global perspective. That dissolving partition that appears and disappears in *Ill Seen Ill Said* suggests the beginning of a new way of placing the body in the world, a fragile form of demarcation and distinction that survives (in a somewhat spectral form) the collapse of national sovereignty. Throughout Beckett's writing, his narrators struggle to give a kind of expression to what they refer to as an 'unspeakable home'. But in later Beckett, this continuing, conflicted search for homeland is balanced against an equally unimaginable totality, what the narrator of *Ill Seen Ill Said* calls the 'unspeakable globe' (NO 95). If Beckett's later works can be seen as a means of expressing a new global perspective, then the possibility of such expression lies in this inchoate relationship in his later writing between home and globe, between entities that lie just on the other side of the speakable, waiting to come to a form of life that is still unthought.

Chapter 8

Knowledge Within Bounds: Beckett, Globalization and the Limits of Perception

I argued in the last chapter that the tendency towards apprehension of the totality that becomes an increasingly central characteristic of Beckett's work through his middle and late periods can be read, to a degree, as a response to the availability of a global perspective in the post-war world. The increasing loss of local placedness in Beckett's work, the increasing fragility of the boundaries that hold the body in remembered landscapes, can be read, I suggest, not only as a feature of Beckett's own aesthetic development, but also as a kind of symptom of the failure of those national boundaries that exert such a powerful positioning force in Joyce, and in earlier Beckett. Seen in a certain light, I would suggest, Beckett's work appears as an early attempt to produce a form in which to express the new possibilities, and the new impossibilities, that are produced by the globalization of culture, and by the globalization of capital. If Bryan McHale sees in Beckett's *Lost Ones* a prophetic vision of a contemporary shopping mall, then perhaps too what McHale calls Beckett's 'microworld' texts, those texts in which Beckett reaches for a totally inclusive picture of a world system, are prophetic glimpses of an absolutely connected globe, and of the global market (globe as shopping mall) which is still now in the process of arriving.[1]

If this argument has any validity, if Beckett's work can be seen as a critique or reflection of the ongoing forces that give rise to globalization, then it might lead us to pose some crucial questions, both about Beckett and about globalization. In his essay 'Cultural Criticism and Society', Adorno sketches a picture of globalization (before the term had currency), that suggests a relation between global culture (what Adorno calls the 'total society') and world systems imagined in Beckett's writing. The 'sinister, integrated society of today', Adorno writes in 1949,

> no longer tolerates even those relatively independent, distinct moments to which the causal dependence of superstructure on base once referred. In the open-air prison which the world is becoming, it is no longer so important to know what depends on what, such is the extent to which everything is one. All phenomena rigidify, become insignias of the absolute rule of that which is.[2]

If the world as open air prison might call to mind the Denmark in which Hamlet feels himself imprisoned, then it is also surely an apt description of Beckett's world systems, in which freedom and imprisonment are one. A characteristic of Beckett's later texts, of *The Lost Ones* and *Imagination Dead Imagine*, is that one is no longer sure whether one is inside or outside, whether one is a cage or in the open, whether the walls that hem one in are those of a narrow prison, or the furthest limits of the seeable and the knowable. Adorno's characterization of globalization as the 'absolute rule of that which is' adds to this Beckettian resonance, predicting of course Beckett's own later attempt to tell it how it is, in a world in which 'everything is one', in which 'all is identical' (HII 121). But if there is a close connection between Beckett's version of how it is and the homogenization, the reification of the world system described by Adorno, does this suggest that Beckett's early expression of globalization is one in which 'phenomena rigidify', one in which the 'absolute rule of that which is' is inscribed, as in mosaic stone? If Beckett's writing can be seen as a dramatization of the waning of the nation state, then does it also suggest the end of democracy, of justice and the good? Can the nostalgia for nation that is shot through Beckett's writing be a seen as a kind of longing for the democratic possibilities that were maintained by the dubious guarantees of national sovereignty? Does this mean that the progressive collapse of boundaries and distinctions intuited by Adorno and dramatized by Beckett spells the end of the possibility both of poetry and of democratic politics? Or do Beckett's representations of world systems contain within them the promise of a new kind of democracy, of a new kind of justice ('meet for now', the narrator of *How It Is* might say, 'meet for here')? Does the collapse of national and other boundaries open onto a new set of possibilities (both political and aesthetic) that the model of the nation state made unavailable or invisible to us? Are Beckett's works restricted to an expression of how it is, or are they animated also by a sense of how it could be, or how it ought to be? Is the version of globalization that Beckett's work helps us to see a dystopian reification of culture, or does it have within it utopian elements, glimpses of Leibniz's and Pangloss's 'best of all possible worlds' in which, as in *The Lost Ones*, 'all is for the best' (CSP 216)? When the narrator of *The Lost Ones* declares that the population of the cylinder is 'enjoined by a certain ethics' (CSP 222), what model of ethics is he invoking, and what post-national mechanism might effect its dissemination? Might this be something like an ethics of globalization?

To begin to respond to these questions is to attempt to understand what happens when we approach the limits of perception, when we seek to apprehend the totality, in political and economic terms, as well as in aesthetic terms. If Beckett's work, his attempt to give an expression to the 'unspeakable globe', has a utopian element, this utopianism is bound up with the attempt to think the totality, to exceed the limits of thought and vision. It requires him to think the limit, despite the fact that, as Andrew Gibson has pointed out via his reading of

Badiou, 'no given world will provide us with the equipment we can use rationally to ascertain its limits'.[3] Ernst Bloch writes in 'Art and Society' that the question posed by utopian art is the question of 'how to complete the world without the word being exploded as in the Christian religious anticipatory illumination, and without disappearing apocalyptically'.[4] The utopian artwork, the utopian image, he argues, allows us to glimpse the completed world, without producing Adorno's rigidification of phenomena. 'In other words', Bloch writes, 'art drives world figures, world landscapes to their entelechical border without causing their demise'.[5] Utopian art allows us to conceive of the world at its limits, at its 'entelechical borders', without experiencing such finishedness as a form of death, or as destruction by fire. In the utopian imagination, the world can be complete, final, over, and yet it can still go on, can still move and breathe and continue to become. The completed world of the utopian artwork, Bloch suggests, is complete because it contains the 'real possibilities' that are not yet perceptible or thinkable. 'Reality', he writes, 'without real possibilities is not complete'.[6] Now, Bloch's dogged optimism, and his somewhat starry eyed faith in the capacity of the utopian art work to anticipate the path of history, might appear decidedly un-Beckettian. Nevertheless, his characterization of the utopian image as one in which the world is both over and still in process is richly suggestive for an understanding of Beckett's treatment of the limit, for his apprehension of a world in a state of completion. One of the features that connect otherwise dissimilar works such as *How It Is*, *The Lost Ones* and *Ill Seen Ill Said* is their shared desire, in Bloch's words, to 'complete the world', to drive the world of the text to its limits, its logical conclusions, or as Gilles Deleuze would have it, to 'exhaust' the world. But this completion, this view of world as total system, does not produce stillness, or total death. The urge towards completion in these works does not open onto the apocalypse, or onto the end of history. Rather, it produces a peculiar surplus, a peculiar 'something', as Hamm puts it in *Endgame*, that continues to 'take its course' (CDW 107) even though it is 'finished', and that is perhaps the province of the utopian in Beckett's writing, and of utopian art and philosophy more generally under contemporary global conditions.

The comedy of *The Lost Ones* derives in large measure from this baffling conjuring of what Bloch would call a surplus, and what Derrida would call a supplement, from a thoroughgoing determination to reveal a self-identical world, a world in which nothing is left out, a world, in Beckett's words, as 'total object, complete with missing parts' (PTD 101). The story is, in a sense, a retelling of Milton's *Paradise Lost*, an attempt to grasp the totality, to apprehend the justice that animates the 'entire system', and through such apprehension, 'unattempted yet in prose or rhyme', to 'justify the ways of God to men'.[7] But, in both Milton's epic and Beckett's story, this attempt to expose the secret mechanics of the universe to narrative or verse leads only to the production of more secrecy, keeping rather than giving away what the narrator of *The Lost Ones* calls 'the secret of the Gods' (CSP 207). In *Paradise Lost*, it is precisely this replication of secrecy at the moment of revelation that the poem sets out to perform. The poem is in fact a defence of the limits of human knowledge (aimed perhaps at the poet himself as the most sceptical of readers, the most ambitious of knowers) rather than an attempt to know a just God. It reaches for the limits of knowledge, seeking to fathom the motivations of a cold and merciless creator, only to hide those limits again, to cloak the beginnings and ends of the universe behind a veil of divine unknowability. As Raphael puts it in Book VII, the poem cannot deliver absolute knowledge, despite the poet's lofty aspirations at the opening of Book I, but only 'knowledge within bounds'.[8] Any knowledge beyond such limits, Raphael warns Adam, we must 'abstain to ask'. Adam, he goes on to assert, must struggle against his own desire for

> Things not revealed, which the invisible king,
> Only omniscient, hath suppressed in night,
> To none communicable in earth or heaven.[9] (7, 120–4)

In *Paradise Lost*, as Bloch suggests, the completion of the world can only be glimpsed as apocalypse, as the destruction of the world that is the condition for the revelation of God's secrets to us who will by then no longer be men. The poem sets out to teach us how much we can know, before we have to accept God's rule as inscrutable. In *The Lost Ones*, however, the peculiarly comic coexistence of the knowable and the unknowable, the fathomable and the unfathomable, is not divided in this way by the occurrence of the apocalypse, that fiery end of history which, for Milton's God, has already arrived. The partial knowledge of the human is not divided by the apocalypse from the total knowledge of God. Rather, knowledge and ignorance, the completed and the ongoing, secrecy and revelation, are one and the same, part of the same fabric. The secret, in *The Lost Ones*, is hidden, as in Poe's *Purloined Letter*, in plain sight.

The patient elaboration of the rules that govern behaviour in the cylinder, for example, does not stave off the irrational and the unknowable. There is no fixed point, or Raphaelean boundary, where the knowable and the unknowable meet. Instead, the rational rules that regulate life in the cylinder give rise at every moment to irrationality, are *inhabited* by irrationality, as order gives rise to chaos, and justice is won from and produces the absence of the very possibility of justice. So, the narrator declares that the 'use of the ladders is regulated by conventions of obscure origin which in their precision and the submission they exact from the climbers resemble laws' (CSP 207). The narrator then goes on to give a detailed, painstaking account of the regulations governing the use of ladders in the cylinder. 'All rests', we are told, 'on the rule against mounting the ladder more than one at a time'. In order that this rule be observed without 'injustice', it is necessary to impose a strict queuing regime. A searcher who uses one of the ladders 'understands', the narrator writes,

> that after a certain interval difficult to assess but unerringly timed by all the ladder is again available meaning at the disposal in the same conditions of him due next to climb easily recognizable by his position at the head of the queue. (CSP 208)

In detailing these rules with such precision, and with increasingly elaborate levels of complexity, the narrator resembles those figures in utopian fictions, from More's *Utopia* onwards, whose task it is to explain the utopian ideal or system of government to the traveller, and by extension to the reader. Like Raphael Hythloday in *Utopia* (another Raphael), or Dick in Morris' *News From Nowhere*, or Dr Leete in Edward Bellamy's *Looking Backward*, or the Master Houyhnhnm in Swift's *Gulliver's Travels*, the narrator outlines the conventions that ensure that 'all is for the best' and that the 'needs' of the cylinder are 'answered' (CSP 215–16). But, as with so many utopian narratives, the more comprehensive the rules become, the more carefully they are worked out in order to ensure justice and fairness, the more clearly they reveal their emptiness, their absurdity. By seeing a world complete, by inventing or describing a system of government in its entirety, the narrator of the utopian narrative is able to imagine the world as it ought to be, is able to balance rights against duties, for example, with no obstacles in the path of justice. As the narrator of *The Lost Ones* puts it, the global utopian narrative allows us to ensure that there is a 'harmony' between 'order and license' (CSP 216). But the effect of this global perspective is not only to achieve such harmony, not only to give a lucid expression to the ethical principles that underlie being in the cylinder, but also to reveal the absence of such ethical principles, to reveal the extent to which such principles defy lucid expression. The utopian narrative is in a sense a response to a need to think the rules clearly. Our cultures and systems of government come into being organically and messily, and are burdened by traditions and histories that make discrimination and ethical clarity difficult. The utopian world, on the other hand, is born entire and whole, a simple manifestation of a set of principles unclouded by historical compromise. But what happens when a world is modelled to illustrate such principles, when the ethical imperatives that animate a system of government are brought out of hiding, as it were, is that ethical thinking itself reveals itself to be impossible, or groundless. It is as if such guiding, animating principles can only be seen in the shadows, can only be intuited indirectly. The narrator of *The Lost Ones* tells us that 'access to the climbers' reserve is authorized only when one of them leaves it to rejoin the searchers of the arena' (CSP 216). This is a very sensible rule, one that is familiar to all of us who have queued to enter the multi-storey car park of Bryan McHale's shopping mall. But here in the cylinder the practicality of the rule is exposed mercilessly to the groundlessness of all rules, to the absence of a guiding principle that makes entry to the 'climbers' reserve' – or to the shopping precinct – valuable or necessary or good, that provokes our desire to shop, to climb ladders, to search for our lost ones. The queuing of the searchers, their stupefied obedience, their willingness to take the place of their fellow searchers when they reach the head of the queue, becomes an exercise in self-perpetuating redundancy, again, not unlike the experience of shopping in malls. From the overarching perspective of the narrator, the narrator who sees the world whole and from whom nothing is hidden, what becomes visible is not only the way that the rules work, but also the lack of a motivating principle behind them. The rules, the narrator says, 'in their precision and the submission they exact from the climbers resemble laws' (CSP 207), just as the searchers are 'enjoined by a certain ethics not to do unto others what coming from them might give offence' (CSP 222). But what is missing here is that moment at which these laws are engraved upon a Mosaic tablet, that source from which the ethic of reciprocity that operates in the cylinder might originate. In *Paradise Lost*, this source is preserved by remaining hidden, remaining beyond the reach of prose or verse. The word of God is not the guarantor of justice in the poem, but is rather a veil that hides its unknowability, as Beckett's word-veil disguises the nothingness that lies behind it (Di 171). But in *The Lost Ones* the animating principle is not 'banished' to what Kristeva calls an 'exorbitant outside'.[10] It is present in the cylinder, present as a perceptible absence, as a flaw in the closely woven texture of the cylinder, a missing element that inhabits ethical thinking, that makes ethical thinking possible as surely as it empties it out. It is in this sense that the 'completion' of the world here does not lead, in Bloch's words, to 'the world's demise'. The gift of the utopian image is that it offers us a completion which contains, by virtue of its very completeness, a missing element that is not yet thinkable, a missing element that is the only trace of a justice that, in Derrida's terms, is still to come. *The Lost Ones* seeks to think the totality, to present us a word entire, a world in which 'all is for the best'. It is through this attempt to grasp the totality, this determination to tear apart the veil that hides what the narrator of *Ill Seen Ill Said* describes as the 'source of all life', that the work makes visible a certain darkness, a certain absence at the source. In the cylinder 'all is for the best', but at the same time, and without apparent contradiction, it is also that case that in the cylinder, 'this old abode', 'all is not yet quite for the best' (CSP 223). The 'not yet', that province for Bloch of the utopian possibility, is threaded into the now of the cylinder, part of the fabric of the completed world. It is the apprehension of the totality that brings an absent justice, the 'not yet', to the point of perceptibility.

In *The Lost Ones*, and across Beckett's later prose, this collapsing boundary between the knowable and the unknowable, the perceptible and the imperceptible, the now and the not yet, conditions and is conditioned by a delicate poetics of perception, of narrative perspective. These works are concerned, perhaps above all, with the act of looking, and with the limits of perception. In *The Lost*

Ones, of course, this obsession with looking is manifested most obviously by the searchers themselves, compulsive, insatiable lookers as they are, lookers who look so hard that their eyes turn red and sore with the effort. The looker in this work, however, whose vision troubles most effectively that trembling boundary between the seen and the unseen is not one of the searchers but the narrator him/her/itself, if this figure can be said to exist, and if the narrator is not to be thought of after all as a compatriot of 'this little people of searchers' (CSP 223). The narrator of *The Lost Ones* appears, at first glance, to be an omniscient narrator, usurping that mode of seeing that Milton's Raphael reserves for God, the 'invisible king, / Only omniscient'. Indeed, the narrator of this work seems to take omniscient narration to its logical conclusion, reducing the act of narration to a bare, telegrammatic description of how it is. At the opening of the work the narrator sets out on this narrative task, without unnecessary preliminaries:

> Abode were lost bodies roam each searching for its lost one. Vast enough for search to be in vain. Narrow enough for flight to be in vain. Inside a flattened cylinder fifty metres round and sixteen high for the sake of harmony. (CSP 202)

But even here, where the description of a world is at its barest and fullest, narrative perspective brushes up against the limits of its purview. This is a description of a world, of a closed cylinder, which, as Bryan McHale has commented, has no exterior, that is 'meant to be experienced from within, not without'.[11] It is a version of the 'total space', the 'complete world'[12] that Jameson suggests is given another kind of form by the Westin Bonaventure Hotel, a space which requires us to 'grow new organs', a new perceptual apparatus, in order to see it.[13] Being in the Bonaventure hotel, in Jameson's account, one is subject to the same kinds of disorientation suffered by the lookers in Beckett's cylinder. The 'latest mutation in built space' represented by the hotel has succeeded, Jameson writes, 'in transcending the capacities of the individual human body to locate itself [. . .], to map the great global multinational and decentered communicational network in which we find ourselves caught as individual subjects'.[14] The cylinder is all there is, the opening direction of *The Lost Ones* suggests, and to find oneself, to locate oneself within it, is to tune oneself to this global totality. The narrator comments later in the story that 'in the cylinder alone are certitudes to be found and without nothing but mystery' (CSP 216). If there is an outside, if there is something beyond this world, then it lies in that dark province that God has concealed from us, that the 'Only omniscient, hath suppressed in night'. But while the limits of the cylinder are presented as the limits of the knowable, it is also the case that, here, at the very opening of the story, such limits are transgressed, as Milton himself transgresses the boundaries of knowledge at the ludicrously audacious opening of *Paradise Lost*, like a male, middle-aged Eve. The narrator's knowledge of the limits of the system, his understanding of its simultaneous vastness and narrowness, suggest already that he has a privileged view of the cylinder (a privilege that is surely denied the searchers, else why would they continue vainly to search, vainly to flee?), that his view is from that very outside that the narrator avers is clouded in mystery. And that last phrase, which resurfaces throughout the story, 'for the sake of harmony'. What are we to make of that? That the narrator is able to penetrate the divine wisdom that is responsible for the harmoniousness of the globe (the cylinder is designed this way according to a celestial harmony, which it is the task of the narrator to 'justify' to 'men')? Or that the narrator himself has arranged the cylinder in this happily harmonious fashion (the narrator and 'deviser' of the cylinder decides upon these measurements 'for the sake of harmony', rather than for the sake of narrative accuracy)? As the narrator of *Imagination Dead Imagine* moves in a panic from the impossible inside to the impossible outside of his dimensionless rotunda – 'go back out', he says, 'go back in' (CSP 182) – so here, at the opening of *The Lost Ones*, the limits of the cylinder are set only through a certain narrative confusion between inside and outside.

As the story continues this uncertainty about the limits and the positioning of narrative perspective develops, to become one of the work's central preoccupations. Throughout the story, the narrator sets limits to his knowing only to exceed them, just as he poses as an absolute knower only to reveal the partiality of his knowledge. When giving an initial description, a 'first aperçu' of the abode, the narrator devotes some time to detailing the arrangement of the niches or alcoves that riddle the higher part of the cylinder, and to which the searchers climb on their ladders. 'These are cavities', the narrator writes, 'sunk in that part of the wall which lies above an imaginary line running midway between floor and ceiling' (CSP 203). They are disposed, he goes on,

> In irregular quincunxes roughly ten metres in diameter and cunningly out of line. Such harmony only he can relish whose long experience and detailed knowledge of the niches are such as to permit a perfect mental image of the entire system. But it is doubtful that such a one exists. (CSP 204)

This is a passage which borders on the schizophrenic, in its vacillation between knowing and unknowing. The narrator gives us a god's eye view of the cylinder, complete with its arrangement of alcoves (alcoves, incidentally, which are invisible from the floor of the cylinder, where the searchers congregate. We are told later that 'Seen from below the wall presents an unbroken surface' [CSP 220]). The narrator notes the slight irregularities in the disposition of the alcoves. They are, he says, 'cunningly out of line', and that word cunning suggests not only that the cylinder is designed by a subtle, even sly divine intelligence, but also that the narrator is in on the joke, that he understands the nature of the deviser's cunning. The wonderful delicacy of their placement is such, he goes on, that to appreciate it would require a 'perfect mental image of the entire system', that mental image that the narrator is trying to pass on to us. But, just at the moment that the narrator seems most confident in his understanding of the cylinder, just as he finds himself grasping the 'system' in its entirety, the narrative implodes. 'But it is doubtful', he says, 'that such a one exists'. The narrator admits doubt here – he is not sure whether or not there could be such a person – just at the moment that his own narrative reach fails. It is probably not possible, he says, to know the cylinder perfectly, to penetrate and to 'relish' the obscure reasoning behind its cunning architecture. So his own description of the 'entire system', his own relish of its cunning irregularity, falls into a kind of abyss, a kind of flaw in the very possibility of narration. The narrator presents himself at once as a searcher, whose knowledge is partial, and as an observer (or even deviser) whose knowledge is absolute; as both 'witness', in Steven Connor's terminology, and 'agency'.[15] The entire rhythm of the narrative, its 'harmony', the 'twofold vibration' that determines the movement in the cylinder from calm to storm, is driven by this impossible contradiction, and this impossible harmony, between different modes of knowing and seeing.

It is in the narrator's attention to the plight of religion in the cylinder that this contradiction in modes of knowing, appropriately enough, announces itself most starkly. There are two religions in the cylinder, two traditions of belief in the possibility of a 'way out' that leads 'in the words of the poet to nature's sanctuaries' (CSP 206). One tradition has it that escape from the cylinder is possible via one of the tunnels that lead from the niches into the 'thickness of the wall' (CSP 204), and the other avers that freedom is possible via a 'trapdoor hidden in the hub of the ceiling' (CSP 206). In describing these two doctrines, the narrator suggests that there is a gradual conversion from the former to the latter, as part of a larger failure of religious conviction among the searchers. The searchers' belief in the way out casts a 'fatuous little light' which will 'be assuredly the last to leave them' (CSP 207), such is the tenacity of the religious instinct. But the shift from tunnel to trap door is the sign of the gradual death of belief, as the trapdoor is 'out of reach', and so can be believed in without being tested. The 'partisans of the trapdoor', the narrator says are spared the burden of proof, because 'the hub of the ceiling is out of reach' (CSP 207). Thus faith declines in the cylinder, as 'by insensible degrees the way out transfers from the tunnel to the ceiling prior to never having been' (CSP 207). But while the narrator casts himself as a disinterested atheist who dispassionately observes this death of faith, disabused of the illusion, the *igniis fatuous*, that inspires such touching but pathetic loyalty in the hearts of the searchers, his description of religion in the cylinder itself troubles the narrator's relationship to God, or to the gods. The 'fact remains', the narrator declares, that

> of these two persuasions that former is declining in favour of the latter but in a manner so desultory and slow and of course with so little effect on the comportment of either sect that to perceive it one must be in the secret of the gods. (CSP 207)

This is an extraordinarily self-cancelling passage. The inexorable decline of religion in the cylinder, the dying of that fatuous little light, is so gradual as to be perceptible only to the divine intelligence whose inexistence is gradually, inexorably revealed. In perceiving this decline of the belief in a way out, the narrator casts himself as a privileged seer and knower, one who is in the 'secret of the gods'; but as he does this, he denies the very possibility of such a perspective, of such a godly form of vision and knowledge. He is in on the secret of the gods, the secret that there are none. In divining the impossibility of the way out that would lead to 'nature's sanctuaries', as it would lead to the fabulous outside where there is 'nothing but mystery' – in acknowledging that the exterior of the cylinder where the gods are to be found is so much fabrication and 'myth' – the narrator positions himself in that very outside whose existence he denies. The secrets of the gods, those secrets that Milton hides behind an impenetrable wall, are preserved here, but only by virtue of the collapse of the boundary that separates outside from inside, the perceptible from the imperceptible, certitudes from mystery, the hidden from the revealed. Just as the wall of the cylinder 'presents an unbroken surface' even as it is riddled with holes, seeing in *The Lost Ones* is made possible by the construction of boundaries which dissolve at the moment that they divide. The missing element, the not yet, the province of Bloch's utopian possibility, is brought into a kind of vibrating, impossible, unboundaried co-existence with that which is already here, with Adorno's 'that which is'.

It is in *Ill Seen Ill Said* that this trembling co-existence, this simultaneous transparency and opacity of the boundary, finds its strangest, but also perhaps its most compelling form. Like *The Lost Ones*, *Ill Seen Ill Said* is about looking, about marking and exceeding the tremulous limits of what can be seen. The fictional landscape of the novella is divided by a number of imaginary boundary lines, which demarcate a number of 'zones'. These zones are housed within one another, as circles within circles. At the centre of the landscape is the woman's 'abode', which is located in the first circular zone, the 'zone of stones'. This circular zone is located within a larger circular zone, known as the 'pastures'. These in turn have a far horizon, beyond which lies a third zone, referred to as the 'unknown' (NO 59), or as 'the haze', or, at one point, as 'paradise' (NO 73). The 'two zones' – the pastures and the zone of stones – 'form a roughly circular whole. As though outlined by a trembling hand' (NO 59). (See Figure 8.1.) Everything that happens in the story is organized around the marking and the testing of these boundaries that divide the zones from one another. The story is driven by a kind of contest between the stones that spread from the centre of the landscape, as if from the woman's abode itself, and the haze that seeps inwards from the outside, from the unknown to the known. Both stones and haze are spreading, both threatening to engulf the landscape, to obliterate all trace of the woman and her abode, in either a triumphant whiteness ('Light in its might at last' [NO 88]), or in a triumphant dark ('Blackness in its might at last' [NO 96]). The stones 'increasingly abound', the 'white stones more

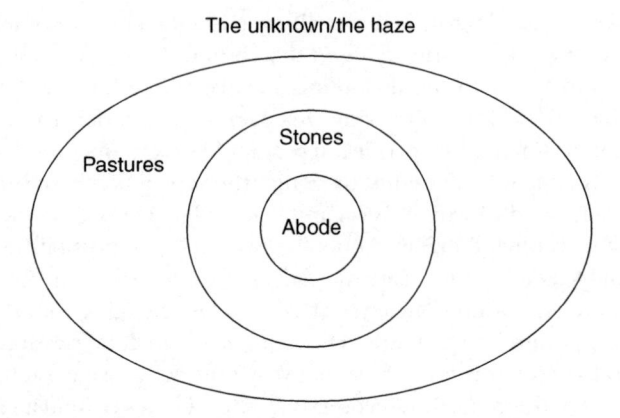

FIGURE 8.1 *Ill Seen Ill Said*

plentiful every year. As well say every instant. In a fair way if they persist to bury all' (NO 71). The 'meagre pastures' hem round the zone of stones, giving it is shape and definition, but the stones 'slowly gain' on the pastures, emanating from the abode at their centre 'as from an evil core' (NO 58). But while the stones nibble away at the pasture from within, the haze, which the narrator describes in an inverted reflection of *The Lost Ones* as the 'sole certitude', obliterates the pasture from without. 'Haze sole certitude', the narrator says: 'the same that reigns beyond the pastures. It gains them already. It will gain the zone of stones. Then the dwelling through all its chinks' (NO 88).

So, the movements of the woman in this bleak, empty landscape, take her across the contested ground between stone and haze. Her mournful trips backward and forward, from her abode where she kneels and prays, to a memorial stone lost somewhere in the unknown beyond the 'further confines' (NO 73), cross these shifting divisions between absolute opposites – between presence and absence, between darkness and light, the seen and the unseen. The central drama of the story – as in *The Lost Ones* the drama of a search for a lost one – is choreographed by the woman's navigation of these boundaries. There are two kinds of searching going on in the story: the woman searches for a missing one, or registers his loss, at gaze in her empty abode, or leaning against a desolate grave; the observer in the story, the narrative presence who sees the scene, and who says what he sees, searches for the woman, struggles to bring her into being. It is as if the observer and the woman are on either side of a divide, a divide between the seen and the unseen, between life and death, and they struggle to reach each other, to see across this boundary. The observer struggles to make out a trace of the woman, to retrieve her from memory or from absence as M conjures his lost one's face from the darkness of his 'little sanctum' in . . . *but the clouds* . . . (CDW 419). The woman sits gazing out to the further confines, struggling to perceive 'him' in the absence, in the haze. 'Eyes closed' the narrator asks, 'does she see him?' (NO 84). She sits at the boundary between stones and pastures, with her 'Face to the north. The tomb. Eyes on the horizon perhaps. Or closed to see the headstone' (NO 73), scanning the darkness for traces of her lost one. At one moment, the gaze of the observer and the woman are brought together through a transparent window pane, in a faint echo of that moment in James' *The Turn of the Screw* at which life and death regard each other through the open and closed boundary of a window – a moment which has grazed the surface a few times in this book already (see p. 43, p. 82). The narrative eye looks in from without, on the woman looking out from within: 'the eye rivets the bare window. Nothing in the sky will distract it from it more. While she from within looks her fill' (NO 66). The possibility of vision in *Ill Seen Ill Said* derives from this encounter across the threshold between outside and inside, between known and unknown, the threshold that is formed in the contest between stone and haze. The story sets out to discover a 'trace' of the woman, to find a mark that has been made in the universal bareness and emptiness by 'home' (NO 70). As stone and haze vie for supremacy, as they spread a contagion of uniformity across the 'formless place' (NO 58) in which the story is set, it is this gaze across the threshold, this attempt to communicate or to see across the boundary, that allows for the possibility of trace, that allows us to divine feature and shape and locality in the 'general dark', the 'unbroken night', the 'universal stone' (NO 90).

This struggle to see, to maintain particularity and distinction in the midst of encroaching uniformity, is expressed in the story as a form of trembling. The trembling of the unseen hand which draws the scene, which separates the zones from one another, is communicated to the scene itself, which trembles throughout with a suppressed energy, a kind of immanent life. The effort to see is an effort to tune oneself to this trembling, to feel the current that runs through the story, animating it as if it were Frankenstein's monster. The elements that comprise the scene, the pallet, the window, the buttonhook, the woman herself, all give themselves to the gaze by exhibiting this trembling, by coming to a faint movement or to a faint life that is imparted to a degree by the gazing eye itself. The buttonhook, we are told, 'hangs by its hook from a nail. It trembles faintly without cease. As if here without cease the earth faintly quaked' (NO 65). This trembling, this version of the 'twofold vibration' (CSP 223) that thrills through the cylinder of *The Lost Ones*, is held against the stillness, the opacity, the lifelessness of stone and of haze, that unbroken uniformity that encroaches on the scene, threatening or promising death, blindness, stillness. The gradual becoming-stone of the landscape, the 'muffled thud of stone on stone. Of those spilling their excess on those emergent' (NO 72), is cast as a kind of calcification, a kind of freezing, in which the trembling is finally stilled. This, in Ernst Bloch's terminology, is the failure of the artwork to preserve those utopian possibilities which are not yet seen, not yet known; this is what Bloch calls the 'will to become like stone', a will which he finds manifested in Egyptian sacred art. In 'all Egyptian figures and faces', Bloch writes,

> nameless fear of death prevails, and there is no other salvation than the affirmation of death, the suppression of inner life, the will to become like stone [. . .] a dead, fixed quietness essentially remains as an overall impression, an overall essence of the Egyptian sacred art.[16]

The woman herself is caught between these two states, between a trembling near animation, and a stony deathliness. As she sits in the cabin, she falls into the fixity of Bloch's Egyptian sacred art; she adopts, the narrator says, a 'rigid Memnon pose' (NO 78), the pose of those Egyptian colossi that guard the tomb of Ahmenotep III. But the narrator's gaze seeks to stir her from such rigor mortis, to bring her again to a trembling life. Seeing her visiting the tomb of her lost one, the narrator compares the quality of the woman's body to the stone of the tomb, an echo of that tomb guarded by the Egyptian Colossi of Memnon. 'See them again', he says, woman and memorial stone, 'side by side. Not quite touching'. In a kind of panic, the narrator frets that the two are 'indistinguishable', that the woman has become of a piece with the stony tomb at which she mourns, the tomb that marks, to some degree, the absence in death of the observer and narrator himself. But the narrator wills the woman to manifest her difference from stone, to become-woman through the force of the gaze itself. 'Indistinguishable the twin shadows', he says, 'Till one at length more dense as if of a body better opaque. At length more still. As faintly at length the other trembles under the staring gaze' (NO 86). 'And the old body itself', the narrator says. 'When it seems of stone. Is it not in fact ashiver from head to foot?' (NO 74).

The story, then, comes to life, comes to a trembling animation, in the space of a struggle between woman and observer, between inside and outside, between absolute presence and absolute absence. The observer, we might say, exists in a kind of outside, in the haze, looking in to the woman who lives in the zone of stones. Both observer and woman tremble on the brink of disappearance, the one into unbroken haze, the other into unbroken stone. The space of the story, the woman, the abode, the buttonhook, are all conjured into a kind of fleeting existence by this oscillating, trembling movement between observer and woman, between inside and outside, a movement that is ever on the point of dying, of becoming still, as it is given over to the global uniformity of stone, or of haze.

As a way of understanding the architecture and movement of the story, this kind of spatial organization makes a certain amount of sense. It is troubled, however, by another level of complexity, another kind of difficulty that bedevils the drawing of boundaries in this story. It is difficult to maintain the idea that the observer is on one side of a boundary – between, say, inside and outside, or life and death – and the woman is on the other, because boundaries in this novella, as in *The Lost Ones*, are always on the point of collapsing, always uniting what they divide, so outside becomes, repeatedly, a feature of the inside, rather than simply its opposite. This kind of collapse is evident in the passage that I quoted above (see pp. 144–145), at which the partition that divides the woman's cabin both resolves and dissolves:

> Next to emerge from the shadows an inner wall. Only slowly to dissolve in favour of a single space. East the bed. West the chair. A place divided by her use of it alone. How more desirable in every way an interior of a piece. The eye breathes again. But not for long. For slowly it emerges again. Rises from the floor and slowly up to lose itself in the gloom. The semigloom. It is evening. The buttonhook glimmers in the last rays. The pallet scarce to be seen. (NO 68)

If, as I argued earlier, this dissolving of the partition has a geopolitical echo, summoning in spectral shadow both the partition of Ireland and the partition and reunification of Germany, then it is also the case that this open boundary is conditioned by the poetics of vision that I have been exploring here. The rising and falling of the partition suggests, of course, the blinking of an eye. The eye 'breathes again' as the partition dissolves, before the partition falls again, 'So to say of itself. With no help from the eye' (NO 92), a reflex blinking. The partition, then, like the window through which the observer and the woman regard one another, can be seen as the eye lid, or better still the skin of the eye, the transparent skin that separates the Shakespearean 'vile jelly' (NO 91) from the woman's abode. On the one side of the boundary the observer, on the other the observed. But to read the partition in this way threatens to destroy the fragile demarcations that allow for seeing and saying, that allow for narration to take place at all. When the eye is opened, this suggests, then the eye and what the eye sees become one, the vile jelly floods out into the scene, surely destroying the conditions that allow for vision rather than creating them. As in Beckett's 1974 poem 'Something there', in which the opening of the 'whole globe' of the eye ensures that there is 'in the end / nothing more', that the 'something there somewhere outside' has been eradicated by global vision, so in *Ill Seen Ill Said* global seeing leads to an undoing of the possibility of vision (CP 65). The opening of the eye effects the collapse of outside into inside, the collapse of haze into stone, of stone into haze, the prevention of which has allowed for the narrator to divine a 'trace', to outline the trembling lines which allow us to see the abode, the zone of stones, the buttonhook. Indeed, later in the story, the narrator suggests just this, that looking erodes the very boundaries between zones upon which vision depends. The gaze of the narrator is the force that brings life in this story, but the narrator also suggests that looks can kill, that his gaze might erode the woman's presence rather than sustain it. The narrator wills the woman into being, but he also sets out to 'see her to death' (NO 74), to wipe away that 'tenacious trace' of woman and abode. Despairing of the woman's absence, he struggles to bring her back to life; but despairing of her presence, of the persistent trace of woman, of abode, and of all the props that clutter this little story, the narrator wants nothing more than to wipe the slate clean, to summon the pure whiteness, the 'shroud of radiant haze', in which one might 'melt into paradise' (NO 73). And just as it is looking that summons animation, so it is looking that produces calcification, that turns quivering flesh to marmoreal stone. 'The buttonhook', he says, in his desperation to find stillness and emptiness, 'The nail',

> They are there again. Still. Worse than ever. Unchanged for the worse. Ope eye and at them to begin. But first the partition. It rid they too would be. It less they by as much. (92)

The opening of the eye, the 'ridding' of the partition that separates the observer from the observed, does not allow for the narrator to see here, does not impart imperceptible, trembling animation, but rather it produces that extraordinary, impossible union of outside with inside, viewer and viewed, that causes the dissolution of trace, that leads both to 'light in its might at last', and to 'blackness in its might at last'. As *The Lost Ones* brings the outside into the inside, summoning unknowing from knowing and knowing from unknowing, so in *Ill Seen Ill Said* the boundary between the observer and the observed is always under a kind of erasure. The outside, from which the narrator gazes at his lost one, and into which the woman gazes in search for her lost one, repeatedly floods into the inside, joining with it in an impossible unity, making of narrator and woman a single, unboundaried entity.

The image which captures most precisely this coincidence of inside and outside, this excruciating coexistence of difference and identity, is the image of an eye, which resurfaces throughout the story in a number of ways. When the narrator finally persuades the woman to offer her face up to his gaze, for example, the focus is on her eyes, and then on her eye:

> Hidden from chin to foot under a black covering she offers her face alone. Alone! Face defenceless evening and night. Quick the eyes. The moment they open. Suddenly they are there. Nothing having stirred. One is enough. One staring eye. Gaping pupil thinly nimbed with washen blue. No trace of humour. None any more. Unseeing. As if dazed by what seen behind the lids. The other plumbs its dark. Then opens in its turn. Dazed in its turn.

This extraordinary moment is a reprise of that earlier encounter between narrator and woman through the window of the abode. The eye of the woman and the eye of the narrator (here the 'other') are brought into the closest possible contact, the one looking at the other across the boundary between the outside and the inside, between stone and haze. Like the gaze unsharingly shared by Murphy and Mr Endon in *Murphy* (Mu 140), or the moment at which Krapp gazes at his lover's eyes in *Krapp's Last Tape* vainly urging her to 'let me in' (CDW 223), this exchange between narrator and narrated suggests, to a degree, the failure of communication between one person and another. Both eyes are 'unseeing', both narrator and narrated are lost in their separate darks, hidden behind their separate lids. The membrane of the eye is an impermeable boundary between narrator and narrated, a boundary across which light and vision cannot pass. But even as the distinction between the two gazing eyes is at its sharpest, there is an insistent suggestion here that the ground for such a distinction is weak, trembling, as if here without cease the earth faintly quaked. The 'gaping pupil thinly nimbed with washen blue' is suggestive, surely, not only of the eye but also of the landscape of the story itself, those concentric zones outlined by an unseen, trembling hand (see Figure 8.1). Seen in a certain light, the ground of the story is itself an eye. The eye of the woman, the eye at the centre of the abode, which is at the centre of the zone of stones, which is at the centre of the pastures, which is surrounded by the unknown, by the shroud of radiant haze, by paradise, threatens here to become one with the landscape itself, with the 'entire system' (CSP 204), to absorb everything into its gaping pupil, to absorb all, including finally the eye of the narrator itself, located beyond the furthest boundaries, beyond the 'further confines'. As both the eye of the narrator and the eye of the woman threaten to reveal their identity with the landscape they look upon, their two separate darknesses tremble on the brink of becoming one, encompassing dark, as Vera and Austerlitz imagine themselves housed within the darkness of a single pupil in Sebald's novel *Austerlitz* (see p. 123). The eye, like the landscape, undergoes a kind of homogenization, an approach towards uniformity, as if eye and landscape are locked into a kind of unity. As the haze threatens to absorb the pastures and the stones, and as the stones threaten to encroach upon pastures and haze, so the discrete zones that make up the eye are under threat of erasure. The pupil in the above quotation is 'gaping' encroaching into the iris, the 'nimb of washen blue'. 'No trace of humour' may suggest the failure of the comic in Beckett's later writing ('Thalia', pleads the narrator of *How It Is*, 'for pity's sake a leaf of thine ivy' [HII 42]), but it also suggests the encroachment of the pupil into the visual apparatus of the eye, the vitreous humour, the 'vile jelly' itself. By the end of the story, this encroachment is almost complete. As the abode nears its final dissipation, as we approach the moment when there is 'no more trace. On earth's face' (NO 96), we find that there is

> Ample time none the less a few seconds for the iris to be lacking. Wholly. As if engulfed by the pupil. And for the sclerotic not to say the white to appear reduced by half. Already that much at least but at what cost. Soon to be foreseen save unforeseen two black blanks. (NO 96)

As the landscape approaches its final end, in which there is finally no trace left upon a triumphant darkness – a 'perfect dark' in which there is 'no more to be seen' – so the centre of the eye expands out to absorb all, to absorb into its darkness iris and sclerotic, pastures and haze, making of this darkness both blindness and total, all encompassing vision. It is this expanded eye that becomes, in *Worstward Ho*, the last instalment of Beckett's second trilogy, the 'whole narrow void' (NO 127), a nothingness that is also everything, an 'empty profusion' (NO 79). It is this pupil that becomes a 'black hole agape on all. Inletting all. Outletting all' (NO 127), a black hole in which it is possible to see, at once, 'Nothing and yet a woman' (NO 127).

At the close of *Ill Seen Ill Said*, this peculiar accord between the eye and the landscape is given its most concise expression, as the eye of the woman, which is also the eye of the narrator, becomes an 'Unspeakable globe' (NO 95). The tendency towards uniformity that threatens the possibility of trace, here, is cast as a globalization, a globalization both of space and of vision. At the limits of perception, at the limits of geographical uniformity, the narrator brushes up against the unspeakable whole that can neither be seen or said, however ill, a uniformity which would make, finally, the leaving of a trace, the drawing of a trembling line, impossible. This unspeakable globe, this unbroken whiteness, might recall the snowy whiteness at the end of Joyce's 'The Dead' – the whiteness that figures in that story as a kind of universal death. It might also recall Adorno's rigidification of phenomena, his discovery in the tendency towards global uniformity of the end of the possibility of a critical art. And indeed, it is the case that the production of global vision does threaten, in Beckett, a rigidity, the rigidity of tombal stone, the stilling of trembling movement. But while Beckett's representation of the global is in part an imagination of the frozen limits of perception – a presentiment of a global death that is carried in the image of stone spreading across the earth, evoking another ice age or a generic global ecological disaster – it is also, and at every point, a performance of a surplus, or a supplement, a continued trembling movement that arises from the erosion of the partition – that same erosion that opens on to the rigidity of stone. His depiction of a 'completed world', in Bloch's terminology, always carries within it something that is missing, Bloch's 'real possibilities', even as it denies the possibility of the missing element. The mechanics which lead to the global in later Beckett - the variously political and aesthetic forces which erode the boundaries between zones and between nation states – produce at once a stony rigidity and trembling movement, a vibrating movement between elements which maintain their difference, even within the identity produced by Beckett's globalization. The apprehension of the whole in Beckett, the tearing apart of the Miltonic veil that separates the known from the unknown, the seen from the unseen, produces an early image of global homogenization, which is also the performance of a new kind of utopian possibility. The collapse of the partition brings inside and outside, self and other, face and face, into a new kind of relationality. Self and other brush up against each other here, unseparated by the boundaries which have melted away, unseparated by the borders between zones and by the skin that covers the eye. This extraordinary intimate contact is always on the point of becoming identity, becoming stony oneness, but it also always resists such unity. It is a contact which demands a new understanding of the nature of the face to face, a new understanding of ethical reciprocity, a new understanding of the sovereignty of the self. As national boundaries collapse, as the local enters into a new relationship with the global, as the sovereign nation state loses its power to act as guarantor of democratic justice, it is this kind of difference in unity, this reshaping of the relation between the local and the global, that has become our most pressing political and ethical priority. The tendency towards the globalization of our referents that runs through Beckett's writing leads to the reification of the mind, to the 'absolute rule of that which is'. But it is also this urge towards the thinking of the limits, the thinking of the totality, that produces utopian possibilities in Beckett's writing, the possibility, glimpsed at the extraordinary end of *Ill Seen Ill Said*, that one might 'know happiness' (NO 97).

Chapter 9

Slow Man, Dangling Man, Falling Man: Beckett in the Ruins of the Future

I argued in the last chapter that Beckett's work suggests the possibility of a new kind of ethical relation between self and other, under the conditions determined by the globalization of capital. His work traces the increasing porousness of the boundaries that separate people and spaces from one another, while inventing new, utopian forms in which to express a continuing, trembling dialogue between discrete geographies and subjectivities that are ever on the point of collapsing into blank identity, or into blank, undialectical opposition.

The need to produce such forms, the need to develop a new ethical basis for relations between self and other in a globalizing world, has arguably become more urgent, or urgent in a new way, at the beginning of the twenty-first century. The terrorist attacks that occurred in New York and Washington on 11 September 2001 effectively rebalanced the equation between globalization and utopian possibility. Those theorists, such as Francis Fukuyama, who regarded the globalization of liberal democracy as a benign process, leading to the foundation of a perfect universal state, have struggled to account for the newly organized resistance to globalization that the attacks seemed to many to express. In his massively influential 1992 work *The End of History and the Last Man*, Fukuyama reprised and defended the argument that he first made in 1989, that the global spread of western democracy would lead to the 'end of history', to a condition in which, as Beckett's narrators would have it, 'all is for the best', in which it would be possible finally to 'know happiness'. 'While earlier forms of government were characterized by grave defects and irrationalities that led to their eventual collapse', Fukuyama wrote in 1992, 'liberal democracy [is] arguably free from such fundamental contradictions'. Western democracy is an 'ideal' condition that represents the 'end point of humankind's ideological evolution', and the 'final form of human government',[1] (a finality that is foreshadowed at the close of *The Lost Ones* as the 'last man' in Beckett's cylinder surveys the universal, post-historical calm [CSP 223]). There has been, Fukuyama writes, a 'remarkable consensus concerning the legitimacy of liberal democracy as a system of government', such consensus that the spread of western markets and ideologies across the globe has met with little resistance. 'Liberal democracy', he argues,

> remains the only coherent political aspiration that spans different regions and cultures around the globe. In addition, liberal principles in economics – the 'free market' – have spread and succeeded in producing unprecedented levels of material prosperity, both in industrially developed countries and in countries that have been, at the close of World War II, part of the impoverished Third World.[2]

After September 11, however, Fukuyama was forced to defend this vision of a global consensus on the legitimacy and the self-evident rectitude of liberal democracy. On 11 October 2001 Fukuyama wrote an article in *The Guardian* newspaper, brassily entitled 'The West has Won', in which he argued that, despite the level of hostility to the west – and particularly to the United States – evidenced by the attacks, they do not constitute any serious opposition to western ideology, and that they do not break the global consensus upon which he bases his claim that the west has established the best of all possible forms of government. The attacks might suggest that 'there is something about Islam' that makes 'Muslim societies particularly resistant to modernity', he writes, but it remains the case that 'radical Islam' does not constitute a 'serious alternative to western liberal democracy'. 'We remain at the end of history' after 9/11, he concludes, 'because there is only one system that will continue to dominate world politics, that of the liberal-democratic west'.[3]

The effect of Fukuyama's defence of his 'end of history' thesis, however, tends to emphasize how difficult it is to sustain a utopian conception of globalization in the new century, rather than to make a convincing case for continued faith in the power of the 'free market' to deliver an ideal global democracy. Fukuyama sees the main alternative to his vision of global democracy to be what he describes as the 'clash of civilisations thesis', a thesis that Fukuyama identifies with another influential right-wing thinker, Samuel Huntington.[4] Huntington argues, Fukuyama writes, that 'rather than progressing toward a single global system, the world remain[s] mired in a "clash of civilisations" in which six or seven major cultural groups [. . .] co-exist without converging and constitute the new fracture lines of global conflict'. 'Since the successful attack on the centre of global capitalism was evidently perpetrated by Islamic extremists unhappy with the very existence of western civilisation' Fukuyama goes on, somewhat sulkily, 'observers have been handicapping the Huntington "clash" view over my own "end of history" hypothesis'.[5] But what Fukuyama does not recognize in his article of October 2001 is that the utopian possibilities of global democracy have come to seem threatened not simply by some non-western, 'other' civilization, but by globalization itself. It is not simply Huntington's xenophobic conception of a hostile and bellicose rank of 'other' civilizations who are perversely resistant to the benefits of modernization that troubles the conception of global, consensual democracy after 9/11; rather the idea itself that globalization might have utopian potential, that it might lead to universal peace and prosperity, suffers an internal collapse. Jean Baudrillard, for example, speaks in part to Fukuyama's engagement with Huntington when he seeks to shift the critical focus from a battle between the west and its various others, to an understanding of the ways in which the globalization of capital produces its own limits, produces in an automatic fashion the collapse of its own utopian fantasies. 'This is not', Baudrillard writes, in a typically intemperate response to September 11,

> A clash of civilizations or religions, and it reaches far beyond Islam and America, on which efforts are being made to focus the conflict in order to create the delusion of a visible confrontation and a solution based on force. There is, indeed, a fundamental antagonism here, but one which points past the spectre of America (which is, perhaps, the epicentre, but in no sense the sole embodiment, of globalization) and the spectre of Islam (which is not the embodiment of terrorism either), to *triumphant globalization battling against itself.*[6]

For Baudrillard, the global hegemony of the west is not threatened by Huntington's hostile civilizations, nor does it enjoy Fukuyama's immunity to ideological resistance. Rather, he sees 9/11 as a symptom of a global system which has overreached itself, which has become vulnerable precisely because of its own power. 'The more concentrated the system becomes globally', he argues, 'ultimately forming one single network, the more it becomes vulnerable at a single point'[7] (as DeLillo has his version of Mohammad Atta think, in his novel *Falling Man*, 'the more power, the more helpless' [FM 81]). Baudrillard sees the collapse of the towers on September 11 as a symbolic version of this failure of the utopian project of globalization. The collapse, he argues, was a kind of suicide, a mirror of the suicide of the hijackers rather than a death at their hands. It is

> as if the power bearing these towers suddenly lost all energy, all resilience.... So the towers, tired of being a symbol which was too heavy a burden to bear, collapsed [...] The symbolic collapse came about, then, by a kind of unpredictable complicity – as though the entire system, by its internal fragility, joined in the game of its liquidation.[8]

While Fukuyama seeks to maintain the utopian possibilities of globalization against the gathering evidence that there is no consensus on the self-evident superiority of western democracy, and while Huntington preaches a defensive retreat of the west from the failed project of global dominance in the face of the innately undemocratic character of other civilizations,[9] Baudrillard sees September 11 as a sign of the failure of the very idea of globalization, a sign that the 'west has become suicidal and declared war on itself'.[10]

Don DeLillo, in his early response to September 11, casts the attacks as a corrective to the utopian tendencies of global structures pre-9/11, and in so doing brushes against the positions adopted both by Baudrillard and by Huntington. 'In the past decade', DeLillo writes in a 2001 essay entitled 'In the Ruins of the Future',

> The surge of capital markets has dominated discourse and has shaped global consciousness. Multinational corporations have come to seem more vital and influential than governments. The dramatic climb of the Dow and the speed of the internet summoned us all to live permanently in the future, in the utopian glow of cyber-capital, because there is no memory there and this is where markets are uncontrolled and investment potential has no limit.
>
> All this changed on September 11. Today, again, the world narrative belongs to terrorists.[11]

This collapse of a utopian, American future back towards a benighted age of terrorism, DeLillo suggests, has come about partly because of tendencies inherent in utopian globalization. 'We like to think', he writes, 'that America invented the future. We are comfortable with the future, intimate with it'.[12] The towers themselves, DeLillo has suggested in earlier novels – in *Players*, in *Mao II*, in *Cosmopolis* – belong in that intimate, unbodied American future that the virtualization of global capital appears to make spectrally present.[13] 'They were made to be the last tall things' Eric Packer thinks in *Cosmopolis*, 'made empty, designed to hasten the future. They were the end of the outside world. They weren't here, exactly. They were in the future, a time beyond geography and touchable money and the people who stack and count it'.[14] In disappearing, in collapsing, or in Baudrillard's suggestively fiscal phrase, in 'liquidating', the towers were really only revealing that they have never been here. Their disappearance is not the failure of the idea they represent, but its consummation. 'You build a thing like that', insists a character in DeLillo's 2007 novel, 'so that you can see it come down' (FM 116), recalling Sebald's narrator's observation, in *Austerlitz*, that 'outsize buildings cast the shadow of their own destruction before them, and are designed from the first with an eye to their later existence as ruins' (A 24).[15] The ruins of the towers, DeLillo suggests, the strands of bent filigree that were all that remained of the towers in the weeks after 9/11, tell us that our intimacy with the future is over. The World Trade Center, DeLillo writes in 'The Ruins of the Future', was a 'justification for technology's irresistible will to realize in solid form whatever becomes theoretically allowable'.[16] The collapse of the towers marks the separation of vaporous technological spirit from solid form, the escape of the utopian American future from the structures which briefly made it palpable and inhabitable.

DeLillo's reading of 9/11, then, shares with Baudrillard's a sense of automaticity, a sense that the collapse of the towers was to a degree a realization of their own internal logic. Unlike Baudrillard, however, DeLillo suggests an ideological political context to the attacks, one which bears some comparison with Huntington's work. While for Baudrillard the attacks are symptomatic of 'globalization battling against itself' in a political and ideological vacuum, for DeLillo they mark the collision of two distinct 'worlds', worlds which align loosely with Huntington's 'civilizations', which might be given the names 'America' and 'Islam', as well as 'future' and 'past', 'us' and 'them'. As a consequence of the attacks, DeLillo writes, as a consequence of the impact of plane with building, 'our world, parts of our world, have crumbed into theirs'. There are, DeLillo argues, 'two forces in the word, past and future':

> With the end of communism, the ideas and principles of modern democracy were seen clearly to prevail, whatever the inequalities of the system itself. This is still the case. But now there is a global theocratic state, unboundaried and floating and so obsolete it must depend on suicidal fervour to gain its aims.[17]

The attacks of September 11, DeLillo writes in 2001, open the faultline between these two 'forces' – between global democracy and global theocracy, as well as between America and Islam. In a formulation which echoes George W. Bush's rallying cry 'You are either with us or against us in this war on terror',[18] DeLillo writes that, as a result of 9/11, the 'sense of disarticulation we hear in the term "Us and Them" has never been so striking, at either end'.[19] While the attacks stage a certain 'crumbling' of one world into another, a certain erosion of the boundary that sees the future returned to the past, that sees 'us' flung into a terrible intimacy with 'them', they also produce this 'disarticulation', this absolute separation between a past and a future, between technological spirit and archaic solid form, that were given a brief joint articulation in the peculiarly fragile reach of the World Trade Towers.

DeLillo's early response to the attacks, then, is an uneasy and unstable mix of the structural and the ideological. The utopian possibilities of cyber capital expire both because of the inherent tendency of the utopian will to reach beyond its own structural limits, to inhabit a future which it cannot quite summon into material existence, and because of the hostile political will of a people who 'want to bring back the past',[20] a multitude of 'countless thousands massing in anger and vowing revenge'.[21] A sign of this mix between Baudrillard and Huntington, between the structural and the ideological, is the confusion here between convergence and separation, between a coming apart and a falling together. The project of American globalization is threatened both by the splitting of one world into two, and by the crumbling of two worlds into the liquidated ruins of one. Already in this essay, however, written in December 2001, DeLillo points towards the possibility of another kind of response to 9/11, a response that is missing from the somewhat gleeful fatalism of Baudrillard, and from the retrenched jingoism of Huntington. Rather than viewing the 9/11 attacks – and the demise of 'the principles of modern democracy' that they seemed to presage – as either the inevitable consequence of the globalization of power, or a symptom of the untranslatability of democracy to other 'civilizations', DeLillo suggests that the attacks require us to produce what he calls a 'counternarrative'. The 'narrative' of globalization, DeLillo writes, 'ends in the rubble, and it is left to us to create the counternarrative'.[22] It is this counternarrative, DeLillo suggests, that offers a means of reimagining our predicament, of maintaining a commitment to the utopian possibilities of global democracy that seemed to fail on September 11, and that were in any case only partly shadowed forth in the 'glow of cyber-capital' that illuminated the heady days of late century. If the 9/11 attacks produced at once the crumbling of 'our' world into 'theirs', and the radical separation of 'us' from 'them' – a collapse into a kind of ruined identity that is also an undialectical, 'disarticulated' opposition – then it is this 'counternarrative' that might suggest a new kind of accommodation between us and them, between self and other. DeLillo writes that, after September 11, 'there is something empty in the sky'.[23] This emptiness, of course, marks the absence of the towers, and their failure to sustain the difficult relation between past and future, between technological will and solid form that, for DeLillo, was the condition of their possibility. But, DeLillo argues, it is the duty of the writer to preserve that emptiness, as a means of negotiating between blank identity and blank opposition, and as a space in which to build utopian poetic forms. 'There is something empty in the sky', DeLillo writes. 'The writer tries to give memory, tenderness and meaning to all that howling space'.[24]

DeLillo's 2007 novel *Falling Man* emerges, to a degree, from his 2001 essay, and constitutes his attempt to build in the howling space vacated by the towers of the World Trade Center. I suggested at the opening of this chapter that September 11 rebalanced the equation between globalization and utopian possibility, and *Falling Man* is, in a sense, a response to this recalibration, a response to the failure of US global dominance post-9/11, and an attempt to construct a counternarrative, a kind of poetic utopianism, built on emptiness, that is the negative reflection of Fukuyama's persistent, belligerent faith in the universal good of western liberal democracy. I also suggested at the opening of this chapter that Beckett's writing, in its tracing of the simultaneous convergence and separation of geographies and bodies, might be thought of as shadowing forth utopian forms which articulate a new kind of relation, under global conditions, between self and other, between here and there, between us and them. Beckett's later work, I have been arguing, responds, however obliquely, to the decline of the post-war nation state, by imagining global scenarios, scenarios in which the boundary between here and there, between, in DeLillo's terms, our world and theirs, is ever on the point of dissolving, of crumbling. Beckett's global texts perform this dissolution of boundaries, but they also perform and witness the emergence of new subjectivities and geographies from and within a borderless world, whose failing presence is conjured from the absence, the inadequacy, the expiry of the boundaries that hold discrete bodies in discrete places. DeLillo's attempt, in *Falling Man*, to create a 'counternarrative', I would argue, emerges, after a particular fashion, from those almost transparent shapes that Beckett invents in his late work, shapes that are born fleetingly from the collapse of trembling difference and contradiction into white uniformity, or into absolute, antinomial opposition. DeLillo seeks, in *Falling Man*, to imagine a world that can survive the simultaneous separation and convergence of geographies that he registers, in somewhat dazed fashion, and more as symptom than as analysis, in his 2001 essay. The novel is an attempt to build such a world in the ruins of an American future – to give a shape and a form to the empty Manhattan sky – and it is an attempt to imagine the kind of body that might live in it, to give articulation to the kind of subjectivity that can withstand both the new intimacy and the new estrangement between self and other that is produced by globalization post-9/11. In imagining such bodies, living in such worlds, DeLillo's novel is haunted by those figures bequeathed to us by Beckett, those figures, trembling on the verge of imperceptibility, who summon themselves into being in the midst of their own ruins, the ruins of self that Beckett's Molloy describes as a 'place with neither plan nor bounds' (Mo 40). In a piece for radio written in 1946, entitled 'The Capital of the Ruins', Beckett reflected on the difficulties of communication and accommodation between different 'peoples', between 'us' and 'them', at a time when war has 'disarticulated' the planet. In an uncharacteristically benevolent mood, Beckett writes that the Irish and French staff of a Red Cross hospital in bombed out St-Lô, for which he worked from 1945–46, had to find ways of overcoming the obstacles that were placed in the way of trans-national relations in the immediate post-war. 'What was important' in the French–Irish accord, he writes,

> was not our having penicillin when they had none, nor the unregarding munificence of the French Ministry of Reconstruction (as it was then called), but the occasional glimpse obtained, by us in them and, who knows, by them in us (for they are an imaginative people), of that smile at the human conditions as little to be extinguished by bombs as to be broadened by the elixirs of Burroughes and Welcome, – the smile deriding, among other things, the having and the not having, the giving and the taking, sickness and health. (CSP 277)

This glimpse of a piece of 'us' in 'them', and of a piece of 'them' in 'us', predicated on the shared, trans-economic, trans-cultural and trans-biological currency of the smile, does not sound typical of 1946 Beckett; neither does it set the stage for what has seemed to many to be the fierce, 'uncompromising' solipsism of the fiction that he writes in the late 1940s and the 1950s. But this radio piece, in demanding a form in which to express a collective response to the war, a form 'in which our condition is to be thought again' (CSP 278), remains suggestive for a reading of relations between 'us' and 'them' in Beckett's post-war writing. Beckett here is reaching for a mode of collective being that is summoned, as he puts it in the same essay, 'from the simple and necessary and yet so unattainable proposition that their way of being we, was not our way and that our way of being they, was not their way' (CSP 277). The task of thinking our condition again – the task of imagining a 'way of being we' and a 'way of being they' that can emerge from the disarticulation between 'us' and them' – is one which requires us, as Daniel Katz has eloquently demonstrated in his reading of 'The Capital of the Ruins', to dismantle not only our conception of 'them', but also our conception of 'us'.[25] In 1946, Beckett glimpses a kind of conjoined subjectivity for which there is not yet a grammar, a kind of collective condition to which our ways both of being we and of being they might approximate, but which remain beyond the interpellating power of any pronoun. His writing after 1946, his fiction and his drama, might be regarded as an extended effort to summon this unnamable, this 'unattainable' conjunction into being, to imagine a protoplasmic 'we' that emerges from the accelerating decline of the nation state after World War II, a 'we' stripped of the pronominal clothing that makes it distinguishable, separable from 'they'. It is this 'we' – at once conjoined and disjoined – that becomes barely perceptible in Beckett's late work, and that lingers on since Beckett, emerging, in various forms, across the spectrum of contemporary cultural activity, emerging, quietly, in DeLillo's response to the new global conditions inaugurated by 9/11. It is this 'we' that points towards a utopian conception of globalization, that takes us beyond the imperial optimism of Fukuyama, the postmodern fatalism of Baudrillard, and the regressive isolationism of Huntington.

Beckett's utopian figures come to a kind of life, then, in DeLillo's *Falling Man*, and as this final part and this book draws to a close, I want to trace some of the ways that Beckett's broader legacy, as I have articulated and animated it here, is passed on to us after 9/11 – a time, as DeLillo puts it in *Falling Man*, when 'everything is measured by after' (FM 138). I want here to put into a kind of critical motion not only the utopian forms that emerge from Beckett's imagining of globalization, but also some of those other thought forms that Beckett has left us, and that I have returned to throughout this book. The 'unattainable' utopian 'we' that is Beckett's response to globalization can be thought, I would suggest, alongside some of his other gifts to those of us who come after, some of his other strategies for leaving, as he has put it, a 'stain upon the silence'. The 'we' that Beckett imagines here is one that is conjured from the unthinkable or barely thinkable body that he imagines in his work, the body won from an impossible cleavage between face and back, between self and other, between man and woman. It is a 'we', also, that is made thinkable, or barely thinkable, by the peculiar temporality that Beckett fashions in his writing, a temporality in which before achieves a kind of conjunction with after, in which chronological sequence gives way to a kind of simultaneity, a kind of temporality for which, as Molloy recognizes, there is not, or not yet, a tense (Mo 36). It is a 'we' that is fashioned from contraction, from reduction, from Bernhardian correction. And it is a we that is joined, articulated, by those 'back roads' that I have traced as they work through Beckett's writing, as they connect Beckett with Bowen and Edgeworth and Kleist, with Banville, Bernhard and Sebald, with DeLillo, Coetzee, Yeats and Joyce, as they place Ireland in a peculiar adjacency with Europe and with America, as they bring the past into a new relationship with the present, and with the future. So in tracing the movement of Beckettian utopian forms in *Falling Man*, I will hope to strike a resonance with my earlier chapters, a resonance that might suggest a kind of conclusion, if a book dedicated to the 'after', to the 'since', can ever be said to conclude. It is also my intention here, in the spirit of such resonance, in the spirit of such open conclusions, in the spirit of the 'we', to approach *Falling Man* as a multiply occupied novel, as a novel which is haunted not only by Beckett, but by other voices and other figures – in particular those left to us by Saul Bellow and J. M. Coetzee – with whose Beckett's strike a kind of balance. If there is a 'counternarrative' to emerge after 9/11, a way of being we that is adequate to the challenges of this new century, then this balance, this difficult combination of Beckett with Bellow, Coetzee and DeLillo, might suggest one means of conceiving of it, might gesture towards the 'terms', as Beckett puts it in 1946, 'in which our condition is to be thought again' (CSP 278).

In *Falling Man*, then, I would suggest that it is possible to hear a number of voices, a number of echoes, among which Beckett's refracted presence mingles. The first time that the falling man of the title appears in the narrative suggests some of the novel's polyvalence, its crowdedness. DeLillo's falling man is a performance artist who appears periodically throughout the novel, and at various venues across New York City, as the novel charts the process of recovery – both of the city and of a particular family – in the months and years after 9/11. One of the protagonists, Lianne, first encounters the Falling Man early in the novel:

> [Lianne] edged along a storefront and looked up toward the green steel structure that passes over Pershing Square, the section of elevated roadway that carries traffic around the terminal in both directions.
>
> A man was dangling there, above the street, upside down. He wore a business suit, one leg bent up, arms at his sides. A safety harness was barely visible, emerging from his trousers at the straightened leg and fastened to the decorative rail of the viaduct. (FM 33)

This first glimpse of the Falling Man, held in a peculiar suspension over the city, is of course an image that is already populated, an image that, in a recurrent

DeLillian trope, is already 'something else'.[26] 'He brought it back, of course', Lianne thinks, 'those stark moments in the burning towers when people fell or were forced to jump' (FM 33). The falling man 'brings back' not only the collective spectacle of people falling, jumping from the towers, but also, in its specific gestural shape, the iconic image of one particular faller who became known as 'Falling Man', and who was photographed in mid fall, head first, one leg bent up, arms at his side, dressed for the day's interrupted business. If it is the case the novel charts post-traumatic recovery, it is staged against this recurrent image of the falling man, who brings the event back, as if in a kind of déjà vu. The body of the artist, suspended in mid fall, and occupied overwhelmingly by the absent body of an unnamed other,[27] suggests that the narrative time in which recovery might take place has been suspended, arrested. This is the double time of *Hamlet*, the time of mourning, the time that is 'out of joint', the time in which an original trauma continues to emerge, refusing to be over, refusing to be left behind in the narrative stream. The image, then, the body of DeLillo's falling man, is one in which the dead live on, and in which the past persists, interrupting and deforming the attempt to enter into a 'post' phase, to enter into the world which is measured by 'after'. But if the falling man summons the photograph of that victim of the attacks, plunging to his death on the morning of 9/11, it also summons other ghosts, producing an effect not only of déjà vu, but of déjà lu. The falling man, in this first appearance, is described not as 'falling', but as 'dangling': 'A man was dangling there', Lianne thinks, and remembers that earlier 'he'd been seen dangling from a balcony in a hotel atrium' (FM 33). This tension between falling and dangling that is registered in Falling Man's first appearance runs throughout the novel. The performance enacts falling, it evokes, Lianne thinks, 'the single falling figure that trails a collective dread, body come down among us all' (FM 33), but it does this by suspending the fall, freeze-framing it just as the original photograph froze the original falling man in the private and intimate midst of his plunge. The barely visible string that runs from Falling Man's straight leg, and that is attached to the rail of the viaduct from which he is suspended, is the mark here of the difference between photographed bodies and bodies in space. The flimsy string bears the weight of the dangling body, a weight that is lifted by the magic of photography, a magic that makes that string not 'barely visible', but invisible, inexistent. Photography renders the Falling Man's plunge endless and weightless; DeLillo's Falling Man, in recreating the spectral recurrence of the image in the city's mourning imagination, feels the pull of gravity, the force of a body in the time and space 'after', wanting to fall. The tension, then, between falling and dangling has to do with the novel's interest in photography, and balances the set of relations that are articulated here between the original falling man, DeLillo's fictional performance artist, and the extant photograph that had such a haunting presence in the cultural imagination in the aftermath of September 11. But it also, and equally powerfully, suggests the relationship between *Falling Man* and Saul Bellow's novel, *Dangling Man*, a work that is intricately threaded through DeLillo's novel, and that forms a constant counterpoint to it. Just as the body of DeLillo's Falling Man is inhabited by the absent body of the photographed victim, so it is inhabited by the body of Joseph, Bellow's Dangling Man, the alienated intellectual who finds himself suspended, in 1942–43, waiting to join World War II.

This presence of Bellow's novel in DeLillo's is a haunting one; Bellow's Joseph lingers on, inflecting DeLillo's Kleistian centre of gravity, influencing gesture, shape and tone, just as the unnamed victim of 9/11 inhabits and shapes DeLillo's Falling Man, and *Falling Man*. But in the case of Bellow's novel, the shaping is mutual, a haunting that works both backwards and forwards. If DeLillo's *Falling Man* turns around the space made by a dangling man, then Bellow's *Dangling Man* orbits around a centre formed by the body of a falling man. Joseph encounters this falling man on a walk across the city, somewhere in the middle of his long wait:

> I walked along East Randolph Street, stopping to look at the rich cakes and the tropical fruits. When I came to the smoky alley alongside the library where the southbound cars emerge, I saw a man sprawl out in front of me, and at once I was in the centre of a large crowd and, from a distance that could not have been as great as it seemed, a mounted policeman standing before a Cottage Grove car was gazing down.
>
> The fallen man was well dressed and above middle age. His hat lay crushed under his large bald head, his tongue had come forward between his lips, his lips seemed swollen. I stooped and tore at his collar and sprang away. By this time the policeman had pushed his way forward. I drew back, wiping my hands on a piece of paper. Together, we stared at the fallen man's face. (DM 94–5)

This encounter with the fallen man in Bellow's novel moves through DeLillo's performances of falling, the elements of Bellow's falling scene recurring insistently. There is a connection, a minor route, that runs from DeLillo to Bellow, a connection that is determined by the tension between dangling and falling. DeLillo's dangling man shapes to become Bellow's fallen man, looking to this earlier incarnation as if to free him from his temporal and spatial suspense, to return him to a fallen form that belongs not to 'after', but to 'before'. It is as if DeLillo is building backwards here, cutting this narrow path back from early twenty-first century global America, to an America on the point of emerging from the post-war ruins of the European nation state. But if DeLillo builds backwards towards Bellow, there is also a sense that Bellow is building forwards, in *Dangling Man*, towards the future, and towards DeLillo. Bellow's Joseph is incarcerated in his room in Chicago, removed from the European theatre of war, from the world history that is in the process of being made on the other side of the door, and on the other side of the Atlantic. His suspension, his 'dangling', is an effect of this removal. But at moments throughout the novel, Joseph is given a glimpse of the future that is waiting for him when he re-enters the world, when as he puts it he is finally 'cut down' (DM 10). Joseph has a series of dreams that take him away from his room, from his seclusion and his suspense, that take him forward along what he calls 'the path of a grey draught' (DM 100), into the time to come. In these dreams, Joseph sees visions of the war in Europe, of the terrors of combat that await him, of bodies in piles, but he also sees again the falling man that he encounters in the street, the falling man that is given another kind of life by DeLillo, in 2007. The encounters that Joseph has with this figure take place, he tells us, in a 'muddy back lane':

> Our encounter was in a muddy back lane. By day it was a wagon thoroughfare, but at this evening hour only a goat wandered over the cold ruts that had become as hard as the steel rims that made them. Suddenly I heard another set of footsteps added to mine, heavier and grittier, and my premonitions leaped into one fear even before I felt a touch on my back and turned. Then that swollen face that came rapidly towards mine until I felt its bristles and the cold pressure of its nose; the lips kissed me on the temple with a laugh and a groan. Blindly I ran, hearing again the gritting boots. The roused dogs behind the snaggle boards of the fences abandoned themselves to the wildest rage of barking. I ran, stumbling through drifts of ashes, into the street.
>
> Could the fallen man of last week have seen, had he chanced to open his eyes, his death in the face of that policeman who bent over him? (DM 100–1)

The muddy back lane, here, takes Joseph out of his room, both towards the European theatre of war, and towards his own death. The swollen face of the falling man that he encountered in the street, this dream suggests, is the irruption of the future, of death itself, into the present. When the fallen man sees his death reflected in the face of the watching policeman, the novel brings the future into a kind of facial contact with the past, a kind of adjacency effected by that muddy back lane, by that path of grey draught. It is in the space of this back lane, in the presence of a watchful death, that Bellow might be thought of as reaching towards DeLillo. Indeed, this back lane emerges in DeLillo, towards the end of *Falling Man*. Keith, Lianne's estranged husband who was trapped in the World Trade Center on the morning of 9/11, imagines returning to the scene of his incarceration in the towers, and in doing so evokes, obliquely, Bellow's back lane (and recalls the back roads that signal a return to the Beckettian maternal home in Banville's *Eclipse*). He imagines returning from his unanchored life in the disorientated days 'after', to see the woman with whom he had a brief affair after the attacks, a woman who, like him, had been trapped in the stair well of the north tower as the building burned. He thought of 'returning' to see her, we are told:

> He'd thought of it in a remote way, like landscape, like thinking of going back to the house where you grew up and walking along the back lanes and across the high meadow, the kind of thing you know you'll never do. (FM 227)

The back road, here, offers an inaccessible route back from the days after, to the time before, just as the back road in Bellow offers a path to the future, to the moment when the dangling man falls.

So, it is possible to imagine this back lane as a place where DeLillo and Bellow meet, as a passage that opens up between them, allowing for this mutual haunting, this mutual shaping. It is a lane that brings DeLillo's dangling to Bellow's falling, just as it leads from DeLillo's after to his before, and from Bellow's before to his after. To imagine this encounter between DeLillo and Bellow in this way, however, is perhaps to read against the grain of *Dangling Man*. Joseph is afforded a vision of the future in that back lane, but, one might argue, this is not a future that takes him forward, that reaches towards the America that DeLillo is to inherit. The death that Joseph encounters here is not what Maurice Blanchot would call 'death as possibility',[28] death as a marker of the undecidable and inexhaustible future. Rather, the muddy lane and the grey path lead only to death as annulment, to a muddy European death that is a denial of the American future in which DeLillo is waiting – the global American future that the World Trade Towers summon into premature existence – rather than a passage to it. The 'path of a grey draught' in *Dangling Man* suggests a passage to vaporous, unformed future, but it also suggests the military draft that denies the future of an entire generation. In the spatial and gestural logic of *Dangling Man*, it is Joseph's dangling that leads to America's global future, and his falling, his journey down that back lane, that signals a refusal of such a future. Throughout the novel, Joseph returns obsessively to his perception that the European war is an economic opportunity for America – that the conflict which exhausts the European nations will give rise to a new economic superpower, to a new imperialism that will rise from the ashes of the old. In his attempt to navigate the ethics of the war, and of his suspended relation to it, it is this sense that the United States benefits economically and culturally from the conflict that is one of the most persistent difficulties for Joseph. He reflects that 'we have easily accustomed ourself' to the mass slaughter of the war, because, he says, 'we are, after all, after some fashion, the beneficiaries of that slaughter' (DM 68). His dangling, his dallying at home while the allies fight abroad, is thus a complicated gesture; it is spiritually and intellectually a form of principled ethical withdrawal from the world – from the barbarity of the war as well as from the US culture that capitalizes on it – but it puts him in the position of becoming a passive beneficiary of the very cultural, economic and military violence that his withdrawal is in part a protest against. Joseph acknowledges this problem. He insists that 'Myself, I would rather die in the war than consume its benefits' (DM 69). He does not have, he recognizes, a simple choice between participation and withdrawal, between 'us' and 'them'. George Bush's 'you are either with us or against us' is based on an ethical and moral clarity that Joseph recognizes is not available to him. 'When I am called', he writes, 'I shall go and make no protest. And, of course, I hope to survive. But I would rather be a victim than a beneficiary'. 'Between our imperialism and theirs', he says, between global fascism and global capitalism, 'I would take ours'. 'Alternatives', he says, clear alternatives between opposing ideologies, 'grow only on imaginary trees' (DM 69). The falling that Joseph sees in his vision, in the muddy back lane that leads to the European front, is thus cast as a blunt end to the ethical and moral suspension that allows Joseph to hang between alternative visions, the suspension that gives him a temporary, weightless immunity from the ethical imperative to decide, to act. To read his vision of the fallen man as a glimpse of a future that takes Joseph toward DeLillo's dangling man is thus to overlook the fact that falling here is a rejection of the very economic future that DeLillo inhabits, the future that is predicated on the failure of the European nation states in the aftermath of the war, and the growth of a US global superstate as a result. Whatever happens in that back lane, one might argue, it leads Joseph not forward to global America, but backward towards a European nation state in its death throes.

The attempt to understand the presence of Bellow in DeLillo, to map the passage that is opened up between them, is further complicated by the aesthetic and political co-ordinates of Joseph's dangling. His withdrawal into his room is coloured not only by his political stance in relation to the war, but also by an intellectual attitude that he develops over the period of his incarceration. His long wait to enlist is the occasion for his incarceration in his room, and his opinions on what it means to fight germinate during this time. But, he says, the 'seven months' delay' in his military career 'is only one of the sources of my harassment'. 'I sometimes think of it', he writes, 'as the backdrop against which I can be seen swinging' (DM 10). The war, and the politics of the US involvement in it, is cast here as the frame for the more abstract concerns that run through *Dangling Man*, namely the nature of the self, the nature of individual, existential freedom, and the nature of the relationship between the self and the world. The war produces, Joseph writes, a predicament in which 'there is nothing to do but wait, or dangle, and grow more and more dispirited' (DM 10). It is this predicament, this experience of enforced waiting, that grants Joseph a privileged insight into the nature of being in the world. Like Vladimir and Estragon in *Waiting for Godot*, Joseph is cast into a kind of temporal, spatial, political vacuum, in which there is 'nothing to be done' (CDW 11), in which the furniture and business of the world is removed to reveal the bare outline of being itself. It is possible, indeed, to think of *Dangling Man* and *Waiting for Godot* as virtual companion pieces, works which both respond to the war by undertaking a forensic examination of the texture of waiting, of ethical, political and spiritual suspension. Both *Dangling Man* and *Waiting for Godot* draw such analyses partly from an engagement with a contemporary European tradition, with the variously nuanced blends of existentialism and absurdism developed by Sartre, by Camus, by Kafka, by Ionesco. Bellow's Joseph can be thought of as a cousin of Beckett's Murphy, or perhaps his little brother. Murphy, we are told at the opening of Beckett's *Murphy*, 'sat out of it, as though he were free, in a mew in West Brompton' (Mu 5), and Beckett's novel goes on to chart the retreat of Murphy from the 'big world' into the silence and darkness of withdrawal and insanity. Joseph, similarly, 'sits out of it', in his Chicago room, and, similarly, brushes against the border between sanity and insanity. *Dangling Man* ends, like *Murphy*, with its protagonist retreating to a room in the attic, and sitting in a rocking chair, preparing to abandon himself to death and to insanity. Joseph concludes, as he sits in his attic room, that there is 'no trusting' the 'objects of common sense', that the only guarantee of a sane life in the 'big world' is through what he calls 'wide agreement'. It is, he reflects, 'my separation from such agreement [that] had brought me perilously far from the necessary trust, auxiliary to all sanity' (DM 158). But while Beckett's depiction of men incarcerated in rooms has been read as leading towards ever more violent versions of solipsism, and ever more extreme depictions of the crazed alienation of self from world, Bellow's work, it has been argued, takes him in the opposite direction. It may be that Joseph's rocking chair is modelled on Murphy's, but at the close of *Dangling Man*, Joseph opts to leave the chair and the room and to re-enter the world, rather than rocking like Murphy towards the dubious freedom of death and non-existence. In his penultimate diary entry, Joseph records that, as he sits in his rocking chair, he is afforded a Beckettian vision of diminishment in which 'the room, delusively, dwindled and became a tiny square, swiftly drawn back, myself and all the objects in it growing smaller' (DM 158). But Joseph does not abandon himself to the obliterating power of the rock, as Murphy arguably does. Rather, he writes, he 'rose rather unsteadily from the rocker', marking both Joseph's and Bellow's refusal of Beckettian withdrawal. 'I had not done well alone', Joseph writes,

> I doubted whether anyone could. To be pushed on oneself entirely put the very facts of simple existence in doubt. Perhaps the war could teach me, by violence, what I had been unable to learn during those months in the room. Perhaps I could sound creation through other means. Perhaps. But things now were out of my hands. The next move was the world's. (DM 158)

So, when Joseph falls, when he is finally 'cut down' from his dangling and released from his room, he makes a gesture that is at once political and aesthetic.

His return to the world is a pragmatic acceptance that one cannot abstain from ethical decisions, even when one is not presented with an alternative that one finds palatable: it is a determination that the native hue of resolution should not be sicklied o'er with the pale cast of thought. But it is also an attempt, more on the part of Bellow, perhaps, than of Joseph, to plot a literary path beyond what Bellow thinks of the impasse reached by Beckett, and by the tradition to which Bellow suggests Beckett belongs. In a 1963 essay on 'Recent American Fiction', Bellow argues that Beckett, with Andre Gide, Sartre, Sarraute and Robbe-Grillet, are involved in a campaign of sorts to effect the alienation of self from world, and the disintegration of the very concept of the individual, of the self-identical subject. These writers, he says, expand on the 'theme of annihilation of the Self, and the description of the inauthentic life which can never make sense'.[29] But if these concerns are 'predominantly European and particularly French', Bellow implies that it is the task of the American novel to somehow engage with and emerge from this tradition. 'Writers like Sartre, Ionesco, and Beckett or like our own William Burroughs and Allan Ginsberg are only a few of the active campaigners on this shrinking front against the self', Bellow writes. 'One would like to ask these contemporaries, 'After nakedness, what?' 'After absurdity, what?'.[30] 'We have so completely debunked the idea of the old self', he goes on,

> that we can hardly continue in the same way. Perhaps some power within us will tell is what we are now that old misconceptions have been laid low. Undeniably the human being is not what he commonly thought a century ago. The question nevertheless remains. He is something. What is he?[31]

Bellow's own work, he implies, is an attempt to answer this question, and perhaps to give a form to this 'power within us' that might tell us who we are. Joseph's unsteady rise from Murphy's rocker is an attempt to find a way of reuniting self with world after Beckettian absurdity, destruction and nakedness. Where Beckett's Unnamable narrator suggests that there is a 'partition' between mind and world ('on the one hand' he says wittily 'the mind, on the other the world' [U 386]), Bellow's Joseph looks for the fusing between mind and word, searches for an ethical response to the fact that the mind is *in* the world, made of the world, as the world is in the mind. Murphy 'sat out of it', but Joseph writes that 'you can't banish the world if it's in you'. 'Whatever you do', he writes, 'you can't dismiss it' (DM 113).

This political and aesthetic context to Joseph's dangling determines, to an extent, the nature of the encounter that is staged, in *Falling Man*, between DeLillo and Bellow. When DeLillo opens this passage to Bellow, this back lane, he seeks a kind of union with a writer who appears at once to refuse the forms of aesthetic withdrawal that are putatively offered by Beckett, and to accept 'our imperialism' as the only possible ethical choice given the alternative between 'us' and 'them'. When Joseph falls, or when he is 'cut down', he concedes with a terrible enthusiasm that 'I am no longer to be held accountable for myself', that his 'freedom' has been 'cancelled'. 'Hurray for regular hours!', he shouts, 'And for the supervision of the spirit! Long live regimentation!' (DM 159). When DeLillo summons Bellow's ghost, in the aftermath of 9/11 and in the shadow of 'Operation Enduring Freedom', his aesthetics of falling are shaped by Joseph's fall, Joseph's plunge from the suspended isolation of his Beckettian room to the mud of a European battlefield. If it is dangling, or aesthetic suspension, that allows for a kind of coming together between DeLillo and Bellow – if their encounter in the back lanes of *Falling Man* and *Dangling Man* is made thinkable by the kind of immunity from the world and from world history that Joseph enjoys and endures during his wait – then perhaps what DeLillo is performing in *Falling Man* is the failure of this encounter, the impassability of this back lane. Joseph falls to a European death that marks the end of a historical era; DeLillo's man falls into the new world that is made on 11 September 2001. While the gestures of Falling Man and dangling man might rhyme, this may not suggest a coming together, a kind of continuity between before and after, but rather a separation, a disarticulation, in which Bellow's man is condemned to his fate – to the straits of his imperialism – as DeLillo's is to his. The possibility that one might craft an aesthetic space of Beckettian withdrawal from the world, a utopian critical space in which one is free from the demand to choose between undesirable alternatives – between us and them – is perhaps cancelled by the plunge both of DeLillo's and Bellow's men. *Falling Man* opens as the towers collapse, as the building comes flooding into the street, and this opening evokes the overwhelming sense that there is no gap, no partition, between the self and the world, that the violence of 9/11 has exposed or abandoned us to our world as the violence of World War II returned Joseph to his. The novel opens with the displaced, dislocated declaration that 'It was not a street anymore but a world' (FM 3). As for DeLillo, writing in 2001, 9/11 meant that 'bits of our world have crumbled into theirs', so the partitions that separate the world have come down, returning us to a terrible, unanchored homogeneity from which there is no withdrawal, a 'time and space of falling ash and near night'. 'This', the narrator writes at the opening of *Falling Man*, 'This was the world now' (FM 3).

To read such complete disarticulation between Bellow's and DeLillo's versions of falling, however, would be to misread both Bellow's and DeLillo's representation of falling, and of dangling. It may be that finding in *Dangling Man* a suspended, minor relation between Bellow and DeLillo requires us to read against the grain of Bellow's novel, but it is equally a violence against both Bellow and DeLillo to overlook the extent to which falling continues to be balanced, for both writers, against dangling, the extent to which entering the world remains balanced against and inhabited by a withdrawal from it. *Dangling Man* might set itself against Beckettian diminishment, as it might prioritize resolution over thought, worldliness over writerliness; but the beauty and delicacy of this novel is its forensic attentiveness to the unresolved tensions and contradictions between withdrawal and participation, between the writer and the world, between falling and dangling. Even when Joseph is cut down – even when he welcomes servitude and the terrible monocular vision required, he implies, of the soldier willing to die for a cause – what the novel leaves us with is not a final conclusion, but a kind of suspense. Joseph's agreement to fight for his country is an agreement to give 'certain blood' for 'uncertain reasons' (DM 69), and it is this careful and delicate combination of certainty and uncertainty, of necessarily deciding and necessarily failing to decide, that is the novel's legacy to DeLillo, rather than the adoption or rejection of a final position, gesture, or stance. Bellow's appearance in shadow form in *Falling Man* bestows this simultaneous certainty and uncertainty, this combination of weight and weightlessness. The critical tradition that has opposed Bellow's worldliness to Beckett's writerliness – 'Bellow's kinetic heroes', in Sarah Cohen's words, to 'Beckett's progressively immobile figures'[32] – has tended to obscure how much Bellow's writing shares with Beckett's, just as the critical insistence on Beckett's refusal of the world has occluded how much Beckett shares with Bellow. Bellow has appeared to be a writer who enters the world, as Beckett has appeared to withdraw from it. But Bellow's ghostly appearance in DeLillo suggests just how unsustainable this distinction is, just how porous this 'partition' is – in Beckett, in Bellow, and in DeLillo – between the 'mind' and the 'world'. In *Falling Man*, and in the fleeting shapes that those spectral figures that move within it make, it is possible to glimpse a realignment between Bellow and Beckett, in which Beckett partly enters into the world (or as DeLillo has put it in a recent letter to Gary Adelman 'extends into the world'[33]), and in which Bellow partly withdraws from it, in which the political and aesthetic connotations both of falling and dangling, of withdrawal and participation, are rethought, reshaped for the global conditions that operate after 9/11.

In *Falling Man*, this collapsing relationship between mind and world is thought through a difficult relationship between 'us' and 'them' – between the New York family whose story takes up the majority of the novel, and one of the 9/11 terrorists, Hammad, whose story is told in much briefer, curiously evacuated episodes spaced through the novel. The novel is balanced around its depiction of the relationship between these two worlds. The New Yorkers and the terrorists are confined to their separate rooms and to their separate sections in the novel, as Bellow's Joseph is confined to his room, as Beckett's characters are confined to theirs. But both the New Yorkers and the terrorists seek to build out from the room into the world, to make the world in their own image. Martin (an international art dealer, and Lianne's mother's lover) comments of the terrorists that 'They want their own place in the world, their own global union, not ours' (FM 116), and the novel is, in a sense, a performance of this struggle between two different visions of global union, a struggle which has some resonance with Huntington's 'clash of civilisations'. Hammad belongs to a long line of DeLillian artists/terrorists, plotters who are confined to their rooms, as Bill Gray and Abu Rashid are confined to their rooms in *Mao II*, as Bucky Wunderlick is confined to his room in *Great Jones Street*, as Taft is confined to his grey, Beckettian room in *End Zone*. This aesthetic of isolation in the room that runs through DeLillo's work is one of his most visible inheritances from Beckett,[34] but here, in *Falling Man*, the man in the room seeks, like Bellow's Joseph, to enter the world rather than to retreat from it. Hammad is told by Mohamed Atta that

> A man can stay forever in a room, doing blueprints, eating and sleeping, even praying, even plotting, but at a certain point he has to get out. Even if the room is a place of prayer, he can't stay there all his life. Islam is the world outside the prayer room as well as the *sūrahs* in the Koran. (FM 79–80)

The plot that builds in the novel towards the moment of impact between plane and building on the morning of September 11 is one which seeks to extend Hammad and Atta's vision of a global union out of the room and into the world. 'The time is coming', Atta says to Hammad, when 'each man becomes the other, and the other still another, and then there is no separation' (FM 80). Against this vision of an Islamic global unity, the New Yorker's seek to defend their own version of the world, a world steeped in that bourgeois individualism that Bellow's Joseph saw arising from the battlefields of Europe. Just as Hammad's world grows from a room in which one plots, and from the mind of the isolated plotter – 'the world changes first in the mind of the man who wants to change it', Hammad thinks – the New Yorker's world also unfolds from the room. At the heart of the New York sections of the novel is Lianne's mother's apartment, at the heart of which in turn hang two still lives by Giorgio Morandi. The paintings are represented in the novel in terms of their capital value. Lianne, we are told late in the novel, 'thought of the dollar value of the paintings' (FM 209), and the narrative dwells on the global transactions by which the paintings are acquired and sold by Martin, the international art dealer. But if their value and their meaning derives partly from their status as currency in a global market place – the market place, in Martin's terms, that forms 'our global union' – they also offer an aesthetic form in which the world might be composed, a means of conceiving the world which is balanced against that version of global union that is composed in the terrorist cells. The paintings hang on the wall in Lianne's mother's room, but they also appear, at times, to contain the room rather than be contained by it, to give a still life to the room and to the world, as the Remedio Varos painting 'Embroidering Earth's Mantle' produces the world which contains it in Thomas Pynchon's novel *The Crying of Lot 49*. Standing in her mother's room, gazing at the paintings, the 'two dark objects, the white bottle, the huddled boxes', Lianne experiences a curious kind of reversal, in which the artwork becomes the source of the world, rather than an object in it. 'Lianne turned away from the painting', we are told, 'and saw the room itself as a still life, briefly' (FM 111). Seeing Morandi's paintings hanging in a gallery later in the novel, Lianne again experiences this sense that the room and the world have their source, somehow, in painted forms. 'She noted the nature and shape of each object', we are told,

> the placement of objects, the tall dark oblongs, the white bottle. She could not help looking. There was something hidden in the painting. Nina's living room was there, memory and motion. (FM 210)

And if Lianne sees her mother's room held inchoately in the formal balance of the painting, as if through a Carrollian looking glass, then both she and Martin find in the painting a shape, a suggestion of the towers of the World Trade Center, again recalling the tower in Pynchon's Varos. 'Two of the taller items' in the painting 'were dark and somber, with smoky marks and smudges, and one of them was partly concealed by a long-necked bottle'. It is these 'two dark objects, too obscure to name' (FM 49) that become, for both Martin and Lianne, a presentiment and an after image of the towers, the towers that summon the future into being.

The climax of the novel depicts the clash of these two versions of the world, one unfolding from Hammad's terrorist cell, the other from Lianne's mother's New York apartment and Morandi's still lives. The last section of the novel, entitled 'In the Hudson Corridor', stages the collision of the unequal halves of the novel just as it stages the collision of plane and building. The chapter is fashioned, at its opening, as the last of the sections detailing the terrorist plot. 'In the Hudson Corridor' takes the terrorists to the very brink of the consummation of the plot, as the earlier sections – 'In Nokomis' and 'On Marienstrasse' – follow its long gestation in Germany and then in Florida. As the novel reaches the critical moment at which the plane strikes the tower, however, there is a seam in the narrative, at which the perspective passes from Hammad to Keith, from the terrorists to the New Yorkers. The impact occurs in the middle of a paragraph, which starts with Hammad sitting in the jump seat of the aircraft as the plane heads towards the tower:

> A bottle fell off the counter in the galley, on the other side of the aisle, and he watched it roll this way and that, a water bottle, empty, making an arc one way and rolling back the other, and he watched it spin more quickly and then skitter across the floor an instant before the aircraft struck the tower, heat, then fuel, then fire, and a blast wave passed through the structure that sent Keith Neudecker out of his chair and into a wall. He found himself walking into a wall. He didn't drop the telephone until he hit the wall. The floor began to slide beneath him and he lost his balance and eased along the wall to the floor. (FM 239)

This is arguably the most important paragraph in the novel, the moment at which the terrorists meet with their victims, before meets with after, 'us' meets with 'them'. It is also the passage in the novel in which the nature of the 'partition' between mind and world, between self and other, comes under the closest scrutiny. It is, however, a difficult passage to read, a passage which leads in opposite directions. In one sense, this moment constitutes a kind of aesthetic and political failure, an abandonment of the possibilities of ethical suspension that recalls Joseph's eventual forsaking of the intellectual freedom of his room for the brutal certainties of the battlefield. One can read this moment as the failure to think oneself into the mind and the space of the other, the recognition that the violent impact of plane with building makes it no longer possible to understand the world in what Bellow calls the 'spirit of alternatives'. For many of the novel's early reviewers, the central weakness of *Falling Man* is its failure to give any life to the sections of the novel which detail the terrorists' plot – the oddly formulaic and static quality of its portrait of Hammad.[35] While DeLillo's earlier portrayal of Lee Harvey Oswald in *Libra* is remarkable for its capacity to enter Oswald's skin, to bring the assassination of JFK to a vivid life from Oswald's perspective, the portrait of Hammad remains distant and stilted, as if the narrator cannot quite inhabit his mind or his space, as if 9/11 is an atrocity that overwhelms the poetic capacity to suspend judgement. This moment, the moment at which the narrative perspective slides from Hammad to Keith Neudecker, can be read as an acknowledgement or performance of this failure. As the event that is known as 9/11 begins to take place, the ability and the will to adopt Hammad's position – always in any case weak, reluctant, half-hearted – gives way altogether, returning us to the perspective – that of the bourgeois New Yorker – in which the narrative has always been at home. The moment of impact is one at which partitions give way, the steel partitions that separate the inside of a plane from the inside of an office building, as well as the papery partitions that separate the different sections of DeLillo's novel. With the collapse of these partitions, the novel perhaps suggests, it is no longer possible to withdraw from the world, to retreat to the room, to give oneself the intellectual freedom not to choose between undesirable alternatives, between 'us' and 'them'. To return to that structural contradiction that runs through DeLillo's essay on 9/11, the collapse of the partition here produces both the folding of two worlds into one – the 'crumbling' of their world into ours – and a new and violent disarticulation between 'us' and 'them', a disarticulation which, in an echo of George Bush's famous ultimatum, forces you to choose whether you are with us or against us, to suffer and perpetrate the intellectual and poetic violence of adopting a position.

There is, however, another and almost directly opposite way of reading this passage. The shift in narrative perspective at the moment of impact might suggest the failure of the novel to imagine or understand the perspective of the other – to let the subaltern speak – but it also produces an extraordinarily intimate and unboundaried coming together of them and us, of self and other. The violence of the impact – the violence that causes a 'blast wave' to pass through the 'structure' – inaugurates a kind of impossible unity between the oppositions that have driven the novel, a unity that is registered in the invisible, unnamable junction that the narrative forges here between Hammad and Keith Neudecker. The very impact that leads to a global 'disarticulation' – that, for DeLillo, produces a new antagonism between Islam and the West, between past and future – engenders also a peculiar kind of unity that is forged in the heat of that violent impact, but that does not have a language in which it might speak. At this moment, the worlds that unfold from Hammad's room and from Lianne's mother's room enter into a kind of conjunction. The bottle that skitters along the floor in the seconds before impact, animated by the energy of the hot fusion that is about to take place, is inhabited in some fashion by the bottle in Morandi's still life, as if the painting, which contains the towers in its smudged forms as well as Lianne's mother's room, is reaching across the partition into the galley, seeking to animate, to give life. And the world that Hammad and Atta prepare in their rooms in Germany and Florida is also realized, in a sense, as the impact occurs, as the walls of the building and of the narrative give way. Atta tells Hammad that the 'time is coming' when 'each man becomes the other, and the other still another, and then there is no separation' (FM 80), and this moment in the narrative lives out precisely this unity, this loss of separation between self and other, between victim and perpetrator, between Hammad and Keith. The global melding that Hammad and Atta seek is of course not the unity that emerges here; indeed it is no more a way of imagining 'their' global union than it is a way of conceiving 'ours'. This is an unboundaried aesthetic unity – a 'way of being we' shadowed forth by the peculiar conjunction between inside and outside, between stone and haze, fleetingly fashioned in Beckett's *The Lost Ones* and *Ill Seen Ill Said* – rather than the unity imagined either by Atta and Hammad, or by the architects of the global market place. But the beauty of DeLillo's depiction of the collision here is that the brutality of the impact between two worlds gives rise both to a political and aesthetic failure to imagine an accommodation between self and other, between past and future, and this delicate new form in which precisely such accommodation might yet be thought, in which we might attain the 'glimpse' of 'us in them' and of 'them in us' that Beckett imagines in 1946. The attacks, as DeLillo writes in 2001, open up a new global 'front', producing a scenario in which there are 'two forces in the world, past and future'; but it also brings past and future, 'before' the impact and 'after' into this new continuity, this new simultaneity. The junction in the narrative here marks the partition between the time before, and the new time in which 'everything is measured by after', but it also produces an immeasurable, untensed continuity, bringing the novel back to the moments with which it started, making of the narrative a kind of Joycean loop.

To understand the doubleness of this moment, to find a way of accommodating these two different readings of DeLillo's dramatization of the moment of impact, requires us to respond to the aesthetics of suspension – of arrested motion – that is developed in the novel. *Falling Man* is driven, to a degree, by the gravitational force that brings the tower down after its impact with Hammad's plane. The narrative opens in the midst of the tower's collapse, when 'the roar was still in the air, the buckling rumble of the fall', and this falling, this tumbling, is in a sense the medium in which the novel takes place. This, the narrator writes at the opening of the novel, 'was the world now. Smoke and ash came rolling down streets and turning corners, busting around corners, seismic tides of smoke, with office paper flashing past' (FM 3). This depiction of a world in the grip of an extended demolition, of what Beckett's Molloy calls an 'endless collapse' (Mo 40), resonates with the sense, at the close of the novel, that Hammad's and Keith's world's collide, that the moment of impact constitutes a brutal assault in which the possibility of convergence or accommodation between self and other suddenly and radically expires. This gravitational force that thrills through the novel calls to Joseph's fall in Bellow's novel, his final acceptance of the world over the mind, action over thought, us over them. But, throughout the novel, this engagement with the staggering kinetic forces that transformed New York into a ruin – so suddenly and so devastatingly – is balanced against an opposite investment in a kind of anti-gravitational poetics. Just as Joseph's fall in Bellow's novel remains inhabited by or weighed against his dangling – just as the need to decide is weighed against the continuing failure to decide – so the heavy momentum of falling in *Falling Man* is countered, throughout, by a certain weightlessness, an aesthetic suspension in which the brutality of impact gives way to the possibility of an unnamable, utopian convergence. Even as the novel opens into the unfurling chaos of September 11 – into what the narrator describes as the 'writhing core' of the event itself – this weightlessness, this stillness makes itself felt. Keith thinks to himself that the event 'happened everywhere around him', but this sense of overwhelming activity, of being in the grip of fundamental physical forces, does not amount to an experience of presence, a sense that one is thrust into the world. Rather, it produces an experience of that 'something less than presence' that Shane Weller finds in Beckett's work (see p. 130). The event is everywhere around him, but, Keith thinks, 'things inside were distant and still, where he was supposed to be' (FM 3). The entire scene, even in the midst of such frenzy, exhibits this distance, this stillness, this peculiar slowness. 'Paper cups', we are told, 'went bouncing oddly by', catching at the movement of that Morandian bottle in the final pages of the novel, a movement at once energized and peculiarly slowed down. Similarly, the path of a falling shirt – presaging the arrested plunge of DeLillo's Falling Man, whose act performs a strange combination of motion and arrested motion – seems at once to suggest flight and descent: a 'shirt came down out of the high smoke', we are told, 'a shirt lifted and drifting in the scant light and then falling again toward the river' (FM 4). Keith's dazed attention in those first moments takes in the fleeing crowds, the panicked pandemonium, but he also sees in the crowds a kind of evacuated stillness, just as the plunge of the falling shirt seems to carry within itself a lightness, a disinclination to fall. 'He saw members of the tai chi group from the park nearby', we are told, 'standing with hands extended at roughly chest level, elbows bent, as if all this, themselves included, might be placed in a state of abeyance' (FM 4).

It is in this empty space, this frozen abeyance at the heart of things, that one can glimpse the possibility of a utopian convergence between us and them – that one can begin to read the 'counternarrative' that DeLillo seeks to hang in the emptiness of the post-9/11 sky. It is also in this slow motion, this arrested fall, that one can most clearly divine Beckett's spectral presence in *Falling Man*, a shadowy presence that is merged strangely with Bellow's simultaneously falling and dangling forms, and that resonates with a wider slow current in contemporary writing. When Molloy talks of an 'endless collapse', he is referring to what he calls his 'ruins', the ruins of the Beckettian self that Bellow argues lead us to an impasse. But Molloy's vision of a world and a self in ruins points, already, to a kind of new beginning, a kind of suspended continuation that is born out of the ruin. 'I listen', writes Molloy,

> and the voice is of a world collapsing endlessly, a frozen world, under a faint untroubled sky, enough to see by, yes, and frozen too. And I hear it murmur that all wilts and yields, as if loaded down, but here there are no loads, and the ground too, unfit for loads, and the light too, down towards an end that can never come. For what possible end to these wastes where true light never was, nor any upright thing, nor any true foundation, but only these leaning things, forever lapsing and crumbling away, beneath a sky without memory of morning or hope of night. (Mo 40)

It is this combination of stillness and motion that underlies the poetics of the suspended fall in *Falling Man*. The world that Molloy envisions here, in which there are no more 'upright things', a world in which all is leaning, all is falling, a 'world at an end' (Mo 40), as Molloy puts it, is the world that is brought about, in DeLillo's novel, by the collapse of the World Trade Center. The ruins of DeLillo's future are also Beckett's ruins, from *Molloy*, from his 'Capital of the Ruins', the ruins that are the 'true refuge long last' of *Lessness* (CSP 197–8). In DeLillo's collapsing, crumbling world, there are no more upright things; the 'strands of bent filigree' that are the remains of the towers, he writes, are the 'last standing things' (FM 25). But in *Molloy*, and in *Falling Man*, the experience of 'lapsing', of 'crumbling' of 'falling', opens onto the opposite experience of continuation, of suspension. 'These leaning things', Molloy writes, are 'forever lapsing', as DeLillo's Falling Man is forever falling. The freezing of the world, in Molloy's vision, suggests a global endedness, an arrival at the becalmed end of history evoked, in a somewhat different fashion, by Francis Fukuyama. But freezing here suggests also a kind of extended duration – the stretched, distended time granted to the visual imagination by the development of the freeze frame, and of cinematic slow motion. The kinetic energy of collapse, in Beckett and DeLillo, is sustained but also countered by the weightless suspension of the frozen, suspended image, as the depiction of the end of history opens onto a peculiar, wordless surplus, a new time and space that emerges from collapse, unnamed, untensed and unlocated. Molloy's ruins are a 'world at an end', but they are also a world that cannot end – 'its end brought it forth', he writes, 'ending it began' (Mo 40). DeLillo's ruins, similarly, bring forth a kind of still stirring – the kind of still movement that is glimpsed in the heart of Morandi's still lives, as it is brought to an arrested life by the figure of DeLillo's dangling performance artist, frozen in an endless fall over the mourning city.

Throughout *Falling Man*, it is possible to feel the influence of this slowness – the 'slow going' that Steven Connor identifies as a formal quality shared by Beckett and 'other arts and artists of the dilatory'.[36] Connor suggests that *The Lost Ones*, in its depiction of the infinitely slow passage of time in the cylinder, acts as a 'kind of interval, a turbulent suspension in the senseless and insensible unspooling of things in general',[37] and it is this interval, this turbulent suspension, that Beckett leaves to DeLillo, and to other contemporary 'artists of the dilatory'. J. M. Coetzee's recent novel *Slow Man* is perhaps one of the more striking examples of this development of a slow current in contemporary culture, a current which is bound up with and emerges from Beckett's static motion, his still stirring. Like *Falling Man*, Coetzee's *Slow Man* turns around a temporal split, a brutal disjunction between past and future, between before and after. The novel tells the story of an accident which leaves the protagonist, Paul Rayment, with one leg amputated above the knee, and of Rayment's adjustment to a circumscribed life in the accident's wake, a life in which, like so many of Beckett's characters (although unlike Beckett's one-legged circumnavigator), Rayment will have to get about, if at all, on crutches, or by other artificially assisted means. It is this accident, and even more this amputation, that makes a temporal disjunction in the novel, a cut in time as much as a cut in flesh. 'In his case', Rayment reflects, 'the cut seems to have marked off past from future with such uncommon cleanness that it gives new meaning to the word *new*' (SM 26). This schism between before and after, between past and future, produces in Rayment a sensation of falling that again resonates with DeLillo's *Falling Man*. The accident, Rayment thinks, has caused him to become '*unstrung*':

> That is the word that comes back to him from Homer. The spear shatters the breastbone, blood spurts, the limbs are unstrung, the body topples like a wooden puppet. Well, his limbs have been unstrung and now his body is unstrung too. His spirit is ready to topple.[38]

As Bellow's Joseph experiences his entry into the war as an unstringing, so here Rayment feels that the event of the accident and the surgery causes him to be cut down, causes a severing of the muscly strings that hold his body upright.

But while the novel performs this entry into the newness of disability as a form of falling, it also investigates the possibilities of a kind of Kleistian suspension, a suspension that, as in DeLillo, is both opposed to and won from the act of falling. As in Coetzee's earlier work *The Master of Petersburg* – in which Coetzee's Dostoevsky figure seeks to reclaim his son from the fall that led him to his death by counteracting falling with a kind of suspended poetic temporality[39] – so in *Slow Man* the fall to illness, death, inertness, is held against a slow suspension that is produced by the artwork itself. The novel produces such slowness as a response to the time of mourning, that disjunct time that finds an earlier manifestation in *Hamlet*. Rayment's response to his injury becomes a mourning for his lost body part, a body part that continues to haunt him as if it were a phantom limb.[40] As Dostoevsky seeks to slow time down in order to hold his son suspended on the brink of annihilation (to 'keep Pavel alive, suspended in his fall'),[41] so Rayment seeks to hold on to his lost body by refusing the narrative of recovery, refusing to be fitted with a prosthesis, refusing to re-enter the temporal stream, to belong to the time when 'everything is measured by after'. Instead, he adopts the position of one of Beckett's indolent characters, resisting the pull of plot, resisting all attempts by Elizabeth Costello (the novel's writer figure and Coetzee's 'alter ego') to make him behave like a good dramatic character. As Belacqua refuses to conform to the demands of the plot in *Dream of Fair to Middling Women*, as Viktor Krapp refuses to obey the demands of the script and of the audience in Beckett's first full-length play *Eleutheria*, so Rayment frustrates all of the various figures and forces in the novel that seek to move him along, to return him to health and motion in the here and now. Costello complains that Rayment becomes less and less functional as a protagonist as the novel continues, that he goes 'slower and slower, till by now you are almost at a halt' (SM 100), and that the people who are drawn into his gravitational field are struck by a similar inertia. The characters in the story, she complains, become 'four people in four corners, moping, like tramps in Beckett, and myself in the middle, wasting time, being wasted by time' (SM 141). Costello suggests to Rayment that she should tell his stories for him, that she should take his slowed life and speed it up. 'You can tell me more stories from your treasure hoard', she says to Paul, 'which I will afterwards tell back to you in a form so accelerated and improved that you will hardly recognise them' (SM 232). Costello's capacity, however, to inject such pace is undermined by another kind of haunting, another phantom limb. The words that Costello uses here, in her anxiety to move things along, echo that refrain in Beckett's *Murphy* which the narrator repeatedly inserts into his own story, interjecting to insist that he is speeding things up while, as Steven Connor has pointed out, actually slowing things down.[42] Like Costello, the narrator of *Murphy* insists that all of his stories are 'expurgated, accelerated, improved and reduced' (Mu 70), but, in *Murphy* and in *Slow Man*, such narrative improvement, such acceleration, leads only to a stalled circling around the empty time marked by Murphy, and by Rayment.

Such slowness, such resistance to the onward thrust of time, frustrates Costello. Like her character, she too feels like the tensile strength has drained from her body as a result of such stasis; she too feels that she has been '*unstrung*' (SM 160), that 'the bowstring that used to be taut has gone as slack and dry as a strand of cotton' (SM 160). But if this slowness, if this refusal of the conventions and the temporality of narrative leads to a certain disarticulation between before and after, between narrator and narrative, then it is also from this suspension that the novel points to a new form of accommodation between them. When Rayment is in his immediate recovery phase, and is making the decision to refuse his prosthesis, a nurse named Madeline urges him to give up on his old body, to embrace what she call his 'new body', and what Rayment refers to as his 'truncated old body'. Madeline admits that 'limbs have memories', but says that her 'job' is

> To reprogram old and now obsolete memory systems that dictate to us how we balance, how we walk, how we run. 'Of course we want to hold on to our old memory systems', she says. 'Otherwise we would not be human. But we must not hold on to them when they hinder our progress. Not when they get in our way'. (SM 60)

The slow going in *Slow Man* is built around an ardent refusal of this conception of the relationship between memory and progress. The stasis around which the novel revolves is one which seeks to imagine a form in which 'obsolete memory systems' remain in contact with the current, with the contemporary. The slow suspension that Coetzee develops in *Slow Man*, and in his later fiction more generally, becomes a medium in which past and future, in which narrator and narrated, in which self and other, human and animal, enter into a new kind of relationship, a relationship which points towards a radical new conception of the ethical and political possibilities of fiction.

In *Falling Man*, DeLillo crafts a poetics of gesture – of the body in space and time – that resonates richly with Coetzee's, and that is shaped, throughout, by Beckett's slowness, as if a current of slow motion runs through the text, catching at every pose, at every sentence, lending to every falling, moving thing a fleeting immunity from the twin demands of gravity and of passing time. This is the immunity that Dorothy Richardson finds in early cinematic slow motion, the 'most priceless offering to date of the film considered as a vehicle for revealing to mankind that in man which is unbounded'.[43] The falling flight, the lifting fall of the shirt that comes down from the tower in the opening pages of DeLillo's novel is shaped by this slow current, held in abeyance like the bodies of the tai chi group members in the park, like Rayment's newly balanced, Kleistian body, and this current that lifts and holds in the opening pages of the novel shows itself time and time again. Keith Neudecker, injured in the maelstrom in the tower, is given a course of physiotherapy to help heal a postsurgical wrist, and these exercises become a form of physical mantra, a set of slow movements that turn around a still centre; programmed, repeated movements that recall the poetics of gesture in DeLillo's earlier novel *End Zone*, which is in turn organized around the slowness of movement in Beckett's late work – in his Rotunda texts, and his late pieces for stage and television. These exercises, termed by the physiotherapists the 'gentle fist', are a meditative, gestural response to the brutality of the impact, an attempt to find a gentle 'countermeasure', to find in the fury of 9/11 a kind of slowed calm. 'He sat alongside the table', the narrative reads, 'left forearm placed along the near edge, hand dangling from the adjoining edge, curled into a gentle fist. He raised the hand without lifting his forearm and kept it in the air for five seconds'. The narrative attention to bodily detail, to the angle that bodies make to floor and to ceiling, produces a kind of suspension in the narrative, a restorative lightness made from slowness, from mantric repetition, from counting out seconds and ritual movements. It recalls that Beckettian, mathematical concentration on bodily placement in DeLillo's earlier fiction, his sense that 'history is the placement of bodies'.[44] 'He found these sessions restorative', the narrative goes on,

> four times a day, the wrist extensions, the ulnar deviations. These were the true countermeasures to the damage he'd suffered in the tower, in the descending chaos [. . .] His injury was slight but it wasn't the torn cartilage that was the subject of this effort. It was the chaos, the levitation of ceilings and floors, the voices choking in smoke. He sat in deep concentration, working on the hand shapes, the bend of the wrist toward the floor, the bend of the wrist toward the ceiling, the forearm flat on the table, the thumb-up configuration in certain setups, the use of the uninvolved hand to apply pressure to the involved hand. (FM 40)

The 'levitation' of floors and ceilings in the moments of impact, as a 'blast wave passed through the structure', is recreated here, but in slow motion, in a gestural meditation that works back to the event, that holds the event open, feeling for the possibilities of gentle convergence that are held, in abeyance, in the violent coming together of plane and building.

Again and again the narrative enters into the influence of this lifting slowness, in which one can glimpse the possibility of a utopian convergence, of a world ordered differently. Keith Neudecker's immersion in the world of poker, Lianne's immersion in her work with Alzheimer's patients, Lianne and Keith's son's concentration on speaking slowly, in single syllables (speaking in single syllables, Justin says to his father, 'helps me go slow when I think' [FM 66]); all these forms of rigour, these forms of contraction, erasure and concentration, are attempts to tune according to the narrative's slow current, the current that runs backwards, lifting the novel's falling particles, working into the endless moments of the tower's collapse. Lianne thinks of the forgetfulness, the unfolding of self brought about by Alzheimer's as a kind of falling, a kind of 'rough tumble through space' (FM 187), that recalls the fall of the photographed falling man on the morning of September 11, the 'ideal falling motion', Lianne thinks 'of a body that is subject only to the earth's gravitational field' (FM 221). But the falling brought about by Alzheimer's is a kind of slow, antigravitational falling, the kind of falling diminishment that Beckett's Murphy and Bellow's Joseph experience in their rocking chairs, that Lianne thinks of elsewhere as a 'falling out of the world', and that Keith thinks of as a 'going slow, an easing inward' (FM 66). Rosellen S., one of the Alzheimer's patients, describes an episode of acute forgetfulness, in which, she says,

> the world was receding, the simplest recognitions. She began to lose her sense of clarity, of distinctness. She was not lost so much as falling, growing fainter. Nothing lay around her but silence and distance. (FM 94)

This sense of a slow falling, an endless lapsing, produces a kind of weightless evacuation of the self, the condition that Keith recognizes at the opening of the novel, in which 'things inside were distant and still'. Lianne's patients speak of the difficulty they have aligning their diminishing selves with their bodies in the world. In a passage that is ghosted by Vladimir and Estragon's comic business in *Waiting for Godot*, their trying on of hats and of boots, Benny T. describes how difficult it is for him to fit inside his clothes, to fit inside his body. 'He was in a mind and body', he tells the group,

> that were not his, looking at the fit. The pants did not seem to fit right. He took them off and put them on. He shook them out. He looked inside them. He began to think they were someone else's pants, in his house, draped over his chair. (FM 94–5)

Curtis B., another patient, describes how difficult it is for him to attach his wristwatch to his wrist. 'There it was', he says, 'the watch':

> He said this gravely. There it was in my right hand. But the right hand could not find its way to the left wrist. There was a spatial void, or a visual gap, a rift in his field of vision, and it took him some time to make the connection, hand to wrist, pointed end of wrist band into buckle. (FM 95)

The slow current that runs through the novel opens this spatial void, this gap between bodies in space, producing an odd emptiness, an oddly unmade space and time in which the displaced, endlessly falling elements of the novel hang, estranged from themselves and from each other, waiting for a form to emerge in which their new alignment might find itself spoken, and embodied.

The image, of course, in which this evacuated, displaced slowness finds its most arresting expression is that of the Falling Man himself, an image in which the shades of Beckett and Bellow find a kind of community, a way of being we, and which reaches also to other contemporary writers, other 'artists of the dilatory' who are seeking to fashion an ethical response to global politics after 9/11. The simultaneously falling and dangling man is caught in the novel's slow current, prevented from falling both by the frozen magic of photography, and by the novel's own formal capacity to slow down time, or as DeLillo's Beckettian artist Bucky Wunderlick puts it, to 'stretch a given minute', to separate its 'unstuck components' (GJS 121). In planing in such a way on the poetic thermals of the novel, in giving an expression both to the gravitational need to fall and the poetic and ethical imperative to dangle, DeLillo's falling man carves open a new space – a utopian space in which Hammad and Keith, Beckett's Murphy and Bellow's Joseph, mind and world, inside and outside, enter into an unbounded conjunction. Lianne sees the Falling Man as he prepares to make his final fall in the novel, and she sees the possibility of this conjunction written in his face:

> The man stared into the brickwork of the corner building but did not see it. There was a blankness in his face, but deep, a kind of lost gaze [. . .] She thought the bare space he stared into must be his own, not some vision of others falling. (FM 167)

As the Falling Man prepares to jump here, Lianne sees in his gaze the absence from self that Keith feels in the opening page of the novel, and that infects the whole city – the absence from self that Lianne finds in the line she adapts from Basho, 'even in New York I long for New York'. If post-9/11 New York is a city that is distant from itself, that is not there even when one is standing in it, then the Falling Man, too, finds that he is distant from himself as he prepares to enter the body posture of a hauntingly absent other, or a host of absent others. As so many of DeLillo's characters find that they are 'there', rather than 'here',[45] as Molloy finds that he is 'there' rather than 'here' at the opening of *Molloy*, so the Falling Man finds himself not inside his own body, not inside his own blank face, but projected onto the 'bare space' of the city, a city which itself is undergoing a displacement, a dislocation. His lost gaze might recall the gaze of those lost ones in Beckett's cylinder, who experience a similar evacuation of self, who find themselves similarly projected onto their bare environment ('None looks within himself' the narrator writes, 'where none can be' [CSP 211]). As he jumps and falls, the Falling Man, and Lianne, and the other spectators of the scene, all enter into a kind of shared stillness, a shared evacuation of self, in which each 'becomes the other, and the other still another, and then there is no separation' (FM 80). As he falls to the end of his rope, as his body feels 'the jolt, the sort of mid air impact and bounce, the recoil, and now the stillness' – the peculiar physical effects of his adopting the weightless attitude of a man in a photograph – Lianne feels the weight and the weightlessness in her own body. As Mrs Dalloway experiences in her body the suicidal fall of Septimus Warren Smith in *Mrs Dalloway*,[46] so Lianne's body goes through the Falling Man's plunge, feels 'her body go limp' (FM 168), in the same way that she feels the impact of the plane with the building when she watches the event on television ('This was the footage', she thinks, 'that entered the body, that seemed to run beneath her skin' [FM 134]). And another spectator, a 'derelict on the street', enters also into this collective, uncentered body, this distance from self which becomes also a peculiar fusing with the other, an entering into the body space of the other that prepares for and is built upon the merging of Hammad's and Keith's minds and bodies at the looped beginning and end of the novel. The 'derelict', we are told, 'seemed to be in a pose of his own', a pose that shapes itself to the pose of the falling man:

> His face showed an intense narrowing of thought and possibility. He was seeing something elaborately different from what he encountered step by step in the ordinary run of hours. He had to learn how to see it correctly, find a crack in the world where it might fit. (FM 168)

The intense, narrowing face of the spectator here mirrors the blank face of the Falling Man, as the two figures arrange themselves, pose themselves, around the shared space that the performance opens in the world. What Falling Man's performance and DeLillo's novel are searching for here is a new poetics of vision – a way to think and see – that can tune itself to the Darwinian, Bowenesque 'fit' that is made here between self and other, between self and world, a new way of being we. The performance marks the voided space of an accommodation between falling and dangling, between us and them, between self and other, an accommodation which exceeds the existing conditions, in the words of the above quotation, of 'thought and possibility'. This is a space which is found in that 'rift' that opens in Curtis B.'s field of vision, the rift that opens when the forces that hold the world together in its current form become unstuck. It is a space which is simultaneously withdrawn from the world and thrust into it, a space which is conjured from the collapse of the partitions that separates east from west in *Ill Seen Ill Said*, the dissolution of the partitions that divide and fail to divide inside from outside in *The Lost Ones*. Watching the tower falling, Keith experiences that same identity with the building that Lianne feels when she watches the attacks on television, and that Martin finds in the Morandi still life. As the sound of the fall is 'trembling in the air' Keith thinks that there was 'something critically missing from the things around him' (FM 5). But this emptiness in the sky, this emptiness that witnesses the irruption of the unseen other into the very heartland of the self, does not only produce evacuation, or distance; it also produces an unknown, unnamed, utopian unity, that is neither our global union or theirs, but the world as it might be, the world as it ought to be, the world as it cannot yet be. As he hears the 'sound of the second fall, or felt it in the trembling air', Keith thinks of himself as at one with the building, as it enters into its long, distended fall, its endless lapsing. 'That was him coming down', Keith thinks, 'the north tower' (FM 5).

The identity that is imagined here, the 'we' that is formed in the slow merging of falling and dangling, is the ghosted image of a democracy that, in Derrida's formulation, is still to come. This is a we that knows nothing of Huntington's 'clash of civilizations', that does not find itself enfranchised within Fukuyama's global liberal democracy, nor disarticulated by Baudrillard's conception of a globalization battling against itself. It is a trembling, unformed 'we' that is shaped in Beckett's imperceptible unities, and that returns in the spatial voids, the rifts in the field of vision, that DeLillo opens in the New York sky. At the opening of his recent book on democracy and the 'rogue state', Derrida suggests that the '"major event" dated "September 11, 2001"' has 'mediatheatricalised' elements of the relationship between globalization, sovereignty and democracy that have had a long gestation in the culture, and brought certain questions to a new urgency. 'What is happening', Derrida asks,

> to the notions of the 'political' and of 'war' (whether world war, war between nation-states, civil war, or even so-called partisan war)? What happens to the notion of 'terrorism' (whether national or international) when the old phantom of sovereignty loses its credibility?[47]

Should we address these questions, he asks (with an implicit reference to Hardt and Negri's response to the same problems) through reference to an existing political vocabulary? Can we think about 'globalisation', or 'the "question of the United States," the question of their "right of the strongest"', in terms of 'Hegemony? Supremacy? A new figure of Empire or imperialism?'. 'Should we be satisfied with this vocabulary', he asks, 'or should we, with no compass to orient us, seek something else?'.[48] The book that Derrida goes on to write after he poses these questions is an attempt to orient himself, without a north, to this something else, this possibility of a democratic 'we'. Democracy, he argues, as a way of being we, has never been properly thinkable, it has never 'presented itself'.[49] The contradictions that run through the very concept of democracy make it impossible for us to imagine or theorize a democratic condition – a condition in which we are both absolutely free and absolutely equal. 'Equality', Derrida writes, 'tends to introduce measure and calculation (and thus conditionality) whereas freedom is by essence unconditional, indivisible, heterogeneous to calculation and measure'.[50] As Jean Luc Nancy puts it, 'freedom measures itself against nothing'.[51] This unthinkability, this 'aporicity' at the heart of democracy, means that democracy has remained unknown to us, even though it continues to enjoin us, to make of us a people. 'We do not yet know what we have inherited', Derrida writes:

> We are legatees of this Greek word and of what it assigns to us, enjoins us, bequeaths or leaves to us, indeed delegates or leaves over to us. We are undeniably the heirs or legatees, the delegates, of this word, and we are saying 'we' here as the very legatees or delegates of this word that has been sent to us, addressed to us for centuries, and that we are always sending or putting off until later. There are, to be sure, claims or allegations of democracy everywhere, everywhere 'we' are; but we ourselves do not know the meaning of this legacy, the mission, emission, or commission of this word or the legitimacy of this claim or allegation.[52]

It is our inheritance of the word democracy that instantiates us as a 'we', but, Derrida argues, the word has always named something that is not yet in the world – has always functioned, he writes, as a 'claim or allegation, a deferral to later, a utopia, indeed the fiction of a democracy to come'.[53] The failure of democracy to 'present itself', the unthinkability, or even impossibility of democracy, however, does not free us from our responsibility to it, or free us from the ethical injunction to act in its name, to struggle towards it even though we don't know what it is, even though there is no compass to point us in its direction. 'Even though we know so little about what "democracy" should mean', Derrida writes, 'it is still necessary, through a kind of precomprehension, to know something about it'. We must, he enjoins, 'move toward the horizon that limits the meaning of the word, in order to come to know better what "democracy"' will have been able to signify, what it *ought*, in truth, to have meant'.[54]

It is this unthinkable, unbounded democracy, this being we, that is Beckett's legacy to us, even if a legacy that he himself is yet to inherit, an injunction or imperative to which he himself could only fail to respond. Beckett's writing glimpses a democracy, glimpses the possibility of a post-sovereign, post-national global union, through a kind of Derridean precomprehension, an intuitive articulation of what Bloch calls the not yet conscious. His work annexes the future in which that unthinkable 'justice' that animates the crawl through the mud in *How It Is*, the ceaseless searching in *The Lost Ones*, is at home, free from the contradictions that bedevil our attempts to think democracy. It brings the time to come into a kind of unthinkable contact with the here and now, as DeLillo suggests the towers of the World Trade Center summoned us all to live prematurely in the future, as DeLillo's *Falling Man* makes an odd suture between past and future, between before and after. In making this future available, Beckett produces some of the forms in which 'our condition is to be thought again', some of the forms that emerge and re-emerge across the range of contemporary cultural expression, the forms in which we reach for an articulation of an ethical life, reach towards that democracy that remains beyond our grasp. Beckett, of course, does not provide for us a language in which a global democracy might be spoken, does not give us any clues about how to form what Fukuyama thinks of as the best of all possible forms of government. He does not tell us how it ought to be. But his writing does bring us toward the 'horizon that limits the meaning of the word' democracy, does allow us, in Blanchot's terminology, to hear a call from that future where democracy is present to itself, so that we might, as Derrida puts it, have 'some *idea* of democracy', an idea without which we 'would never seek to elucidate its meaning or, indeed, call for its advent'.[55] Beckett contents himself with saying how it is, rather than troubling himself with speculating on how it ought to be; but in denying the 'ought', in refusing to give us a picture of the future, or to tell us what we should hope for, his work reveals the extent to which 'is' is shadowed and formed by 'ought', the extent to which the present is inhabited, oriented by a future which lives within it, but which cannot speak. As the narrator of *How It Is* finds that his story comes to him from somewhere beyond the far horizon of the work, somewhere beyond part three where, he says, he 'has his life', so Beckett's writing derives, in part, from a place and time that is still to come, and is spoken by an unbodied, silent voice which we are still learning to hear. To be 'since Beckett', as in Derrida's haunted reading of Marx, is to be since that 'post-mortem' voice which comes to us from a democratic future that has not yet presented itself, to be since the future that Beckett's work brings to the trembling verge of the perceptible.

Notes

Introduction: Since Beckett

[1] There is a large body of critical work dedicated to following the figuring of the end in Beckett's writing. For a response to this question of persistence in Beckett, which includes a useful gloss on the various critical positions in relation to it, see Russell Smith, 'Beckett's Endlessness: Rewriting Modernity and the Postmodern Sublime', in Uhlmann, Anthony, Sjef Houppermans and Bruno Clément, eds, *After Beckett / D'apres Beckett, Samuel Beckett Today / 'Aujourd'hui'*, vol. 14, 2000, pp. 405–20.

[2] See Martin Esslin, 'Samuel Beckett: The Search for Self', in Martin Esslin, *The Theatre of the Absurd*, third edition (London: Penguin, 1991) pp. 50, 52, where Esslin writes that the 'subject' of *Waiting for Godot* 'is not Godot but waiting, the act of waiting as an essential and characteristic aspect of the human condition'. 'Waiting', Esslin argues, 'is to experience the action of time, which is constant change. And yet, as nothing real ever happens, that change itself is an illusion. The ceaseless activity of time is self-defeating, purposeless, and therefore null and void. The more things change, the more they are the same'. See also Alain Robbe-Grillet's essay 'Samuel Beckett, or Presence on the Stage', in which Robbe-Grillet argues that Beckett's drama allows us to 'see man'. We can see man, he argues, 'alone on stage, standing up, futile, with no future or past, irremediably present' (Alain Robbe-Grillet, 'Samuel Beckett, or Presence on the Stage', in Alain Robbe-Grillet, *For a New Novel: Essays on Fiction* [Salem: Ayer Company Publishers, 1965], trans. Richard Howard, p. 119).

[3] There have been a number of seminal publications which have defined the theoretical approaches to Beckett's work. See for example, Steven Connor, *Samuel Beckett: Repetition, Theory and Text* (Oxford: Blackwell, 1988), Leslie Hill, *Beckett's Fiction: In Different Words* (Cambridge: Cambridge University Press, 1990) and Andrew Gibson, *Beckett and Badiou: The Pathos of Intermittency* (Oxford: Oxford University Press, 2006). Anthony Uhlmann, in *Beckett and Poststructuralism* (Cambridge: Cambridge University Press, 1999), sets out to produce a poststructuralist reading of Beckett which is also historically located.

[4] Theodor Adorno, 'Cultural Criticism and Society', in Theodor Adorno, *Prisms* (Cambridge: The MIT Press, 1983), trans. Samuel and Shierry Weber, p. 34. The Benjaminian dialectic that Adorno refers to here is drawn from Benjamin's essay,

'Theses on the Philosophy of History', where Benjamin writes that 'there is no document of civilization which is not at the same time a document of barbarism' (Walter Benjamin, 'Theses on the Philosophy of History', in Walter Benjamin, *Illuminations* [London: Pimlico, 1999], trans. Harry Zorn, p. 248).
5. Adorno, 'Cultural Criticism and Society', p. 34.
6. Theodor Adorno, 'Trying to Understand *Endgame*', in Theodor Adorno, *Notes to Literature*, vol. 1 (New York: Columbia University Press, 1991), trans. Shierry Weber Nicholsen, p. 247.
7. W. J. McCormack, From Burke to Beckett: Ascendancy, Tradition and Betrayal in Literary History (Cork: Cork University Press, 1994), p. 413.
8. Adorno, 'Trying to understand *Endgame*', p. 247.
9. See Anthony Cronin, *Samuel Beckett: The Last Modernist* (London: Harper Collins, 1996). The title of the biography is indicative of Beckett's iconic status as the last modernist, but the biography itself touches only fleetingly on Beckett's engagement with modernism.
10. Richard Begam, *Samuel Beckett and the End of Modernity* (Stanford: Stanford University Press, 1996), p. 7.
11. Begam, Samuel Beckett and the End of Modernity, p. 187.
12. Begam, Samuel Beckett and the End of Modernity, p. 186.
13. Begam, Samuel Beckett and the End of Modernity, p. 186.
14. For a recent reading of Jameson's symptoms, see Ian Buchanan, *Frederic Jameson: Live Theory* (London: Continuum, 2006), pp. 89–102.
15. See Matthew Feldman, *Beckett's Books: A Cultural History of Samuel Beckett's 'Interwar Notes'* (London: Continuum, 2006), and Matthew Feldman and Mark Nixon, eds, *Beckett's Literary Legacies* (Cambridge: Cambridge Scholars Press, 2007).
16. Daniela Caselli, *Beckett's Dantes: Intertextuality in the Fiction and Criticism* (Manchester: Manchester University Press, 2006).
17. See James Knowlson and Elizabeth Knowlson, eds, *Beckett Remembering / Remembering Beckett: Uncollected Interviews with Samuel Beckett and Memories of Those Who Knew Him* (London: Bloomsbury, 2006), and Anthony Uhlmann Sjef Houppermans and Bruno Clément, eds, *After Beckett / D'apres Beckett, Samuel Beckett Today / Aujourd'hui'*, vol. 14, p. 200.
18. For a reading of Pinter's work in a Beckettian absurdist tradition, see Martin Esslin, 'Harold Pinter: Certainties and Uncertainties', in Esslin, *Theatre of the Absurd*, pp. 234–64. For a reading of Stoppard's place in such a tradition, see Richard Dutton, *Modern Tragicomedy and the British Tradition* (Brighton: Harvester Press, 1986) and Michael Hinden's review essay, 'After Beckett: The Plays of Pinter, Stoppard, and Shepard', in *Contemporary Literature*, vol. 27, no. 3, Autumn, 1986, pp. 400–408, which suggests the presence of Beckett in these dramatists. For a reading of 'Christine Brooke-Rose's *Thru* in relation to Beckett, see Shlomith Rimmon-Kenan, 'Ambiguity and Narrative Levels: Christine Brooke-Rose's *Thru*', in *Poetics Today*, vol. 3, no. 1, pp. 21–32.
19. For a discussion with Pinter about the 'political turn' in his theatre, which is orientated to a degree to Beckett's writing, see Harold Pinter, 'A Play and its Politics: A Conversation between Harold Pinter and Nicholas Hern', in Harold Pinter, *One for the Road* (London: Methuen, 1984), pp. 5–24.

[20] Graham Saunders comments that 'Samuel Beckett's influence looms large in all of Sarah Kane's work', in his recent book *Love Me or Kill Me: Sarah Kane and the Theatre of Extremes* (Manchester: Manchester University Press, 2002), p. 55. Kane has remarked herself on the primacy of Beckett's influence in an interview with Nils Tabert ('Gespräch mit Sarah Kane', in Nils Tabert, ed., *Playspotting: Die Londoner Theaterszene der 90er* (Reinbeck: Rowohlt Taschenbuch Verlag, 1998), pp. 8–21, quoted in Saunders, *Love Me or Kille Me*, p. 54.

[21] See Vaclav Havel's play *Mistake*, written in response to Beckett's *Catastrophe* (the dedication to Havel in that play itself suggests how responsive Beckett's drama is to context). *Mistake* is collected in Vaclav Havel, *Selected Plays 1963–1983* (London: Faber and Faber, 1992).

[22] Bruce Naumann showed his 'Clown Torture', and his piece 'Slow Angle Walk (Beckett Walk)', at the exhibition entitled 'I Not I' in the Gallagher Gallery, at the Royal Hibernian Academy, from 24 March to 1 May 2006. See http://www.royalhibernianacademy.com/html/exhibitions/inoti07.html. Hirst's production of *Breath* was screened at the same exhibition.

[23] For an indication of David Mamet's indebtedness to Beckett, see David K. Sauer, and Janice A. Sauer, eds, *David Mamet: A Research and Production Sourcebook* (Westport: Greenwood, 2003). For Lynch's relationship with Kafka, see Chris Rodley, ed., *Lynch on Lynch* (London: Faber and Faber, 1997), p. 56, where Lynch says 'The one artist that I feel could be my brother [. . .] is Franz Kafka. I really dig him a lot. Some of his things are the most thrilling combos of words I have ever read. If Kafka wrote a crime novel, I'd be there. I'd like to direct that for sure'.

[24] For a reading of Beckett's influence on Mahon, see Mark Nixon, '"A brief glow in the dark": Samuel Beckett's Presence in Modern Irish Poetry', in Ronan McDonald, ed., *Irish Writing Since 1950*, special issue of *Yearbook of English Studies*, vol. 35, 2005, pp. 43–57. For a penetrating analysis of the relationship between Beckett and Susan Howe, see Nicky Marsh, '"All Known – Never Seen": Susan Howe, Samuel Beckett and an Indeterminate Tradition', in Peter Boxall, ed., *Beckett/Aesthetics/Politics, Samuel Beckett Today / Aujourd'hui*, vol. 9, 2000, pp. 239–54. For Susan Howe's reception of Emily Dickinson, see Susan Howe, *My Emily Dickinson* (Berkeley: North Atlantic Books, 1985).

[25] See Ismail Kadare, *Broken April* (London: Vintage, 2003), trans. J. Hodgson, and Ismail Kadare, *Spring Flowers, Spring Frost* (London: Vintage, 2003), trans. David Bellos.

[26] For Beckett's influence on Coetzee, see Coetzee's own discussion of Beckett that runs through his collection *Doubling the Point: Essays and Interviews* (Cambridge, Massachusetts: Harvard University Press, 1992). See also J. M. Coetzee, 'Eight Ways of Looking at Samuel Beckett', in Minako Okamuro, Naoya Mori, Bruno Clément, Sjef Houppermans, Angela Moorjani and Anthony Uhlmann, eds., *Samuel Beckett Today / 'Aujourd'hui'*, vol. 19, 2008.

[27] For a recent reading of Beckett and Duras, see Andrew Slade, *Lyotard, Beckett, Duras, and the Postmodern Sublime* (New York: Peter Lang, 2007). For Auster's own reflections on Beckett, see Paul Auster, *The Art of Hunger: Essays, Prefaces, Interviews and The Red Notebook* (London: Penguin, 1997).

[28] William Gibson, *Pattern Recognition* (London: Penguin, 2004), p. 29. For an essay which reflects astutely on the relationship between Beckett and science fiction,

see Bryan McHale, 'Lost in the Mall: Beckett, Federman, Space', in Henry Sussman and Christopher Devenny, *Engagement and Indifference: Beckett and the Political* (Albany: State University of New York, 2001), pp. 112–25. McHale traces relationships between Beckett, Raymond Federman and J. G. Ballard.

29 See Mark Osteen, *American Magic and Dread: Don DeLillo's Dialogue with Culture* (Philadelphia: University of Pennsylvania Press, 200), p. 209. Osteen suggests here and elsewhere, though, that we should not too readily accept Gray's comments about Beckett in *Mao II*, arguing that it is extremely unlikely that Beckett had any measurable impact on mass consciousness.

30 For an example of this response to Gladney and Suskind, see for example Leonard Wilcox, 'Baudrillard, DeLillo's "White Noise," and the End of Heroic Narrative', in *Contemporary Literature*, vol. 32, no. 3, Autumn, 1991, pp. 346–65.

31 See Rita Cirio, 'Austria Infelix', in Sepp Dreissinger (Hg.), *Von einer Katastrophe in die andere. 13 Gespräche mit Thomas Bernhard* (Witra: Bibliothek der Provinz, 1992), p. 102. Quoted in Jopling, 'Bernhard as Company for Beckett', p. 49, and in Wulf, *The Imperative of Narration*, p. 1.

32 Jacques Derrida, Spectres of Marx: The State of the Debt, the Work of Mourning, and the New International (London: Routledge, 1994), trans. Peggy Kamuf, p. 17.

33 Harold Bloom, *The Anxiety of Influence: A Theory of Poetry*, second edition (Oxford: Oxford University Press, 1997), p. 11.

34 Bloom, *The Anxiety of Influence*, p. 11.

35 See for example, Ihab Hassan, *The Dismemberment of Orpheus: Towards a Postmodern Literature* second edition (Wisconsin: The University of Wisconsin Press, 1982), p. 210, where he characterizes Beckett as 'a supreme example of the postmodern artist'. Tyrus Miller, in *Late Modernism: Politics, Fiction and the Arts Between the World Wars* (Berkeley: University of California Press, 1999) characterizes Beckett as an 'uncompromising postmodern minimalist', but also suggests that Beckett's work might be regarded as late modernist, arguing that 'the concept of late modernism helps us to situate and understand the majority of Beckett's works' (p. 170).

Chapter 1

1 See David Wills, *Dorsality: Thinking Back through Technology and Politics* (Minneapolis: University of Minnesota Press, 2008).

2 James Joyce, *Portrait of the Artist as a Young Man* (Harmondsworth: Penguin, 1992), p. 276.

3 For a striking account of temporality in *Castle Rackrent*, which suggests that the novel's 'strange, fractured, and unstable narrative, is *the* symptomatic discrepancy of the nineteenth century novel', see Seamus Deane, *Strange Country: Modernity and Nationhood in Irish Writing since 1790* (Oxford: Clarendon, 1997), pp. 38–41.

4 See W. J. McCormack, From Burke to Beckett: Ascendancy, Tradition and Betrayal in Literary History (Cork: Cork University Press, 1994).

5 See Elizabeth Bowen, *To The North* (London: Gollancz, 1932), p. 49. For a reading of this spectral continuity, in relation to Derrida's *Spectres of Marx*, and in dialogue with Andrew Bennett and Nicholas Royle's book on Bowen, *Elizabeth Bowen and*

the Dissolution of the Novel (Basingstoke: Macmillan, 1995), see Andrew Gibson, 'Ethics and "The Dissolution of the Novel"', in Andrew Gibson, *Postmodernity, Ethics and the Novel: From Leavis to Levinas* (London: Routledge, 1999), pp. 85–108.

[6] Elizabeth Bowen, *The Mulberry Tree: Writings of Elizabeth Bowen* (London: Vintage, 1999), selected and introduced by Hermione Lee, p. 282.

[7] Bowen, *The Mulberry Tree*, p. 282.

[8] Bowen, *The Mulberry Tree*, p. 283.

[9] Bowen, *The Mulberry Tree*, p. 276.

[10] Bowen, *The Mulberry Tree*, p. 276.

[11] Declan Kiberd, *Inventing Ireland: The Literature of the Modern Nation* (London: Vintage, 1996), p. 377. For a nuanced and informed reading of Bowen's and Beckett's belonging to a shared tradition, see W. J. McCormack, 'Infancy and History: Beckett, Bowen and Critical theory', in McCormack, *From Burke to Beckett*, pp. 375–433.

[12] Kiberd, *Inventing Ireland*, p. 531.

[13] Kiberd, *Inventing Ireland*, p. 530.

[14] Kiberd, *Inventing Ireland*, p. 531.

[15] Kiberd, *Inventing Ireland*, p. 539.

[16] Kiberd, *Inventing Ireland*, p. 538.

[17] Kiberd, *Inventing Ireland*, p. 531.

[18] Bowen, *The Mulberry Tree*, p. 282.

[19] See Bowen, *The Mulberry Tree*, p. 282, where Bowen says that the places in her stories are scattered between England and Ireland, noting that 'Nothing (*at least on the surface*) connects them' (my italics).

[20] Bowen, *The Mulberry Tree*, p. 281.

[21] Bowen, *The Mulberry Tree*, p. 282.

[22] Bowen, *The Mulberry Tree*, p. 283.

[23] McCormack, *From Burke to Beckett*, p. 413.

[24] There are a number of recent studies which have reassessed Beckett's relationship with Ireland. See for example, Eion O'Brien, *The Beckett Country* (Dublin: The Black Cat Press, 1986), John P. Harrington, *The Irish Beckett* (New York: Syracuse University Press, 1991), David Lloyd, 'Writing in the Shit: Beckett, Nationalism and the Colonial Subject', in David Lloyd, *Anomalous States: Irish Writing and the Post-colonial Moment* (Dublin: The Lilliput Press, 1993), pp. 41–58, Sinead Mooney, '"Integrity in a Surplus": Beckett's (Post-) Protestant Politics', in Boxall, ed., *Beckett/Aesthetics/Politics*, pp. 223–37, Peter Boxall, 'The Existence I Ascribe: Memory, Invention and Autobiography in Beckett's Fiction', in *The Yearbook of English Studies*, vol. 30, 2000. Anna McMullen contributes to this reassessment, and offers an excellent survey of such approaches; see Anna McMullen, 'Irish/Postcolonial Beckett', in Lois Oppenheim, ed., *Palgrave Advances in Samuel Beckett Studies* (Basingstoke: Palgrave, 2004), pp. 89–109.

[25] For a reading of the back in *Company*, and in Beckett's work more generally, see Nicholas Royle, 'Back', in *Oxford Literary Review*, vol. 18, nos. 1–2, 1996, pp. 145–57.

[26] See for example, James Knowlson, *Damned to Fame: The Life of Samuel Beckett* (London: Bloomsbury, 1996), pp. 651–3.

[27] The discussion of these plays refers throughout to the version broadcast by the BBC on 17 April 1977.

28. Gilles Deleuze and Félix Guattari, *Kafka: Toward a Minor Literature* (Minneapolis: The University of Minnesota Press, 1986), p. 73.
29. For a fuller reading of the relationship between the Yeats poem and . . . *but the clouds* . . ., see Richard Bruce Kirkley, 'A *catch in the breath*: Language and Consciousness in Samuel Beckett's . . . *but the clouds* . . .', in *Modern Drama*, vol. 35, no. 4, December 1992, pp. 607–16.
30. W. B. Yeats, 'The Tower', in W. B. Yeats, *Collected Poems* (London: Picador, 1990), p. 219.
31. For a discussion of cinematic suturing, see Stephen Heath, 'On Suture', in Stephen Heath, *Questions of Cinema* (Basingstoke: Macmillan 1981), pp. 76–112, and Kaja Silverman, 'Suture', in Kaja Silverman, *The Subject of Semiotics* (New York: Oxford University Press, 1983), pp. 194–236.
32. Kirkley, 'A *catch in the breath*', p. 615.
33. Yeats, 'The Tower', p. 225.
34. McMullen, 'Irish/Postcolonial Beckett', p. 107.

Chapter 2

1. See Banville, *Eclipse*, p. 31. There are several Beckettian echoes, but perhaps the strongest is from *All That Fall*, where Mrs Rooney reflects that while it is 'suicide to be abroad', to remain at home would be a 'lingering dissolution' (CDW 175).
2. See Ronan Sheehan, 'Novelists on the Novel: Ronan Sheehan talks to John Banville and Francis Stuart', in *Crane Bag*, vol. 3, no. 1, 1979, pp. 76–84, p. 80. This interview, and the interview with Hedwig Schall, is cited at the opening of Kersti Tarien Powell's essay 'Not a Son but a Survivor': Beckett . . . Joyce . . . Banville', in McDonald, ed., *Irish Writing Since 1950*, pp. 199–211, p. 199. This essay gives a useful and comprehensive sense of the critical response to the twin influences of Beckett and Joyce on Banville's work, in the context of Banville's ambivalent belonging to an Irish tradition, glossing readings of Banville by Seamus Deane, Joseph McMinn, Richard Kearney and Ingo Berensmeyer.
3. Hedwig Schall, 'An Interview with John Banville', in *European English Messenger*, vol. 6, no. 1, Spring 1997, pp. 13–19, p. 17. The interview took place at Shelbourne Hotel on 18 December 1996.
4. Joseph McMinn notes this overlaying of Banville's and Beckett's landscapes, suggesting that the two writers produce shared 'versions of Irish pastoral, Banville's Wexford providing him with the landscape of childhood as do the Dublin mountains for Beckett' (Joseph McMinn, *The Supreme Fictions of John Banville* [Manchester: Manchester University Press, 1999], p. 162).
5. John Banville, *The Sea* (London: Picador, 2005), p. 9.
6. See John Banville, *Ghosts* (London: Picador, 1998), and John Banville, *Athena* (London: Picador, 1998). The obsessive focus on the space of the threshold, of the doorway and the window, has led *The Body of Evidence*, *Athena* and *Ghosts* to be known collectively as the 'Frames Trilogy'.
7. See Henry James, *The Turn of the Screw* (New York: Norton, 1999). Quint first appears framed by a window at the 'very top' of a tower (p. 15), and second outside the dining room window (p. 20).

[8] For the mapping of a tradition that includes James and Bowen, see for example, John Bayley, *The Short Story: Henry James to Elizabeth Bowen* (Brighton: Harvester, 1988). For an analysis of the 'strong affinities' (p. 170) between Bowen and James, see Glen Cavaliero, *The Supernatural and English Fiction* (Oxford: Oxford University Press, 1995), pp. 158–81.

[9] For examples of work in this tradition, see Bowen, *The Last September*, E. OE. Somerville and Martin Ross, *The Real Charlotte* (London: Zodiac Press, 1972) and *The Big House of Inver* (London: W. Heinemann, 1925). For a critical account which traces the big house tradition from Edgeworth up to Banville and to William Trevor, see Vera Kreilkamp, *The Anglo-Irish Novel and the Big House* (Syracuse: Syracuse University Press, 1998).

[10] Yeats, 'The Tower', p. 219.

[11] Yeats, 'The Tower', p. 221.

[12] Yeats, 'The Tower', p. 222.

[13] Yeats, 'The Tower', p. 220.

[14] T. S. Eliot, 'Marina', in T. S. Eliot, *Collected Poems 1909–1962* (London: Faber and Faber, 1974), p. 116.

[15] For a rich analysis of the uncertain referents of the phrase 'my daughter' in Eliot's poem, see Stephen Thomson, 'The Adjective, My Daughter: Staging T. S. Eliot's "Marina"', in *The Yearbook of English Studies*, vol. 32, 2002, pp. 110–26.

[16] See W. B. Yeats, 'Leda and the Swan', in Yeats, *Collected Poems*, p. 241.

Chapter 3

[1] In insisting that the tradition that he belongs to is one that is 'manufactured' by himself, Banville draws attention to this fusion in his work between Irish and wider European literary traditions, saying that 'I feel part of my culture. But it's a purely personal culture gleaned from bits and pieces of European culture of four thousand years' (Sheehan, 'Novelists on the Novel', p. 80). Powell outlines the critical debate that has emerged over whether Banville should be considered part of an Irish or of a European tradition. See Powell, 'Not a son but a survivor', pp. 199–201.

[2] See John Banville, *God's Gift: A Version of* Amphitryon *by Heinrich von Kleist* (Oldcastle: The Gallery Press, 2000).

[3] See Banville, *Eclipse*, p. 89. See Heinrich von Kleist, *Amphitryon*, in Heinrich von Kleist, *Five Plays* (New Haven: Yale University press, 1988), trans. Martin Greenberg, p. 63, where the line is translated as 'And who except myself's Amphitryon'. See also Molière, *Amphitryon*, in *The Plays of Molière* (Edinburgh: John Grant, 1907), trans. A. R. Waller, p. 399, where the line is translated 'And who, besides myself, may this Amphitryon be?'.

[4] See Knowlson, *Damned to Fame*, pp. 632–3.

[5] Knowlson, *Damned to Fame*, p. 633.

[6] For an elaboration of Bloch's theorization of the relationship between the 'not-yet conscious' and the 'utopian function' in art and aesthetics, see Ernst Bloch, 'The Conscious and Known Activity within the Not-Yet-Conscious, the Utopian Function', in Ernst Bloch, *The Utopian Function of Art and Literature: Selected Essays*

(Cambridge, Massachusetts: The MIT Press, 1988), trans. Jack Zipes and Frank Mecklenburg, pp. 103–41.
7. Gilles Deleuze, 'The Exhausted', in Gilles Deleuze, *Essays Critical and Clinical* (London: Verso, 1998), trans. Daniel W. Smith and Michael A. Greco, p. 168. For another essay in which Deleuze and Guattari expand their theory of 'faciality', see Gilles Deleuze and Félix Guattari, 'Year Zero: Faciality', in Gilles Deleuze and Félix Guattari, *A Thousand Plateaus: Capitalism and Schizophrenia* (London: Continuum,1988), trans. Brian Massumi, pp. 167–91.
8. Knowlson, *Damned to Fame*, p. 682.
9. De Man does not have an essay by the title 'Effacement and Real Presence', but the title that is perhaps suggested here is 'Autobiography as De-Facement', in Paul de Man, *The Rhetoric of Romanticism* (New York: Columbia University Press, 1984), pp. 67–81.
10. For a robust critical assessment of the impact of the Celtic Tiger economy on Irish cultural formations, see Peadar Kirby, Luke Gibbons and Michael Cronin, eds, *Reinventing Ireland: Culture and the Celtic Tiger* (London: Pluto 2002), and Colin Coulter and Steve Coleman, *The End of Irish History? Critical Reflections on the Celtic Tiger* (Manchester: Manchester University Press, 2003). See also Declan Kiberd, 'The Celtic Tiger: A Cultural History', in Declan Kiberd, *The Irish Writer and the World* (Cambridge: Cambridge University Press, 2005), pp. 269–88.
11. Michael Cronin, 'Ireland, Globalisation and the War Against Time', in Kirby et al., *Reinventing Ireland*, p. 65. For Virilio's influential analysis of the relation between speed and politics, see Paul Virilio, *Speed and Politics: An Essay on Dromology* (New York: Semiotext(e), 1986), trans. Mark Polizzotti.
12. Terry Eagleton, *Crazy John and the Bishop and other Essays on Irish Culture* (Cork: Cork University Press, 1998), p. 313. Eagleton's argument for the importance of maintaining fidelity to nationalist specificity under post-national, global conditions is starkly opposed to Richard Kearney's enthusiastic embrace of the possibilities of post-nationalism, in his book *Postnationalist Ireland: Politics, Culture, Philosophy* (London: Routledge, 1997), which emerged at about the same time as Eagleton's.
13. See Michael Hardt and Antonio Negri, *Empire* (Cambridge, Massachusetts: Harvard University Press, 2000).
14. For Hardt and Negri's discussion of the politically progressive possibilities of global networks, see their work *Multitude: War and Democracy in the Age of Empire* (London: Penguin, 2006), which builds upon their earlier *Empire*.

Chapter 4

1. For an early reading of Beckett's engagement with Kafka, see for example, George H. Szanto, *Narrative Consciousness: Structure and Perception in the Fiction of Kafka, Beckett, and Robbe-Grillet* (Austin: University of Texas Press, 1972). See also Daniel Albright, *Representation and the Imagination: Beckett, Kafka, Nabokov, and Schoenberg* (Chicago: Chicago University Press, 1981), and Hans H. Hiebel, 'Beckett's Television Plays and Kafka's Late Stories', in Marius Buning, Matthijs Engelberts, Sjef Houppermans and Emmanuel Jacquart, *Samuel Beckett: Crossroads and Borderlines*.

L'OEuvre Carrefour/L'OEuvre Limite, special issue of Samuel Beckett Today/Aujourd'hui, vol. 6, 1997, pp. 313–27. It is possible to see Kafka and Beckett mingling in Auster's essays, *The Art of Hunger: Essays, Prefaces, Interviews and The Red Notebook* (London: Penguin, 1997), as well as throughout his novels. There is a similar set of cross influences apparent in Coetzee's collection of essays *Doubling the Point: Essays and Interviews* (Cambridge, Massachusetts: Harvard University Press, 1992). See also Coetzee's Kafkaesque piece 'At the Gate' in *Elizabeth Costello* which also takes something from Beckett (EC 193–225). Ihab Hassan memorably characterizes the joint influences of Joyce, Proust and Kafka on Beckett's writing when he suggests that 'Joyce may be Beckett's transubstantial father and Kafka closer to his secret self, but it is Proust who helps to define his artistic conscience' (Ihab Hassan *The Dismemberment of Orpheus: Toward a Postmodern Literature*, second edition (Wisconsin: The University of Wisconsin Press, 1982), p. 214.

[2] A number of critics have examined Beckett's relationship with Kleist. Perhaps the most influential of these has been James Knowlson and John Pilling's essay 'Beckett and Kleist's essay "On the Marionette Theatre"', in James Knowlson and John Pilling, *Frescoes of the Skull: The Later Prose and Drama of Samuel Beckett* (London: Calder, 1979), pp. 277–85. For a reading of the relationship between Beckett and Wittgenstein, see Marjorie Perloff, 'Witt-Watt: The Language of Resistance / The Resistance of Language', in Marjorie Perloff, *Wittgenstein's Ladder: Poetic Language and the Strangeness of the Ordinary* (Chicago: The University of Chicago Press, 1996), pp. 115–43.

[3] Beckett's relationship with Proust is suggested most directly by his short book on Proust, entitled *Proust*. Nicholas Zurbrugg's *Beckett and Proust* (Gerard's Cross: Smythe, 1988) is a full reading of the dialogue between the two writers. Beckett's influence on Marie Redonnet and Jean-Philippe Toussaint is traced by Jean-Louis Hippolyte in *Fuzzy Fiction* (Lincoln: University of Nebraska Press, 2006). For a recent reading of Beckett and Duras, see Andrew Slade, *Lyotard, Beckett, Duras, and the Postmodern Sublime* (New York: Peter Lang, 2007).

[4] See Esslin, *The Theatre of the Absurd*, where Beckett's work is located in an absurdist tradition that includes Arthur Adamov, Eugène Ionesco, Jean Genet and Harold Pinter.

[5] A number of studies have examined the relationship between Beckett and Bernhard. See for example, Michael Jopling, '"Es gibt ja nur Gescheitertes": Bernhard as company for Beckett', in *Journal of European Studies*, vol. 27, 1997, pp. 49–71, Catharina Wulf, *The Imperative of Narration: Beckett, Bernhard, Schopenhauer, Lacan* (Brighton: Sussex Academic Press, 1997), and Martin Esslin, 'Beckett and Bernhard: A Comparison', in *Modern Austrian Literature*, vol. 18, no 2, 1985, pp. 67–78. There has been less-sustained treatment of Beckett's relation with Sebald, although the comparison is made by a number of critics, including Thomas Osborne, who likens Sebald to the 'different yet curiously parallel case of Samuel Beckett' (Thomas Osborne, 'Literature in Ruins', in *History of the Human Sciences*, vol. 18, no. 3, 2005, pp. 109–118, p. 116).

[6] See Ludwig Wittgenstein, *Philosophical Investigations* (Oxford: Blackwell 2001), trans. G. E. M. Anscombe, p. 109. See also Norman Malcolm's *Nothing is Hidden: Wittgenstein's Criticism of his Early Thought* (Oxford: Blackwell, 1986), which reads Wittgenstein's rethinking of the *Tractatus* through this moment in *Philosophical Investigations*.

⁷ See Beckett, *Watt*, pp. 162–7, where Sam details Watt's peculiar modes of speech, whose obscurities mean that 'I missed I suppose mush I suspect of great interest' in the narration. At Watt's most incomprehensible, his language 'seemed so much balls' to Sam. At his clearest, Sam understood 'fully one half of what won its way past my tympan' (W 167).
⁸ Dante Alighieri, *The Divine Comedy*, 3 vols, vol. 1, *Inferno* (New York: Oxford University Press, 1961), trans. John D. Sinclair, Canto 1, lines 1–3, p. 22/23.
⁹ Daniela Caselli, *Beckett's Dantes: Intertextuality in the Fiction and Criticism* (Manchester: Manchester University Press, 2005), p. 124.
¹⁰ Caselli, *Beckett's Dantes*, p. 124.
¹¹ Caselli, *Beckett's Dantes*, p. 144, n. 11.
¹² Knowlson, *Damned to Fame*, p. 633. See also Knowlson and Pilling, *Frescoes of the Skull*, p. 281, where they report that 'Beckett stressed that the 'figure in *Ghost Trio* looks up from the pallet to the mirror, it should be in a smooth, unbroken, graceful movement.'
¹³ Pilling and Knowlson, *Frescoes of the Skull*, p. 284.
¹⁴ John Milton, *Paradise Lost* (Harlow: Pearson Longman, 2007), ed. Alastair Fowler, I, 5, p. 57.
¹⁵ See Heinrich von Kleist, 'Über das Marionettentheater', in Heinrich von Kleist, *Gesammelte Werke* (Berlin: Aufbau-Verlag, 1955), p. 388.
¹⁶ See Samuel Beckett, 'Dante . . . Bruno. Vico . . Joyce', in Samuel Beckett and Others, *Our Exagmination Round his Factification for Incamination of Work in Progress* (London: Faber, 1929), pp. 3–22.
¹⁷ See Thomas More, *Utopia* (Cambridge: Cambridge University Press, 2002), eds, George M. Logan and Robert M. Adams.
¹⁸ Paul de Man, 'Aesthetic Formalization: Kleist's *Über das Marionettentheater*', in de Man, *Rhetoric of Romanticism*, p. 277.

Chapter 5

¹ See for example, McHale, 'Lost in the Mall', p. 120, where McHale suggests the recurrence of Beckett's relationship with the Holocaust, saying that 'It is, of course, nothing new to suggest an affiliation between the worlds of Beckett's fiction and the concentration camp world; this has been a commonplace of Beckett criticism since Adorno first gave the idea currency'. McHale seeks, in ways that have some parallels to my own reading here, to suggest how Beckett's dramatization of the concentration camp merges with later representations and configurations. 'What *is* new', he writes, 'is the implication that the space of this particular Beckett fiction [*The Lost Ones*] models *both* the death-camp space *and also*, by a kind of double-exposure, the shopping-mall space of commerce and circulation'.
² Eelco Runia, 'Spots of Time', in *History and Theory*, vol. 45, no. 3, 2006, p. 316.
³ Eelco Runia, 'Presence', in *History and Theory*, vol. 45, no. 1, 2006, p. 16.
⁴ Zuckerman is quoted in Jacqueline Rose, *The Last Resistance* (London: Verso, 2007), pp. 4–5, where Rose seeks to develop a theoretical means of understanding how to 'draw a line' (p. 5) from the Holocaust to contemporary Palestine,

how to respond to her conviction that testimonies such as Zuckerman's 'cannot, and should not, be held to their originating moment, but instead become part of an ongoing history' (p. 4).

5. See Paul Auster, *The Locked Room*, in Paul Auster, *The New York Trilogy* (London: Faber and Faber, 1987).
6. See Jean Michele Rabaté's foreword to Wulf, *The Imperative of Narration*, p. viii, where Rabaté comments that 'one is bound to fail, but, failing, one desires to fail again, to fail even better. And, as Beckett and Bernhard keep repeating, this is not sad'.
7. See Ludwig Wittgenstein, *Tractatus Logico-Philosophicus* (London: Routledge, 2001), trans. D. F. Pears and B. F. McGuinness, p. 89, where he famously ends with the remark 'What we cannot speak about we must pass over in silence'.
8. Jopling, 'Bernhard as company for Beckett', p. 50.
9. Jopling, 'Bernhard as company for Beckett', p. 50.
10. Wulf, *The Imperative of Narration*, p. 11.
11. Wulf, *The Imperative of Narration*, p. 11. The quotation from Bernhard is taken from Sepp Dressinger, *Von einer Katastrophe in die andere. 13 Gespräche mit Thomas Bernhard* (Vienna: Bibliothek der Provinz, 1992), p. 109.
12. Thomas Bernhard, *Der Italiener*, quoted in Wulf, *The Imperative of Narration*, p. 14. The translation is Wulf's.
13. Wulf, *The Imperative of Narration*, p. 14.
14. Wulf, *The Imperative of Narration*, p. 174.
15. Jopling, 'Bernhard as company for Beckett', p. 49.
16. Jopling, 'Bernhard as company for Beckett', p. 68.
17. Jopling, 'Bernhard as company for Beckett', p. 69.
18. Jopling, 'Bernhard as company for Beckett', p. 51.
19. Jopling, 'Bernhard as company for Beckett', p. 68.
20. Ludovic Janvier, 'Place of Narration/Narration of Place', in Ruby Cohn, ed., *Samuel Beckett: The Comic Gamut* (New Brunswick: Rutgers University Press, 1962), p. 101.
21. Jopling, 'Bernhard as company for Beckett', p. 51.
22. Thomas Bernhard, *Wittgensteins Neffe: Eine Freundschaft* (Frankfurt: Suhrkamp Verlag, 1982), p. 8.
23. This structure, whereby a narrator enters into a relationship with a quoted speaker, emerges across Bernhard's oeuvre, beginning with the relationship between the narrator and 'Prince Saurau', in Bernhard's first published novel *Gargoyles* (London: Vintage, 2006). Thomas Cousineau's *Three Part Inventions: The Novels of Thomas Bernhard* (Newark: The University of Delaware Press, 2008), reads this relation between narrator and interlocutor, pointing out that this is almost always conducted as a three-way conversation (in *Gargoyles*, e.g., the narrator, the Prince and the narrator's father are present; in *Old Master's* the trio is Reger, Atzbacher and Irrsigler).
24. Perloff, *Wittgenstein's Ladder*, p. 145.
25. See Franz Kafka, 'In the Penal Settlement', in Franz Kafka, *Metamorphosis and Other Stories* (London: Minerva, 1992), trans. Willa and Edwin Muir.
26. See Sigmund Freud, 'A Note Upon the "Mystic Writing Pad"', in Sigmund Freud, *On Metapsychology*, in *The Penguin Freud Library*, 15 vols, vol. 11 (Harmondsworth: Penguin, 1991), pp. 429–34.

27 See Franz Kafka, 'The Burrow', in Kafka, *Metamorphosis and Other Stories* pp. 128–66. In both *How It Is* and 'The Burrow', the protagonists crawl through a muddy environment that doubles as the artwork of their own construction. In both texts, also, there is a confusion between the surface from which they burrow downwards, and the depths from which they, in a sense, emerge.

28 See Ludwig Wittgenstein, *Briefwechsel mit B. Russell, G. E. Moore, J. M. Keynes, F. P. Ramsay, W. Eccles, P. Engelmann und L. von Ficker* (Frankfurt: Suhrkamp, 1980), ed. B. F. McGuinness and G. H. von Wright, pp. 96–7. This English translation is from Ray Monk, *Ludwig Wittgenstein: The Duty of Genius* (London: Vintage, 1991), p. 178.

29 Bernhard, *Wittgensteins Neffe*, p. 161.

Chapter 6

1 See W. J. McCormack, review of *Austerlitz*, in *The Post.ie: Sunday Business Post Online*, Sunday 20 January 2002, http://archives.tcm.ie/businesspost/2002/01/20/story41667728.asp.
  The characterization of Bernhard as an 'Alpen Beckett' arises in a number of places. It was originally coined in *Der Spiegel* in 1972, and is quoted, for example, in Wulf, *The Imperative of Narration*, p. 1.

2 The interview took place on Thursday 6 December 2001. It can be heard at: http://www.kcrw.com/etc/programs/bw/bw011206w_g_sebald

3 Amir Eshel, 'Against the Power of Time: The Poetics of Suspension in W. G. Sebald's *Austerlitz*', in *New German Critique*, vol. 88, Winter 2003, pp. 71–96, p. 95.

4 See William Ray, 'Suspended in the Mirror: Language and the Self in Kleist's "Über das Marionettentheater"', in *Studies in Romanticism*, vol. 18, no 4, Winter 1979, pp. 521–46.

5 See Thomas More, *Utopia*, (Harmondsworth: Penguin, 1965), trans. Paul Turner, n. 4, p. 135.

6 Adorno, 'Trying to Understand *Endgame*', p. 275.

7 John Keats, 'Ode on a Grecian Urn', in John Keats, *Selected Poems and Letters of John Keats* (Oxford: Heinemann, 1966), ed. Robert Gittings, p. 127.

8 Milton, *Paradise Lost*, I, 63, p. 64.

9 Emily Dickinson, 'From Blank to Blank', in Emily Dickinson, *The Poems of Emily Dickinson* (Cambridge, Massachusetts: Harvard University Press, 1998), ed. R. W. Franklin, poem 484, line 10, p. 222.

10 Quoted in Maya Jaggi, 'Recovered Memories', in *The Guardian*, Saturday 22 September 2001. See http://www.guardian.co.uk/books/2001/sep/22/artsandhumanities.highereducation

11 Runia, 'Presence', pp. 11–12.

12 Russell J. A. Kilbourn, 'Architecture and Cinema: The Representation of Memory in W. G. Sebald' *Austerlitz*', in J. J. Long and Anne Whitehead, eds, *W. G. Sebald: A Critical Companion* (Edinburgh: Edinburgh University Press, 2004), p. 145.

13 Caroline Duttlinger, 'Traumatic Photographs: Remembrance and the Technical Media in W. G. Sebald's *Austerlitz*', in Long and Whitehead, *W. G. Sebald*, p. 170.

14. Quoted in Jaggi, 'Recovered Memories'.
15. Richard Eder, 'Excavating a Life', in *New York Times*, 28 October 2001. See http://query.nytimes.com/gst/fullpage.html?res=9B0CE2D9153EF93BA15753C1A9679C8B63&sec=&spon=&pagewanted=2
16. Julia Kristeva, *Proust and the Sense of Time* (London: Faber and Faber, 1993), trans. Stephen Bann, p. 65. This passage in Kristeva is quoted in Gibson, *Postmodernity, Ethics and the Novel*, p. 118, where Gibson goes on to develop a rather different view of the unities in Proust's work, one based on a keener awareness of the 'incommensurability' of the worlds that Proust brings together.
17. For a reproduction of this photograph of Beckett and his mother, see O'Brien, *The Beckett Country*, p. 12.
18. C. G. Jung, *The Symbolic Life: Miscellaneous Writings* (London: Routledge and Kegan Paul, 1977), trans. R. F. C. Hull, p. 95.
19. Jung, *The Symbolic Life*, p. 96.
20. See Primo Levi, *The Drowned and the Saved* (London: Abacus, 1989), trans. Raymond Rosenthal.
21. Shane Weller, *A Taste for the Negative: Samuel Beckett and Nihilism* (London: Legenda, 2005), p. 133.
22. John Banville, 'The Rubble Artist', in *The New Republic Online*, 6 December 2001, http://www.powells.com/review/2001_12_06
23. See Thomas Tresize, 'Unspeakable', in *The Yale Journal of Criticism*, vol. 14, no. 1, 2001, pp. 39–66.

Chapter 7

1. See Steven Connor, 'Beckett and the World', p. 12, http://www.bbk.ac.uk/english/skc/beckettworld/beckettworld.pdf. See Emer Nolan, *James Joyce and Nationalism* (London: Routledge, 1994), and Andrew Gibson, *Joyce's Revenge: History, Aesthetics and Politics in* Ulysses (Oxford: Oxford University Press, 2005). See also Andrew Gibson and Len Platt, eds, *Joyce, Ireland, Britain* (Gainesville: University of Florida Press, 2006).
2. Connor, 'Beckett and the World' p. 13.
3. Connor, 'Beckett and the World', p. 12.
4. The conference, entitled 'Borderless Beckett', took place in Tokyo from 29 September to 1 October 2006. Selected papers from the conference are published in Minako Okamuro, Naoya Mori, Bruno Clément, Sjef Houppermans, Angela Moorjani and Anthony Uhlmann, eds, *Samuel Beckett Today/'Aujourd'hui'*, vol. 19, 2008.
5. Richard Ellmann, *James Joyce*, new and revised edition (Oxford: Oxford University Press, 1983), p. 253. Nolan, *James Joyce and Nationalism*, p. 32.
6. See Benedict Anderson, *Imagined Communities: Reflections on the Origin and Spread of Nationalism*, revised edition (London: Verso, 1991), where Anderson extends an analysis of the connection between the development of print media and the forging of the nation. The reading of the newspaper, Anderson argues, is performed in isolation, in the 'lair of the skull', yet 'at the same time, the newspaper

reader, observing exact replicas of his own paper being consumed by his subway, barbershop or residential neighbours, is continually reassured that the imagined world is visibly rooted in everyday life' (pp. 35–6).
7. See for example, Emer Nolan, *James Joyce and Nationalism*, and Declan Kiberd, 'James Joyce and Mythic Realism', in Kiberd, *Inventing Ireland*, pp. 327–55.
8. See Gilles Deleuze, 'The Exhausted', in Gilles Deleuze, *Essays Critical and Clinical* (London: Verso, 1998), pp. 152–74, for Deleuze's reading of Beckett's depiction of an 'any-space-whatever'.
9. See Samuel Beckett, *Company* (NO 18), where the narrator describes himself as being 'Nowhere in particular on the way from A to Z'.
10. There are various ways of thinking about the relationship between the decline of the nation state and the development of globalization. Michael Hardt and Antonio Negri, in *Multitude* (London: Penguin, 2004), claim that 'the sovereign authority of nation states is declining and there is instead emerging a new supra-national form of sovereignty, a global Empire'. While for most thinkers there is a relationship between the waning of the nation state after World War II and the production of global relations, there is some disagreement about the history of globalization, and how far back this history reaches. For a useful account of different positions on this question, see Frank J. Lechner and John Boli, eds, *The Globalization Reader*, second edition (London: Blackwell, 2004), pp. 55–119.
11. Michael Hardt and Antonio Negri give a rather patchy but sometimes insightful account of the possibilities of democracy in the transition from sovereignty to globalization in *Multitude*. Jacques Derrida gives a different account of the same problems in his recent work *Rogues: Two essays on Reason* (Stanford: Stanford University Press, 2005).
12. John Donne, 'A Valediction: Forbidding Mourning', in John Donne, *The Complete English Poems* (London: Penguin, 1971), p. 85.
13. Deleuze, 'The Exhausted', p. 162.

Chapter 8

1. McHale, 'Lost in the Mall', p. 114.
2. Adorno, *Prisms*, p. 34.
3. Andrew Gibson, *Beckett and Badiou*, p. 177.
4. Bloch, The Utopian Fiction of Art and Literature, p. 73.
5. Bloch, The Utopian Function of Art and Literature, p. 73.
6. Bloch, The Utopian Function of Art and Literature, p. 155.
7. Milton, *Paradise Lost*, I, 16, 26, p. 59, 60. For a reading of *The Lost Ones* that reads at once through Milton's *Paradise Lost* and Kafka's 'In the Penal Colony', see Gary Adelman, 'Fearful Symmetry: Beckett's *The Lost Ones*', in *Journal of Modern Literature*, vol. 26, no. 2, 2003, pp. 164–9.
8. Milton, *Paradise Lost*, VII, 120, p. 396.
9. Milton, *Paradise Lost*, VII, 120–4, p. 396.
10. Julia Kristeva, *Powers of Horror: An Essay on Abjection* (New York: Columbia University Press, 1982), trans. Leon S. Roudiez, p. 1.

11. McHale, 'Lost in the Mall', p. 119.
12. Frederic Jameson, *Postmodernism: Or the Cultural Logic of Late Capitalism* (London: Verso, 1991), p. 40.
13. Jameson, *Postmodernism*, p. 39.
14. Jameson, *Postmodernism*, p. 44.
15. Steven Connor, 'Slow Going', *The Yearbook of English Studies*, vol. 30, 2000, p. 163.
16. Bloch, The Utopian Function of Art and Literature, p. 89.

Chapter 9

1. Francis Fukuyama, *The End of History and the Last Man* (London: Penguin, 1992), p. xi.
2. Fukuyama, *The End of History*, xiii.
3. Francis Fukuyama, 'The West Has Won', in *The Guardian*, 11 October, 2001, http://www.guardian.co.uk/Archive/Article/0,4273,4274753,00.html
4. See Samuel Huntington, *The Clash of Civilizations and the Remaking of the World Order* (New York: Simon and Schuster, 1996).
5. Fukuyama, 'The West Has Won'.
6. Jean Baudrillard, *The Spirit of Terrorism* (London: Verso, 2002), p. 11.
7. Baudrillard, *The Spirit of Terrorism*, p. 8.
8. Baudrillard, *The Spirit of Terrorism*, p. 49.
9. See Huntington, *The Clash of Civilizations*, pp. 21–21, where Huntington argues that 'The survival of the West depends on Americans reaffirming their Western identity and Westerners accepting their civilization as unique not universal and uniting to renew and preserve it against challenges from non-Western societies'.
10. Baudrillard, *The Spirit of Terrorism*, p. 50.
11. Don DeLillo, 'In the Ruins of the Future', in *Harper's Magazine*, December 2001, p. 33. For an early reading of DeLillo's essay, in response to DeLillo's 'rhetoric of seeing', see Marco Abel, 'Don DeLillo's "In the Ruins of the Future": Literature, Images, and the Rhetoric of Seeing 9/11', in *PMLA*, vol. 118, no. 5, 2003, pp. 1236–50.
12. DeLillo, 'In the Ruins of the Future', p. 39.
13. See Don DeLillo, *Players* (London: Vintage, 1991) p. 19, Don DeLillo, *Mao II* (Mao 187).
14. Don DeLillo, *Cosmopolis* (New York: Scribner, 2003), p. 36.
15. This sense in both *Austerlitz* and *Falling Man* that structures are designed with an eye to their destruction can be traced back to DeLillo's earlier novel *White Noise*, where Jack Gladney refers it back further, to Nazi architectural aesthetics. Gladney says that 'Albert Speer wanted to build structures that would decay gloriously, impressively, like Roman ruins [. . .]. The ruin is built into the creation, which shows a certain nostalgia behind the power principle, or a tendency to organize the longings of future generations' (WN 257–8). See also Albert Speer, *Inside the Third Reich* (London: Phoenix, 1995), trans. Richard and Clara Wilson
16. DeLillo, 'In the Ruins of the Future', p. 37.
17. DeLillo, 'In the Ruins of the Future', p. 40.

18. George Bush made this comment on several occasions and in different contexts. See for example, *The Guardian*, 26 June 2002, p. 4, where Bush is reported to have made the comment in his Middle East policy statement, made on 24 June 2002.
19. DeLillo, 'In the Ruins of the Future', p. 34.
20. DeLillo, 'In the Ruins of the Future, p. 33.
21. DeLillo, 'In the Ruins of the Future', p. 39.
22. DeLillo, 'In the Ruins of the Future', p. 37.
23. DeLillo, 'In the Ruins of the Future', p. 39.
24. DeLillo, 'In the Ruins of the Future', p. 39.
25. See Daniel Katz, *Saying I No More: Subjectivity and Consciousness in the Prose of Samuel Beckett* (Illinois: Northwestern University Press, 1999), pp. 46–8. Katz argues that, in 'The Capital of the Ruins', Beckett 'refuses all rhetoric which might pose a "native" culture as being natural or naturalized in a manner which would place a "foreigner" in an irremediable relationship to it of exteriority, mediation, and artifice. Yet Beckett *also* rejects any appeal to nonhistorical, nonculturally specific criteria of "universal human values," which can so easily serve to erase the distinct specificities and very real divergences that collectively constitute 'universal' human culture and history' (p. 48).
26. This phrase remerges across DeLillo's oeuvre. See DeLillo, *Americana*, p. 205, where David Bell says that the idea for his avant-garde film came when 'I saw a woman trimming a hedge. Almost immediately it became something else. And it's still changing'. In DeLillo's late novel *The Body Artist*, the protagonist Lauren Hartke has a similar revelation when she sees a Japanese woman watering the garden, a sight, she thinks, that was 'something that is also something else' (Don DeLillo, *The Body Artist* [London: Picador, 2001], p. 36).
27. Andrew O'Hagan, in an angry review of *Falling Man* in the *New York Review of Books*, insists on providing the name of 'real' Falling Man, arguing that DeLillo had failed to respond to the reality of the event, or do justice to the life and death of the victims: 'the person inside the legend was a man from Mount Vernon who worked in the North Tower restaurant, Windows on the World. He was flesh and blood, not just an idea. He was born on 5 March 1958. He was six feet five. His father was a preacher. He suffered from asthma and had a wife called Hilary. He died sixty-five minutes twenty seconds after Mohamed Atta, and is currently awaiting a writer sufficiently uncoerced by the politics of art to tell his story'. Andrew O'Hagan, 'Racing Against Reality', in *New York Review of Books*, vol. 54, no. 11, 28 June 2007, http://www.nybooks.com/articles/20310.
28. See Maurice Blanchot, 'Death as Possibility', in Maurice Blanchot, *The Space of Literature* (Lincoln: University of Nebraska Press, 1082), trans. Ann Smock, pp. 87–107.
29. Saul Bellow, 'Some Notes on Recent American Fiction', in Malcolm Bradbury, ed., *The Novel Today: Contemporary Writers on Modern Fiction*, revised edition (London: Fontana, 1990), pp. 53–69, p. 53.
30. Bellow, 'Recent American Fiction', p. 61.
31. Bellow, 'Recent American Fiction', p. 69.
32. Sarah Blucher Cohen, *Saul Bellow's Enigmatic Laughter* (Urbana: University of Illinois Press, 1974), p. 12.

33 See Gary Adelman, 'Beckett's Readers: A Commentary and Symposium', in *Michigan Quarterly Review*, vol. 54, no. 1, Winter 2004, p. 54.
34 For a genealogy of the Beckettian room in DeLillo's prose, see Peter Boxall, *Don DeLillo: The Possibility of Fiction* (London: Routledge, 2006). For a reading of Beckett's shaping presence in early DeLillo, see Peter Boxall, 'DeLillo and media culture', in John N. Duvall, ed., *The Cambridge Companion to Don DeLillo* (Cambridge: Cambridge University Press, 2008), pp. 43–52.
35 See for example, Toby Litt's review of *Falling Man* in *The Guardian*, 26 May 2007, p. 16, where Litt writes that 'DeLillo's 9/11 terrorists read like a weak echo of earlier DeLillo gangs'.
36 Connor, 'Slow Going', p. 165.
37 Connor, 'Slow Going', p. 165.
38 Coetzee, *Slow Man*, p. 27.
39 See J. M. Coetzee, *The Master of Petersburg* (London: Secker and Warburg, 1994), p. 21.
40 For a sustained and imaginative reading of the phantom limb in Beckett's writing, see Ulrika Maude, *Beckett, Technology and the Body* (Cambridge: Cambridge University Press, 2009).
41 Coetzee, *Master of Petersburg*, p. 21.
42 See Connor, *Samuel Beckett: Repetition, Theory and Text*, p. 22, where Connor points out that 'the account of how Celia's narrative has been 'expurgated, accelerated, improved and reduced' squanders rather than saves time'.
43 Dorothy Richardson, 'Slow Motion', in *Close Up 1927–1933: Cinema and Modernism* (London: Cassell, 1998), ed. James Donald et al., pp. 182–3. Richardson dwells in this essay on the capacity of slow motion to reveal to us the shapes that a body makes in motion. The slow motion film of 'Mr Jones winning the high jump', allows us to see the 'whole elastic body [. . .] poised in the air upon the outstretched toe that sought and lightly found the earth'.
44 See Don DeLillo, *End Zone* (London: Penguin, 1986), p. 45.
45 This is a refrain that is found in virtually every DeLillo novel. For a reflection on the phrase in DeLillo, see Laura Barrett, '"Here, But Also There": Subjectivity and Postmodern Space in *Mao II*', in *Modern Fiction Studies*, vol. 45, no. 3, 1999.
46 See Virginia Woolf, *Mrs Dalloway* (London: Grafton, 1976), p. 163: 'Always her body went through it, when she was told, first, suddenly, of an accident; her dress flamed, her body burnt'.
47 Derrida, *Rogues*, p. xiii.
48 Derrida, *Rogues*, p. xiii.
49 Derrida, *Rogues*, p. 9.
50 Derrida, *Rogues*, p. 48.
51 Derrida, *Rogues*, p. 47.
52 Derrida, *Rogues*, p. 9.
53 Derrida, *Rogues*, p. 13.
54 Derrida, *Rogues*, p. 18.
55 Derrida, *Rogues*, p. 18.

Bibliography

Adelman, Gary, 'Beckett's Readers: A Commentary and Symposium', in *Michigan Quarterly Review*, vol. 54, no. 1, Winter 2004, p. 54
Adelman, Gary, 'Fearful Symmetry: Beckett's *The Lost Ones*', in *Journal of Modern Literature*, vol. 26, no. 2, 2003, pp. 164–9
Adorno, Theodor, *Notes to Literature*, 2 vols (New York: Columbia University Press, 1991), trans. Shierry Weber Nicholsen
Adorno, Theodor, *Prisms* (Cambridge: The MIT Press, 1983), trans. Samuel and Shierry Weber
Albright, Daniel, *Representation and the Imagination: Beckett, Kafka, Nabokov, and Schoenberg* (Chicago: Chicago University Press, 1981)
Amis, Marin, *Money* (London: Jonathan Cape, 1984)
Anderson, Benedict, *Imagined Communities: Reflections on the Origin and Spread of Nationalism*, revised edition (London: Verso, 1991)
Auster, Paul, *The Art of Hunger: Essays, Prefaces, Interviews and The Red Notebook* (London: Penguin, 1997)
Auster, Paul, *The New York Trilogy* (London: Faber and Faber, 1987)
Banville, John, *Athena* (London: Picador, 1998)
Banville, John, *The Book of Evidence* (London: Minerva, 1990)
Banville, John, *Eclipse* (London: Picador, 2000)
Banville, John, *Ghosts* (London: Picador, 1998)
Banville, John, *God's Gift: A Version of Amphitryon by Heinrich von Kleist* (Oldcastle: The Gallery Press, 2000)
Banville, John, *The Sea* (London: Picador, 2005)
Banville, John, 'The Rubble Artist', in *The New Republic Online*, 6 December 2001, http://www.powells.com/review/2001_12_06
Banville, John, *Shroud* (London: Picador, 2002)
Banville, John, *The Untouchable* (London: Picador, 1997)
Barrett, Laura, '"Here, But Also There": Subjectivity and Postmodern Space in *Mao II*', in *Modern Fiction Studies*, vol. 45, no. 3, 1999
Barthes, Roland, *Camera Lucida* (London: Vintage, 2000), trans. Richard Howard
Basho, *On Love and Barley: Haiku of Basho* (London: Penguin, 1985), trans. Lucien Stryk
Baudrillard, Jean, *The Spirit of Terrorism* (London: Verso, 2002)
Bayley, John, *The Short Story: Henry James to Elizabeth Bowen* (Brighton: Harvester, 1988)
Beckett, Samuel, *Collected Poems: 1930–1978* (London: Calder, 1986)
Beckett, Samuel, *Complete Dramatic Works* (London: Faber and Faber, 2006)

Beckett, Samuel, *Complete Shorter Prose* (New York: Grove Press, 1995), ed. S. E. Gontarski
Beckett, Samuel, *Dream of Fair to Middling Women* (London: Calder, 1993)
Beckett, Samuel, *Disjecta* (London: Calder, 1983) ed. Ruby Cohn
Beckett, Samuel, *Eleutheria* (Paris: Minuit, 1995)
Beckett, Samuel, *How It Is* (London: Calder, 1964)
Beckett, Samuel, *Mercier and Camier* (London: Picador, 1988)
Beckett, Samuel, *Molloy, Malone Dies, The Unnamable* (London: Calder, 1994)
Beckett, Samuel, *More Pricks than Kicks* (London: Picador, 1974)
Beckett, Samuel, *Murphy* (London: Picador, 1973)
Beckett, Samuel, *Nohow On* (London: Calder, 1992)
Beckett, Samuel, and Others, *Our Exagmination Round his Factificaton for Incamination of Work in Progress* (London: Faber, 1929)
Beckett, Samuel, *Proust and Three Dialogues with Georges Duthuit* (London: Calder, 1965)
Beckett, Samuel, *Watt* (London: Calder, 1976)
Begam, Richard, *Samuel Beckett and the End of Modernity* (Stanford: Stanford University Press, 1996)
Bellamy, Edward, *Looking Backward* (New York: Dover, 1996)
Bellow, Saul, *Dangling Man* (London: Weidenfeld & Nicolson, 1972)
Bellow, Saul, 'Some Notes on Recent American Fiction', in Malcolm Bradbury, ed., *The Novel Today: Contemporary Writers on Modern Fiction*, revised edition (London: Fontana, 1990), pp. 53–69
Benjamin, Walter, *Illuminations* (London: Pimlico, 1999), trans. Harry Zorn
Bennett, Andrew and Nicholas Royle, *Elizabeth Bowen and the Dissolution of the Novel* (Basingstoke: Macmillan, 1995)
Bernhard, Thomas, *Alte Meister: Komödie* (Frankfurt: Suhrkamp Verlag, 1985)
Bernhard, Thomas, *Auslöschung: Ein Zerfall* (Frankfurt: Suhrkamp Verlag, 1986)
Bernhard, Thomas, *Correction* (London: Vintage, 2003), trans. Sophie Wilkins
Bernhard, Thomas, *Extinction* (London: Quartet, 1995), trans. David McLintock
Bernhard, Thomas, *Gargoyles* (London: Vintage, 2006)
Bernhard, Thomas, *Korrektur* (Frankfurt: Suhrkamp Verlag, 1975)
Bernhard, Thomas, *Old Masters* (Chicago: The University of Chicago Press, 1989), trans. Edward Osers
Bernhard, Thomas, *Three Novellas: Amras, Playing Watten, Walking* (Chicago: the university of Chicago Press, 2003), trans. Peter Jansen and Kenneth J. Northcott
Bernhard, Thomas, *Wittgensteins Neffe: Eine Freundschaft* (Frankfurt: Suhrkamp Verlag, 1983)
Bernhard, Thomas, *Wittgenstein's Nephew* (Chicago: The University of Chicago Press, 1990), trans. David McLintock
Bernhard, Thomas, *Wittgensteins Neffe: Eine Freundschaft* (Frankfurt: Suhrkamp Verlag, 1982)
Blanchot, Maurice, *The Space of Literature* (Lincoln: University of Nebraska Press, 1082), trans. Ann Smock
Bloch, Ernst, *The Utopian Function of Art and Literature: Selected Essays* (Cambridge, Massachusetts: The MIT Press, 1988), trans. Jack Zipes and Frank Mecklenburg
Bloom, Harold, *The Anxiety of Influence: A Theory of Poetry*, second edition (Oxford: Oxford University Press, 1997)

Bowen, Elizabeth, *The Collected Stories of Elizabeth Bowen* (London: Vintage, 1999)
Bowen, Elizabeth, *The Last September* (London: Vintage, 1998)
Bowen, Elizabeth, *To the North* (London: Gollancz, 1932)
Bowen, Elizabeth, *The Mulberry Tree: Writings of Elizabeth Bowen* (London: Vintage, 1999)
Boxall, Peter, 'The Existence I Ascribe: Memory, Invention and Autobiography in Beckett's Fiction', in *The Yearbook of English Studies*, vol. 30, 2000
Boxall, Peter, 'DeLillo and media culture', in John N. Duvall, ed., *The Cambridge Companion to Don DeLillo* (Cambridge: Cambridge University Press, 2008), pp. 43–52
Boxall, Peter, *Don DeLillo: The Possibility of Fiction* (London: Routledge, 2006)
Brooke-Rose, Christine, *Thru* (London: Hamilton, 1975)
Buchanan, Ian, *Frederic Jameson: Live Theory* (London: Continuum, 2006)
Carroll, Lewis, *Alice's Adventures in Wonderland* (Ontario: Broadview Press, 2000)
Caselli, Daniela, *Beckett's Dantes: Intertextuality in the Fiction and Criticism* (Manchester: Manchester University Press, 2005)
Cavaliero, Glen, *The Supernatural and English Fiction* (Oxford: Oxford University Press, 1995)
Coetzee, J. M., *Doubling the Point: Essays and Interviews* (Cambridge, Massachusetts: Harvard University Press, 1992)
Coetzee, J. M., 'Eight Ways of Looking at Samuel Beckett, in Minako Okamuro, Naoya Mori, Bruno Clément, Sjef Houppermans, Angela Moorjani and Anthony Uhlmann, eds, *Samuel Beckett Today/Aujourd'hui*, vol. 19, 2008
Coetzee, J. M., *Elizabeth Costello* (New York: Viking, 2003)
Coetzee, J. M., *The Master of Petersburg* (London: Vintage, 1999)
Coetzee, J.M., *Slow Man* (London: Secker and Warburg, 2005)
Cohen, Sarah Blacher, *Saul Bellow's Enigmatic Laughter* (Urbana: University of Illinois Press, 1974)
Cohn, Ruby, ed., *Samuel Beckett: The Comic Gamut* (New Brunswick: Rutgers University Press, 1962)
Connor, Steven, *Beckett and the World*, http://www.bbk.ac.uk/english/skc/beckettworld/beckettworld.pdf
Connor, Steven, *Samuel Beckett: Repetition, Theory and Text* (Oxford: Blackwell, 1988)
Connor, Steven, 'Slow Going', *The Yearbook of English Studies*, vol. 30, 2000
Coulter, Colin, and Steve Coleman, eds, *The End of Irish History? Critical Reflections on the Celtic Tiger* (Manchester: Manchester University Press, 2003)
Cousineau, Thomas, *Three Part Inventions: The Novels of Thomas Bernhard* (Newark: The University of Delaware Press, 2008)
Cronin, Anthony, *Samuel Beckett: The Last Modernist* (London: Harper Collins, 1996)
Dante Alighieri, *The Divine Comedy*, 3 vols (New York: Oxford University Press, 1961), trans. John D. Sinclair
Deane, Seamus, *Strange Country: Modernity and Nationhood in Irish Writing Since 1790* (Oxford: Clarendon, 1997)
Deleuze, Gilles, and Félix Guattari, *A Thousand Plateaus: Capitalism and Schizophrenia* (London: Continuum, 1988), trans. Brian Massumi
Deleuze, Gilles, *Essays Critical and Clinical* (London: Verso, 1998), trans. Daniel W. Smith and Michael A. Greco
Deleuze, Gilles and Félix Guattari, *Kafka: Toward a Minor Literature* (Minneapolis: The University of Minnesota Press, 1986)

DeLillo, Don, *Americana* (London: Penguin, 1990)
DeLillo, Don, *The Body Artist* (London: Picador, 2001)
DeLillo, Don, *Cosmopolis* (New York: Scribner, 2003)
DeLillo, Don, *End Zone* (London: Penguin, 1986)
DeLillo, Don, *Falling Man* (New York: Scribner, 2007)
DeLillo, Don, *Great Jones Street* (London: Picador, 1998)
DeLillo, Don, 'In the Ruins of the Future', in *Harper's Magazine*, December 2001
DeLillo, Don, *Libra* (London: Penguin, 1988)
DeLillo, Don, *Mao II* (London: Vintage, 1992)
DeLillo, Don, *Players* (London: Vintage, 1991)
DeLillo, Don, *White Noise* (London: Picador, 1999)
Derrida, Jacques, *Rogues: Two Essays on Reason* (Stanford: Stanford University Press, 2005)
Derrida, Jacques, *Spectres of Marx: The State of the Debt, the Work of Mourning, & the New International* (London: Routledge, 1994), trans. Peggy Kamuf
Dickinson, Emily, *The Poems of Emily Dickinson* (Cambridge, Massachusetts: Harvard University Press, 1998), ed. R. W. Franklin
Donne, John, *The Complete English Poems* (London: Penguin, 1971)
Dressinger, Sepp, *Von einer Katastrophe in die andere. 13 Gespräche mit Thomas Bernhard* (Vienna: Bibliothek der Provinz, 1992)
Dutton, Richard, *Modern Tragicomedy and the British Tradition* (Brighton: Harvester Press, 1986)
Eagleton, Terry, *Crazy John and the Bishop and other Essays on Irish Culture* (Cork: Cork University Press, 1998)
Eder, Richard, 'Excavating a Life', in *New York Times*, 28 October 2001
Edgeworth, Maria, *Castle Rackrent* (Oxford: Oxford University Press, 1964)
Eliot, T. S., *Collected Poems 1909–1962* (London: Faber and Faber, 1974)
Ellmann, Richard, *James Joyce*, new and revised edition (Oxford: Oxford University Press, 1983)
Eshel, Amir, 'Against the Power of Time: The Poetics of Suspension in W. G. Sebald's *Austerlitz*', in *New German Critique*, vol. 88, Winter 2003, pp. 71–96
Esslin, Martin, 'Beckett and Bernhard: A Comparison', in *Modern Austrian Literature*, vol. 18, no 2, 1985, pp. 67–78.
Esslin, Martin, *The Theatre of the Absurd*, third edition (London: Penguin, 1991)
Feldman, Matthew, *Beckett's Books: A Cultural History of Samuel Beckett's 'Interwar Notes'* (London: Continuum, 2006)
Feldman, Matthew and Mark Nixon, eds, *Beckett's Literary Legacies* (Cambridge: Cambridge Scholars Press, 2007)
Freud, Sigmund, 'A Note Upon the "Mystic Writing Pad"', in Sigmund Freud, *On Metapsychology*, in *The Penguin Freud Library*, 15 vols, vol. 11 (Harmondsworth: Penguin, 1991), pp. 429–34
Friel, Brian, *Translations* (London: Faber and Faber, 1981)
Fukuyama, Francis, *The End of History and the Last Man* (London: Penguin, 1992)
Fukuyama, Francis, *The West Has Won*, in *The Guardian*, 11 October, 2001
Gibson, Andrew *Beckett and Badiou: The Pathos of Intermittency* (Oxford: Oxford University Press, 2006)

Gibson, Andrew, and Len Platt, eds, *Joyce, Ireland, Britain* (Gainesville: University of Florida Press, 2006)
Gibson, Andrew, *Joyce's Revenge: History, Aesthetics and Politics in* Ulysses (Oxford: Oxford University Press, 2005)
Gibson, Andrew, *Postmodernity, Ethics and the Novel: From Leavis to Levinas* (London: Routledge, 1999)
Gibson, William, *Pattern Recognition* (London: Penguin, 2004)
Hardt, Michael and Antonio Negri, *Empire* (Cambridge, Massachusetts: Harvard University Press, 2000)
Hardt, Michael and Antonio Negri, *Multitude: War and Democracy in the Age of Empire* (London: Penguin, 2006)
Harrington, John P., *The Irish Beckett* (New York: Syracuse University Press, 1991)
Hassan, Ihab, *The Dismemberment of Orpheus: Toward a Postmodern Literature*, second edition (Wisconsin: The University of Wisconsin Press, 1982)
Havel, Vaclav, *Selected Plays 1963–1983* (London: Faber and Faber, 1992)
Heath, Stephen, *Questions of Cinema* (Basingstoke: Macmillan 1981)
Hiebel, Hans H., 'Beckett's Television Plays and Kafka's Late Stories', in Marius Buning, Matthijs Engelberts, Sjef Houppermans and Emmanuel Jacquart, *Samuel Beckett: Crossroads and Borderlines. L'OEuvre Carrefour/L'OEuvre Limite*, special issue of *Samuel Beckett Today/Aujourd'hui*, vol. 6, 1997, pp. 313–27
Hill, Leslie, *Beckett's Fiction: In Different Words* (Cambridge: Cambridge University Press, 1990)
Hinden, Michael, 'After Beckett: The Plays of Pinter, Stoppard, and Shepard', in *Contemporary Literature*, vol. 27, no. 3, Autumn, 1986, pp. 400–8
Hippolyte, Jean-Louis, *Fuzzy Fiction* (Lincoln: University of Nebraska Press, 2006)
Howe, Susan, *My Emily Dickinson* (Berkeley: North Atlantic Books, 1985).
Huntington, Samuel, *The Clash of Civilizations and the Remaking of the World Order* (New York: Simon and Schuster, 1996).
Jaggi, Maya, 'Recovered Memories', in *The Guardian*, Saturday, 22 September 2001
James, Henry, *The Turn of the Screw* (New York: Norton, 1999)
Jameson, Frederic, *Postmodernism: Or the Cultural Logic of Late Capitalism* (London: Verso, 1991)
Jopling, Michael, '"Es gibt ja nur Gescheitertes": Bernhard as company for Beckett', in *Journal of European Studies*, vol. 27, 1997, p. 50
Joyce, James, *Dubliners* (Oxford: Oxford University Press, 2000)
Joyce, James, *Finnegans Wake* (London: Minerva, 1992)
Joyce, James, *Portrait of the Artist as a Young Man* (London: Penguin, 1992)
Joyce, James, *Ulysses* (London: Penguin, 1992)
Jung, C. G., *The Symbolic Life: Miscellaneous Writings* (London: Routledge and Kegan Paul, 1977), trans. R. F. C. Hull
Kadare, Ismail, *Broken April* (London: Vintage, 2003), trans. J. Hodgson
Kadare, Ismail, *Spring Flowers, Spring Frost* (London: Vintage, 2003), trans. David Bellos
Kafka, Franz, *Metamorphosis and Other Stories* (London: Minerva, 1992), trans. Willa and Edwin Muir
Kane, Sarah, *Complete Plays* (London: Methuen, 2001)
Katz, Daniel, *Saying I No More: Subjectivity and Consciousness in the Prose of Samuel Beckett* (Illinois: Northwestern University Press, 1999)

Kearney, Richard, *Postnationalist Ireland: Politics, Culture, Philosophy* (London: Routledge, 1997)

Keats, John, *Selected Poems and Letters of John Keats* (Oxford: Heinemann, 1966), ed. Robert Gittings

Kiberd, Declan, *Inventing Ireland: The Literature of the Modern Nation* (London: Vintage, 1996)

Kiberd, Declan, *The Irish Writer and the World* (Cambridge: Cambridge University Press, 2005)

Kirby, Peadar, Luke Gibbons and Michael Cronin, eds, *Reinventing Ireland: Culture and the Celtic Tiger* (London: Pluto 2002)

Kirkley, Richard Bruce, 'A *catch in the breath*: Language and Consciousness in Samuel Beckett's . . . *but the clouds* . . .', in *Modern Drama*, vol. 35, no. 4, December 1992

Kleist, Heinrich von, *Five Plays* (New Haven: Yale University press, 1988), trans. Martin Greenberg

Kleist, Heinrich von, 'Über das Marionettentheater', in Heinrich von Kleist, *Gesammelte Werke* (Berlin: Aufbau-Verlag, 1955), pp. 384–92

Knowlson, James and Elizabeth Knowlson, eds, *Beckett Remembering / Remembering Beckett: Uncollected Interviews with Samuel Beckett and Memories of Those Who Knew Him* (London: Bloomsbury, 2006)

Knowlson, James, *Damned to Fame: The Life of Samuel Beckett* (London: Bloomsbury, 1996)

Knowlson, James and John Pilling, *Frescoes of the Skull: The Later Prose and Drama of Samuel Beckett* (London: Calder, 1979)

Kreilkamp, Vera, *The Anglo-Irish Novel and the Big House* (Syracuse: Syracuse University Press, 1998)

Kristeva, Julia, *Powers of Horror: An Essay on Abjection* (New York: Columbia University Press, 1982), trans. Leon S. Roudiez

Kristeva, Julia, *Proust and the Sense of Time* (London: Faber and Faber, 1993), trans. Stephen Bann

Lechner, Frank J. and John Boli, eds, *The Globalization Reader*, second edition (London: Blackwell, 2004)

Levi, Primo, *The Drowned and the Saved* (London: Abacus, 1989), trans. Raymond Rosenthal

Litt, Toby, review of *Falling Man*, *The Guardian*, 26 May 2007, p. 16

Lloyd, David, *Anomalous States: Irish Writing and the Post-Colonial Moment* (Dublin: The Lilliput Press, 1993)

Long, J. J. and Anne Whitehead, eds, *W. G. Sebald: A Critical Companion* (Edinburgh: Edinburgh University Press, 2004)

McCormack, W. J., *From Burke to Beckett: Ascendancy, Tradition and Betrayal in Literary History* (Cork: Cork University Press, 1994)

McCormack, W. J., review of W. G. Sebald, *Austerlitz*, in *The Post.ie: Sunday Business Post Online*, Sunday, 20 January 2002, http://archives.tcm.ie/businesspost/2002/01/20/story41667728.asp

McHale, Brian, 'Lost in the Mall: Beckett, Federman, Space', in Henry Sussman and Christopher Devenny, *Engagement and Indifference: Beckett and the Political* (Albany: State University of New York, 2001), pp. 112–25

McMinn, Joseph, *The Supreme Fictions of John Banville* (Manchester: Manchester University Press, 1999)
McMullen, Anna, 'Irish/Postcolonial Beckett', in Lois Oppenheim, ed., *Palgrave Advances in Samuel Beckett Studies* (Basingstoke: Palgrave, 2004)
Malcolm, Norman *Nothing is Hidden: Wittgenstein's Criticism of his Early Thought* (Oxford: Blackwell, 1986)
Man, Paul de, *The Rhetoric of Romanticism* (New York: Columbia University Press, 1984)
Marsh, Nicky, '"All Known – Never Seen": Susan Howe, Samuel Beckett and an Indeterminate Tradition', in Peter Boxall, ed., *Beckett/Aesthetics/Politics, Samuel Beckett Today/Aujourd'hui*, vol. 9, 2000, pp. 239–54
Maude, Ulrika, *Beckett, Technology and the Body* (Cambridge: Cambridge University Press, 2009), forthcoming, as this book goes to press.
Miller, Tyrus *Late Modernism: Politics, Fiction and the Arts Between the World Wars* (Berkeley: University of California Press, 1999)
Milton, John, *Paradise Lost* (Harlow: Pearson Longman, 2007), ed. Alastair Fowler
Molière, *Amphitryon*, in *The Plays of Molière* (Edinburgh: John Grant, 1907), trans. A. R. Waller
Monk, Ray, *Ludwig Wittgenstein: The Duty of Genius* (London: Vintage, 1991)
Mooney, Sinead, '"Integrity in a Surplus": Beckett's (Post-) Protestant Politics', in Peter Boxall, ed., *Beckett/Aesthetics/Politics, Samuel Beckett Today/Aujourd'hui*, vol. 9, 2000, pp. 223–37
More, Thomas, *Utopia* (Cambridge: Cambridge University Press, 2002), eds, George M. Logan and Robert M. Adams.
More, Thomas, *Utopia* (Harmondsworth: Penguin, 1965), trans. Paul Turner
Morris, William, *News From Nowhere* (Peterborough: Broadview, 2003)
Nixon, Mark, '"A brief glow in the dark": Samuel Beckett's Presence in Modern Irish Poetry', in Ronan McDonald, ed., *Irish Writing Since 1950*, special issue of *Yearbook of English Studies*, vol. 35, 2005, pp. 43–57
Nolan, Emer, *James Joyce and Nationalism* (London: Routledge, 1994)
O'Brien, Eion, *The Beckett Country* (Dublin: the Black Cat Press, 1986)
O'Hagan, Andrew, 'Racing Against Reality', in *New York Review of Books*, vol. 54, no. 11, 28 June 2007, http://www.nybooks.com/articles/20310
Okamuro, Minako, Naoya Mori, Bruno Clément, Sjef Houppermans, Angela Moorjani and Anthony Uhlmann, eds, *Samuel Beckett Today/Aujourd'hui*, vol. 19, 2008
Osborne, Thomas, 'Literature in Ruins', in *History of the Human Sciences*, vol. 18, no. 3, 2005, pp. 109–18
Perloff, Marjorie, *Wittgenstein's Ladder: Poetic Language and the Strangeness of the Ordinary* (Chicago: The University of Chicago Press, 1996)
Poe, Edgar Allen, *Selected Tales* (Oxford: Oxford University Press, 1998)
Powell, Kersti Tarien, 'Not a son but a survivor': Beckett . . . Joyce . . . Banville', in Ronan McDonald, ed., *Irish Writing Since 1950*, special issue of *Yearbook of English Studies*, vol. 35, 2005, pp. 199–211,
Pinter, Harold, *The Birthday Party* (London: Faber and Faber, 1991)

Pinter, Harold, 'A Play and its Politics: A Conversation between Harold Pinter and Nicholas Hern', in Harold Pinter, *One for the Road* (London: Methuen, 1984), pp. 5–24

Pinter, Harold, *Plays 2* (London: Faber and Faber, 1991)

Proust, Marcel, *Remembrance of Things Past*, 3 vols (London: Penguin, 1983), trans. C.K. Scott Moncrieff and Terence Kilmartin

Pynchon, Thomas, *The Crying of Lot 49* (Philadelphia: Lippincott, 1966)

Pynchon, Thomas, *Mason and Dixon* (London: Vintage, 1998)

Ray, William, 'Suspended in the Mirror: Language and the Self in Kleist's "Über das Marionettentheater"', in *Studies in Romanticism*, vol. 18, no. 4, Winter 1979, pp. 521–46

Richardson, Dorothy, 'Slow Motion', in *Close Up 1927–1933: Cinema and Modernism* (London: Cassell, 1998) pp. 182–3

Rimmon-Kenan, Shlomith, 'Ambiguity and Narrative Levels: Christine Brooke-Rose's *Thru*', in *Poetics Today*, vol. 3, no. 1, pp. 21–32

Robbe-Grillet, Alain, *For a New Novel: Essays on Fiction* (Salem: Ayer Company Publishers, 1965), trans. Richard Howard

Rodley, Chris, ed., *Lynch on Lynch* (London: Faber and Faber, 1997)

Rose, Jacqueline, *The Last Resistance* (London: Verso, 2007)

Royle, Nicholas, 'Back', in *Oxford Literary Review*, vol. 18, nos. 1–2, 1996

Runia, Eelco, 'Presence', in *History and Theory*, vol. 45, no. 1, 2006

Runia, Eelco, 'Spots of Time', in *History and Theory*, vol. 45, no. 3, 2006, p. 316

Rushdie, Salman, *Midnight's Children* (London: Penguin, 1991)

Saunders, Graham, *Love Me or Kill Me: Sarah Kane and the Theatre of Extremes* (Manchester: Manchester University Press, 2002)

Schall, Hedwig, 'An Interview with John Banville', in *European English Messenger*, vol. 6, no. 1, Spring 1997

Sebald, W. G. *Austerlitz*, (London: Penguin, 2001), trans. Anthea Bell

Sebald, W. G. *Campo Santo*, (London: Penguin, 2005), trans. Anthea Bell

Sebald, W. G. *The Emigrants*, (London: Vintage, 2002), trans. Michael Hulse

Sebald, W. G. and Jan Peter Tripp, *Unrecounted* (New York: New Directions, 2004)

Sebald, W. G. *Vertigo*, (London: Vintage, 2002), trans. Michael Hulse

Shakespeare, William, *Hamlet*, (London: Routledge, 1982), ed. Harold Jenkins

Sheehan, Ronan, 'Novelists on the Novel: Ronan Sheehan talks to John Banville and Francis Stuart', in *Crane Bag*, vol. 3, no. 1, 1979, pp. 76–84

Silverman, Kaja, 'Suture', in Kaja Silverman, *The Subject of Semiotics* (New York: Oxford University Press, 1983)

Slade, Andrew, *Lyotard, Beckett, Duras, and the Postmodern Sublime* (New York: Peter Lang, 2007)

Smith, Russell, 'Beckett's Endlessness: Rewriting Modernity and the Postmodern Sublime', in Uhlmann, Anthony, Sjef Houppermans and Bruno Clément, eds, *After Beckett / D'apres Beckett, Samuel Beckett Today / Aujourd'hui*, vol. 14, 2000, p. 405–20

Somerville, E. OE. and Martin Ross, *The Big House of Inver* (London: W. Heinemann, 1925)

Somerville, E. OE. and Martin Ross, *The Real Charlotte* (London: Zodiac Press, 1972)

Speer, Albert, *Inside the Third Reich* (London: Phoenix, 1995), trans. Richard and Clara Wilson

Swift, Jonathan, *Gulliver's Travels* (Oxford: Oxford University Press, 1986)

Szanto, George H., *Narrative Consciousness: Structure and Perception in the Fiction of Kafka, Beckett, and Robbe-Grillet* (Austin: University of Texas Press, 1972)

Tabert, Nils, 'Gespräch mit Sarah Kane', in Nils Tabert, ed., *Playspotting: Die Londoner Theaterszene der 90er* (Reinbeck: Rowohlt Taschenbuch Verlag, 1998), pp. 8–21

Thomson, Stephen, 'The Adjective, My Daughter: Staging T. S. Eliot's "Marina"', in *The Yearbook of English Studies*, vol. 32, 2002, pp. 110–26

Tresize, Thomas, 'Unspeakable', in *The Yale Journal of Criticism*, vol. 14, no. 1, 2001, pp. 39–66

Uhlmann, Anthony, Sjef Houppermans and Bruno Clément, eds, *After Beckett / D'apres Beckett, Samuel Beckett Today/Aujourd'hui*, vol. 14, 2000

Uhlmann, Anthony, in *Beckett and Poststructuralism* (Cambridge: Cambridge University Press, 1999)

Virilio, Paul, *Speed and Politics: An Essay on Dromology* (New York: Semiotext(e), 1986), trans. Mark Polizzotti.

Weller, Shane, *A Taste for the Negative: Samuel Beckett and Nihilism* (London: Legenda, 2005)

Wilcox, Leonard, 'Baudrillard, DeLillo's "White Noise," and the End of Heroic Narrative', in *Contemporary Literature*, vol. 32, no. 3, Autumn, 1991, pp. 346–65

Wills, David, *Dorsality: Thinking Back through Technology and Politics* (Minneapolis: University of Minnesota Press, 2008)

Wittgenstein, Ludwig, *Briefwechsel mit B. Russell, G. E. Moore, J. M. Keynes, F. P. Ramsay, W. Eccles, P. Engelmann und L. von Ficker* (Frankfurt: Suhrkamp, 1980), eds, B. F. McGuinness and G. H. von Wright, pp. 96–7

Wittgenstein, Ludwig, *Philosophical Investigations* (Oxford: Blackwell 2001), trans. G. E. M. Anscombe

Wittgenstein, Ludwig, *Tractatus Logico-Philosophicus* (London: Routledge, 2001), trans. D. F. Pears and B. F. McGuinness

Woolf, Virginia, *Mrs Dalloway* (London: Grafton, 1976)

Wulf, Catharina, *The Imperative of Narration: Beckett, Bernhard, Schopenhauer, Lacan* (Brighton: Sussex Academic Press, 1997)

Yeats, W. B., *Collected Poems* (London: Picador, 1990)

Zurbrugg, Nicholas, *Beckett and Proust* (Gerard's Cross: Smythe, 1988)

Index

Abel, Marco 214n. 11
Act of Union 22–3, 44
Adamov, Arthur 70, 208n. 4
Adelman, Gary 183
   'Fearful Symmetry: Beckett's *The Lost Ones*' 213n. 7
Adorno, Theodor 8, 9, 10, 30, 131, 157, 164, 209n. 1
   'Cultural Criticism and Society' 148–9, 150
   'Trying to Understand *Endgame*' 7, 118
Ahmenotep III 160
Albright, Daniel
   Representation and Imagination: Beckett, Kafka, Nabokov and Schoenberg 207n. 1
Amis, Martin
   Money 3
Anderson, Benedict 137
   Imagined Communities 212–13n. 6
Antonioni, Michelangelo 13
ascendancy, Anglo-Irish 21–4
Ascham, Roger 110
Ashbery, John 11
Atta, Mohammad 168, 184, 187
Atwell, David 15
Auschwitz 7, 130
Auster, Paul 11, 70, 207–8n. 1
   The Art of Hunger 202n. 27, 207–8n. 1
   The Locked Room 87

Bachmann, Ingeborg 109
back 21–45, 56–7, 58–65, 73–7, 79, 80, 82–3, 101–2, 103, 116, 120–1, 129, 173, 177–8, 181, 182
Badiou, Alain 149–50

Ballard, J.G. 202n. 28
Banville, John 11, 13, 14, 21–65, 69, 70, 74, 82, 126, 130, 174, 205nn. 2,3,4, 206nn. 1,9
   Athena 43, 205n. 6
   The Body of Evidence 24, 38, 43, 44, 205n. 6
   Eclipse 24, 38–52, 53–65, 69, 177, 206n. 3
   Ghosts 43, 205n. 6
   God's Gift 54
   The Sea 39
   Shroud 53–65
   The Untouchable 53
Barrett, Laura 216n. 45
Barthes, Roland 117
Basho 195
Baudrillard, Jean 168–9, 170, 171, 173, 194, 203n. 30
Bayley, John 206n. 8
Beckett, Samuel
   All That Fall 57, 129, 205n. 1
   Breath 11, 202n. 22
   . . . but the clouds . . . 24, 31, 32, 33–7, 38, 51, 60, 158
   The Calmative 2–3, 4, 72–3, 95, 117
   'The Capital of the Ruins' 14, 172–3, 174, 187, 189, 191, 197–8
   Catastrophe 60, 202n. 21
   Company 5–6, 24, 31–3, 34, 40–1, 60, 72–3, 101, 103, 120, 128
   'Dante… Bruno. Vico… Joyce' 3, 76
   Disjecta 60, 93, 139, 142, 153
   Dream of Fair to Middling Women 30–2, 94–5, 139–42, 143, 145, 191

Beckett, Samuel (*Cont'd*)
  Eleutheria 145, 191
  Endgame 1, 7, 12, 16, 82–3, 118, 126, 150
  Film 98
  First Love 41–2
  Fizzles 1, 34
  The Four Novellas 31
  Ghost Trio 3, 31, 32, 33–7, 44, 54–5, 70–4, 76, 79–84, 92, 98, 99, 103, 118, 121, 124, 127
  How It Is 32, 72–3, 96, 99, 101–8, 110, 111, 112, 115, 116, 123, 127–30, 146, 147, 149, 150, 163, 198, 211n. 27
  Ill Seen Ill Said 3, 48, 139, 144–7, 150, 153, 157–65, 166, 187, 196
  Imagination Dead Imagine 31, 32, 61, 144, 146, 147, 149, 155
  Krapp's Last Tape 42, 80, 82, 87, 127, 163
  Lessness 189
  The Lost Ones 1–2, 3, 31, 76, 80–1, 83, 144, 146, 148, 149, 150–7, 158, 159, 160–1, 162, 163, 166, 187, 190, 195, 196, 198, 209n. 1
  Malone Dies 8, 31, 89, 94, 97, 105, 146
  Mercier and Camier 11
  Molloy 2, 8, 14, 15, 31, 39, 40, 42, 52, 89, 93, 94, 95, 172, 174, 188, 189–90, 195
  Murphy 8, 60–1, 80, 94–5, 97, 142, 143, 145, 146, 163, 180, 181, 191, 194, 195
  Nacht und Träume 60, 99
  'Neither' 31, 42, 64, 140, 141, 147
  Not I 55
  The Old Tune 32
  Ping 31, 147
  Proust and Three Dialogues with Georges Duthuit 1, 52, 79, 107, 128, 150, 208n. 3
  Quad 3, 147
  'Something there' 161
  Stirrings Still 24, 141, 146
  That Time 60
  'they come' 73
  The Unnamable 1, 2, 3, 4, 8–9, 15, 31, 61, 76, 89, 103, 142–4, 146, 181
  Waiting for Godot 12, 29, 79, 124, 179–80, 194
  Watt 4–6, 8, 9, 69, 70, 72, 84–5, 95, 96, 97–101, 104, 105–6, 110, 123, 128, 129, 138, 208n. 2, 209n. 7
  'What is the Word' 3, 141
  'Whoroscope notebook' 73
  Worstward Ho 4, 62, 76, 90, 93, 146, 164
Beethoven, Ludwig 33, 34, 35, 81, 121
Begam, Richard 8, 16–17
Bellamy, Edward
  Looking Backward 152
Bellow, Saul 14, 174–84, 189, 195
  Dangling Man 175–83, 184, 186, 188, 190, 194, 195
  'Recent American Fiction' 181
Benjamin, Walter 7, 114
  'Theses on the Philosophy of History' 200–1n. 4
Bennett, Andrew, and Nicholas Royle
  Elizabeth Bowen and the Dissolution of the Novel 203–4n. 5
Berensmeyer, Ingo 205n. 2
Bergman, Ingmar 11
Bernhard, Thomas 11, 13–14, 15, 70, 74, 86–108, 109–11, 112–16, 123–6, 130–1, 174
  Correction 87–9, 96–7, 99, 103, 104–8, 110, 112–13, 123, 124
  Der Italianer 93
  Extinction 89–92, 102, 123
  Gargoyles 210n. 23
  Old Masters 91, 92, 105, 110, 114–15, 119, 123, 210n. 23
  Wittgenstein's Nephew 91, 97–8, 104–5, 106, 110, 111
Big House, the 21–4, 25, 44, 206n. 9
Blanchot, Maurice 178, 199
Bloch, Ernst 58, 65, 150, 153, 157, 159–60, 164, 198
  'Art and Society' 150, 151, 153
  The Utopian Function of Art and Literature 206–7n. 6
Bloom, Harold
  The Anxiety of Influence 16
Blunt, Anthony 53
Bosch, Hieronymus 98–101
  'The Crowning with Thorns' 99–101, 102, 114

Bowen, Elizabeth 3, 13, 14, 23, 29–30, 31, 38, 39, 43–4, 46, 51, 61, 64, 69, 174, 196, 203–4n. 5, 204n. 11, 206n. 8
  'The Back Drawing Room' 24–9, 32, 34, 35, 36, 44, 46–7
  The Last September 24, 206n. 9
  The Mulberry Tree 204n. 19
  'Pictures and Conversations' 27–8
  To the North 24, 27
Boxall, Peter
  Beckett/Aesthetics/Politics 202n. 24, 204n. 24
  'DeLillo and Media Culture' 216n. 34
  Don DeLillo: The Possibility of Fiction 216n. 34
  'The Existence I Ascribe: Memory, Invention and Autobiography in Beckett's Fiction' 204n. 24
Brod, Max 87
Brooke-Rose, Christine 10
  Thru 201n. 18
Buchanan, Ian
  Frederic Jameson: Live Theory 201n. 14
Burroughs, William 181
Bush, George W. 170, 179, 186, 215n. 18

Camus, Albert 70, 180
Carrio, Rita 15
Carroll, Lewis 82, 99, 185
Carter, Angela 3
Cary, H. F. 73
Caselli, Daniela
  Beckett's Dantes 10, 73
Cavaliero, Glen 206n. 8
Celan, Paul 130
Celtic Tiger 136, 207n. 10
Coetzee, J. M. 11, 14, 15, 70, 174
  Doubling the Point 202n. 26, 208n. 1
  'Eight ways of Looking at Samuel Beckett' 202n. 26
  Elizabeth Costello 208n. 1
  The Master of Petersburg 191
  Slow Man 120, 121, 190–2
Cohen, Sarah 183
Connor, Steven 135–6, 145, 156, 190, 191
  Samuel Beckett: Repetition, Theory and Text 200n. 3, 216n. 42

Coulter, Colin, and Steve Coleman
  The End of Irish History? Critical Reflections on the Celtic Tiger 207n. 10
Cousineau, Thomas
  Three Part Inventions: The Novels of Thomas Bernhard 210n. 23
Cronin, Anthony 8
  Samuel Beckett: The Last Modernist 201n. 9
Cronin, Michael 63
cyberpunk 11

Dallas 3
Dante Alighieri 10, 72–3, 79, 124
  The Divine Comedy 73
Darwin, Charles 24, 25, 37, 196
dasein 130
Deane, Seamus 205n. 2
  Strange Country 203n. 3
Deleuze, Gilles 6, 139, 147
  'The Exhausted' 60, 99, 150
Deleuze, Gilles, and Felix Guattari 35
  A Thousand Plateaus 207n. 7
DeLillo, Don 12–13, 14, 168, 169–99, 215n. 26
  Americana 12–13, 215n. 26
  The Body Artist 215n. 26
  Cosmopolis 169
  End Zone 184, 193
  Falling Man 168–99, 214n. 15, 215n. 27
  Great Jones Street 184, 195
  'In the Ruins of the Future' 169–71, 172, 186
  Libra 186
  Mao II 9, 12, 169, 184, 203n. 29
  Players 169
  White Noise 13, 203n. 30, 214n. 15
democracy 14, 141, 149, 165, 166–99
Derrida, Jacques 6, 150, 153, 197–9
  Rogues 197–8, 213n. 11
  Spectres of Marx 15–16, 199, 203–4n. 5
Dickens, Charles 25
Dickinson, Emily 11, 51, 120, 202n. 24
Donne, John
  'A Valediction Forbidding Mourning' 143
Dostoevsky, Fyodor 191
Duras, Marguerite 11, 70, 202n. 27, 208n. 3

Duttlinger, Caroline 125
Dutton, Richard 201n. 18

Eagleton, Terry 64, 207n. 12
East Enders 3
Eden 76
Eder, Richard 125
Edgeworth, Maria 13, 14, 30, 37, 38, 39, 48, 51, 61, 64, 69, 70, 74, 174, 206n. 9
  Castle Rackrent 21–4, 44–6, 53, 203n. 3
Eliot, T. S.
  'Marina' 49–51, 59–60, 77, 82
Ellmann, Richard 135, 137, 138
Eshel, Amir 109–10
Esslin, Martin 6, 70, 200n. 2, 201n. 18, 208n. 4
  'Beckett and Bernhard: A Comparison' 208n. 5
Europe 8, 13–14, 24, 30–1, 49, 53–65, 69, 98, 110, 119, 131, 135–47, 174, 176–7, 178, 179, 180, 181, 182, 184

face 26–7, 30, 31–7, 50, 58–65, 73–4, 79, 81–3, 92, 99, 101–2, 104, 112, 127, 162, 163, 164–5, 173, 177, 195, 196, 207n. 7
Falling Man 175, 194
Father Ted 11
Federman, Raymond 203n. 28
Feldman, Matthew
  Beckett's Books: A Cultural History of Samuel Beckett's 'Interwar Notes' 9–10
Feldman, Matthew and Mark Nixon
  Beckett's Literary Legacies 9–10
Ficker, Ludwig von 104
Frankenstein 159
Freud, Sigmund, 'The Mystic Writing Pad' 101, 102
Friedrich, Kaspar David 139
Friel, Brian
  Translations 24
Fukyama, Francis 166–9, 171, 173, 189, 197, 199
  The End of History and the Last Man 166–9
  'The West has Won' 167

Genesis 75
Genet, Jean 208n. 4

Gibson, Andrew 135, 137, 138, 149–50
  Beckett and Badiou 200n. 3
  Postmodernity, Ethics and the Novel 203–4n. 5, 212n. 16
Gibson, William 11
  Pattern Recognition 11
Gide, Andre 181
Ginsberg, Allan 181
globalization 14, 59, 63–5, 135–99
Godard, Jean-Luc 11, 12
Goldsmith, Oliver 28
Guimarães, Adriano and Fernando 11

Hardt, Michael, and Antonio Negri 65, 197
  Empire 207n. 14
  Multitude 207n. 14, 213nn. 10,11
Harrington, John P
  The Irish Beckett 204n. 24
Hassan, Ihab
  The Dismemberment of Orpheus 203n. 35, 208n. 1
Havel, Vaclav 10, 70
  Mistake 202n. 21
Heath, Stephen, *Questions of Cinema* 205n. 31
Heidegger, Martin 53
Hiebel, Hans H. 207–8n. 1
Hill, Leslie
  Beckett's Fiction: In Different Words 200n. 3
Hinden, Michael 201n. 18
Hippolyte, Jean-Louis, *Fuzzy Fiction* 208n. 3
Hirst, Damien 11, 202n. 22
Holocaust 11, 14, 53, 86, 87, 119, 125–6, 130–1, 209n. 1, 209–10n. 4
Homer 190
Houellebecq, Michel 11, 70
Howe, Susan 11, 202n. 24
  My Emily Dickinson 11, 202n. 24
HSBC 64
Huntington, Samuel 167–9, 170, 171, 173
  The Clash of Civilisations 167–8, 183, 197, 214n. 9

Ionesco, Eugène 70, 180, 181, 208n. 4
Ireland 13, 21–65, 98, 130, 135–47, 161, 172–3, 174, 204n. 24
Islam 167–8, 170, 184, 187

Jaggi, Maya 211n. 10
James, Henry 43–4, 206n. 8
   The Turn of the Screw 43, 82, 159, 205n. 7
Jameson, Frederic 9, 154
Janvier, Ludovic 95
Johnson, B. S. 10
Jopling, Michael 93, 94–5, 208n. 5
Joyce, James 3, 8, 13, 14, 16, 39, 69, 70, 117, 126, 130, 135–47, 148, 174, 187, 205n. 2, 208n. 1
   'The Dead' 136–9, 143, 144, 146, 147, 164
   Dubliners 137
   Finnegans Wake 76, 137, 138, 140, 141, 147
   Portrait of the Artist as a Young Man 22, 141, 143
   Ulysses 137, 138, 147
Jung, Karl 128–9

Kadare, Ismail 11
Kafka, Franz 3, 11, 35, 69, 70, 74, 87, 109, 130, 180, 202n. 23, 207–8n. 1
   'The Burrow' 102, 211n. 27
   'In the Penal Settlement' 101
Kane, Sarah 10, 202n. 20
Katz, Daniel 173, 215n. 25
Kearney, Richard 205n. 2
   Postnationalist Ireland 207n. 12
Keats, John
   'Ode on a Grecian Urn' 118
Kelman, James 11
Kennedy, John F. 186
Kenner, Hugh 135
Kiberd, Declan 28–9
   The Irish Writer and the World 207n. 10
Kilbourn, Russell 125
Kirby, Peadar et al.
   Reinventing Ireland: Culture and the Celtic Tiger 207n. 10
Kirkley, Richard Bruce 36, 205n. 29
Klein, George 123–4
Kleist, Heinrich von 13–14, 54–5, 57, 69, 70, 74, 87, 109, 110, 123, 126, 130, 174, 176, 191, 192, 208n. 2
   Amphitryon 54, 74, 99, 206n. 3
   Über das Marionettentheater 54–5, 74–85, 95, 98, 99, 103–4, 110, 121, 208n. 2
Kluge, Alexander 109

Knowlson, James 55, 74
   Damned to Fame: The Life of Samuel Beckett 204n. 26
Knowlson, James and Elizabeth Knowlson
   Beckett Remembering/Remembering Beckett 10
Knowlson, James and John Pilling
   Frescoes of the Skull 208n. 2, 209n. 12
Kreilkamp, Vera
   The Anglo-Irish Novel and the Big House 206n. 9
Kristeva, Julia 126, 153

Lechner, Frank J., and John Boli,
   The Globalization Reader 213n. 10
Leibniz, Gottfried 149
Levi, Primo 130
Lewis, Jim 60
Litt, Toby 216n. 35
Lloyd, David
   Anomalous States 204n. 24
Lowry, Malcolm 10
Lucas, George 3
Lynch, David 11, 202n. 23

McCormack, W. J. 7, 30, 109
   From Burke to Beckett 23, 204n. 11
McDonald, Ronan 202n. 24
McHale, Bryan 148, 152, 154, 202–3n. 28, 209n. 1
McMinn, Joseph 205nn. 2,4
McMullen, Anna 37
   'Irish/Postcolonial Beckett' 204n. 24
MacNeice, Louis 53
Mahon, Derek 11, 202n. 24
Malcolm, Norman
   Nothing is Hidden: Wittgenstein's Criticism of his Early Thought 208n. 6
Mamet, David 11, 202n. 23
Man, Paul de 53, 56, 61, 79, 80
   The Rhetoric of Romanticism 207n. 9
Mann, Thomas 70
Marsh, Nicky 202n. 24
Marx, Karl 15–16
Maude, Ulrika, *Beckett, Technology and the Body* 216n. 40
Miller, Tyrus
   Late Modernism 203n. 35

Milton, John 75, 120, 164
  Paradise Lost 150–1, 153, 154–5, 157
modernism 3, 8–9, 10, 12, 13, 14,
  16, 70, 126, 130–1, 135–7, 138,
  203n. 35
Molière 70
  Amphitryon 54, 57, 206n. 3
Mooney, Sinead, '"Integrity in a Surplus":
  Beckett's (Post-) Protestant
  Politics' 204n. 24
Morandi, Giorgio 184, 187, 188, 190, 196
More, Thomas 77, 78, 103, 110–12,
  123, 127
  Utopia 77, 78, 95, 103, 110, 111–12, 152
Morris, William
  News From Nowhere 152
Murdoch, Iris 3

Nabokov, Vladimir 44
  Lolita 41
Nancy, Jean Luc 197
nationalism 62, 64–5, 135–47
Naumann, Bruce 10–11, 202n. 22
  'Clown Torture' 202n. 22
  'Slow Angle Walk (Beckett Walk)'
  202n. 22
Navridis, Nikos 11
Nazism 7, 91, 96, 112
Nietzsche, Friedrich 53
Nixon, Mark 202n. 24
Nolan, Emer 135, 137, 138

O'Brien, Eion 43
  The Beckett Country 204n. 24, 212n. 17
O'Connell, Daniel 146
O'Hagan, Andrew 215n. 27
One Foot in the Grave 11
Operation Enduring Freedom 182
Oppenheim, Lois
  Palgrave Advances in Beckett Studies
  204n. 24
Osborne, Thomas 208n. 5
Osteen, Mark 12, 203n. 29
Oswald, Lee Harvey 186

Perloff, Marjorie 97–8
  Wittgenstein's Ladder 208n. 2

Pickup, Ronald 54–5
Pilling, John 74
Pinget, Robert 70
Pinter, Harold 10, 70, 201n. 18, 208n. 4
  One for the Road 201n. 19
The Play for Today 3
Poe, Edgar Allan
  The Purloined Letter 151
postmodernism 3, 8–9, 12, 16, 173,
  203n. 35
postnationalism 62, 64–5, 135–47, 198
Poussin, Nicolas 41
Powell, Kersti Tarien 205n. 2, 206n. 1
Proust, Marcel 3, 8, 14, 16, 35, 70, 87,
  124–6, 130, 208n. 1
Prynne, J. H. 11
Pynchon, Thomas 11
  Crying of Lot 49 11, 184, 185
  Mason and Dixon 11

Rabaté, Jean-Michel 90, 210n. 6
Ray, William 110
Redonnet, Marie 70, 208n. 3
revelations 75
Richardson, Dorothy 192, 216n. 43
Riemann surface 103
Rimmon-Kenan, Shlomth 201n. 18
Robbe-Grillet, Alain 6, 10, 70, 181, 200n. 2
Rodley, Chris
  Lynch on Lynch 202n. 23
Rose, Jacqueline
  The Last Resistance 209–10n. 4
Royle, Nicholas
  'Back' 204n. 25
Runia, Eelco 86–7, 91, 92, 101, 115, 121,
  124–5, 126
Rushdie, Salman
  Midnight's Children 3

Sarraute, Nathalie 181
Sartre, Jean-Paul 70, 180, 181
Sauer, David, and Janice Sauer 202n. 23
Saunders, Graham 202n. 20
Schall, Hedwig 39, 205n. 2
Sebald, W. G. 11, 13–14, 70, 86, 87,
  109–31, 174
  Austerlitz 110–31, 163, 169, 214n. 15

The Emigrants 110
Vertigo 110
Sebald, W. G. and Jan Peter Tripp
   Unrecounted 15, 111, 115–16, 128
Shakespeare, William 161
   Hamlet 4, 149, 175, 191
Shaw, George Bernard 28
Sheehan, Ronan 205n. 2, 206n. 1
Sheridan, Richard 28
Silverman, Kaja
   The Subject of Semiotics 205n. 31
Simone, Claud 109
Slade, Andrew 202n. 27, 208n. 3
slow motion 189–95, 216, n. 43
Smith, Russell 200n. 1
Somerville and Ross 44
   The Big House of Inver 206n. 9
   The Real Charlotte 206n. 9
Speer, Albert 214n. 15
   Inside the Third Reich 214n. 15
Spinario 78
Star Wars 3
Stein, Gertrude 3
Stoppard, Tom 10, 201n. 18
suture 36, 61, 82, 119, 205n. 31
Swift, Jonathan 69
   Gulliver's Travels 152
Szanto, George H. 207n. 7

Tabert, Nils 202n. 20
terrorism 166–99
   September 11 166–99
Thalia 163
Thomson, Stephen, 'The Adjective, my Daughter: Staging T. S. Eliot's "Marina"' 206n. 15
Tintoretto
   'White Bearded Man' 114–15
Toussaint, Jean-Philippe 70, 208n. 3
Trevor, William 206n. 9
Trezise, Thomas 130–1

Uhlmann, Anthony, et al., *After Beckett* 10
   Beckett and Poststructuralism 200n. 3

United Nations 141
Utopia 16, 58–9, 62, 64, 103, 110, 112–13, 135–99, 206–7n. 6

Varos, Remedio, 'Embroidering Earth's Mantle' 184–5
Vico, Giambattista 76
Virgil 72–3, 79
Virilio, Paul 63
   Speed and Politics 207n. 11
Voltaire
   Candide 149

Weller, Shane 130, 188
Westin Bonaventure Hotel 154
White, Hayden 86
Wilcox, Leonard 203n. 30
Wilde, Oscar 28
Wills, David 21
Wirtz, Thomas 123
Wittgenstein, Ludwig 13, 70, 72, 101, 107, 109, 111, 113, 115–16, 117, 118, 119, 123, 127, 128, 208n. 2
   Philosophical Investigations 208n. 6
   The Tractatus 92, 104, 107–8, 208n. 6
Woolf, Virginia 3
   Mrs Dalloway 196
World Trade Center 168, 169–70, 171, 175, 177, 178, 182, 185, 189, 196–7, 198
World War II 86, 112–13, 141, 167, 172–3, 176–9, 182
Wulf, Catharina 90, 93, 95
   The Imperative of Narration 208n. 5

Yeats, W. B. 13, 36, 37, 38, 39, 48, 51, 61, 69, 138, 174
   'Leda and the Swan' 57
   'The Tower' 35, 36, 38, 42, 47

Zuckerman 87, 209–10n. 4
Zurbrugg, Nicholas
   Beckett and Proust 208n. 3

Lightning Source UK Ltd.
Milton Keynes UK
UKOW040348130312

188853UK00003B/11/P